Bradt

Slow
Devon
& Exmoor

Local, characterful guides to Britain's special places

Hilary Bradt

Contributing author Janice Booth

Edition 1

uides Ltd, UK

ng Co Ltd, UK

Press Inc, USA

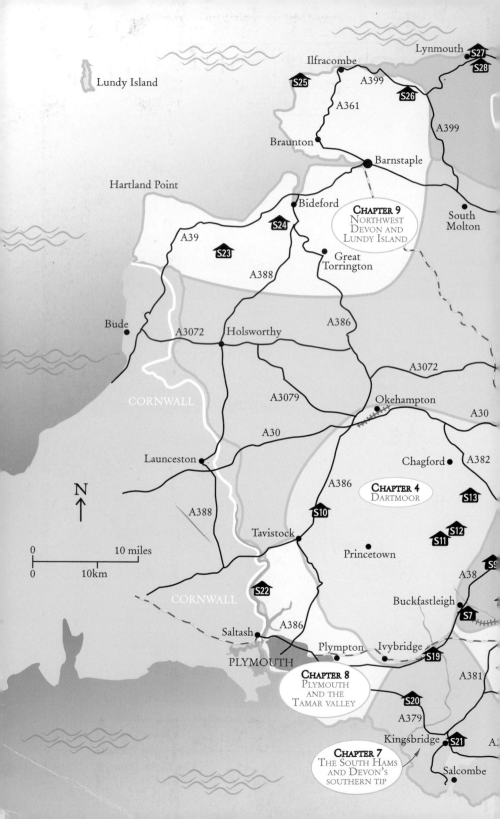

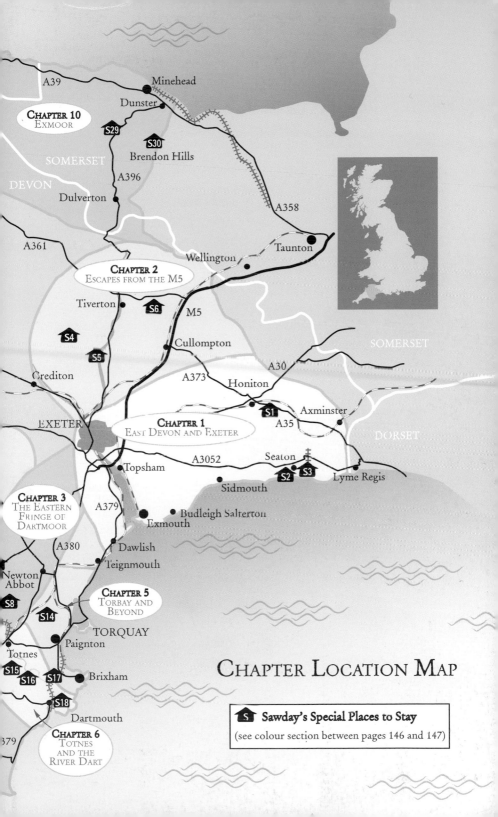

CHAPTER LOCATION MAP

S Sawday's Special Places to Stay

(see colour section between pages 146 and 147)

A Devon & Exmoor Gallery

The South West Coast Path near Salcombe. About two-thirds of this 630-mile-long path is in Devon, providing glorious walks in any season. (HB)

Dartmoor's iconic landmark, Haytor, is an easy stroll from the road and one of the great viewpoints. (DP/PL)

Devon has 150 miles of the National Cycle Network as well as dedicated cycle trails. Whether you hire a bike for an hour or two or do some serious touring, you've plenty of options. (CN/FL)

The Merrivale Stone Rows after a snowstorm. Winter walkers can escape the crowds and appreciate the emptiness of Dartmoor. (DC/PL)

Walking and riding

The ideal Slow way to appreciate the splendid West Country scenery at any time of the year is by walking or taking to the saddle; but for the less energetic, buses and trains give a grandstand view.

Devon is a county of rivers, usually with a helpful waterside footpath such as this one along the River Otter. (HB)

The South Devon Railway at Staverton. Steam trains run from Totnes to the edge of Dartmoor, as well as to Paignton, Dartmouth and into Exmoor. (HB)

Even less experienced riders can enjoy pony trekking on Exmoor or Dartmoor. (DRS)

The Saturday Haytor Hoppa circles through the most scenic parts of Dartmoor, offering some splendid 'bus walks'. (HB)

St Blaise's at Haccombe, once attached to a manor and crammed with monuments and nuggets of history. (HB)

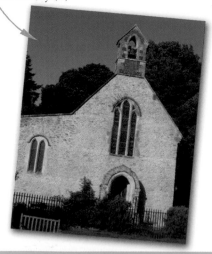

In Higher Ashton's church, St Apollonia, the patron saint of dentists, proudly holds one of her extracted teeth. Vivid paintings of obscure martyred saints decorate many church screens in the region. (HB)

Rural churches

The region's little churches have been part of its landscapes for centuries, and tell us so much about the history of a village and its present-day community.

Carved bench ends such as this enigmatic figure at St Andrew's Church, Colebrooke, are a feature of some Devon churches. This one probably dates from the 15th century. (HB)

The tiny St Beuno's Church at Culbone, 'squatting in a clearing with its spire, set slightly askew, reaching hopefully towards the treetops'. (HB)

Heather Jansch, an artist working with driftwood, occasionally opens her studio near Newton Abbot to visitors. (HB)

Open-air sculptures
The southwest has a generous share of artists and several wonderful sculpture gardens.

These happy ladies cavort in Broomhill while the Mythic Gardens, on the edge of Dartmoor, have a changing exhibition. (HB)

Periwinkle Cottage, Selworthy. A tea room owned by the National Trust in a picture-book-charming Exmoor village.

In 2007–8 the Royal Mail closed many rural post offices. Some villages responded by setting up their own community-run shops staffed by volunteers and well supported by grateful villagers. (HB)

DALWOOD SHOP & POST OFFICE

Darts Farm near Topsham, with its mouth-watering selection of organic fresh vegetables, meat and fish, has been described as 'Selfridges Food Store dumped in the middle of a field'. The food-miles of much of its produce are zero. (HB)

The village pub is often centuries old, serving real ales as well as Slow Food. (ROD)

The village community

The church and the pub are the cornerstones of any English village. In Devon you can add cream teas and, in some enterprising villages, a community shop.

Maritime Devon has more than its share of good seafood restaurants. (NH/PL)

Bowerman's Nose, a natural rock formation on Dartmoor. Legend has it that the eponymous huntsman was turned to stone when he disturbed a coven of witches. (HB)

The moors

Devon's two national parks, Dartmoor and Exmoor, are only an hour or so's drive apart but entirely different in character. What they have in common is superb scenery.

In August the eastern part of Exmoor is ablaze with ling and bell heather. (HB)

Exmoor is the only part of England where large numbers of red deer are found. They're around throughout the year, but are best seen during their autumn rut. (AS/FL)

In prehistoric times Dartmoor was covered in forest, of which only fragments remain. Wistman's Wood is a fairytale grove of gnarled and twisted oaks set among moss-covered boulders. (HB)

Brentor's church of St Michael is the highest in England, thanks to the Devil's intervention. (AB/PL)

This cottage in Branscombe, East Devon, is never without its coat of flowers. (HB)

Villages and towns

Devon villages with their thatched cottages are immediately appealing, but towns have their own charms too.

A Totnes rickshaw en route to a wedding. Totnes has led the way in the Slow movement – its rickshaws run on bio-fuel made from discarded cooking oil. (TRC)

Broadclyst, part of the National Trust's Killerton Estate, has a number of picturesque cottages. (HB)

A La Ronde, near Exmouth, is one of many National Trust properties in the county. (RW/PL)

Dartmouth is not only steeped in history but also uncompromisingly scenic.
Approach it on foot along the cliff path for the best views. (RHPL/SS)

The Old Light on Lundy Island. Owned by the National Trust and managed by the Landmark Trust, car-free Lundy in the Bristol Channel provides an authentic Slow experience. (VE)

Salcombe harbour from the South West Coast Path. (HB)

Beer, east Devon, is a working fishing village despite its beach huts and other visitor facilities. (RHPL/SS)

The sea stacks of Ladram Bay, near Exmouth, were part of a parched desert during the Triassic era. Time and erosion have created some of east Devon's most dramatic coastal scenes. (PB/SS)

Bigbury Bay and Burgh Island. At low tide the expanse of sand attracts the bucket-and-spade brigade, whilst at high tide the island's unique hotel is only accessible by sea tractor. (JH/FL)

The coast

Devon's two coastlines and variety of beaches make it a popular holiday destination, but walkers can still find their own secluded cove.

Hartland Point, with its lighthouse and distant view of Lundy, is set amid northwest Devon's most exciting coastal scenery. The geological turmoil of its cliffs is best seen from this most scenic and rewarding stretch of the South West Coast Path. (PF/PL) (HB)

One of Devon's most bizarre festivals is the Hunting of the Earl of Rone, in Combe Martin. The earl's sufferings include being shot at with muskets and threatened by a hobby horse. (ERC)

At first glance the church clock at Buckland-in-the-Moor, Dartmoor, seems perfectly normal. Look closer and you'll see that the gothic 'numbers' actually spell out 'MY DEAR MOTHER'. (HB)

Quirky Devon

The county has its share of eccentricities, from follies to festivals.

The Highwayman Inn, Sourton. John 'Buster' Jones took 40 years to complete this folly-cum-public house; the inside is as extraordinary as its entrance. (KB/FL)

Author

Hilary Bradt's career as an occupational therapist ended when potential employers noticed that the time taken off for travel exceeded the periods of employment. With her then-husband George she self-published the first Bradt guide in 1974 during an extended journey through Latin America. Since then she has seen Bradt Travel Guides grow to be an internationally recognised and award-winning publisher. In 2008 she was awarded an MBE and in 2009 received the Lifetime Achievement Award from the British Guild of Travel Writers. She lives in Seaton, East Devon.

Author's story

I bought my little house in Seaton in 2005, but it was a while before I could tear myself away from my roots in Buckinghamshire. Now I wonder why on earth it took me so long. It's always fascinating to look back at the process of getting to know a new place. I've done it often enough; it begins with your immediate neighbourhood then gradually radiates out, like ripples, as people tell you about, or show you, their favourite places. Devon has been different. Rather than the dropped pebble with its gentle ripples, it's been more like one of those speeded-up nature films where the greening of my knowledge and appreciation of the county have quickly spread from one point to cover the whole landscape. I started in early April, when the trees were bare, but drifts of white blossom covered the blackthorn and the banks were yellow with primroses, and finished in a blaze of autumnal colours in October. In the interim I've walked many miles of coast and moorland paths, cycled parts of the Tarka Trail and canoed the river Dart. The nature has been marvellous, but above all I'll remember the people I've met who, with their different stories, all share a love of Devon and Exmoor. Like them, I feel so lucky to be here.

Contributing author

Janice Booth initiated and co-wrote the Bradt guide to Rwanda, has had travel articles published at home and abroad, won two national writing contests, edited 20-odd Bradt guides and been on the judging panel for Bradt's annual travel-writing competition. She chose to settle in Seaton in 2001 after much wandering because she had pleasant memories of holidays in Devon: she tasted her first clotted cream in Sidmouth aged eight, rode on Burgh Island's sea tractor aged ten, and loves its mixture of coast and open moorland. She has written the boxes marked JB and several parts of Chapters 1 and 8, including the sections on Plymouth, Exeter and the Exe Estuary.

First published May 2010
Bradt Travel Guides Ltd
23 High Street, Chalfont St Peter, Bucks SL9 9QE, England
www.bradtguides.com
Alastair Sawday Publishing Co Ltd
The Old Farmyard, Yanley Lane, Long Ashton, Bristol BS41 9LR
www.sawdays.co.uk
Published in the USA by The Globe Pequot Press Inc, 246 Goose Lane,
PO Box 480, Guilford, Connecticut 06437-0480

ISBN-13: 978 1 84162 322 1

Photographs, illustrations and maps
Photographs Hilary Bradt (HB); Dean Riding Stables (DRS); Earl of Rone Council (ERC);
Victoria Eveleigh (VE); Flickr: Kelvin Barber (KB/FL), Coldnoodle (CN/FL), John Hale
(JH/FL), Adam Stafford/deerdiaryphotos (AS/FL); Photolibrary: Adam Burton (AB/PL),
David Clapp (DC/PL), Philip Fenton (PF/PL), Nigel Hicks (NH/PL), Dave Porter
(DP/PL), Roy Westlake (RW/PL); Ring of Bells Pub, North Bovey (ROB); SuperStock:
Peter Barritt (PB/SS); Robert Harding Picture Library (RHPL/SS); Totnes Rickshaw
Company (TRC)
Maps and illustrations Chris Lane and Chris Nairne-Clark (Artinfusion Ltd)
Cover artwork Neil Gower (www.neilgower.com)

Typeset from the author's disc by Artinfusion Ltd
Production managed by Jellyfish Print Solutions and manufactured in the UK

Mixed Sources
Product group from well-managed
forests and other controlled sources
www.fsc.org Cert no. SGS-COC-003985
© 1996 Forest Stewardship Council
FSC

CONTENTS

Contributors

Many Devonians have contributed boxes for this book. The following have given readers the benefit of their knowledge on more than one subject.

Victoria Eveleigh (pages 225–30, 234, 237 and 253) lives with her husband, Chris, on an Exmoor hill farm a few miles inland from Lynmouth. They have sheep, cattle and a herd of Exmoor ponies, as well as keeping a couple of horses for fun, stock work and hunting. Victoria has written for several magazines and periodicals, and is the author of the *Katy's Exmoor* trilogy and *Midnight on Lundy*. www.tortoise-publishing.co.uk.

Philip Knowling (pages vii, 20, 37, 83, 116 and 250) writes regularly on follies for *Devon Life* magazine, has visited follies around the world and contributed feature articles to a range of magazines. He is also press officer for Paignton Zoo and Living Coasts.

Tony Soper (pages 155 and 190) is best known as an author and wildlife broadcaster – he was involved with the BBC's Natural History Unit from the start, working with David Attenborough among others – but as a sailor whose roots are firmly in Devon he knows the wildlife of the coast and estuaries better than anyone. www.tonysoper.com

Acknowledgements

So many people whose names I never knew have shared their enthusiasm for what makes Devon and Exmoor special, from fellow bus passengers to the driver who picked up two hitch-hiking authors. Others who patiently answered my queries include a host of vicars, church wardens/historians and museum curators. Those deserving a special mention are Bridget and Jerry Gurney who described their home area in East Portlemouth and John Earle, the veteran author of Dartmoor walking guides, who gave me a great chunk of his time and expertise, as did Dr Michael Tisdall who shared his unique knowledge of the meaning of church carvings. Geoff Billington told me about bat conservation, and Bryan Cath and Mike Harrison between them had the answers to all my walking and cycling queries. The indefatigable Rachel Kelly from the Exmoor Tourist Association filled me in on her part of the world, and Pat Edgar (PR Matters) provided instant answers to all manner of questions. Finally a huge thank you to project manager Tim Locke for his endless patience, skill and knowledge, and to Janet Mears for meticulous proof-reading.

The Slow mindset

From Alastair Sawday, founder of Alastair Sawday Publishing
One of my early literary 'heroes' was John Stewart Collis, a poet who wrote about his work as a farm labourer during World War II. 'Now, as far as I can see in any direction, a plantation free (of entanglements) meets my eye, accomplished by the labour of my hands alone. Nothing that I have ever done has given me more satisfaction than this, nor shall I hope to find again so great a happiness.' If you are a gardener, have an allotment, make things or simply revel in the slow creative labours of others, you will know what Collis meant.

Going Slow is a way of thinking, living, eating and being. It is also a sophisticated response to unsophisticated, vacuous commercialism – the Slow movement offering something that is life-affirming, rooted in a deep understanding of human needs.

Slow is serious, yet it is fun too. The ideas go deep, but so do the pleasures – for Slow can be seen as a 'bridge from panic to pleasure'. These Slow books are awash with stimulating examples of people who have turned their backs on hectic and empty lives to find deep pleasure in living in a different gear.

Sawday's *Go Slow England* book has enabled thousands of people to enjoy themselves innocently, slowly and greatly. This collaboration with Bradt Guides, a delightful company with whom we have much in common, will lure readers more deeply into the crannies and nooks of England in pursuit of deeper and even slower pleasures.

From Hilary Bradt, founder of Bradt Travel Guides
At a Bradt editorial meeting some years ago we started to explore ideas for guides to our favourite country – Great Britain. We pretty much knew what we wanted: to recruit our best authors to write about their home areas. They had shown that they could write wittily and perceptively about distant lands, so why not ask them to explore closer to home? We wanted a series of books that went beyond the usual tourist attractions and found something different, something extraordinary in familiar villages and landscapes. To quote T S Eliot: 'We shall not cease from exploration, and the end of all our exploring will be to arrive where we started and know the place for the first time'. Exactly.

We have long been impressed with Alastair Sawday's approach to life and travel, and he prepared the way for this series. The Slow philosophy matched our concept perfectly: the ideal partnership. So take time to explore. Don't rush it, get to know an area – and the people who live there – and you'll be as delighted as the authors by what you find.

GOING SLOW IN DEVON & EXMOOR

'We Devonians are a bit worried about the title as we think we might stop altogether if we have to go slower!' This comment reminded me that Devonians do, indeed, know how to go slow. I've just taken a break from writing to walk along Seaton's seafront. It's a warm, sunny October day, and people are making the most of it. Some are sunbathing flat out on the shingle, others are eating fish and chips or picnics, closely watched by this year's crop of adolescent herring gulls, and the energetic are striding along the esplanade. Up on the cliffs are the silhouettes of walkers heading for Lyme Regis. It's half term so children are out in force, throwing pebbles into the sea, playing with their dogs or paddling, and a woman is fishing from the beach for mackerel. Yes, Devonians know how to go slow; it's we incomers and visitors who sometimes need a reminder or two.

Delving under the tourism surface of Devon, beyond the brochures and listed 'attractions', I found more and more nuggets of information that I've not seen in other guidebooks. Sometimes a place came alive through its historical background, pieced together from a number of different sources. Or I spotted something new and special in a village, or found myself in an isolated church. And I need to explain my fascination for England's little churches because it feels almost like a personal relationship. When I admitted to a friend that the first sight of Culbone brought tears to my eyes he looked at me pityingly. It has little to do with religion, since I would define myself as a church goer rather than a churchgoer; but I can still look for and find the footprints of history in these places. It's evident in the list of vicars who served that parish, from the Norman-French names of the 12th century to the women priests of today; it's there in the monuments which show so clearly the wealth and power of the old established families, and it shines from the contributions of a community that loves its church: the flower rotas, the kneelers, the hangings made by the WI, and the little messages to visitors. And the visitors' book.

If the Slow movement is about taking time to savour the moment and getting to know a region thoroughly rather than trying to tick off sights, then the usual guidebook's comprehensive approach wasn't going to work here. That's why we have selected ten locales which, in my opinion, hold the most interest within a smallish area. There are parts of Devon that deserve to be here but are omitted. It's not that I think them dull, only that to include everything would defeat the purpose. But there will be more editions, and I am always open to persuasion.

As the book evolved, I – or we, since Janice Booth has been involved from the start – realised that the response we most hope to get from readers who live locally is 'Well, I didn't know that!' I, in turn, hope to find the same response in the feedback that readers send me.

Follies in Devon
Philip Knowling

What are follies? Think of them as landscape jewellery. Like jewellery, follies are manmade and ornamental, designed to adorn and beautify. They come in a range of styles and may be useful (like watches or lockets) or (like brooches) simply decorative. They can be expensive – or just look expensive. Some are meant to make not only the wearer but also the buyer look good.

So what jewellery does Devon wear? The typical Devon folly would be built of granite and stand on a hilltop with a view of the sea, the moors – or both. Devon follies are vernacular rather than sophisticated, rural rather than urban. There are more towers and summerhouses than temples and triumphal arches. Devon follies tend to be – with a few exceptions – the product of unremarkable finances and modest eccentricity.

Haldon Belvedere is arguably the most famous folly in Devon – it's certainly one of the easiest to spot. The triangular crenellated Gothic tower stands out white among the dark trees of the Haldon Hills west of Exeter (see page 37).

Devon has a few garden landscapes of national significance. Generations of Fortescues have created something very special at Castle Hill. The most beautiful Palladian house in Devon stands in a landscape of bridges, follies, temples and ruins. A sham castle and a triumphal arch face each other down a long vista. Castle Hill, at Filleigh near South Molton, has all the élan of Stowe or Stourhead, if not the scale, and is open to the public.

Other Devon folly gardens can be visited, including the Capability Brown landscape at Ugbrooke House, near Chudleigh; Bicton Park (see page 29), in east Devon (its formality inspired by Versailles); and Tapeley Park, in north Devon.

On the north coast, the Pack o' Cards pub in Combe Martin (see page 244) is well known for taking its design from the mathematics of a deck of playing cards. The village of Fairy Cross, west of Bideford, has a beautiful conical bus stop with a painted ceiling and mosaic floor built by the lord of the local manor. It shows that the art of the folly is far from dead.

And then there are the oddities among the oddities. The Rock Nursery, at Chudleigh, is a plantsman's paradise and home to a watery grotto, hidden caves and dramatic lost gardens. Delamore House, near Ivybridge – which holds excellent outdoor art exhibitions – also has a mock prehistoric cromlech that was built to mark the millennium.

Old buildings need new uses to survive, and you can stay in some of Devon's follies. Ellerslie tower at Fremington in north Devon has been turned into a self-catering holiday let. Thanks to the Landmark Trust you can stay (self-catering) in some other Devon follies. Peters Tower, at Lympstone, is a petite bell tower – a night spent here is a little like a night in a grandfather clock. The imposing classical Silverton stables, east of Exeter, is like a courtyarded Roman villa.

Planning your visit

When to go

Most of you will know that the spring and autumn are the best times to visit any popular region in Britain. Our little island can't cope with the summer surge of cars that squeeze their way down lanes created by hoof and foot rather than design. So if you can avoid the school holidays, do. I've been out and about researching this book from April to October, and it's the springtime that has the best memories. So come to Devon and Exmoor as soon as the Easter holidays are over for coastal hillsides awash with purple and yellow from the violets and primroses, and new-leafed trees not yet obscuring the sea views. Most National Trust properties open at Easter, as do museums and other managed attractions. The first sign of spring comes in February, when Exmoor's Snowdrop Valley is carpeted with white, and March gives you snow-like drifts of blackthorn and, in places, expanses of daffodils – or wait until May for the bluebells and tender new beech leaves. Autumn offers quiet, sunny days and the changing leaf colours, but if you want to see heather in bloom you have to break the rule about avoiding summer: go to eastern Exmoor in August for its full purple glory. But of course many people go to this region for the beaches and swimming in the sea. Early September, when the school holidays are over, may be the best time for this.

We're so used to complaining about the weather forecast we often forget just how accurate it generally is. And most visitors have access to a television or at least a radio or some online device, so you just need to plan ahead for wet days. I know people who set out determinedly, booted and waterproofed, into the face of horizontal rain but I'm not one of them. Devon and Exmoor have some of the best walking country in England and it deserves to be seen through slanting sunshine not slanting rain. The county has some wonderful houses, excellent museums and other interesting indoor attractions. Even zoos and wildlife parks can be rewarding on a rainy day, because the animals also hate rain so tend to come inside, nearer the viewer, if they have that option.

Food and drink

The Southwest likes its food (and wine and beer) and hosts a number of food festivals that foodies would do well to incorporate into their holiday plans.

The Celebration of Food is one of the largest food and drink festivals in the country with over 230 events taking place across Somerset, Devon and Cornwall throughout October. See www.celebrationoffood.co.uk.

The region prides itself on its celebrity chefs and holds an annual Exeter Festival of South West Food and Drink, co-founded by *chef extraordinaire* Michael Caines, over three days each April. Three food and drink pavilions showcase the produce of hundreds of regional producers, celebrity chefs demonstrate their skills, and the public can eat and drink themselves into a torpor. See www.exeterfoodanddrinkfestival.co.uk.

Exmoor Food Festival (www.exmoorfoodfestival.co.uk) is Exmoor's response to Devon's indulgence. It's a nine-day happening with forty events all over Exmoor (both Devon and Somerset).

Slow Food in Devon

Marc Millon, a food, wine and travel writer based in Topsham, and a long-standing member of Slow Food.

Slow Food Devon is part of the Slow Food international movement that started in northern Italy in defence of traditional foods and way of life in the face of increasing globalisation and the loss of family values. Devon's Slow Food values have been interpreted by a dynamic group of individuals who believe in the importance of real food in the daily scheme of living. Pleasure lies very much at the heart of the 'slow' philosophy, which seeks not only to champion food that is 'good, clean and fair' but which also aims to bring people around the table for convivial enjoyment, good cheer, and the furthering of knowledge.

Throughout the year, a range of imaginative events takes place, from informal picnics and 'pot luck' suppers, to meals in pubs and restaurants; and from brewery visits and cider tastings, to workshops, masterclasses and more. These events are all open to members and non-members alike. Once a month, a Slow Food Devon market takes place with local member artisan producers bringing their delicious food and drink to Topsham, on the Exe estuary, which is particularly well served for food lovers.

The Slow Food philosophy seems to be particularly relevant in Devon. For this is essentially a relaxed, rural corner of the country where the quality of local food, drink and produce combines with a more laid-back understanding of what is most important in life which is, by nature, 'slow' here – and all the better for it.

Websites: Slow Food in Devon: www.slowfooddevon.co.uk; Slow Food in the UK: www.slowfood.org.uk; the Slow Food international movement and its activities: www.slowfood.com.

Vineyards in Devon and Exmoor

The region's mild climate and south-facing hills makes it an ideal place for wine production and the area has a large number of vineyards that welcome visitors.

Down St Mary near Crediton ☎ 01363 82300 🖑 www.englishvineyard.co.uk. Wine shop, tastings, tours.
Highcroft Vineyard Kilmington ☎ 01297 33944. Tours and tasting by appointment.
Kenton Vineyard Kenton, near Exeter ☎ 01626 891091
🖑 www.kentonvineyard.co.uk. Wine shop, tastings, tours.
Manstree Vineyard (Boyces) Shillingford St George, near Exeter ☎ 01392 832218
🖑 www.boyces-manstree.co.uk. Wine shop, tastings, tours. PYO soft fruit.

Old Walls Vineyard Near Teignmouth ☎01626 770877
⌂ www.oldwallsvineyard.co.uk. Wine shop, tastings, tours.
Pebblebed Vineyards Topsham ☎01392 875908 ⌂ www.pebblebed.co.uk. Wine shop, tastings, tours.
Sharpham Vineyard Ashprington (see page 143) ☎01803 732203
⌂ www.sharpham.com. Wine shop, tastings, tours, café.
Willhayne Vineyard Colyton ☎01297 553463. Tours and tasting by appointment.
Yearlstone Vineyard Bickleigh (see page 58) ☎01884 855700
⌂ www.yearlstone.co.uk. Wine shop, tastings, tours, café.

Some off-beat festivals

Some pretty bizarre and intriguing festivals are held in the region, not all in villages covered in this book. If you're searching for the eccentric side of Devon check out the following.

Hunting the Earl of Rone, Combe Martin (page 245). Spring Bank Holiday.
Patwalloping Festival, Westward Ho! A festival based on the ancient custom of throwing pebbles back onto the town's pebble ridge. This ridge prevented flooding and thus secured grazing rights. Late May.
International Festival of Worm Charming, Blackawton. The aim is to extract as many worms as possible without digging the turf or harming the worms. Contestants come from as far afield as New Zealand. May Bank Holiday.
Hot Pennies Fair, Honiton (page 21). July.
Apple Pie Fair, Marldon (page 116). Last weekend in July.
Birdman Festival, Ilfracombe (page 225). August.
Orange Race, Totnes (page 134). Chasing oranges down the street at breakneck speed. August.
Colyford Goose Fair. Mummers, Morris dancers, medieval costume and more (page 17). Last Saturday in September.
Blazing barrels, Ottery St Mary (page 25). 5 November.
Hatherleigh Fire Festival, blazing barrels are rolled down the streets (rather than carried, as in Ottery). First Wednesday after 5 November.
Sticklepath Fireshow. A combination of fire, puppets and drama. 5 November.
Turning the Devil's Boulder, Shebbear, Nr Holsworthy. A giant boulder, said to have been dumped by the devil, is turned to keep him away. 5 November.

Visiting private houses and gardens

Each year householders from all over England and Wales open their studios or gardens for the **NGS Gardens Open for Charity** scheme.

Since this guide aims to get under the skin of Devon, a visit to one of these open gardens is the perfect way of understanding Devonians or – if you are a visitor from overseas – the English. We are the most passionate gardeners in the world and Devon, with its rich soil and mild climate, makes enthusiasts out of even reluctant horticulturists. The gardens that are open in this scheme come in every size, from manor-house grounds to the kitchen gardens of semi-detached cottages. And it's not just the gardens you'll enjoy. Almost every householder taking part in the scheme adds to the money raised by offering coffee and tea with a wonderful array of cakes. I'm writing this stuffed to the gills with lemon drizzle cake and apricot slice. And full, too, of ideas of how to transform a small garden into a blaze of colour.

The NGS publishes *The Yellow Book* annually which lists all the participating gardens in England and Wales, but there's one for just Devon, which can usually be picked up free at tourist offices, or through the website www.ngs.org.uk. There are gardens to be visited throughout the year, from January to December, although more, of course, in the spring and summer months. Some only open for one weekend a year so you need to plan ahead.

Devon is the home of Heather Jansch, whose sculptures inspire awe and admiration in anyone who sees them. Using curved or chunky pieces of driftwood collected from Devon's estuaries and beaches, she builds horses that prance and leap through her acres of meadow and woodland near Newton Abbot. Her studio is open to the public during Devon's **Open Studios** fortnight in September (www.southwestopenstudios.org) and for the NGS Gardens Open for Charity scheme, under the name of her property, Sedgewell Coach House. She is just one example of the county's artists who invite visitors to see them at work and to buy their art at lower prices than in a gallery.

Walking and cycling

He who walks sees most of the charms of the country and especially of the coast, for he can wander where motoring and cycling are alike impossible, and can more fully appreciate the wonders of a Devonshire lane. In fact, if he be wise, the visiting pedestrian will have as little as possible to do with the main roads – except when a motor-bus service will take him speedily over an uninteresting stretch – but will stick to lanes, bridle-tracks and footpaths.

This advice published in a 1930 *Ward Lock Guide* says it all! There are suggestions for short and medium-length walks in each chapter.

My niece, living in Belgium, was told that it was impossible to cycle in England because of all the traffic. So I took her along the Tarka Way and she loved it. Now she's all set to return and tackle one of the long-distance routes. Devon has a good range of dedicated cycle paths as well as 150 miles of the National Cycle Network being developed by Sustrans, a sustainable transport charity (www.sustrans.org.uk), along with local organisations. All these are listed and described in the booklet *Cycling Trails in Devon*, available from Tourist Information Centres and the VisitDevon website (www.visitdevon.co.uk), as are the cycling guides to areas and towns. Most are free but there's a charge for those covering the long-distance cycle routes: *The Devon Coast to Coast* and *The West Country Way*.

SLOW DEVON & EXMOOR

Those who prefer off-road cycling of a more adventurous sort will find that Exmoor is the region most geared to this. See page 240.

Most of Devon's lanes are narrow with high hedges, so cyclists can feel very vulnerable. I asked two experienced cyclists for tips on safe cycling. Mike Harrison (www.croydecycle.co.uk) said his biggest advice is to make sure you can hear. Then if a vehicle is approaching you have time to pull in to the edge or be more visible. Lanes may be narrow but there is usually space for a slow-moving car to pass a stationary cyclist or pedestrian – after all, the lanes can cope with trucks and tractors. The back lanes carry very little traffic, but coastal roads can be busy. Adrian Silvester told me of a survey done for a biking magazine which found that you are less likely to be knocked off your bike if you don't look as though you know what you're doing. 'So if you ride along confidently, wearing a helmet, motorists won't give you much space but if you ride with arms and legs flailing they'll give you a wide berth.' Probably best to keep the helmet but flail those arms and legs.

Car drivers unused to coping with single-track lanes can find Devon and Exmoor daunting. See box on page 231 for advice.

Local buses

In July 2009 a cat named Caspar made the news by regularly catching the number 3 bus from Plymouth. The drivers knew where to let him off and he enjoyed his free trips for months before his owner found out what he was doing. At 12, Casper probably qualified for a Concessionary Bus Pass in cat years, but in fact the Devon buses provide such a good service, and pass through such lovely scenery, that it hardly matters whether you are paying or not. I took an hour's journey on the south coast for which the fare was £2.70. Most regions have a special deal on their buses (more details in the appropriate chapters) so you can spend a day on them, with some healthy walks in between, for very little. Devon County Council publishes a series of regional bus timetables as well as a bus map of the county. Relevant ones are listed in each chapter and they are also obtainable from www.devon.gov.uk/buses. Traveline (0871 200 2233; www.traveline.info) gives information on routes and timetables, so even if you are standing, in despair, at a deserted bus stop, you can phone them for help.

Top ten churches: a personal choice

My favourite churches are not those with the grandest monuments but the still-loved little churches that combine fascinating examples of rural art and history with evidence of their present-day community.

Luppitt page 22

East Budleigh page 30

Cullompton page 50

Colebrooke page 54

Doddiscombsleigh page 62

Haccombe page 126

Bere Ferrers page 196

Tawstock page 219

Parracombe page 246

Culbone page 262

xii

Reference Books

When researching this book I made use of four entertaining books, sadly long out of print.

Devon: A Shell Guide by Ann Jellicoe and Roger Mayne. 1975, Faber & Faber. The erudite research and literary style that you would expect in a Shell Guide.

Devon by W G Hoskins. 1959. Collins. The authority on Devon. No place is too small or insignificant not to merit an entry in the gazetteer.

Early Tours in Devon and Cornwall edited by R Pearse Chope. 1918; reprinted in 1967. David & Charles. A fascinating look at how early travellers in Devon saw the county. The writers date from John Leland, who travelled from 1534 to 1543, to Robert Southey in 1802. Daniel Defoe in 1724 and Celia Fiennes (1695) are included.

The South Devon Coast by Charles G Harper. 1907. Chapman & Hall. A lengthy and often entertaining look at Devon a hundred years ago.

Request for feedback

Devon and Exmoor are stuffed with people who have specialist knowledge on their part of the county, and although we've done our best to check our facts there are bound to be errors as well as the inevitable omissions of really special places. You can post your comments and recommendations, and read the latest feedback from other readers, online at http://updates.bradtguides.com/devon&exmoor.

How to use this book

The **colour map** at the front of this book shows which area falls within which chapter. Each chapter begins with a more detailed **chapter map** highlighting places mentioned in the text.

① ② ③ To guide you round, each featured place is given a **circled number** corresponding to the same circled number on the map. Points are numbered consecutively as they occur in the text, making it easy to locate them on the map.

⑤ This symbol denotes a **pub** recommended in Alastair Sawday's *Pubs & Inns of England & Wales*.

S1 S2 These symbols appear on the chapter maps at the start of each chapter, as well as on the colour map at the start of the book. These refer to the 30 **Sawday's Special Places to Stay**, which are described fully in the second colour section.

To give clarity to some descriptions of localities – particularly walks – simple **sketch maps** are included. They are intended merely to set the scene rather than to provide detailed information.

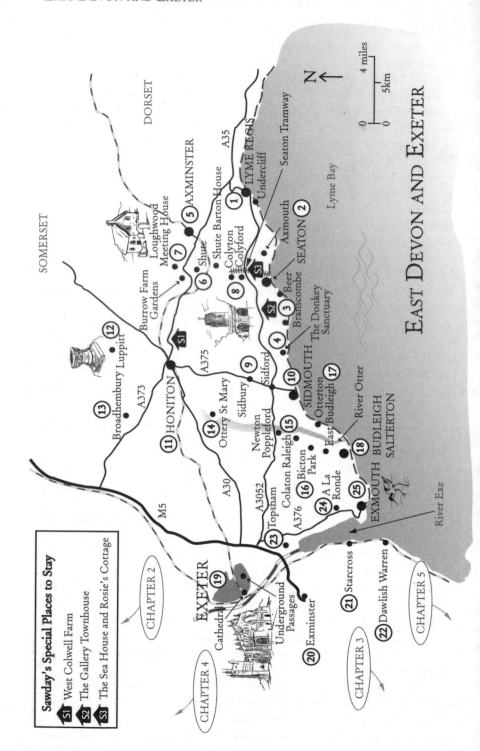

EAST DEVON AND EXETER

Sawday's Special Places to Stay

S1 West Colwell Farm
S2 The Gallery Townhouse
S3 The Sea House and Rosie's Cottage

CHAPTER 2
CHAPTER 3
CHAPTER 4
CHAPTER 5

SOMERSET
DORSET

N

0   4 miles
0   5km

Lyme Bay

River Exe
River Otter

SEATON ②
LYME REGIS
Undercliff
Seaton Tramway
Axmouth
Beer
Branscombe
AXMINSTER
Shute Barton House
Colyton
Colyford
Shute
Loughwood Meeting House
Burrow Farm Gardens
Luppitt
Broadhembury
SIDMOUTH
The Donkey Sanctuary
Otterton
East Budleigh
BUDLEIGH SALTERTON
EXMOUTH
A La Ronde
Bicton Park
Colaton Raleigh
Newton Poppleford
Sidbury
Sidford
Ottery St Mary
HONITON
Topsham
EXETER
Cathedral
Underground Passages
Exminster
Starcross
Dawlish Warren
River Exe

A35
A375
A373
A30
A3052
A376
M5

① ② ③ ④ ⑤ ⑥ ⑦ ⑧ ⑨ ⑩ ⑪ ⑫ ⑬ ⑭ ⑮ ⑯ ⑰ ⑱ ⑲ ⑳ ㉑ ㉒ ㉓ ㉔ ㉕

S1 S2 S3

1. EAST DEVON AND EXETER

East Devon doesn't offer the mystique and isolation of the high moors, the craggy cliffs of the northern coast or the steeply twisting lanes and thatched hamlets of Devon's heartland, and is characterised less by cosy cream teas and fields of red Devon soil, more by the wide Exe estuary with its boating and birdlife, historic Exeter and – excitingly – the internationally famous **Jurassic Coast** (see box below). Exmouth is the western gateway to this fascinating World Heritage Site.

A very large part of the locale also comprises the East Devon Area of Outstanding Natural Beauty. Along the Exe and Axe estuaries are bird-rich marshes and nature reserves, some with hides and walkways, while the coast offers peaceful, traditional seaside resorts such as Budleigh Salterton and Sidmouth, their often shingly beaches framed by high cliffs. Small towns proudly display their historic claims to fame (Honiton its lace, Axminster its carpets, Colyton its reputation as 'the most rebellious town in Devon'...) and villages their flower-filled gardens and ancient churches. All in all, it's a gentle part of Devon.

The Jurassic Coast

Stretching from Orcombe Point in Exmouth (see page 45) to just beyond Swanage in Dorset, the rocks of this 95-mile length of coastline – now a **World Heritage Site** – represent the Cretaceous, Jurassic and Triassic eras: a period covering some 185 million years. The oldest rocks are in Exmouth (Triassic, 250 million years old) and they decrease in age as they go eastward: 200 million years old (Jurassic) at Lyme Regis, 140 million (still Jurassic) at Portland Bill and 65 million (Cretaceous) at the eastern end. There's also a little pocket of Cretaceous at Beer Head. So, if you walk eastward along the coastal path from Exmouth, you're covering an average of two million years in every mile!

In Triassic times the area was a vast desert; then it was flooded by a tropical sea – imagine water creeping in over the red, arid plains – and the earliest Jurassic rocks formed. Towards the end of the Jurassic period (around 140 million years ago), the sea level dropped again and forests grew, where dinosaurs will have roamed. Then, around 100 million years ago, the sea rose again and flooded the entire area – and we're into the Cretaceous period. With so much movement, of course many fossils accumulated, but the best ones are in Dorset and thus outside our scope.

From almost any beach in this locale you can gaze upwards at high cliffs with fascinating rock formations, or see them stretching along the shore. An even better view is from the sea, and it's worth considering a 'Jurassic cruise' – see Stuart Line Cruises on page 39. This amazing chunk of geology (www.jurassiccoast.com) is a great national treasure; don't miss it.

JB

Getting there and around

Drivers have easy access from north (M5 to Exeter), west (A30), east (A35/30 from Lyme Regis to Exeter via Honiton) or south (A38 and A30 to Exeter). More picturesque, because it goes through smaller places, is the A3052 from Lyme Regis to Exeter. For non-drivers, there are good rail and bus links; cyclists and walkers have some well-kept trails and extensive flattish stretches, particularly to the west.

Public transport

By **rail**, Exeter, Axminster and Honiton have direct services from London; Exeter (which offers connections to Exmouth, Topsham and Lympstone) is accessible from just about anywhere in Britain, often without changes. Its **bus** station has services to all parts of Devon and beyond, some of them express and others meandering through villages. Coastlink bus X53, the 'Jurassic Coast' service, runs from Exeter right across to Poole; sit on the top deck for a wonderfully scenic ride. Smaller towns have their own local services, such as the beautiful 899 route between Seaton and Branscombe or the Sidmouth–Whimple 382 round trip via Ottery St Mary. The timetable you need is *East Devon* (www.devon.gov.uk/buses), or of course the ever-helpful Traveline (0871 200 2233; www.traveline.info).

Cycling

Around Exeter and the Exe estuary, cyclists are spoilt for choice. The as-yet incomplete **NCN2** is finished here, with the **Exe Estuary Trail** providing traffic-free cycling and walking. You can start at Exeter Quay and pedal to Topsham, past the unusual double lock and Countess Wear, or bring your bike to Exeter by train and join the trail via the new Miller's Crossing bridge. Or there's Lympstone to Budleigh Salterton via Exmouth, the first (traffic-free) stretch giving panoramic views across the Exe estuary. From Exmouth, you can cross the estuary, plus bike, to Starcross, on the Starcross/Exmouth Ferry.

Further east, the NCN2 should eventually run from Axminster to Budleigh Salterton and the **NCN33** from Seaton to Bristol; NCN33's Seaton–Axminster stretch is already open. For updates see www.sustrans.org.uk. The 82-mile **Buzzard circular route (Regional Route 52)** runs from Exmouth to Sidmouth via Honiton, Axminster and Seaton, some of it on NCN2

Exmouth Cycle Hire 1 Victoria Rd, Exmouth ✆ 02395 225656
⌕ www.exmouthcycles.com. Good selection of bikes including tandems and tricycles. Can collect and deliver. Open daily.
Saddles & Paddles 4 King's Wharf, The Quay, Exeter ✆ 01392 424241
⌕ www.sadpad.com. Open daily; cycle (and canoe) hire; cycle sales and workshop.

Walking

Around Exeter and the estuary are some good river/canal strolls, and an attractive stretch of the Exe Valley Way runs from the Exminster Marshes Nature Reserve to Exeter Quay. More excitingly, the East Devon Way and 30 miles of the South West Coast Path cross right through the locale, making a long circular trip of almost 70 miles. The many shorter walks are covered under their specific areas.

The **East Devon Way** starts at Exmouth and goes to Lympstone, Woodbury and Colaton Raleigh Commons and thence through often hillier country to reach the Dorset border at Lyme Regis: a total of 38 miles.

Walking and cycling maps and guides

The free leaflet *Exmouth Cycle Map and Exeter Cycle Guide and Map* can be picked up at Tourist Information Centres or on line from VisitDevon (www.visitdevon.org.uk then click on 'request brochure'). Through the same website you can order or download *The Exe Valley Way*, most of which is covered by OS Explorer map 114. For the Exe estuary see www.exe-estuary.org. The East Devon Way is partly managed by the East Devon Area of Outstanding Natural Beauty (01395 517557; www.eastdevonaonb.org.uk). The booklet *The East Devon Way* can be bought at Tourist Information Centres or ordered from its Honiton office (01404 46663 or 549173). All but the last few miles of the trail are covered by OS Explorer map 115 and OS Landranger 192.

The far east

A fossil-throw over the Dorset border is Lyme Regis, too deservedly popular to ignore altogether and, for walkers, joined to Devon by the famous Undercliff. The South West Coast Path is the most direct link between Lyme and the seaside resorts of Seaton and Beer, and to flower-bedecked Branscombe, squeezed into its valley between formidably steep hills.

Inland the 'carpet town' of Axminster has its feet well in history, dating back to 1755 when Thomas Whitty wove his first carpet, and nearby villages throw up some curiosities, such as the little church at Combpyne with its sketch of a ship on the wall, possibly drawn by some 14th-century sailor, and the quintessential Devon village of Dalwood.

① Lyme Regis and the Undercliff

Lyme Regis is not in Devon, so I won't linger on the undeniable charms of this most likeable and characterful of seaside resorts, but it has the best claim to being the gateway to the Jurassic Coast since it is here, and around Charmouth to the east, that most fossils are found, so a brief description of the town is appropriate. Since the book by John Fowles and film *The French Lieutenant's Woman*, many will recognise the Cobb, an artificial harbour, and the Undercliff where Meryl Streep brooded in her black cloak. The waterfront manages to be both intimate and impressive, and there's a small sandy beach.

Lyme has a Tourist Information Centre (01297 442138), a museum, a theatre, a teddy bear shop and lots of fossil shops which offer fossil hunts.

Walking the Undercliff to Seaton (seven miles)

Let me say at the start that although this is one of the best-known stretches of the South West Coast Path it's also, for many walkers, one of the dullest. Yes, the feeling of being in an English rainforest is interesting, and on a sunny summer day you should see butterflies and plenty of flowers, but you'll also be slogging up and down hills with the sea views obscured by trees, and the mud, which never seems to dry out, ever-present in the hollows. And there's no escape – once you've committed yourself to the walk, you must stay on the trail until you've reached your destination. The good news is that it is well engineered, with steps cut to deal with the frequent ups and downs, and signs explaining what you are seeing. This has to be a bus walk, with the Jurassic Coast Bus (X53) providing the transport in one direction.

First, a bit of history. On Christmas Day, 1839, after a period of heavy rain, a great chasm opened up in the cliffs just east of the Axe River. The ground had been showing signs of movement for some weeks, and finally around eight million tons of earth and rock slid forward and fell to the beach below. The event utterly changed the nature of this stretch of coast, pitching agricultural land into the abyss and returning it to nature. Over the years the fallen land has been colonised by scrub, ash and hazel, taking their place beside some huge lime and beech trees, survivors from before the landslip. The whole area is now a National Nature Reserve and a true wilderness since no land management is possible here.

Seaton, Axmouth, Beer and Branscombe

The town of Seaton and the villages of Beer and Branscombe, each in its shingly cove, hit the national media in January 2007 when the MSC *Napoli* was beached just off Branscombe and her cargo of wrecked containers littered many miles of coastline. With the subsequent looting (some looters stole wheelie-bins from Branscombe gardens to carry off their booty) and extensive clean-up operation, it was the biggest event in the area since the Seaton landslip of 1839, when about eight million tons of earth crashed down from the cliffs just east of the Axe estuary. Normally things are more peaceful!

The boatbuilders of Seaton

A friend lent me an ancient book on Seaton. Inside was a yellowing page from the local paper dated 1978 and I found, to my astonishment, that it was about my next-door neighbour! I knew that Paul was a boatbuilder, and I remembered him saying 'I've already told Trevor I want that bough' when we were discussing a neighbour's diseased elm with a curve in the lower branch, but I hadn't realised his pedigree. Paul Mears learned his craft from his father, Harold, who in turn learned it from a firm of boatbuilders in Exmouth. In the interview Harold is reported as saying: 'It's not just a question of being a good carpenter, you need to have a good eye to judge the curves and the extent to which the planks must be bent.'

Paul has inherited this good eye. 'I still use oak knees or elbows if I can get them. Yes, there are lots of names we use in boatbuilding, and it's funny how they change in such a short area. For instance we call the frames that go inside the boats ribs, but in Sidmouth they call them stiddles. You also see these differences in the shapes of boats all round the coast. In Hastings you've got the lute-sterned boats which are very similar in shape to ours but they've got a funny stern that overhangs, here we have the normal flat-bottomed beach boats, and in Cornwall you've got the long, narrow, deep boats and I think it's for the different sea conditions. In Cornwall you've got the long, rolling Atlantic breakers and the narrow boats can go straight through them, whereas here we have short seas so our boats can jump over the top of the waves.' Paul uses local wood whenever possible. 'You can't get elm these days. There's some in Cornwall which they use for their gigs – it's traditional to use elm for these. It's a very forgiving timber, very tough and it bends well. Larch is good, but it's not as hard as elm.'

Paul's son Alex is now learning the trade, 'although it's a shame really, he's wasted a hell of a good degree in architecture and engineering.' No, not a shame. There are plenty of good architects around but precious few boatbuilders.

② Seaton and Axmouth

Ther hath beene a very notable Haven at Seton, but now ther lyith between the 2 Pointes of the old Haven a mighty Rigg and Barre of pible Stones in the very Mouth of it, and the Ryver of Ax is driven to the very Est Point of the Haven, callid Whit Clif.
John Leland, 1540.

Indeed, two thousand years ago the Axe was broader and much deeper, and the Romans built a harbour at what is now Axmouth (they called it Uxelis), directly across the river from Seaton; the Saxons expanded it, and by medieval times Axmouth was a busy and important port with apparently as many as 14 inns. But then changing tides began to form Leland's 'barre of pible stones' at the mouth; despite the villagers' efforts to prevent it, the river gradually silted up and shipping dwindled. The first bridge across the estuary was built in 1877, replacing an overhead cable ferry. This old bridge, now a footbridge and a scheduled ancient monument, is the oldest concrete bridge still standing in Britain. The eastern end is in Axmouth, the western end in Seaton.

Axmouth village today has two historic old pubs, including the deservedly popular Harbour Inn, some beautiful old cottages, and a well-kept 12th-century church, St Michael's, with medieval wall paintings and appealing 19th-century windows depicting rural scenes – look out for the hen (improbably) feeding a worm to her chicks. There are good strolls or walks up into the surrounding fields and beyond. On the quay at the tip of the estuary there's a small marine aquarium and café, and walking eastward along the shore from here at low tide you may find fossils.

While its glossier neighbours Sidmouth and Lyme Regis can be described as 'seaside towns', **Seaton** is 'a town by the sea': plainer, unpretentious and less geared for tourism, and since both the author and contributing author live here, we're naturally biased in its favour! Flanked by high cliffs, with the chalky Cretaceous Beer Head on one side and red Triassic on the other, Seaton makes much of its 'Gateway to the Jurassic Coast' credentials. Bathing is safe and uncrowded on its long pebbly beach, which has occasional sand at low tides (for a snapshot of the Esplanade see page vi). Cliff Field Gardens to the west of town are large and peaceful, with a boules pitch and an intriguing labyrinth, and seats on the adjacent cliff give beautiful views out to sea – and as far as Portland Bill in Dorset on a clear day.

Seaton's oldest building, St Gregory's Church, was gazing across the estuary when trading vessels still sailed to and from Axmouth harbour; started in the 13th century to replace an earlier Saxon building, it has been altered or added to in most centuries since then. There's a 19th-century gallery at the west end and a beautiful window, engraved in 2001 by Devon-born Simon Whistler as part of a millennium project, called *The Waters of Life*. By day, the engraving really needs sunlight to set it off, but a lady arranging flowers (the church is lovingly cared for) told me how she'd been there for an evening service when a car outside switched on its rear lights – 'and suddenly it was so lovely, with all the red light shining through'.

In these days of supermarkets and chain stores, Seaton is pretty good at going slow. Its many small independent shops include three butchers, a fishmonger, two bakers, a traditional ironmonger and various cafés. Simply Chocolate in Cross Street sells hand-made local chocolates, Bag End Bags brims with vintage and modern bags and accessories, and the second-hand bookshop named 'The End' is only a beginning in terms of happy browsing. For fresh, home-made light lunches and snacks you could try the licensed Terrace Arts Café (vegetarian) or Pebbles, both in Marine Place just across from the Esplanade.

Summer pitch-and-putt and year-round tennis courts are available in Seafield Gardens, and for cyclists part of the Buzzard Route (see page 6) passes through. Church enthusiasts taking the Buzzard via Musbury and Combpyne should pause there: in **Musbury's** 13th-century St Michael's is an impressive memorial to various Drakes of Ashe (not Sir Francis), while **Combpyne's** small and very appealing 13th-century St Mary the Virgin has some fascinating old murals. Musbury has an Iron Age hill fort too. The helpful Seaton TIC stocks leaflets on local cycle trails and walks – including the popular Undercliff walk to Lyme Regis (see page 4) and the walk up to Holyford Woods, which at bluebell time is particularly scenic. A stroll out to the bird hide on the marshes is rewarding too.

Buses 52A, X53, 885, 899 and 52A all pass through Seaton, but the most scenic link to the big outside is the little **Seaton Tramway** (01297 20375; www.tram.co.uk) whose dozen or so colourful trams shuttle along the estuary to Colyford and Colyton. The views are extensive, and bird-filled (see box below). It runs from April to October and at some weekends in other months. Currently near the tram station, the Tourist Information Centre (01297 21660; www.seatontic.com) may move elsewhere in 2010.

Birdwatching from the Seaton Tramway

These historic little trams run from Seaton to Colyton and back, along the tidal estuary of the River Axe. Every so often there is a special birdwatchers' trip.

I took the bird tram in April. Diehard birders immediately informed me that it wasn't the best time – the widgeons have gone. And if you'd been here in September or October you might have seen the osprey. Nevertheless, in the spring warmth and slanting evening sun it seemed a wonderful way of looking at birds. I left the competitiveness to my fellow passengers who always needed to identify something before the guides. There was plenty of 'No, there. Can't you see. 3 o'clock Yes, a wheatear.' I was happy with the pair of roe deer that no one paid much attention to (no feathers) and with the explanation that the dapper female shelduck can afford to be sartorially equal to the males since they nest in old rabbit burrows so don't need the camouflage. I didn't know that. And I learned how to differentiate a greater black-backed gull from a lesser, and to pick out the redshank (well, yes, the red legs are rather a giveaway) and the ringed plover which was invisible against the shingle until it moved.

Altogether we identified about 40 species which wasn't bad in two hours. And we also saw spring blossom, green fields full of red Devon cattle, and Axmouth church from a new angle.

Be there at least half an hour before departure to make sure of getting a seat near the front, where the guide sits. Dates of the bird trips are on the tramway's website, www.tram.co.uk.

The Grizzly

An almost-marathon run may not seem the ideal 'slow' activity, but the Grizzly is different. No one is trying to beat a world record here, just survive. It is described on the Axe Valley Runners' website as '20 muddy, hilly, boggy, beachy miles of the multiest terrain running experience you will find this side of the end of time'. First of all, the Grizzly is held in March, ensuring the worst possible weather conditions and the most mud; second the course is along shingle beaches, narrow tracks and stretches of the hilly cliff path so you can't go fast, even if you want to; and third, it Includes the Black Bog, a sticky morass which, in some years, encases runners' legs from shoes – if they can keep them on their feet – to crotch with glutinous mud. There's a river to wade down (remember, this is March) and it finishes over a long stretch of Seaton's pebble beach which most of us find hard work just to walk along. For some reason the runners come back year after year, and for us, the spectators, it provides a very jolly picture of suffering. And it's definitely different. As one blogger put it: 'Around the course, there were lots of nice children handing sweets to disreputable-looking men, which is a good bit of role-reversal'. Details from www.axevalleyrunners.org.uk.

③ Beer

Men might get very excited at the name of Seaton's neighbour, a lovely 20-minute walk on the tarmacked coast path. But it derives from the Old English *bearu*, meaning either peninsula or grove, which crops up in one form or another in many Devon names. John Leyland, in 1540, called it Berewood and describes how it once had a pier 'for Socour of Shippelettes... but ther cam such a Tempest a 3 Yeres sins as never in mynd of men had before beene sene in that shore, and tare the Pere in Peaces.' It was never rebuilt, but the fishing and tourism trade manages perfectly well without one.

Beer is utterly delightful – and that's its problem. I first saw it on a sunny March day and was enchanted by the curved bay, enclosed by great chalk cliffs, the fishing boats drawn up on the pebble beach, the fishermen's cottages stacked up the hill and the shack selling fresh fish at the shore's edge: everything a fishing village should be. Running up from the beach is the main street, where a little channelled stream gurgles next to the pavement, and visitors browse in the galleries and small shops. My next visit was in August when it was choked with cars and tourists and almost tawdry.

Pecorama (www.peco.uk.com/pecorama), with its model railway exhibition and passenger-carrying miniature railway, is the village's 'official' attraction. There's plenty here to delight children, but adults will find a different satisfaction in the imaginatively laid out Millennium Garden. Down by Beer beach there's a helpful little **marine interpretation centre**, and in Fore Street are two high-quality art galleries: **Marine House** and **Steam Art Gallery** (01297 625257; www.marinehouseatbeer.co.uk) both under the same management.

Beer Quarry Caves (01297 680282; www.beerquarrycaves.fsnet.co.uk) are about a mile due west of Beer (a pleasant walk along Quarry Lane). Hoskins calls this underground stone quarry 'one of the most exciting things in Devon... a deeply impressive place when one calls to mind what strength and what sunlit beauty have come from its heart over so many centuries.' The quarry has been worked since Roman times for the white, easily carved limestone which is a feature of great buildings throughout the land.

Tours take place whenever there are enough visitors in the summer (coffee is available while you wait), but at set times in spring and winter. The full hour in the caves may be a bit much for some people but the quality of the guide's narrative makes it worthwhile. We learnt little nuggets of information, such as that the expression 'stone deaf' comes from the quarry-men's loss of hearing resulting from being exposed to the relentless echoing bangs of pickaxe on stone. And that the quarrymen had to buy their candles, but were only paid for perfect stone, so some blocks were 'not worth the candle'. We also saw greater horseshoe bats hanging from the electricity wires – no candles these days – and were told that if we'd done a tour in the early spring there would have been scores of them (see page 70 for more on bats). We learned that, behind an enormous pile of rubble, the 400-year-old remains of a quarryman's lunch had been found: rabbit and cider, and that the caves have been used for growing mushrooms and rhubarb as well as storing ammunition during World War II. There is also a secret chapel which was used for centuries by Catholics practising their forbidden religion. Supposedly a tunnel connects with nearby Bovey House, former seat of the Catholic Walrond family, though this has never been confirmed. What is known is that the house is built entirely of Beer stone and has a priest's hole.

If you don't want to walk to Beer from Seaton there is quite a spacious car park near Dolphin Antiques (see below), and the Jurassic Coast bus (X53) stops here every two hours.

Deep-sea fishing Cyril Newton ☏ 01297 21460, or Kim Aplin ☏ 01297 21955.
Dolphin Antiques and Collectables Fore St ☏ 01297 24362
🖥 www.secondhandtools.co.uk/Beer.htm. A treasure-trove of antiques and old tools (Gerry's speciality). Closed Tue and Thu.
Anchor Inn ☏ 01297 20386 🖥 www.anchorinn-beer.com. Outdoor seating overlooking the beach or cosy log fires inside. A varied and good-value menu.

Branscombe

Branscombe is not so much a village as a haphazard line of blossomy cottages folded into a combe. There's nowhere to go but along, so the 'village street' is a mile-long curve between steep hills with a pub at each end, and the church, and a cluster of National Trust properties (01392 881691) – The Old Bakery, Manor Mill and Forge – roughly half way. Branscombe used to have four mills but Manor Mill is the only one remaining. It's in working order and demonstrations are given.

The forge (www.branscombeforge.com) is believed to be the only working thatched forge left in the country – smiths have been hammering their wares here for at least 200 years. Now blacksmith Andrew Hall produces some classy metalwork – not cheap, but beautiful and very varied. Opposite the forge is a small information centre; on audio clips, local people talk about lace-making and smuggling. The Forge is open daily year-round; the Old Bakery, a photogenic yellow thatched cottage (now a café plus museum) 11.00–17.00 Wednesday to Sunday during April to November; the Mill 14.00–17.00 on Sunday March to November, plus Wednesday in July and August.

The **church of St Winifred** squats low on the side of a hill, looking more like a Norman castle than a place of worship; you quite expect arrows to rain down on the approaching congregation. An enclosed spiral staircase giving access to the Elizabethan gallery is on the side of the tower.

St Winifred was one of those saints who were rather casually beheaded, but barely inconvenienced by the fact, simply replacing the head and going on to do good works. She was the niece of St Beuno (see page 262) and one story goes that he restored her head to its rightful place, leaving only a thin red line to show its misadventure, and allowing its owner to live on to become an abbess; another version has it that her head remained on the ground, from where a sacred spring gushed to become the Holy Well.

The original church was probably Saxon, and some interesting drawings inside give an idea how it looked in Norman times, 1150, when it was rebuilt. The rarest feature is a triple-decked pulpit, allowing different levels for the lesson, for prayers, and for the sermon. The wagon roof is lovely, largely constructed from the original, worm-eaten timber. There are also some carved bench ends, one showing an unnervingly well-muscled Adam and Eve. The church has had some colourful vicars, including John Cardemaker who was burned at the stake, and Thomas Puddicombe who supplied a dunce's hat for any member of the congregation who, in his view, was acting inappropriately during the service.

Above the church is a row of cottages one of which, at all times of the year, is almost completely covered in flowers. It must be one of the most photographed private houses in Devon, and deservedly so.

If ever the advice not to travel by car into a village was pertinent, it's here. There is one small car park near the National Trust places, but that's it. The most enjoyable way of seeing the village is to amble down its full length (around three miles) as part of a walk which takes in the Donkey Sanctuary and the coastal path (see below). There is also an occasional bus service, the 899, from Sidmouth or Seaton.

S **Fountainhead** ☎ 01297 680359. At the Sidmouth end of Branscombe, this 500-year-old pub is popular with walkers and their dogs, and has extensive outdoor seating so no need to muddy the flagstone floor. On cold days it has a log fire, and good pub food along with local beers including Branoc ale from the Branscombe Vale brewery.

S **Mason's Arms** ☎ 01297 680300 ⌨ www.masonsarms.co.uk. The Seaton end of town, this 14th-century building became a pub to slake the thirst of the workers in nearby Beer quarry. Plenty of outdoor seating; meat is spit-roasted on the huge fireplace inside and displays of historic photos decorate the walls. Local beers include Otter Bitter and Branoc.

The Donkey Sanctuary

People *love* this place! The animals here must be some of the most pampered in the country, and their longevity proves the care lavished on them. A long list of names testifies to the number of people who remembered donkeys in their wills.

The sanctuary is open year-round (01395 578222; www.donkeysanctuary. org.uk). There's no charge for visiting it and it is blessedly free of commercial trappings apart from the shop. The story of each donkey is told through labels on the enclosures. The Jurassic Coast bus stops here and it's the start of some good walks down to sea.

④ A bus walk around Branscombe and Beer (5 or 7 miles)

The aim here is to find the most scenic stretch of the South West Coast Path and walk the length of Branscombe, so you can enjoy one of the pubs as well

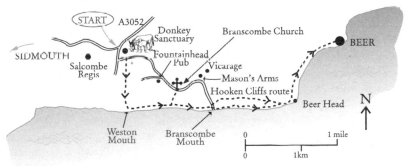

as the church and National Trust places. However, because Branscombe is in such a deep valley, if you want to keep mainly to footpaths you must resign yourself to a steep climb and descent over the hill that separates it from the sea.

Make the most of the free car park at the Donkey Sanctuary, or park in Sidmouth and catch the Jurassic Coast bus (X53) there and take the footpath down to Weston Mouth. The section of coastal path east from here is gorgeous – I think my favourite in all East Devon – passing close to the edge of high cliffs. You have a choice of footpaths to Branscombe, the first being the reasonably level one to Berry Barton which puts you on the lane that dives steeply to the Fountainhead pub. Or, continue along the coast path to the short but steep path that takes you to Branscombe church. The Mason's Arms is further down the road towards Beer. If you are parked in Sidmouth and the timing is right, you can take the 899 bus back to your car from the Village Hall. To return to the Donkey Sanctuary head for Branscombe Mouth (the village beach) where you can pick up the coast path again and continue to Beer – a further two miles. You'll be offered the choice of the high route over the top of Hooken Cliffs which is shorter and more level, or the longer, more undulating Undercliff. This is a spectacularly tumbled landscape, well worth it if you're still full of boundless energy, but I'm very happy with the high path and its gorgeous views, and watching the hang-gliders from Beer Head in the summer. From Beer, catch the bus X53 back towards Sidmouth and the Donkey Sanctuary.

Shorter, circular walks around Branscombe are described in *Shortish Walks in East Devon* and you can also head west on the coast path from Weston to walk the three miles into Sidmouth, high on the cliffs with superb views. Be warned, however: this stretch is rated as 'severe' – the toughest – by the South West Path Association.

⑤ Axminster and around

Axminster is the rail hub for the east of the locale, with regular trains arriving from Exeter and Waterloo, and buses from the railway station then heading off to Taunton, Lyme Regis, Honiton and Seaton. Long ago the area was a hub for less mechanised transport: it's at the crossing of two ancient roads, adopted by Romans as the Fosse Way to Aquae Sulis (the modern Bath in Somerset) and Isca Dumnoniorum (Exeter).

Axminster

The manufacture of this place is chiefly carpets, and esteemed superior to the Wilton, being worked by the pliant fingers of small children, from patterns and colours laid before them.
The Reverend S Shaw, 1788.

Alas, child labour on our own home ground! But indeed at the time Axminster was busily involved with carpets, for it was in 1755 that Thomas Whitty, a local weaver, wove his first carpet, and thus laid the foundations for a product that became renowned worldwide. They quickly became the furnishing of choice for wealthy English homes, as well as in many other countries. King George III visited the factory in 1789, with his whole family, and the Prince Regent ordered huge carpets for Brighton's Royal Pavilion. Axminster was on the itinerary of anyone visiting the southwest. An American visitor wrote, in 1864, 'Passed through Axminster, famous for giving an everlasting name to the carpets of royal palaces and mansions of nobility and gentry'. For the full carpet history, see the website www.axminster-carpets.co.uk. Quietly bustling in the peaceful beauty of the Axe valley, this market town has some attractive old buildings (but some bland modern stuff too), lovely walks out into the countryside, and a strong feeling of community. A farmers' market takes place in the central square every Thursday, and small independent shops are holding their own against the big chains. The well-stocked Tourist Information Centre in the Old Courthouse building (I was helped by someone so enthusiastic that she'd have described every inch of the town if I'd had time) can supply information about walks and all local activities. It's next to the really excellent Archway Bookshop, tucked in a rambling old building, which can order instantly whatever it hasn't got in stock, and between them is the Arts Café, providing snacks and light meals.

There are records of a Minster (monastic convent) here in 786, and its present Minster Church of St Mary the Virgin dates from the 13th century. The fine tower dominates the town from its position in the central square. Like so many churches in the area, every century has left some traces of alteration or acquisition. The interior is peaceful, beautiful and well used; lunchtime concerts are held every Thursday in summer, and evening concerts throughout the year.

A very much newer arrival in Axminster is Hugh Fearnley-Whittingstall and his **River Cottage** of TV fame (01297 631715; www.rivercottage.net). His shop in Axminster's central square is the essence of Go Slow, with its fresh local produce. The canteen attached to the shop – very busy at lunchtimes – follows the philosophy through and offers good, wholesome, unpretentious local food. Out at River Cottage itself, roughly between Axminster and Lyme Regis, a wide range of day courses and evening events (and some delectable meals) are held; check the website for the current programme.

The **Axe Vale Festival** in June is well worth catching if you're in the area (www.axevalefestival.org.uk). The showground buzzes with displays and activities of all kinds, showcasing local products, trades, crafts and activities; the food hall alone justifies the entrance fee, with its mouth-watering spread of meats, fish, preserves, cheeses, baking, vegetables.

Tourist Information Centre The Old Courthouse, Church St ✆ 01297 34386 🖰 www.axminsteronline.com.
Archway Bookshop Church St ✆ 01297 33744 🖰 www.archwaybookshop.co.uk.

⑥ *Shute and area*

If you feel like exploring around Axminster, start by heading a couple of miles west to **Kilmington**, a peaceful and pretty village where you can see traces of the old Roman road that ran from Exeter to London. A little further on there's the National Trust's medieval manor at **Shute Barton** (EX13 7PT; 01392 883126; www.nationaltrust.org.uk), with allegedly Britain's largest fireplace where two oxen could be roasted side by side, and the attractive little church of St Michael in Shute itself; and then the relaxing **Burrow Farm Gardens**, in almost ten acres, landscaped and with beautiful views of the surrounding countryside. This is an exceptionally peaceful place for just wandering among the different features and pausing in the coffee shop if you want refreshment. There's a woodland garden, a courtyard garden, a rill garden, lawns, borders... none of it too manicured or artificial. Finally, reasonably close to both Shute and Burrow Gardens there's the extremely tempting **Lyme Bay Winery**, selling specialist country wines, draught and bottled ciders, preserves and much more. The apple juice is wonderful! By car, you can load up your boot; if you're cycling, you may prefer to use their mail order service. Their Jack Ratt cider and scrumpy are named after the notorious West Country smuggler Jack Rattenbury.

Burrow Farm Gardens EX13 7ET ✆ 01404 831285 ⌂ www.burrowfarmgardens.co.uk. Open Apr–Oct.

Lyme Bay Winery EX13 7PW (signposted from the A358 between Seaton and Axminster) ✆ 01297 551355 ⌂ www.lymebaywinery.co.uk. Open daily in summer, Mon–Fri in winter.

⑦ *Loughwood Meeting House and Dalwood*

With the suppression of Catholicism following the Reformation, and the disruption of society in the Civil War, England was ripe for the emergence of non-conformist beliefs in the 17th century. The Baptists could only risk worshipping in secret in remote locations, and their Meeting House (EX13 7DU) at Loughwood, built around 1653, is certainly remote. The visitor book is full of comments such as 'worth the long search'. The little thatched building, tucked into the side of a hill, is now in the care of the National Trust. It is utterly delightful, as is the whole area. Inside is completely simple, as you would expect, with plain box pews and a gallery for musicians, complete with music rests. As in some churches, a hole has been cut to accommodate the bass viol. On the wall is a memorial to the Reverend Isaac Hann who died in 1778 at the ripe old age of 88, with a charming epitaph. The 380 bus from Axminster passes close by the Meeting House. If you are driving from Axminster the turning is off the A35, on the right, one mile from Kilmington. It is never locked.

The narrow, unsignposted lanes around **Dalwood** are not designed for car drivers who don't know where they're going but are perfect for walkers with a map or *Shortish Walks in East Devon*. Leave your car in the Loughwood car park and head out (continuing along the lane) for this village a mile away. It is the quintessential English community, not particularly pretty but with everything a village needs: shop, church, village hall and pub. Plus the meandering Corry Brook and miles and miles of open rolling countryside.

At the top of the lane is a proud sign pointing to the Dalwood Shop and Post Office. This is a Community Shop run by volunteers, 49 of them so the chap manning the till that Saturday told me. 'But only about 35% of the village uses it. It's a shame, really.' The church of St Peter is described by Hoskins as 'of no great interest'. That's true of the interior, although I liked the way that the carved capitals were at eye level because of the low roof, but the outside is fascinating:

gargoyles are quite unusual on village churches, but this church's gargoyles are all farmyard animals! Or I think they are. There are a couple of cows, a sheep (or maybe a goat) and a chicken! How appropriate in this farming community.

In the village I saw a lane sign: Lower Lane leading to Rising Sun. I liked that.

I chose to explore Dalwood because Loughwood is so near, but throughout Devon there are hundreds of such villages, ignored by visitors and guidebook writers, yet all with something special if you just take the time to look.

Tucker's Arms Dalwood ☎ 01404 881342 ✆ www.tuckersarms.co.uk. A thatched, 13th-century pub with flagstone floors and a generous fireplace, serving good food with a particularly yummy selection of desserts.

⑧ The two Colys (Colyton and Colyford)

In fact there are three, because Colyton and Colyford are both on the River Coly, whose valley offers some beautiful walks. There are also good – though hilly – cycle rides in the area. Bus 885 (Seaton–Axminster) runs through both Colyton and Colyford, as does the Seaton Tramway (see page 11).

Colyton

The little town of Colyton, with its steep, twisty streets and beautiful old cottages, oozes history from every brick and cobble. Prehistoric man used its veins of hard flint to fashion axes and arrowheads, then the Romans settled nearby and linked it by road to Exeter, Sidmouth and Lyme Regis. The present layout of its streets harks back to Saxon times; in 827AD it had a Saxon Parliament, and it appears in Domesday Book.

Wealthy families who came over with William the Conqueror settled and became Lords of the Manor. By the 15th century Colyton was Devon's third richest wool town. In 1549 its Chamber of Feoffees (local government) was established and still meets regularly today. Colyton was involved in the Civil War of 1643 (it supported Parliament), and at the time of the Monmouth Rebellion earned the reputation of being 'the most rebellious town in Devon' (see box on page 16). See www.colyton.co.uk for an excellent account of its history.

Colyton today is a town with the soul of a village: warm, friendly, active and community minded. Its old houses (some dating from the 16th and 17th centuries) cluster confidentially together in the narrow lanes. The unusual octagonal tower of 12th-century **St Andrew's Church** (one of only three in the UK) looks down on a patchwork of little rooftops, some still thatched. Inside the light, spacious interior of the church is a beautifully carved Saxon cross, as well as interesting memorials and two fine brass chandeliers, purchased in 1796 for £82. Its west

window is one of the largest in Devon. Concerts are held here, the music echoing evocatively around the old stonework.

Back in the mid 19th century, Colyton had butchers, bakers, a candlemaker and just about every other shop or business a small town could possibly need, including hairdressers and bookstores. The list is somewhat less exhaustive today, but still the several small, independent shops provide a service gloriously far removed from that of supermarkets and chain stores. The town has three royal market charters, granted by King John, Edward III and Henry VIII; its monthly **market** is one of the largest open-air local food markets in the southwest.

The most rebellious town in Devon

During the 16th and 17th centuries, religious dissent and persecution were rife in England, seesawing according to which religion (broadly, Catholicism or Protestantism) was uppermost. When James II came to the throne on the death of Charles II in 1685, there were general fears that he would give more weight to Catholicism. The (Protestant) Duke of Monmouth, illegitimate son of Charles II, hoping to overthrow James, landed at Lyme Regis and tried to raise a rebellion. He had stayed briefly in Colyton five years before on a visit to gauge public support, so the (Protestant) people of Colyton felt involved, and 105 marched off to join him in the fight for religious freedom. This was a larger number than from any other parish in Devon, hence 'the most rebellious town...'. None had military experience, but this was not a 'rabble army'; several were skilled craftsmen and one a doctor. But the Duke's army was routed at Sedgemoor, and 71 Colyton men were sent to face trial by the notorious Judge Jeffries. He sentenced 14 to be hanged (two were hanged, drawn and quartered in Colyton itself), and 22 to be transported to the West Indies as slaves. Two of the slaves eventually escaped captivity, pirates and numerous other hardships and made it back to Colyton – and how welcome the return to their quiet rural life must have been! The Duke was beheaded, an incompetent executioner taking five blows of the axe to complete the deed. Gruesome times.

JB

Art galleries and antique shops include the Dolphin House Gallery (www.dolphinhousegallery.co.uk) in picturesque old Dolphin Street, with the paintings and detailed, distinctive etchings of Roger St Barbe, and the long, rambling Colyton Antiques Centre down at the end of the Tramway platform. Another treasure down near the Tramway is The Tool Box (www.thetoolbox.org.uk), selling an assortment of ancient and modern tools for all crafts, and manuals of many kinds. Drawer upon drawer brims with old and new chisels, hacksaw blades, planes, nails, hinges... a veritable emporium! Haynes of Colyton in Market Place (www.haynesofcolyton.co.uk) is a good source of leaflets on walks and other local attractions.

Cream teas abound (try Liddons Dairy Tea Room down by the Tramway,

The Olde Corner Shoppe in Market Place or The Old Bakehouse in Lower Church Street, among others); the 16th-century Kingfisher in Dolphin Street (01297 552476; www.kingfisherinn.co.uk) and other pubs provide main meals.

Colyford

Colyford is equally rooted in history. Back in 1341, it was granted a charter to hold a Goose Fair – which it does now, annually, generally on the last Saturday in September. This medieval-inspired romp features mummers, Morris dancers, strolling players, displays of traditional crafts such as felting, weaving and thatching, a ram-roast, lots of people in medieval costume and a ceremonial opening by the Mayor. The surroundings are beautiful and, weather permitting, it's a fun afternoon, with all profits going to help the community.

A few old buildings survive in the short main street (it's the A3052, so watch out for fast traffic) including a 1950s-style petrol station, unfortunately not dispensing petrol at 1950s prices (the pumps no longer work) but housing a small transport museum. At the Tramway station at the bottom of the hill is a historic iron urinal – rather beautiful in its way! The little St Michael's Church, built as a private chapel in Arts and Crafts style in 1889, still has many of its original features.

Colyford Common Local Nature Reserve offers good views over the Axe estuary from a footpath and some boardwalks, which are being extended at the time of writing. It's between the tramline and Colyford village, accessed from Seaton Road roughly opposite its junction with Pope's Lane. Despite the boardwalks, it can get muddy.

The Wheelwright Inn in Swan Hill Road (01297 552585) is a popular place locally, serving good food in pleasant surroundings. On potentially busy evenings, it's safest to book beforehand.

The Sids

As you may guess, Sidbury, Sidford and Sidmouth are all located on the River Sid. If you catch the 52B bus from Sidmouth up to Sidbury, you can walk back to Sidmouth along the Sid Valley, passing Sidford and its 14th-century Blue Ball Inn *en route*. The website www.walkingindevon.co.uk/sidmouth.htm gives full details of the walk (just under four miles). Rather surprisingly, given the apparently flattish terrain, the river tumbles its way over several weirs. Its final stretch runs through The Byes, a pleasant and popular area of National Trust parkland between Sidford and Sidmouth.

⑨ Sidbury

The great treasure here is what's believed to be a Saxon crypt in the apparently 12th-century church of St Giles. One of only six known in England, it was discovered in 1898, and a guided tour of it is given on Thursday afternoons in summer; otherwise it's closed to the public. I found the tiny, plain underground chamber unexpectedly moving; who knows what Saxon voices may have echoed there some 1,400 years ago? The church itself has Norman features but has been much altered over the years. Rather surprisingly, gunpowder was stored above the porch during the Napoleonic wars. Elsewhere in Sidbury, the attractive Kingfisher Gallery (www.kingfishergallery.fsnet.co.uk) housed in an old working watermill, displays local art and crafts.

⑩ Sidmouth

Sidmouth is not a staring jerry-built town. Its streets are fringed with shops of sober appearance and houses not of yesterday's build, many of them gay with flowers in the summer months; it bears an air of quiet, decent prosperity, and is essentially restful and comfortable.
From a 1930 guidebook.

Today's Sidmouth has strayed somewhat from the description above. It's such a popular resort that it's not particularly Slow; at busy tourist times the beach and promenade are buzzing with people. But indeed it is still a pleasant place. Its curving, shingly bay is beautifully positioned between red cliffs (such a contrast to Beer's chalky white ones), it's full of flowers and floral displays, and there are some charming, dignified old buildings: in fact it calls itself a 'Regency Town by the Sea' and is rich in commemorative 'blue plaques'. John Betjeman loved it. There's a small traditional indoor food market in – yes – Market Place, and its narrow shopping streets have plenty of original independent businesses including a bookshop, Paragon Books, that is strong on the local area and personal service. The happily old-fashioned Fields Department Store also has painted on its wall 'For Service as it used to be'. In summer, the Manor Pavilion Theatre runs a season of weekly repertory, including plays that were already rep stalwarts almost fifty years ago.

However, the Sidmouth annual **FolkWeek** (www.sidmouthfolkweek.co.uk) is strictly 21st-century and is one of England's best Folk Festivals. Ideally, come in by bus rather than trying to park, but if you're in the area at the beginning of August don't miss it.

Sidmouth Museum is fascinating and worth a slow visit. Exhibits include sketches by Beatrix Potter (who used to holiday in Sidmouth), antique dolls, lace-making, local memorabilia, and of course the geology, archaeology and history of the area. Author R L Delderfield has a section, as does the artist Lawson Wood, whose cartoons and comic art remain so collectable. It's by the lych-gate of the parish church and is open from April to the end of October; guided strolls around Sidmouth also take place from here.

Cafés, pubs and restaurants are plentiful. Among many others, you could try (in Old Fore Street) Grants Café Brasserie or the pre-reformation Old Ship Inn; or (in Fore Street) Osbornes Coffee House & Restaurant or Brown's. Or buy picnic food from the Cheese Board (64 High St), a cheerful little deli with a variety of products from local farms.

A couple of miles outside Sidmouth, on the A3052 towards Exeter, is the award-winning **Sidmouth Garden Centre** (www.sidmouthgardens.co.uk). The café/restaurant is excellent, with an outside terrace overlooking the gardens and good, homemade food. Further towards Exeter look out for the **Farm Shop** (0796 9024749) on the same side of the road. This is the retail outlet for East Hill Pride, who are licensed slaughterers which means that their free-range animals have the best possible life before appearing on our dinner tables. John and Cynthia Coles have kept their business a small, family concern, and deliberately eschewed technology. Don't go looking for a website or email address – there isn't one – but turn up there and you'll find first-class meat and veg, pick-your-own fruit, and picnic tables overlooking the spacious Otter valley where you can munch on homemade cakes while admiring the view.

Dame Partington and her mop

In November 1824, there was a terrible storm in Sidmouth. Gale-force winds coincided with a high tide, and waves lashed up from the shore into the streets. One lone soul struggled vainly to protect her cottage. The Rev Sydney Smith, speaking out against the Lords' rejection of the Reform Bill in 1831, recalled the story:

'In the midst of this sublime and terrible storm, Dame Partington, who lived upon the beach, was seen at the door of her house with mop and pattens, trundling her mop, squeezing out the sea-water, and vigorously pushing away the Atlantic Ocean. The Atlantic was roused: Mrs Partington's spirit was up. But I need not tell you that the contest was unequal; the Atlantic Ocean beat Mrs Partington. She was excellent at slop or puddle, but should never have meddled with a tempest.'

Leaving aside the fact that Sidmouth is actually on the English Channel, presumably the ocean represented the Reform Bill that the Lords were trying to reject. And 'Dame Partington and her mop' thus came to mean some futile attempt, similar to that of King Canute in trying to stop the tide from rising.

JB

Just outside the town, the **Norman Lockyer Observatory** perches on the top of Salcombe Hill. Built by Sir Norman Lockyer in 1912 and now manned entirely by volunteers (luckily it seems that plenty of people of astronomical bent retire to Sidmouth), this is such an inspiring little place. Lockyer started with virtually nothing – he was actually a linguist and a clerk in the War Office – except a lively interest in the heavens. Quite by chance he used to commute to London with one George Pollock who, it turned out, had a 3½-inch telescope. He lent this to Lockyer, thus fuelling his interest. Then in 1862, aged 26, Lockyer met Thomas Cooke, a telescope manufacturer – who promised him a 6¼-inch lens if he could build his own tube to house it. This Lockyer did, in papier mâché, using a telegraph pole as a mould! He constructed the stand from scrap metal. And this telescope, almost 150 years old, is in the Norman Lockyer Observatory today, working perfectly and being used by visitors. Lockyer himself is buried in nearby Salcombe Regis, where the tower of beautiful St Mary and St Peter's Church points steeply to the stars.

The Observatory now has several telescopes, including a donated 20-inch Newtonian telescope, as well as a lecture theatre and planetarium, and is open to the public at least twice a month. Events include a spring moon watch, meteor watch, and observing the Milky Way. The entry fee (£5) is what keeps it going. Courses and tutorials are also held: the year's calendar is on the website.

Tourist Information Centre Ham Lane ✆ 01395 516441 🖰 www.visitsidmouth.co.uk.
Sidmouth Museum Church St ✆ 01395 516139 🖰 www.sidvaleassociation.org.uk.
Norman Lockyer Observatory ✆ 01395 579941 🖰 www.normanlockyer.org.

Sidmouth *Orné*

Philip Knowling

Sidmouth may be the little cousin of Torquay and Exmouth, but it has benefited from the way in which development largely passed it by. It was nearly fashionable in the late 18th century but never quite made it. The harbour was never expanded, the railway came late. The twentieth century failed to ruin the town.

Thanks to this, Sidmouth is truly Picturesque. The *Picturesque* was an early 19th-century fad for the rural, the rose-tinted and the rustic. To some the style is fey and sentimental; to others it is painterly and gloriously indulgent.

This the best place in Devon to spot *cottages orné*. The *cottage orné* of the Picturesque period is an organic, asymmetric blend of genteel gothic and tidied-up rustic. The style blends simple thatch-cottage charm with pointed windows, ornamental gables, Regency balconies and crenellations. You'll see them, for example, in Coburg Terrace. On occasion the *cottage orné* bears little resemblance to a cottage; Knowle, built in 1810 and now home to East Devon District Council, has 40 rooms.

Thanks to fashion, Sidmouth acquired a mix of Picturesque mock cottages, Regency terraces and crescents and Arts and Crafts villas. Also thanks to fashion, this is one resort that has kept its period character.

Honiton and the northern villages

Honiton sits in the middle of East Devon, with the beautiful rolling countryside of the southern Blackdown Hills to its north and the River Otter starting to make its presence known. The area is little visited by tourists so makes an ideal summer retreat whilst the woodlands are a mass of bluebells in May and golds and russets in the autumn.

⑪ Honiton

Honiton is a neat market town situate on the river Otter; the country around it is beautiful. The present condition of this town is indebted to a dreadful fire, which broke out on July 19 1747, and reduced three parts of it to ashes, to the great distress of several hundred industrious inhabitants. The houses now wear a pleasing aspect, and the principal street extending from east to west is remarkably paved, forming a small channel well shouldered up on each side with pebbles and green turf, which holds a stream of clear water with a square dipping place opposite each door; a mark of cleanliness and convenience I never saw before. The first manufacture of serges was introduced into Devonshire at this town, but at present it is employed chiefly in making lace.
The Reverend S Shaw, 1788.

That says it all, really! Beautiful countryside, a pleasing aspect, serge, lace – it just needs adding that Honiton today is well known for its antique shops, of which there are enough to delight any browser's heart. The High Street is fascinating: long, wide, and lined with a mixture of old buildings and (mainly) small, busy shops. Whatever you want, it'll be here, particularly if it's antique.

Honiton's earliest known inhabitants were the Honiton Hippos, dating back around 100,000 years. Their bones, now in Allhallows Museum, were found in the 1960s when a bypass was being built. Jumping forward several millennia, medieval Honiton was one of the main centres of the woollen cloth trade, then later became known for lace-making. 'Honiton lace' is a guarantee of quality worldwide. It was greatly in demand during the 17th and 18th centuries, both at home and abroad; in fact at the end of the 17th century over half of Honiton's inhabitants were earning their living from lace. However, in the 19th century machines had begun producing a cheaper version of what had been made so painstakingly by hand, and the lace-making industry declined, with many families losing their main source of income. There's plenty on lace-making in **Allhallows Museum**, which in fact is interesting as much for itself as for its exhibits. It's the oldest building in Honiton, dating from before 1327, and was first a chapel and then a school before being opened as a museum 50 years ago. Its collection of Honiton lace is one of the finest in the world, demonstrations of lace-making are given during summer months, and you can even try your hand at making it. Other displays include the history and archaeology of the town and area, and a very fine Victorian dolls' house from around 1840.

A lively Honiton event is its apparently inflation-proof **Hot Pennies Fair**, held annually in July and probably dating back to the 13th century, when hot pennies are thrown out of various inns in the High Street to the waiting crowds. Ouch. The following Saturday is **Charter Day**, marking the signing of the market charter some 750 years ago, when people dress in medieval costume and merry-make appropriately. Normal markets are held in the High Street on Tuesdays and Saturdays, with a local farmers' market on the third Thursday of the month.

Basics

Honiton Tourist Information Centre Dowell St ☎ 01404 43716
🖰 www.honitontic.org.uk. Open Mon–Sat, shorter opening hours in winter. The
website is adequate, but a more informative one is www.honiton.com.
Allhallows Museum High St, beside St Paul's Church ☎ 01404 44966
🖰 www.honitonmuseum.co.uk. Open from Easter to end October.

Food and drink

s♀ The Holt 178 High St, Honiton ☎ 01404 47707 🖰 www.theholt-honiton.com. An
unpretentious-looking pub serving superior food. The Otter connection is not so much
because of the river but because the McCaigs own the Otter Brewery, so as you would
expect, beer has a prominent presence here.
Honiton Wine Bar 79 High St ☎ 01404 47889 🖰 www.honitonwinebar.co.uk.
In one of the town's oldest houses, built around 1766, this atmospheric place has
antique maps and photos of old Honiton on the walls. Menus are mostly traditional
with a modern twist. It's popular locally, so gets busy.

Luppitt and Broadhembury

Any number of the villages in this large area northwest of Honiton could be
picked out for description, so Luppitt and Broadhembury are just samples. A
journey on the Fridays-only bus 863 will take you on a Magical Mystery Tour of
the region.

⑫ *Luppitt*

The village consists of a few houses strung along a deep valley, but
the church is sheer delight. The first thing that strikes you on
entering is the cruciform design set off by the dark timbered
cradle roof of the nave and transepts which are said to date
back to the 14th century. Then you notice the bell ropes. In
most churches these are hidden away in the tower but here
they hang close to the font, and a sign proclaims that the eight bells were rung
for three hours three minutes on 19 February 1960 to celebrate the birth of
Prince Andrew. Another notice tells us that the chimney apparatus was installed
in 1928 and extended in 1974. This allows tunes to be played by one operator.

The font is thought to be about a thousand years old and, to the unschooled
eye, looks delightfully pagan. It is four-sided, with a bearded head at each corner.
On one side a very cross-looking dragon, with a second head on what could be
its tail, is hotly pursued by a determined man with a spear. This is, so they say, a
double-headed monster which represents the evils of duplicity. Then there are
some violent goings-on with a club and a severed head or two (probably a
martyrdom). The next is said to be a hunting scene, although it's not easy to know
what animal is being hunted; a boar, maybe. Finally the carver seems to have run
out of inspiration and there an abstract design which looked to me to be a
giant tapeworm, though the official description is that it's the tree of life.

Whatever it's all about, it's a delightful piece of work and thrillingly old.

New, but equally impressive in its way, is the millennium *Tapestry of Luppitt*, a book of photos and descriptions showing every aspect of the community.

The bell ringers of Devon

If you're a 'church crawler' like me, you start to notice unusual features. I was struck, for instance, by the floor-level bell ropes in Luppitt and Lustleigh, and wondered if they were a rarity. Usually, I thought, the bell ringers climb up to the tower. The opportunity to learn more about this and bell ringing in general came when I met David Trist, a keen bell ringer. 'There are a lot of ground floor rings in Devon' he said. 'This arose because the fashion in Devon was for relatively short solid towers as opposed to Somerset which liked tall towers. The Devon fashion may well have sprung from the local building materials, in this case granite, being both difficult to work and very heavy.' I joked that I knew all about bell ringing because of the ongoing story line in *The Archers*. 'You're thinking of method ringing,' said David. 'That's not what we do. In Devon we do call-change ringing.'

'What's the difference?'

'Call-changes are a repeated pattern of ringing which then introduces a slight change. Method ringing does not repeat its patterns and is constantly changing its sound on every stroke of the bell. Our tradition of call-changes is probably what all churches used to ring.' David went on to explain that the tradition was passed down through families and communities but because ringing the old bells was hard work, it used to be the 'working' community that did it. Old rules that survive on tower boards state that it was an offence to swear, curse, fight, and draw knives or pistols in church. This says a lot about the bell-ringing community. The gentry and clergy decided to take up bell ringing in order to introduce a more sophisticated style, better suited to people with an education. This was a blatant attempt to exclude the rougher element. Devon was barely affected by the changes of population brought about by the agricultural and industrial revolutions in other counties, so a strong tradition of ringing continued to be handed down through families — which continues to this day with the Trouts, Sharlands, Pascoes and Adams' dynasties. 'As a result,' said David 'we maintained our tradition which is now recognised throughout the country as being uniquely skilful.'

⑬ Broadhembury

The hembury part of the name comes from Hembury Fort to the south (considered the finest hillfort in Devon), but there is another, nearer earthwork, Dumpdon Hill, which was also a hillfort.

Broadhembury is the only village in this region which attracts substantial numbers of coach parties, and understandably so: it's very, very pretty. The Drewe family built this typical estate village, which has rows of thatched cottages abutting the road, the lack of front gardens more than compensated for by the profusion of roses and creepers up the walls. The Grange, the Drewes' ancestral home, is still an imposing presence south of the village. It was built in 1603 by Edward Drewe, legal officer of Queen Elizabeth, who is buried in Broadclyst church (see page 52). The church is unimpressive, though the list of 'Donations to the Poor of this Parish' was interesting, from £10 per annum in 1725 to the interest on £300 in 1836. The popular pub **The Drewe Arms** (01404 841267; www.thedrewearms.co.uk) serves classy food.

The mid Otter

By the time the River Otter reaches Ottery St Mary it has become a focus for the area and an invitation for walkers.

⑭ Ottery St Mary

At first acquaintance the grandeur of the cathedral-like church doesn't really fit this ordinary little Devon town, but Ottery punches above its weight. It is one of Devon's Transition Towns, with Sustainable Ottery promoting the same values as Totnes: a community market (held in the Institute Hall on the last Saturday of the month), a reduction in energy use, and other initiatives. It produces a good free news sheet, the *Ottery Gazette*, and there's a helpful **Tourist Information Centre** (01404 813964).

Near the river is a unique 'tumbling weir' which supplied power to the nearby wool factory. The weir is in the form of a circular hole in the middle of the stream, allowing water to sluice down to a tunnel and then to the river.

The **Church of St Mary** is undoubtedly what draws visitors to the town. The manor of Ottery was given to the cathedral of Rouen by Edward the Confessor, and wrested back in 1334 by Bishop Grandisson who set about rebuilding the church, modelling it on Exeter Cathedral. It was added to in the 16th century and in the Victorian era. And repainted in 1977. And here, for me, is the problem. I don't like this church as much as I should; the whole is not equal to the sum of its parts and it lacks a feeling of spirituality. The stonework is too white, the crossings on the roof too brightly painted, the bosses too well restored. This view was not shared by my companions, however, and the parts that I did like are splendid. No one can miss the two monuments to the Grandissons who lie on each side of the aisle under elaborately carved canopies. Sir Otho de Grandisson was the bishop's younger brother. He died in 1359 and lies there in full armour, with his luxuriant moustache draped over his breastplate. He has the knight's usual lion at his feet, symbolising strength, although it has lost its head. His wife, Lady Beatrix, looks as uncomfortable in death as she probably was in life: her hair is incorporated into a square headdress which has the effect of a pair of blinkers; this, along with the high collar of her dress, must have ensured that she faced life looking straight ahead at all times. Two little dogs nuzzle each other at her feet, their liveliness contrasting with their poor inanimate mistress. Another notable monument, although carved in marble 500 years later, is to Jane Fortescue, Baroness Coleridge. The carving is very fine, and it's interesting to see that her feet rest on an otter rather than the usual dog (see box below).

All visitors will pick out their favourite things from the detailed guide. Don't miss the little medieval encaustic tile showing a spear-wielding knight on a charger (you'll also see his image on the kneelers), behind the altar screen, and the very cute little elephant with human ears on one of the capitals.. The astronomical clock is also impressive for its age (perhaps as early as the mid 14th century) and its complexity. On the south wall is a brass memorial to a young soldier who died in action in Afghanistan – in 1880.

The Coleridge family

Although of humble origins, the poet's father, the Reverend John Coleridge, was headmaster of the local grammar school and vicar of the church in Ottery St Mary from 1760 until his death in 1781. He married twice and had a total of 13 children. By the time the youngest, Samuel Taylor (named after his godfather), was born in 1772, his father was already in his mid-fifties and his mother, a farmer's daughter, was 45. John Coleridge seems to have been an affectionate and well meaning father and vicar, but decidedly eccentric. He insisted on reading the Bible in Hebrew to his flock of farm labourers, saying that it was 'the language of the Holy Ghost'.

The young Samuel grew up in and around the church, but took refuge from bullying by reading adult books, so that he had 'all the docility of the little child but none of child's habits. I never thought as a child, never had the language of a child.' The religious sub-plot of the *Rime of the Ancient Mariner* reflects his upbringing.

The whole south transept of St Mary's church is given over to Coleridge memorials, including the questionable mosaic tiled walls and the stained glass window. These were the gift of Lord John Duke Coleridge, the eldest son of John Taylor Coleridge and a great nephew of the poet. He sensibly chose law and politics as his career path and rose to become Lord Chief Justice of England as well as a Baron. It is his wife, Jane Fortescue Coleridge, whose marble memorial lies in the church. The otter was part of the family heraldry.

Ottery's blaze of glory comes each 5 November (Guy Fawkes night) when it holds its annual **Tar Barrel Event** when flaming tar barrels are carried through the town streets. This is said to date from 1688, and continues despite apparently flying in the face of health and safety issues.

Seasons 9 Silver St ✆ 01404 815751. Breakfast, lunch, tea (gardens). One of the few good places to eat in Ottery.

Stagestruck 19 Broad St ☏ 01404 811311 **e** stagestruck99@hotmail.com. Run by Joyce and David Pomeroy and Nick Lawrence, keen members of Ottery Choral Society. An extraordinary collection of essentials for the actor: wigs, stage makeup, clothing and dance shoes. A fascinating browse even if you're not involved in theatre.

Around Ottery: Cadhay Manor and Escot

A mile from Ottery is **Cadhay Manor**, a privately-owned Tudor house, famous for its gardens and courtyard with statues of Henry VIII and his three children (who all became monarchs). Just north of the A30 is **Escot**, a hybrid of garden, adventure playground and small zoo. The otters were hiding when I visited, as were the red squirrels, but what I really liked about the place was the unstructured adventures available for gutsy children. There's the Forest Leap, a woodland drop slide which scared the pants off me just looking at it, but as a 12-year-old I would have loved it. There are natural slides down woodland slopes, and ropes, and above all a lack of adult supervision and very few warnings. The owners very sensibly expect parents to take responsibility for their children, and the policy works.

><><><

Cadhay Manor EX11 1QT ☏ 01404 813511 ⌂ www.cadhay.org.uk. Open Fri May–Sep plus late spring and summer bank hols, 14.00–17.30.

Cuckoo Down Farm Yurts West Hill, EX11 1UE ☏ 01404 811714 or 0773 868 7246 ⌂ www.luxurydevonyurts.co.uk. A huge field with three luxury yurts set up to suit the most fastidious camper: Persian carpets, big double beds, two sofas and, surprisingly, a wood-burning stove. Outside is a little covered kitchen, and a compost loo. It's utterly peaceful, and great for children who can be as adventurous as they want, or more domestic collecting eggs from the free-range hens.

Escot EX11 1LU ☏ 01404 822188 ⌂ www.escot-devon.co.uk. Open daily.

⑤ Jack in the Green Inn Rockbeare EX5 2EE ☏ 01404 822240 ⌂ www.jackinthegreen.uk.com. Some way west from Ottery and on the other side of the A30, this may not look impressive from the outside but the food is worth going out of your way for. Smart and foody, it has modern variations of tried and trusted pub favourites as well as more ambitious restaurant offerings.

A walk down the Otter

A good path runs along the west bank of the River Otter to Tipton St John, and a not-so-good one returns the other side. This, in 2009, had been diverted 'for health and safety reasons' (I think the bank is collapsing) by the old mill, necessitating walking an unrewarding stretch of road to just short of Wigaton. Apart from this diversion the route is scenic and varied.

Tipton St John is a very small village with a heart of gold. Or at least in the person of the lady running the village shop (formerly the post office). Seeing our crestfallen faces when we asked if there was a teashop in the village, she provided cups of tea, doughnuts and chairs. There is a village pub, but it stops serving lunches at 2pm.

Perhaps the best way of enjoying the Otter is to combine the walk with one of the prettiest bus trips in east Devon. Bus 382 runs roughly every two hours on a circular route, taking in Ottery St Mary, Tipton St John and Bowd, just off the A3052. So you can park in Ottery, take the bus to Bowd, and walk back to Ottery via the East Devon Way to Harpford and then up the River Otter to Ottery via Tipton St John. It's a distance of about five miles. The whole bus circuit from/to Ottery takes an hour and if you stay on the bus you'll see some lovely countryside and small villages.

The lower Otter

The River Otter splices this region lengthwise, adding character to the little villages to its west and giving the town of Budleigh Salterton a nearby birdwatching attraction to add to its beach. The coast to the east of the Otter is a place of dramatic red sea-stacks and devoid of any settlement apart from Otterton. The region is also known as the birthplace of Sir Walter Raleigh, and the home of the pre-Raphaelite artist Sir John Everett Millais, whose famous painting *The Boyhood of Raleigh* is identifiably set in his home town of Budleigh Salterton – there's a bit of red east-Devon cliff in its left hand side and the wall on which the sailor sits to tell his tales is still there. He is pointing, accurately, towards the New World.

⑮ Newton Poppleford, Colaton Raleigh and ⑯ Bicton Park

Newton Poppleford is one of those places people drive through on the A3052, smile at the name (*popple* is a smooth, rounded pebble used as decoration) then

East Devon's heathland

The county's pebble-bed heaths are composed of sand and pebbles, so are relatively infertile. They have just escaped cultivation and have evolved as a precious habitat for endangered species, particularly if they include ponds which attract dragonflies and damselflies. Rare birds include the Dartford warbler, and there are also stonechats, linnets and wheatears. Nightjars also breed in this habitat. Among the heathland butterflies you may see are graylings, small heath and silver-studded blues. You may also see slowworms.

Collectively known as the East Devon Common or Heathland, these places include **Aylesbeare Common** (an RSPB reserve), which is ablaze with gorse in the early summer, and networked by footpaths, **Harpford Common** and the broad expanse of **Woodbury Common** which is purple with heather in the late summer and has numerous (confusing) walking trails. The East Devon Way crosses many of these heaths.

forget about, a fact that irritates its residents. And indeed, Newton Poppleford is an attractive large village with some cob-and-thatch cottages including arguably the oldest tollhouse in the county (1758) on the western edge of the village. Also on the western edge, on the left as you head towards Exeter, is a garden containing a local eccentricity: a clock set in a red phone box. It's the work of Ken Woodley, a local clockmaker.

Sir Walter Raleigh

Out of many variations this spelling of Sir Walter's surname has become the best known. Facts about his early life are vague: he was born sometime between 1552 and 1554, in Hayes Barton near East Budleigh (see below), and is thought to have studied law. Next he spent time as a soldier and landowner in Ireland, where he is credited with planting the first potato – but probably didn't. Nor was it he, as is often claimed, who first brought tobacco to England: Sir John Hawkins did. There's a story that one of Raleigh's servants doused him with water because the smoke from his pipe made her think he was on fire; it's said to have happened at his home in Ireland – or in Wiltshire – or in Dorset. Who knows!

Returning to England from Ireland, he was introduced at court and quickly found favour with Queen Elizabeth. This is the Raleigh with whom we're more familiar: the dashing, gallant courtier beloved of the Queen. Whether or not he actually flung his cloak into a puddle so she could walk on it, he certainly charmed her. He also spied for her, and uncovered the Babington plot to replace her with Mary, Queen of Scots. She knighted him, and gave him lucrative positions and land.

In 1592 he secretly married one of the Queen's ladies in waiting, for which offence Elizabeth sent him briefly to the Tower. After his release, he was elected to Parliament, and also spent three years as Governor of Jersey. He also went to sea, first to seek (unsuccessfully) a fabled 'golden city' in Guiana, now Venezuela; his *Discoverie of the Large, Rich and Bewtiful Empyre of Guiana* became a best-seller. Embracing piracy, he was involved in the sack of Cadiz.

When James I succeeded Elizabeth he demoted Raleigh, eventually imprisoning him in the Tower under death sentence for alleged treason. In his 13 years there Raleigh started writing his mammoth *Historie of the World*. Released in 1616, he was sent off to seek gold again in Guiana, but the expedition failed and his death sentence was reinstated. He was executed in 1618. It's said that his wife had his head embalmed and carried it with her in a bag for the rest of her life.

Raleigh was undoubtedly a skilful soldier, seaman, explorer and administrator, who played a leading role in Elizabethan history and society. Also he painstakingly recorded current events, and Tennyson's poem *The Revenge* is based closely on an account by him. But what has lasted until the present day is his poetry: straightforward, evocative, well shaped and often charming. The charismatic courtier and adventurer was also one of the foremost Elizabethan poets – and perhaps this is his greatest legacy.

JB

Colaton Raleigh is a pleasant village with some cob-and-thatch houses, but would be ignored if it wasn't for the Raleigh connection (see box on page 28). Sir Walter may or may not have been christened in the chapel of Place Court, a nearby manor.

The splendid gardens of **Bicton Park** (01395 568465; www.bictongardens.co.uk) are open year round. It's a mini-Kew with glass houses for different climates – arid, temperate and tropical – plus a palm house which is actually older than Kew's. So even if it's pouring with rain, as it was when I last visited, there's plenty of under-cover enjoyment including a good restaurant. On a sunny day the spacious formal gardens are always rewarding, featuring plants from different parts of the world. A list of rules for gardeners, dated 1842, makes entertaining reading. Infringements included smoking a pipe at work, coming to work on Monday in a dirty shirt or with untied shoes, swearing or 'in any way mutilating or defacing the above rules'. The fines were deducted equally from the pay of all workers at the end of the year and put 'to some useful purpose'.

Finally there's a very good countryside museum, full of intriguing old farm machinery. Don't miss the horrendous spiked man trap of 1790, used to catch poachers and trespassers. And you can speculate over the 'egg trap' until you realise that it traps egg eaters rather than eggs. There are some beautiful steam engines, a huge cider press, early threshing machines, and all the implements and machinery of Devon's agricultural heritage.

Moores' Restaurant 6 Greenbank, High St, Newton Poppleford ✆ 01395 568100 ⌂ www.mooresrestaurant.co.uk. Upmarket and well regarded.

The Otter Inn Colaton Raleigh ✆ 01395 568434 ⌂ www.otterinn.co.uk. Family friendly, with a large garden, and good-value food served 12.00–21.00.

⑰ Otterton and East Budleigh

Otterton's relative isolation as the only village on the east side of the southern Otter gives it an additional appeal. There's a fine walk from here to the coast and those famous sea-stacks. The village is most attractive, with whitewashed cottages set beside the green, but the reason most people visit here is **Otterton Mill** (01395 568521; www.ottertonmill.com). This converted mill is a 'green' complex of restaurant, bakery (using flour ground at the mill), Devon organic produce, and an art and craft gallery. Everything smacks of quality, from the local produce and bakery, to the meals in the restaurant (open for lunch only; 01395 567041). The chef, Ed Chester, likes to use wild food including grey squirrel and plants foraged locally by Robin Harford. The galleries exhibit the work of different artists and crafts people and, like everything else here, this is seriously good-quality stuff. The Mill also describes itself as one of the country's leading roots music venues.

East Budleigh is both the prettiest – lots of whitewashed thatched cottages – and the most interesting village in this region, and one that has a flourishing community shop (always a good sign). In the 15th century, ships could penetrate this far up the river, or so John Leland claimed in the mid 1500s: 'Lesse than an Hunderith Yeres sins Shippes usid this Haven, but it is now clene barrid.' These days the only connection East Budleigh has with the sea is as the birthplace of Sir Walter Raleigh. The church, which stands above the town on a steep hill, has a Raleigh pew, with the family coat-of-arms and Sir Walter's dates, and even a Raleigh kneeler. He was born in Hayes Barton, now a private house about a mile to the west of the village, and his father was church warden here.

However, it is not Raleigh that makes this church a 'must-visit', nor even the very beautiful gilded bosses, but the wonderful 16th-century carved bench ends. These are quite extraordinary, and deserve as much time as you can give them. While some other churches may have half a dozen or so, the **Church of All Saints** has around 60. Bring a torch so you can study the detail. They are thought to have been carved by local people and almost all are of secular subjects: a unicorn, dragons and monsters, tradesmen with their tools, a peacock, and a 'pelican in her piety' (a religious symbol). There's a detailed sailing ship, and several carvings of heads including, hidden behind the piano, a bearded man wearing what seems to be a feathered headdress. It's hard not to think 'Red Indian!' A sailor returning from the New World would have remembered the more flamboyant aspects and perhaps described them to the local craftsmen. But the 'feathers' could also be foliage. There is also a carving which is described by J Stabb, in his book *Some Old Devon Churches* (1908), as 'a man's head with the mouth open, showing the teeth with something between them, whether his tongue or a substance he is supposed to be swallowing it is difficult to say'. But if you look carefully you'll see that he is definitely eating something. Dr Michael Tisdall, the authority of the unusual in English churches, supports this: 'It is my idea that it is a banana. Bananas would have been known to Raleigh's crew. They sailed via the Azores where bananas were in production and some were taken across to these new West Indies and planted there. So either a banana or a drawing or other memory of a banana would be very likely in East Budleigh.' Fascinating stuff! Although most authorities date the carvings from the mid 16th century, some could well have been done after Raleigh made his voyages and came back with stories about the wonders of the New World.

The Otter and Ladram Bay: a walk from Otterton

The length of this walk can be varied; at its shortest it takes in the well-known view of Ladram Bay's famous sea-stacks and a short section of the South West Coast Path, before looping back to Otterton, but the full length (about six miles) follows the coast path (along one of its gentlest stretches) to the mouth of the Otter then returns to Otterton along either side of the river.

The route is very straightforward so you don't need a detailed map. From Otterton Mill continue through the village and follow signs to Ladram Bay (to reach the view point you need to go through the caravan park). The coast path is signposted and from there you'll see one of the most photographed views in Devon; the orange-red sandstone has been eroded into lumps and chunks like

pieces of cake. Turn right along the coast path and, if you're taking the short route, follow it for a short distance until you see the footpath leading back to Otterton. For the longer walk, keep going for 2½ miles to the Otterton Estuary Nature reserve. This is the best habitat for saltmarsh vegetation in Devon, and with the tidal mudflats this makes it an important place for over-wintering birds; there are hides, so if you're a bird watcher bring binoculars.

To return you can stay on the east side of the river, which is also a cycle route, or cross at the first opportunity and walk up the footpath on the west side; most walkers prefer this option.

⑱ Budleigh Salterton

This village is caullid Salterne, and hath beene in tymes past a thing of sum Estimation.
John Leland, 1540.

Towns have different specialities. One may have a historic church, another some picturesque cottages, a third particularly fine gardens. Budleigh Salterton has – pebbles. It's attractive in other ways too, but the stones on its beach are remarkable: smooth, multi-hued and rather smug, as they gleam up at you with an air of 'yes we *know* we are beautiful'. In fact they're probably saying 'nous sommes beaux', because they're foreigners; they originated over 400 million years ago when sandstones formed in what is now Brittany. These rocks were then eroded and, during the Triassic era, carried by vast rivers to form the Budleigh Salterton Pebble Beds. They're found along other parts of the Jurassic Coast too, but not in such quantities.

And no, you must not collect them! A local woman told me with horror in her eyes of someone who had been spotted going to the beach with – gasp – a *wheelbarrow*. Just not done. Apparently a freak storm a while ago stripped them away in the night leaving just grey silt. In the morning the townspeople were appalled. Where was their beach? Fortunately Neptune was on their side and the sea threw back the pebbles on the next rising tide.

Walking along Fore Street with its shops and businesses, you'd never guess that two miles of curving beach were just a stone's throw (sorry) away. Residents use it extensively, walking, exercising dogs, flying kites – it's the town's biggest asset. But there's history here too, and some beautiful old houses. The

Fairlynch Museum, for instance, is one of very few thatched museums in existence, and is a typical example of a marine *cottage orné*. Its displays include an unusual costume collection, dating back to the 1700s, and it's strong on the archaeology and geology of the area.

This is an artistically minded town: there are some good galleries, and an important Music & Arts Festival is held in the summer.

The Long Range Hotel in Vales Road offers cream teas overlooking a pleasant garden and The Cosy Teapot in Fore Street offers them off Royal Albert Bone China, but a walk along the beach will work off the calories.

Tourist Information Centre Fore St ☎ 01395 445275 🖰 www.visitbudleigh.com.
Fairlynch Museum and Arts Centre Fore Street ☎ 01395 442666
🖰 www.devonmuseums.net/fairlynch. Open afternoons, Easter to October.

⑲ Exeter

When the Romans rowed their great galleys up the Exe, bent on subjugation, Exeter was the capital of the Damnonii (their territory stretched throughout Devon and Cornwall) who had named it Caerwisc or 'city of the waters'. Renaming it Isca Damnoniorum and the Exe the Isca, the Romans – inevitably – built a fortress, which from around AD55 to AD70 accommodated some 5,000 men, most of them legionnaires originating from Italy, Spain and France. After the legionnaires had been moved to sites of new Roman conquests elsewhere in Britain, Isca gradually spread beyond the fortress; a protective wall was built to enclose its wider area, together with new housing, temples, bath-houses, markets and administrative buildings. Living was good. However, by the end of the 4th century (with the departure of the Romans) the city had declined and pretty much reverted to farming. There was a Saxon monastery in Exeter in the 7th century, King Alfred created it a Royal Borough in 877, and by the end of the 17th century the woollen cloth trade had made it one of England's biggest and busiest cities. The imaginative website www.exeter.gov.uk/timetrail allows you to explore its historic growth in detail. Many traces of its Roman past can still be seen in Exeter today, nearly 2,000 years later, including parts of the city wall. As you stroll along it you may be following the footsteps of some ancient sandaled centurion or slave.

By their nature cities aren't go-slow places and Exeter does bustle. During World War II it was severely bombed (on one night in 1942 alone, it lost almost 2,000 shops and houses) and some of the modern replacements are soulless, but attractive old buildings remain tucked away around the city centre and are easily accessible on foot. Signposts show 'walking minutes' rather than distances, for example ten minutes from the Cathedral to the Quay. Almost 70% of the city wall survives, while the old quayside has been developed into a pleasant area of traditional shops and workshops. Above all the great cathedral, started by the Normans in 1114 and remodelled in Gothic style in 1270–1369, is magnificent: an unmissable part of any visit. The Visitor Information Centre has a good stock of leaflets and maps.

Exeter Visitor Information and Tickets Dix's Field (near bus station) ☎ 01392 665700 🖰 www.exeter.gov.uk/visiting and www.exeterandessentialdevon.com.
Exeter Red Coat Guided Tours c/o Exeter Visitor Information above ☎ 01392 265203 🖰 www.exeter.gov.uk/guidedtours. Enthusiastic local guides cover the places of interest and describe their history.
Quay House Visitor Centre 46 The Quay ☎ 01392 271611 🖰 www.exeter.gov.uk/quayhouse.

Getting around

If you've driven to Exeter, you'll find **car parks** well signposted, but the one-way systems can be confusing; you may prefer to use one of the Park and Ride parks on the outskirts, at Honiton Road, Matford and Sowton, with frequent bus connections to the centre (see www.devon.gov.uk/park_and_ride).

Exeter has two main **train** stations, Central and St David's, about 20 minutes' walk apart; some long-distance trains stop at both, some at only one. Central is 10–15 minutes' walk from the central bus station, St David's nearer 30 minutes; taxis and buses are available. There's a good network of city **buses**; they leave from inside (or sometimes just outside) the central bus station.

Exeter is one of six National Cycling Demonstration Towns in England and so does cater for **cyclists**, who can also visit nearby Haldon Forest Park (see *Haldon Belvedere*, page 37). All the main places of interest around the centre are within walking distance of each other, and there are plenty of seats if your feet get weary. The Exeter Green Circle consists of five linked **walks** forming a 13-mile circle round the outskirts of the city, giving good views to the surrounding countryside; individual sections aren't more than three miles each but do include some roughish stretches. Within the city you can do a self-guided walk round the remains of the city wall (under two miles), the Medieval Trail or the Woollen Trail, or take walks to the main sites led by expert Red Coat Guides. The Visitor Centre has leaflets on all of these.

What to see and do

If you arrive at the central bus station, you're handily close to the **Visitor Information Centre** (just across the main road), from where it's only a short walk to the Underground Passages (see below). If you've got time to spare, you could then turn up Sidwell Street (Sidwell or Sidwella meant 'full of virtue'), just because at **St Sidwell's Community Centre**, a short way along on the left, is an imaginative little vegetable and flower garden. It was created a few years ago on derelict wasteland, largely as a therapeutic project for troubled youngsters:

somewhere they could work together, get support and learn new skills. As a sideline it has brought wildlife, including bees, back into this inner-city area, and the Centre's small café benefits from the fresh produce.

From the High Street, a narrow covered alley between Boots and the Halifax leads you through to pleasant **Northernhay Gardens**, the first public gardens in the country and the site of the annual Exeter Festival of South West Food and Drink (see page 1), where you'll see the side of **Exeter Castle** and some of the old city wall. Turn left when you emerge from the far end of the gardens, in Queen Street, and you're beside the impressive **Royal Albert Memorial Museum**, currently closed for renovation but due to reopen by the end of 2010. It was wonderful before – very strong on the history of Exeter – and I assume it will be even better. Meanwhile, some exhibits are housed in the Central Library. There's not much to see of the castle interior: it's partly administrative offices and partly used for art exhibitions and other events. Nearby **Gandy Street** – it describes itself as the Carnaby Street of Exeter – has some attractive small independent shops, and marks the line that the Roman soldiers followed when they were patrolling the wall of their fortress.

The 11th-century **St Nicholas Priory** has skipped a few centuries and now offers three reconstructed rooms illustrating Tudor life. **St Bartholomew's Cemetery** is now a park, housing Exeter's **catacombs**. These were built in 1835–7, against the city wall, and were the first cemetery buildings in Britain to be built in Egyptian style. The entrances resemble Egyptian tombs, and the pointed granite gate pillars reflect Egyptian obelisks. They're only open to the public on a Red Coat tour three times a week, April to October; contact the Tourist Visitor Centre for details. In the lower part of the High Street is the impressive **Guildhall**, where Exeter's affairs have been run for over 800 years, and not far away, roughly opposite St Petrock's church, is what's claimed to be the world's narrowest street: Parliament Street, 25 inches wide at one end increasing to a maximum 45 inches. (It all depends on your definition of 'street'...)

Underground passages

If you like putting on a hard hat and going down into a very narrow passage (I did) these are interesting. They were built in the 14th and 15th centuries to bring fresh water into the city, and the guide (extremely good, the day I visited) fills in a lot of fascinating background. For example, during the 1549 Prayer Book Rebellion, rebels broke into the tunnels and stole lead to make bullets. The builders were hot on brickwork but poor at pipes: the old joints used to leak a lot. There's a small museum, too. Opening times vary: check with the Visitor Centre or on www.exeter.gov.uk/passages.

Exeter University Sculpture Walk

The university's spacious Streatham Campus, around ten minutes' walk from St David's rail station, is considered by many to be the most beautiful in the country, so it is fitting that its stately trees, ponds and gardens should also be the setting for sculptures by leading artists including Barbara Hepworth and Henry Moore. Twenty-five works of art are displayed inside and outside; it takes about two hours to see them on a self-guided walk. Ask at the office in the library building for a leaflet giving their locations and an audio guide. Opening hours are normally 9–6pm on weekdays, and Saturday mornings, but it's wise to check beforehand: 01392 263999 or 01392 263584; www.exeter.ac.uk/sculpture.

Exeter Quayside

I love this place. The old quayside, dating back to Roman times, has been turned into a relaxed, pleasant leisure area, with traditional workshops (furniture, metalwork, mirrors...) in the old warehouses. You can take a boat trip along the canal, paddle off in a canoe or kayak, or hire a bike and pedal down the old towpath. There are bars, cafés and restaurants with fresh local food, and antiques and curios galore. The old **Quay House** (built in 1680) has a good exhibition of the area's history, and the TIC in the same building is well-stocked and helpful.

The cannons in front of the old customs house don't indicate battle; they were brought in by boat from Glasgow, ready for shipping to the continent, but their shippers couldn't pay the necessary fees so they were just left there – long, long ago. A few minutes' walk away, **Cricklepit Mill** is home to the Devon Wildlife Trust and has recently been restored for visitors.

The little flat-bottomed **Butts Ferry** that is hauled across the canal on a wire is the oldest wire ferry in Britain, dating from at least 1641. It was nearly retired when a bridge was built nearby in the 1970s, but a Councillor Butt saved it – hence its present name. In bad weather a year or so back it broke loose and drifted down to Topsham, to end up nestling cosily among six pedalos painted to resemble large black swans. Nice picture! It runs from Easter to October and the crossing takes all of three minutes. Or you can use the bridge, but that's boring.

If you don't fancy the uphill walk from the quay back to the centre, there is a bus, but it's only hourly, doesn't run on Sundays, and the last of the day leaves in mid afternoon.

Exeter Cathedral

I've saved the best till last. This great building with its massive carved frontage sends my spirits soaring as soon as I step into Cathedral Yard. It's hunkered solidly there on the green, the weight of centuries pressing it into Exeter's earth, yet when you step inside the door your eye swings immediately up to the space and grace of its amazing roof: the longest unbroken stretch of Gothic vaulting in the world.

Devon's first cathedral was built in Crediton, in 909, but in 1050 the See moved to Exeter and the cathedral temporarily occupied a large Saxon Minster church in the present Cathedral Yard. The Normans started building their new cathedral in 1114 and completed it around 66 years later. Then from 1270 to 1369 it was remodelled in decorated Gothic style, and the vaulting dates from that time. When you've recovered from the impact of its size and grandeur, you can focus on small, intimate details: animals on the choir stalls, sweet-faced angels playing musical instruments, sad swans with entwined necks, intricate roof bosses, the centuries-old hole in the door of the north tower to allow access for the Cathedral cat... so many, and so absorbing. (And just imagine how beautiful it can be at a Christmas service, by candlelight...)

Allow plenty of time here, because one thing will draw you to another and the place is best savoured slowly. You may want simply to gaze and absorb the atmosphere, but you'll gain far more from your visit if you get a guidebook from the Cathedral shop. There is an entrance fee (£5 at the time of writing), and personally I'm happy to help maintain this treasure-house of history and human faith.

Markets

Exeter Farmers' Market, with local produce from all around the area, takes place every Thursday morning at the junction of Fore Street and South Street. There's home-reared meat, fish from the Devon coast and all manner of fresh seasonal vegetables, as well as baking and dairy goods. Last time I was lured there by the smell of pasties. The **Sidwell Street Market** is an informal affair, Monday–Saturday, selling just about everything, including flowers and secondhand books.

Where to eat and drink

My favourite for a quick snack is the little mobile pavement **Crêperie** in Castle Street, just off the High Street. And it's solar powered! The chef has been serving pancakes there for 20 years; just watch his speed and dexterity as he spreads, flips and folds them on their griddle. If you're of more carnivorous bent, the **Hot Sausage Company** operates from a traditional cart beside him. Both get quite a queue at lunchtime. Otherwise Exeter is packed with eating places, old and new; you'll spot them everywhere. Below are three very different ones, all close to the cathedral (the area gets busy at touristy times).

The Cathedral Café Exeter Cathedral ☎ 01392 285988. Set right inside the historic cloisters of this beautiful building, the café prides itself on a friendly atmosphere and fresh, homemade food: snacks, light lunches and cream teas. Open Mon–Sat, 10.00–16.45.

Exeshed Restaurant Bedford St, Princesshay ☎ 01392 420070. A light, bright, modern, good-value restaurant and cocktail bar in the new Princesshay shopping area. Mainly European cuisine but giving new twists to old favourites. Good curries too.

Michael Caines Restaurant ABode Exeter (formerly Royal Clarence Hotel), Cathedral Yard ☎ 01392 223638 ✆ www.michaelcaines.com. Top-class dining opposite the cathedral, and understandably not cheap, but the fine menu at ABode Exeter is based on locally sourced food whenever possible. The two- or three-course lunches will be served within the hour if you say you're in a rush: reassuring if you've a bus or train to catch. Supports the charity *Families for Children.*

Haldon Belvedere

Philip Knowling

Drive southwest from Exeter on the A38 and in Haldon Forest Park you'll see Haldon Belvedere, high on the ridge, limewashed and rising proudly above the trees. This is perhaps Devon's most famous folly. It is also something of a folly success story. A few years ago it was almost in ruins, today – restored and cared for by the Devon Historic Buildings Trust – the tower is a showcase visit.

Haldon Belvedere was built in 1788 by Sir Robert Palk, a poor local lad who made his career and his fortune in the army in India and rose to become Governor of Madras. It commemorates his mentor, friend and colleague, Major-General Stringer Lawrence (hence its alternative name, Lawrence Castle), who spent time at Palk's Haldon estate; when he died in 1775 he left his riches to Palk's children. Palk in turn honoured Lawrence by building the tower on the site of one of the old soldier's favourite viewpoints.

The building is triangular, with corner turrets and Gothic windows. Its interior is impressive, with marble sent by the Nizam of Hyderabad (another admirer of Lawrence) and mahogany from the East Indies. There's even an artificial stone statue of Lawrence dressed as a Roman general. Climb the 99 steps to the roof on a clear day and you'll see Dartmoor, Exmoor, the Blackdown Hills and Portland Bill.

When I first visited Haldon Belvedere it was home to the elderly Dale brothers who lived in it like an old farm cottage. The render was falling away, windows were stuffed up with old socks and the rooftop crenellations moved when you leant on them. Serene decay and wistful neglect can add romance to a folly. Many a tower achieves a natural maturity only when it becomes overgrown and abandoned. Your sense of personal discovery is heightened as you push through undergrowth and startled pigeons take flight through an empty roof. Renovation clears the brambles, repairs the roof and brings a new identity. Some people say repair also drives out character. Today Haldon Belvedere is neat and tidy and has a car park. The private peculiarity has become a public attraction. Has it lost some of its character? In truth, ruins are romantic but decay is deadly. Without renovation the tower would have collapsed. Instead it has been saved – and, what's more, returned to something approaching its original glory, but with public access.

Haldon Belvedere EX6 7QY ☎ 01392 833668 🖰 www.haldonbelvedere.co.uk. Six miles from Exeter off the A38 (take Exeter Racecourse turn-off and follow brown signs). Open Feb to end Oct, Sun and bank holidays 13.30–17.30.
Haldon Forest Park ☎ 01392 834251 🖰 www.haldonforest.org.uk. Directions as above. Has a bird-of-prey viewpoint and five cycle trails; bike hire from Forest Cycle Hire (☎ 01392 8337680).

The Exe estuary

The broad Exe estuary stretching south from Exeter is a haven of birdlife, easy trails for cyclists and walkers, and exceptional views across the water. **Buses** serve towns along both banks. Seasonal **foot ferries** operate to/from Exeter, Exmouth, Topsham, Starcross and Exminster: see listing below. Double-check current times and availability before planning your journey. When you buy bus, train or ferry tickets, ask about Exe Estuary Circular tickets allowing a linked trip on all three systems. **Walkers** and **cyclists** are spoilt for choice: between them they have parts of the South West Coast Path, the East Devon Way and the Exe Valley Way, as well as the new Exe Estuary Trail which will eventually run from Exeter to Dawlish; it's still to be completed at the time of writing, though the sections from Exeter to Topsham and from Lympstone to Exmouth are open. It takes in the various nature reserves and offers wonderful estuary views. Some of the cycle routes (both on-road and off-road) are suitable for wheelchairs and pushchairs. Check its current state of development on www.exe-estuary.org, which also offers an excellent series of downloadable leaflets and maps covering public transport, wildlife, trails, ferries etc; you should also find them in Tourist Information Centres. OS Landranger map 192 covers the area; the larger-scale OS Explorer map 110 maddeningly just misses the estuary's start in Exeter.

From Exeter, two **train trips** down the Exe estuary are far more beautiful than the same routes done by road. Both run close to the water, with some platforms right on the edge. The tiny stretch to **Exmouth** is known as the Avocet Line – with good reason. In winter, around 15,000 waders and waterbirds come to the estuary, and the train windows offer a tremendous view. During the 30-minute journey you should spot a variety of species – including avocets – and even the occasional peregrine as it seeks out its prey. Numbers dwindle in summer, but the view is wonderful anyway. The little two-coach train shuttles along half-hourly by day, hourly at evenings and weekends. Most tickets let you get off at intermediate stations and continue your journey later; for example you could visit historic Topsham (see page 42) or tranquil Lympstone, where villagers in homes bordering the estuary walk out on to the silt when the tide is low, hang their washing on tall lines there, leave it to flap above the water as the tide rises, and collect it a few hours later once the tide has ebbed! The train takes up to two cycles if there's room, but it can be jam-packed with Exeter commuters at peak times, so travel off peak if you can. From Exeter, sit on the right-hand side.

The line to **Dawlish** gives similar views from the opposite side: Lympstone nestles between its red cliffs, colourful yachts are scattered against the distant backdrop of Exmouth and gradually estuary turns to sea. In Dawlish, probably best known as the town where the railway runs so close to the sea that trains get seriously splashed in winter storms, the station is right by the beach; from here you can start your return to Exeter by following the South West Coast Path back to Dawlish Warren (page 41), mostly along the sea wall. At low tide you can do part on the beach, which is good for paddling, shells and even a quick dip. Just before Dawlish Warren the little Red Rock Café – open every day of the year (even Christmas Day) – provides drinks and hot snacks. At Dawlish Warren you can catch a train or bus (number 2) or else continue on the South West Coast Path to Starcross (page 40). It's on a quiet road, not particularly scenic, but blackberries offer a free snack in season. You'll pass (unless the smell of cooking tempts you inside) the popular Anchor Inn (see page 41), overlooking Cockwood's harbour. Finally, from Starcross you can rejoin the train for more estuary views, catch a bus, or take the ferry across to Exmouth, where the station (about 20 minutes' walk) is home to the Avocet Line. Approaching Exmouth you'll see a colourful new housing complex on the headland, with some distinctive architecture.

Ferries and cruises

Butts Ferry ☎ 07984 368442 www.exetercruises.com. A 'pull' ferry from Exeter Quay to Haven Banks, operating since at least 1641. Also see page 35.

Exeter Cruises ☎ 07984 368442 www.exetercruises.com. From Exeter Quay to Double Locks. Connects with White Heather (below).

Exmouth/Starcross Ferry ☎ 01626 774770 www.exe2sea.co.uk. Runs daily (hourly) from Apr to late Oct; carries cycles.

RSPB ☎ 01392 432691 www.rspb.org.uk. Runs birdwatching cruises from Topsham.

Sea Dream II Ferry ☎ 07778 370582 www.topshamtoturfferry.co.uk. From Topsham to Turf Locks for Turf Inn, also RSPB birdwatching cruises.

Stuart Line Cruises ☎ 01395 222144 www.stuartlinecruises.co.uk. From Exmouth, coastal cruises; day trips to Topsham, Sidmouth and Torbay; summer Jurassic Coast cruises; guided birdwatching cruises.

Topsham Ferry ☎ 07801 203338. Topsham to Exminster Marshes. Also water taxis.

White Heather Ferry ☎ 07884 164255 and 07909 608095. From Double Locks pub to Turf Inn. Connects with Exeter Cruises (above).

⑳ Exminster

From Exminster you can walk or drive to the edge of the RSPB's Exminster Marshes Nature Reserve (see box below), where a footpath continues to the Topsham Ferry. You can also walk or cycle to one of the few pubs in the country that can't be reached by car: the amazingly located **Turf Inn**. Right on the edge of the Exeter Ship Canal, it has provided refreshment to lock keepers and passing vessels since 1827. It's served by two seasonal ferries from Topsham, and one that shuttles along the canal from the Double Locks pub; see above. A few miles south of Exminster, in **Kenton**, you'll see the entrance to **Powderham Castle** (www.powderham.co.uk), built in 1391: tours of the interior are available, and the well-kept grounds offer scenic strolls and various family-friendly attractions. Kenton's 14th-century church, incorporating walls from two earlier churches and described by John Leland as 'a right goodly church', has a very fine screen.

S) The Turf Exeter Canal, Exminster ✆ 01392 833128 ✆ www.turfpub.net.
A unique, rambling old pub overlooking the mudflats, and reached by a mile's walk along the towpath. Big windows for birdwatching. Top-notch Otter ales. Virtually all food is homemade.

Bird reserves around the Exe estuary

If you're walking or cycling round the estuary, you'll pass some of the best mudflats and wetland habitats in Devon. Make a day of it and see how many species you can spot from the RSPB hides and along the boardwalks.

The RSPB's Exe Estuary Nature Reserve is two areas of coastal grazing marsh on opposite sides of the river: Exminster Marshes on the west side and Bowling Green Marsh on the east, in the pocket of wetlands south of Topsham between the River Clyst and the Exe. A summer ferry from Topsham connects the two.

Spring is a good season: you can see lapwings and redshanks and – if you're a serious twitcher – listen for the rare Cetti's warbler. But winter is the most rewarding time when, at high tide, there are thousands of waterbirds including black-tailed godwits, widgeons, shoveler ducks and Brent geese. Recently the RSPB built two lagoons to encourage wildfowl to return to the area, and they've been a great success.

The ace in the pack, however, is the avocet and you have a good chance of seeing some in the winter (in spring they go to East Anglia and the Netherlands to breed), especially if you take a special RSPB cruise from Topsham, Exmouth or Starcross (see below). Bird cruises are also run by the Stuart Line.

Other wetlands around the estuary include the evocatively named Old Sludge Beds and the Powderham Marshes, as well as the extensive and accessible Exmouth Local Nature Reserve, one of Devon's largest, with its constantly changing tidal mudflats and sands. Finally there's the Dawlish Warren National Nature Reserve (see page 41), centred on a 1½-mile sand-spit at the estuary's mouth. And all within easy reach of a major city: not bad!

Devon Wildlife Trust ✆ 01392 279244 ✆ www.devonwildlifetrust.org.uk.
Exe Estuary Management Partnership ✆ 01392 382236 ✆ www.exe-estuary.org.
Their leaflet, Exe Wildlife, is available from Tourist Information Centres.
RSPB ✆ 01392 432691 ✆ www.rspb.org.uk. For details of birdwatching cruises, search on their website (top right-hand corner) for Avocet+Exe+cruise. The RSPB shop at Darts Farm (✆ 01392 879438) runs nature walks, normally at 14.00 on Sat.
Stuart Line ✆ 01395 222144/279693 ✆ www.stuartlinecruises.co.uk.

㉑ Starcross

Starcross has two pubs and a handful of small shops, plus – importantly – the **Exmouth–Starcross Ferry** (01626 774770; www.exe2sea.co.uk). This runs daily from April to late October, and carries bikes as well as pedestrians. It docks just a stone's throw from the railway station; walk down the platform and along a pier and you're there. With it you can do a variety of circular trips (combinations of train, bus, cycling and walking) around the two shores of the estuary.

The reddish building with a tower, opposite the garage, was the old pumping station of Isambard Kingdom Brunel's **atmospheric railway** (see box below). The chimney was once much taller, but was damaged in a storm in the 1890s. The Atmospheric Railway pub has – of course! – some related memorabilia.

A mile or so south of Starcross, by Cockwood's small harbour, is the deservedly popular and award-winning **Anchor Inn** (01626 890203; www.anchorinncockwood.com), specialising in seafood. It can get very busy; if you're eating there before catching the Starcross Ferry, leave plenty of time as it'd be a shame to rush your meal.

The Atmospheric Railway in Devon

The first atmospheric railway opened in Ireland in 1844, followed by one on the outskirts of Paris and another on five miles of the London and Croydon Railway. The trains literally ran on air, with a combination of partial vacuum and atmospheric pressure; they were practically silent, and with no nuisance of steam or smuts. Isambard Kingdom Brunel then recommended the use of the system on a much longer stretch, planned to run from Exeter to Torre and Totnes. At stations along the route, including Exeter, Turf, Starcross and Dawlish, pumping houses were built and steam-driven pumping engines were installed in them. The first train ran in September 1847.

There were always difficulties. Among others, the pumping engines used far more coal than expected, communication between pumping houses was poor, and the leather flap valves sealing the traction pipes deteriorated from use and the salty atmosphere. Treated with oil to prevent this, they then attracted rats and mice, which got sucked in to the tube and thus jammed the piston – at which point third-class passengers might have to dismount and push the train to the next station. At the system's peak, nine trains a day ran between Exeter and Teignmouth at up to 70mph; but for reasons of cost and many operational problems it just wasn't viable. The last train ran in September 1848. Gradually the machinery was removed and the pumping houses were closed and dismantled; the one at Starcross is the only one that has survived in situ.

JB

㉒ Dawlish Warren

Grit your teeth and ignore the raucous 'amusement' area with its gaming arcades and razzmatazz; the **nature reserve** beyond it is a peaceful and interesting place, and the long, sandy, dune-edged shoreline is superb. The reserve has a visitor centre and is an internationally important area for wildlife: the main roosting site for the huge numbers of wading birds and wildfowl that spend the autumn and winter on the estuary. It's also designated as a Special Area of Conservation

(SAC) for its dune grassland, humid dune slacks and the tiny, rare 'petalwort' that grows there. An out-of-season visit is best, because Dawlish Warren is a popular holiday resort and fills up in summer.

㉓ Topsham

Exeter... is a small city...about ten miles from the sea. The river there empties itself into a large bay, up which the largest vessels, even those of three hundred tons burden, can pass safely as far as Topsham, a village three miles from Exeter; whence merchandise is conveyed in smaller boats quite up to the city.

Cosmo III, Grand Duke of Tuscany, 1669, as reported by Count L Magalotti.

The Devil's footprints?

...Deep snow fell all over Devon that night, and when folk in Topsham and elsewhere along the Exe estuary awoke in the morning of 7 February 1855 an unaccountable sight met their eyes. In the snow, stretching along roads, gardens and even roofs, were strange hoof-like footprints. Once it became clear how widespread they were, people armed themselves with whatever implements were to hand and set off to track the intruder – but found nothing. Based on reports it received (which may well have been considerably embroidered) *The Times* wrote up the event the following week. News had come in from other areas, reporting footprints around Teignmouth and Dawlish too. Altogether their alleged trail stretched for around 100 miles. Some, near Powderham, appeared to cross the Exe estuary (there's no record of whether it was frozen over). They were about 2½ inches wide, 4 inches long and 8 inches apart, generally travelling in a straightish line, apparently made by a biped rather than a quadruped. Individual stories – whether true or false – emerged, as of dogs in Dawlish backing away from them in terror. A local vicar claimed them as 'the devil's footprints' in his sermon the following Sunday, and this became their nickname.

There have been a few reports of similar phenomena around the world at different times, but none so comprehensive. The chronicler Ralph of Coggeshall, who was Abbot at Coggeshall (Essex) from 1207 to 1218, wrote of an occurrence in a small area after an electrical storm in July 1205. Many suggestions have been made as to the origin of the Devon prints, the strongest being that a weather balloon accidentally pulled loose from Devonport Dockyard and drifted over the area, its tether lines trailing so that they scratched the snow; but the route of the footprints apparently didn't match the direction of the prevailing wind. To this day, no explanation has been satisfactory. Since the weather was too bad for him to sunbathe on Tarr Steps (see page 258), perhaps they were indeed those of Old Nick on some grumpy nocturnal ramble.

JB

Topsham's position at the mouth of the River Exe ensured its place in history. A Roman port was established here in the first century AD to serve Exeter, and the present Topsham Road into the city is of Roman origin. Its prosperity increased in 1282, when the Countess of Devon, Isabella de Fortibus, built a weir across the Exe just below Exeter, rendering the city inaccessible to shipping, so all vessels had to unload at Topsham. The Countess and her weir account for the area called 'Countess Wear', and an old local jingle tells the tale:

Once the haughty Isabella – she of Countess Weir renown,
Had a quarrel, as they tell us, with the 'cits' of Exon town;
And preferring - God forgive her! – private rights to public weal,
In her arrogance the river from the City sought to steal...

Don't take it as gospel! But anyhow Topsham became the main port for the wool trade, and evidence of its wealth can still be seen in the Dutch-style merchants' houses along the waterfront. These date from the early 1700s when Holland was the largest buyer of Devonshire serges.

For a Slow-intentioned visitor, the best way to arrive is from Exeter Quay by foot or bike along the canal. That way you see the most attractive part of the town with its Dutch-style houses first as you approach along Ferry Road and The Strand. The town **museum** is here, in a group of 17th-century buildings. It gives a good overview of local history and wildlife. Rather surprisingly, there's a Vivien Leigh room; the museum's founder was her sister-in-law. Above Ferry Road and The Strand is **Fore Street**, with its classy boutiques, galleries and restaurants; the monthly Topsham Slow Food Market is held here, in Matthew's Hall in the morning up to 13.30. For ferries to and from Topsham, see page 39.

The train station is a walk of five minutes or so from the centre. About half a mile beyond it, on the eastern edge of town, is one of the most famous pubs in Devon, the **Bridge Inn**, overlooking the River Clyst. Pink-washed, rambling, and 16th century or earlier, it found its niche in the 1950s or thereabouts, and stayed determinedly that way. The two rooms are tiny, the licensing hours are strictly last century, and no food is served in the evenings (it would be hard to know where to eat it, for one thing). But there's a huge selection of beer, real ale and cider, and traditional pub grub is served at lunchtime. It does have a nod at modern times in its warning that 'Fresh food is SLOW food... please be patient'. And another sign tells customers to switch off their mobile phones: 'A pub is a place for conversation between people, not machines.' Photos on the wall show a visit here by the Queen in 1998 (there's a delightful account of this on the website). The pub has been in the Cheffers-Heard family since 1897, and I can't imagine it ever being sold. Or not crammed with customers.

Looking eastward along the road from the inn, you can see the complex of **Darts Farm**. *The Guardian* described this as 'finding Selfridges' food store dumped in the middle of a field'. It comprises a farm shop, delicatessen, butchers, fishmongers, specialist cider and ale house, and various other retailers, all as organic as they come and top quality. The shelves of luscious vegetables reminded me of a continental food market in their colour and freshness. Look outside and you'll see the fields where they are grown: food miles – zero. Expect your wallet to be considerably lighter when you leave, but you'll eat very well indeed for the next few days. There's also an RSPB shop here (01392 879438) which organises regular nature walks; normally at 14.00 on Saturdays, but check beforehand. They'll also have details of the RSPB birdwatching cruises from Topsham.

Basics

Topsham information ⌕ www.topsham.org.
Darts Farm Bridge Hill, off the A376, EX3 0QH ✆ 01392 878200
⌕ www.dartsfarm.co.uk. Open Mon–Sat 08.30–17.30, Sun 10.00–16.30.
Topsham Museum 25 The Strand ✆ 01392 873244
⌕ www.devonmuseums.net/topsham. Open Apr–Oct.

Food and drink

ⓢ **Bridge Inn** EX3 0QQ ✆ 01392 873862 ⌕ www.cheffers.co.uk. See description above.
Oliva Restaurant 6–7 Fore St ✆ 01392 877878 ⌕ www.olivarestaurant.co.uk. Fine Mediterranean menu; paella a speciality. Open Wed–Sat lunch, Mon–Sat dinner.

㉔ A La Ronde

This fascinating 16-sided house was built for two artistic spinster sisters, the Misses Parminter, in the 1790s. They'd just brought back all manner of souvenirs from an extensive Grand Tour of Europe, and these are on show, along with later acquisitions; for example the walls of the 'Shell Gallery' are studded with almost 25,000 shells, so fragile that they're only viewable on closed-circuit television. Immediately intriguing from outside, with its unexpected shapes and angles, the house is even more surprising inside: the decoration and furnishings (refurbished in the 1990s) reflect the sisters' enthusiasm for blending materials such as feathers, shells, découpage, seaweed, stones, glass – and more. They enjoyed cutting out silhouette pictures, some very fine, and you can see the little scissors they used. The walls of the rooms are packed with paintings, etchings, miniatures and photos, and there's some beautiful furniture. Shelves and cupboards overflow with trinkets and memorabilia, from an Inuit family modelled in wood and sealskin to stuffed birds and rare old books. Really, there is nothing like it!

The house, a National Trust property, is down a short, narrow lane just off the A376, roughly two miles north of Exmouth; the East Devon Way runs past and the South West Coast Path is less than a mile away. Everything is small – the house, the rooms, the parking area – so at busy times it can become uncomfortably crowded and there may be delays.

A La Ronde EX8 5BD ✆ 01395 265514 ⌕ www.nationaltrust.co.uk. Open Feb–Nov, closed Thu and Fri. Other days and times vary seasonally; check before visiting.

㉕ Exmouth

Bathing at Exmouth is good, but the curious old bathing machines, those round houses on wheels divided into compartments, are one by one disappearing. There are ordinary bathing machines, and tents may be used almost all along the extensive shore... Attendants in boats ... may be of assistance to swimmers in difficulties.

So it was described in a 1930 guidebook, and Exmouth's wonderful long, sandy shore is still its greatest asset, although nowadays it hosts the likes of surfing, windsurfing and kite-surfing. And not a single bathing machine. Signs of the dignified Victorian resort still remain in stretches of the promenade and a few roads, but the centre has been pretty much modernised. Some ferries and cruises from Exmouth serve the estuary (see page 39), and its local nature reserve (page 40) is important – it's easy to reach from the train and bus stations, and the A376. However, Exmouth's biggest 21st-century claim to fame is as the westernmost gateway to the fabulous **Jurassic Coast**. This World Heritage Site (see box on page 1) officially starts at a 'geoneedle' set on the cliff at Exmouth's Orcombe Point. Follow the two-mile promenade and sandy beach eastward from the harbour (a lovely stroll in its own right) and when the paved promenade ends, take the steps that zigzag up the cliff. At the top, keep right and follow the coast eastward; after ten minutes or so you'll see the tall, pointed geoneedle ahead. Unveiled by the Prince of Wales in 2002 to inaugurate the Site, it's made of the different stones found along the Jurassic Coast and demonstrates their time sequence. The red rock of the cliff beneath it was once part of a bare, baked desert – remember that as you gaze seaward from the storm-swept headland, rain trickling down your neck and this book a soggy lump in your pocket!

Good tidings

Devon is the only English county with two separate coastlines, so it's particularly tempting for any visitors fascinated by cliffs, beaches and the shore. However, lifeboats are all too often called out to rescue people who've wandered too far and are trapped by the incoming tide. The danger and cost of the rescue could have been avoided if they'd checked the **Tide Tables** beforehand; used sensibly, these make possible a wealth of safe exploring. Get them from local shops and TIC's.

Non-seawise visitors don't always realise that the extent and timing of a tide's ebb and flow vary with the phases of the moon. The fact that you could walk past the tip of that promontory yesterday at midday and return safely doesn't mean you can do the same tomorrow, even if you calculate the time correctly: the tide may not ebb so far, or may rise higher, and you'll be trapped. (If this happens, don't try wading, particularly in rough weather; there can be dangerously deep pools close to rocks.) These timings and differences vary from place to place and from day to day, throughout the year, so – better safe than sorry!

JB

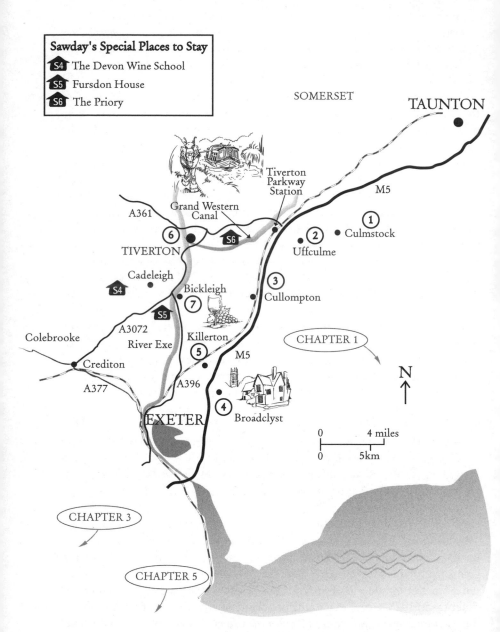

Sawday's Special Places to Stay

S4 The Devon Wine School
S5 Fursdon House
S6 The Priory

SOMERSET

TAUNTON

Tiverton
Parkway
Station

M5

Grand Western
Canal

A361

① Culmstock

⑥ TIVERTON

S6

② Uffculme

Cadeleigh

S4

Bickleigh

⑦

③ Cullompton

S5

A3072

River Exe

Killerton

⑤

M5

CHAPTER 1

N
↑

Colebrooke

Crediton

A377

A396

EXETER

④ Broadclyst

0   4 miles
0   5km

CHAPTER 3

CHAPTER 5

Escapes from the M5

2. ESCAPES FROM THE M5

M
any visitors burst upon Devon via the M5 intent on reaching their holiday destination as speedily as possible. Indeed, the motorway does give easy access to Exmoor, Dartmoor and eastern Devon including Exeter, and has allowed some of the most attractive small towns and villages of the area, once snarled with traffic, to sink back into a state of relative tranquillity. So only a few minutes from the motorway there are quiet villages, a castle, and a mansion with one of the best gardens in Devon.

The whole region was shaped by the wool industry. The great churches were built with wool wealth, and inconsequential villages became important market towns through this white gold. Industry needs power, and the wool industry needed water to drive the mills. Before the arrival of the motorway, this region was defined by two great rivers, the Culm and the Exe, which provided this power. One of these mills is still operating.

Getting there and around

The title of this chapter assumes that you are in a car, but in fact just about every place described here can be visited from one **bus** route: the 1, 1A and 1B which runs frequently between Exeter and Tiverton. It follows the B3181 which in turn more or less follows the M5, and it takes its time: the full journey takes between one and one-and-a-half hours, depending on the route. If you are in a car, be warned that there is no exit between the A30 junction, near Exeter, and Cullompton. It's easy to be caught out and end up driving much further than you intended. So if visiting several places in this section, stick to the B3181.

The area is easily accessed by **rail**. The Paddington line to Plymouth and Penzance runs past **Tiverton Parkway** (an exceptionally hassle-free station just off the motorway with good parking) and cycles can be carried on the train.

Cycling and walking

This is a great area for cycling, with a stretch of the **Grand Western Canal** being within minutes of Tiverton Parkway (see above). The canal towpath forms part of the West Country Way (NCN3) which runs along the canal from the Somerset border to Tiverton. The canal was closed as a commercial waterway in 1925, giving way to the popularity of the railways. The canal area is now a country park, providing 11 miles of safe cycling for all the family; bikes can be hired at Halberton from **Abbotshood Cycle Hire** (01884 820728; www.abbotshoodcyclehire.co.uk). They will pick up bikes at the end of the trail with prior notice, and have an adult tricycle and duet bikes for people with disabilities.

The *Tiverton and Culm Valley Cycle Map* is available free from tourist information centres or www.devon.gov.uk/tiverton_cycling_leaflet.pdf.

The 50-mile-long **Exe Valley Way** runs from the Exe estuary to Exford, and is ideal for cycling as well as walking since it runs along small lanes for part of its lower length, as well as an alluring stretch above Tiverton. And, as it follows the river, it's mostly blissfully flat – a rarity in Devon. However, the lower stretch towards Exeter has some relentlessly steep hills, which cyclists can't avoid if doing a circular trip. The National Cycle Network (NCN) Route 3 runs fairly close to the Exe, so here you have a ready-made round trip: up the Exe Valley Way from Tiverton to the bridge at Cove, and back down NCN3, with a few steep hills to keep your muscles in shape. The OS maps Explorer 114 and Landranger 181 cover this route.

The Culm Valley

The River Culm snakes its way down from the Blackdown Hills, becoming broader and more leisurely near Culmstock before joining the Exe above Exeter. It gives its name to several villages in the area, which is a quiet and relatively little-known part of the county.

① Culmstock

The village is famous for having a yew tree growing from its church tower and a very good inn, but little notice is taken of it otherwise. However, I found it to be just the way a Devon village should be: attractive in an unpretentious way, with the river forming a central focus, a garden with a hazel bush clipped to the shape of a teapot, and the village shop doing just what a village shop should do – serving the community.

It was the teapot bush that made me yearn for a cuppa and the sign outside the Strand Stores suggested that cream teas were on offer. Immediately obvious in the village's only shop was that the goods had been selected to reflect what people in the village actually want to buy. There were tins of organic tomatoes and chick peas, gluten- and wheat-free brown flour, ethical plain white flour, and imaginative snacks on the menu. This former post office was a victim of the post-office closures two years ago, much to the dismay of the villagers, and was reopened in its new guise early in 2009. It's a perfect example of village initiative and how to turn a disaster into a triumph. The feeling of community was strengthened by the rows of home-made jam on the shelves. 'Sometimes local people will buy up the tail end of our fruit, when it's starting to go soft,' said the assistant, 'and then sell us the jam they've made.'

The shop sells a little booklet of walks in the area, including one that goes to **Culmstock Beacon**, a local landmark. The beehive-shaped hut was built in the reign of Queen Elizabeth I to act as a lookout and warning against attack by the Spanish Armada. A chain of such beacons stretched across the county, and if the enemy entered the English Channel a watchman would light the first beacon, triggering the lighting of the next and so on. This was the signal for all able-bodied men to arm themselves and gather in the church to await instructions. The roofed structure gave shelter to the watchman in this exposed place, but there was a hole in the roof for the beacon pole, and slits at each side providing views of the neighbouring beacons of Upottery and Blackborough. The chain of beacons was lit for the 400th anniversary of the Spanish Armada in 1988, and for the Queen's Golden Jubilee.

The church with its yew tree has a story too: the yew apparently started growing soon after the spire was taken down in 1776. It has been well looked after – during particularly dry summers villagers have carried up buckets of water so that it doesn't dry out. The reason it's small for its age is that the constricting masonry has a 'bonsai' effect. In 1835 the father of R D Blackmore (of *Lorna Doone* fame) became curate at Culmstock, and Blackmore lived there from the age of ten; he mentions the tree in his novel *Perlycross*, which is set in the area.

><><><

S⁹ Culm Valley Inn Culmstock ✆ 01884 840354. A cosy local inn serving really good food in convivial surroundings. There's an unusually good wine list and a grand array of specialist spirits and many local beers tapped from the cask. Credit cards not accepted. **The Strand Store** ✆ 01884 840232· 🖥 www.thestrandstore.co.uk The shop/café is open from 07.00 to 19.00; closed Mon.

② Uffculme

If you come here by bus, you may like to know that the wooden bus shelter in the central square was once a butcher's shop! Dating back to the 18th century, it was a roofed and open-sided 'counter' where he could come in from the country and sell his wares. It fell out of use when the butchery business moved to a proper shop; the counter was replaced by benches on which you can now wait comfortably for your Number 1 to Exeter.

Coldharbour Mill

Should you be looking for socks, this is the place for you. In the shop are socks of every colour imaginable, every pattern and of every sort of wool: alpaca and a whole range of sheep breeds. No wonder John Arbon was described to me as 'the sock man'. This label belies the fact that this talented man has a First Class Honours Degree in Textiles and Apparel, as well as a post-graduate diploma in Fashion and Textiles. He always had an interest in alpaca wool and the luxuriously soft yarn that it produced, and set up UK Alpaca to buy and process fleece from this country's alpaca herds before the opportunity came up to start a business in Coldharbour Mill.

John Arbon Textiles (www.jarbon.com) is an integral part of the restored woollen mill, built in 1799, which is partly a museum and partly a working mill producing a range of yarns which are sold in the shop as well as tea cosies, scarves and, of course, socks. John has bought up some old spinning machines (descendants of the famous 'spinning jenny' that started the Industrial Revolution) from the north of England and brought them, in pieces, to Devon where they have been painstakingly reassembled.

There's a self-guided tour of the mill which introduces you to the process of machine carding and spinning, and includes the original water wheel, powered by the River Culm, which was built in 1821. Several times a year the old steam-driven engines which originally drove the machines are powered up. Phone 01884 840960 for dates of the Steam Up Days.

A restaurant at the mill was busy serving a happy group of cyclists when I was there. **Christine's Cuisine** is a popular eating venue for locals (07866 684488) and for cyclists tackling NCN3, which passes nearby.

③ Cullompton

Cullompton's splendid church stands as a landmark for miles around and is the reason to visit this small town. The *Shell Guide* describes the top of the tower as 'pinnacled, crocheted, gargoyled and pierced' and this lavish decoration continues on much of the exterior. Constructed of local red sandstone, this is a 'wool church' and wool merchant John Lane left his mark with carvings of sheep shears as well as ships.

The interior is stunning. The church was built in the perpendicular style, with two different families competing in their displays of wealth and piety. There is a Moore chapel, with lots of angels and the family coat of arms, and the Lane chapel which is really an entirely new aisle, with a fan-vaulted roof to rival King's College Chapel, and angels and twiddly carvings crammed into every space. Whilst the Lane chapel/aisle is all creamy-coloured sandstone, the rest of the church is done up in muted green, blue, red and gold. The barrel roof, with a criss-cross pattern of feathered wooden braces, is dull gold and sky blue, and wherever there's room for an angel you'll find one. The screen is very finely carved with entwined foliage and also painted. Every pillar is topped with vines or a figure – there is some very splendid facial hair in this church, particularly in the wood carvings on the organ screen. Of the stained glass windows, one depicting the evangelists on the south side of the Lane chapel stands out because of its rich colours: it's by the Pre-Raphaelite artist Edward Burne-Jones.

I almost missed what was, for me, the *pièce de résistance*. At the back of the south aisle is a trunk of oak, carved along its length with skulls, bones and rocks. The boldness of the carving looks modern, and is quite different from anything else in the church, yet it is said to be just as old. It is called Golgotha and supposedly once supported the rood. I'm glad it's now at eye level where it can be properly admired. It's a stunning piece of sculpture in its own right.

Devonshire's Green Lanes

Valerie Belsey

There are at least a thousand miles of accessible green lanes in Devon – lanes with an unmade surface, bounded by hedgerows. Many form part of the network of public rights of way, and those which once appeared on the OS maps as 'white roads' of uncertain status have become byways.

When you step into Devon's green lanes you enter a network of ways which once thronged with travellers, drovers, miners, quarrymen, lime-kiln burners, drovers, sailors, pedlars, thieves, smugglers, workers and traders of all kinds, who used them day and night. When the majority of the population lived and worked in the countryside, travellers came from the towns into the villages, not the reverse as is the case today. There are lanes leading from village to village, to churches, and to the small settlements which are a feature of the Devon countryside. There are ways which lead to the sea, such as those in the South Hams in the Slapton area or in the north leading to the dramatic Atlantic beaches below Braunton and Georgeham, and others with granite stone walling leading up to Dartmoor, or soft beech-lined ways on to Exmoor. But there are many small moors in Devon which also have their green lanes, such as at Witheridge and around Newton Poppleford.

They are often steep, taking the most direct route over a hill, and nearly always muddy and stony, worn down by generations of humans, cattle, packhorses and wagons. Many are cobbled, but not in the Clovelly sense of the word. Look carefully and you will see where the wagons once ran over these well-worn local stones, from sandstone, limestone, ironstone, granite, basalt.

Drovers' roads surviving as green lanes can be up to 15 yards wide and others as narrow as gullies snaking around the edge of a wood. Some are bordered by big boundary or marker beeches, oaks or ashes towering over you, while others have hedgerows made up of just honeysuckle or dogwood.

Green lanes are wildlife corridors and you will find many species of birds living at different heights in the hedgerows. There are dragonflies attracted to the wet patches and glow-worms to the mud. Kestrels and peregrines hunt along them like farmers' sons revving up their motor-cross bikes to overtake each other. The variety of flowers, especially in spring, is breathtaking and you will always find some red campion in bloom at any time of the year.

Each area has a different type of lane. In the south they are sunken, in the north often more exposed, in the west are very wooded and in the east have lower hedgerows. But above all they are silent ways into the heart of the countryside. As the great Devonian historian W G Hoskins said: 'Every lane has its history; it is not just there by accident: and every twist it makes once had some historical meaning which we can sometimes decipher today, but not often.' Happy exploring.

Valerie Belsey is the author of Exploring Green Lanes in N & NW Devon, Exploring Green Lanes in the South Hams *and* Exploring Green Lanes in S & SE Devon, *all published by Green Books (www.greenbooks.co.uk).*

Broadclyst and the Killerton Estate

This whole area is infused with signs of the Acland family, who held land here since the reign of Elizabeth I. The last Acland was Sir Richard, who gave the whole estate, which includes Broadclyst village and Killerton to the National Trust in 1944.

④ Broadclyst

It is surprising to find such a picturesque and peaceful village so close to Exeter. There are thatched cottages galore, including the medieval **Marker's Cottage**, and **Clyston Mill** which still produces flour. Both are now cared for by the National Trust.

The **church** is tucked away next to the Red Lion pub, its 16th-century tall and elegantly pinnacled tower providing a landmark for miles around. I popped in just as the chairman of the local history society, John Jones, was locking up. 'It was built with money at the time when people had money – pre-Reformation – and its virtue, perhaps, is that the village didn't develop particularly, so no one came along who wanted to knock it all down and Victorianise it.'

The interior of the church is splendid: large, light, and stuffed with monuments. The oldest, a knight in the armour of the 14th century tucked away in the sanctuary near the altar, is probably Sir Roger de Nonant. He has a toothy lion gazing at him adoringly, and a cluster of attentive cherubs. On the north side of the sanctuary is a small monument to Henry Burroughs, who founded the village almshouses, along with his wife Elizabeth. Then there's Edward Drewe with his splendid moustache and ruff, together with his wife who has a rather sweet, bear-like dog at her feet. He was Queen Elizabeth's legal officer and the Recorder of Exeter, a position he agreed to on the proviso that if the Queen needed him in London he would have to go. And go he did. His son inherited the estate and sold it to the Aclands. Sir John Acland lies in an elaborately carved monument by the north wall, propped on one elbow, with his large family above him.

Every capital is different, with intriguing faces and foliage. 'There's a mason's joke here,' said Mr Jones, 'See, that's a Staffordshire knot. The bishop at the time [the early part of the 15th century] was Bishop Stafford.'

The rood screen has gone but the door to it remains, now isolated on the north wall. Opposite are photocopies of large fragments of parchment from an illuminated missal used in 15th-century worship, which were found ignominiously providing the cover for a church warden's account book.

Broadclyst is really easy to get to by bus from Exeter. The 1, 1A and 1B run four times an hour so you'll never have to wait long, and you can continue on the same bus to visit Killerton and Budlake (below).

⑤ Killerton

Killerton Estate (01392 881345; www.nationaltrust.org.uk) covers a huge area and includes part of the villages of Broadclyst and Budlake. Formerly the home of the Acland family, it was given to the National Trust in 1942. Although the house is Georgian, the interior was redesigned in 1924, following a fire, so it now represents the way of life of an aristocratic family between the wars.

The **house** with its swathes of wisteria and other creepers has a welcoming look, and inside are some interesting bits and pieces including a Broadwood piano made in 1802, which is thus the oldest surviving piano made by John Broadwood and Sons. This is too fragile to be played but in the Music Room is a nice little chamber organ which you can ask to play (assuming you know how!). Likewise the Bechstein piano. My favourite room was the library, largely because of the joke titles of the fake books that conceal a drinks cupboard. These include *Hard Nuts to Crack*, *Authors not Generally Known*, *Sermons on Hard Subjects* and two reference books: *Crabb on Fishes* and *Hobble on Corns*.

Upstairs there's a good collection of costumes from the 18th to 20th century.

The best part of Killerton is undoubtedly the **garden**, all 20 acres of it, with huge lawns sloping down from a multi-coloured copse. There are numerous large and rare trees dotted around, herbaceous borders, and a folly. Once called 'The Hermitage' this is now known as the **Bear's Hut** because, so they say, the child Gilbert Acland kept a pet bear here. It's hard to believe that a large, long clawed Canadian black bear would not demolish such a delicate building. This delightful thatched summer house was originally built by Sir Thomas Acland for his wife Lydia. Each tiny room is made from different materials. The floors are sections of logs, cobble stones, and – extraordinarily – hundreds of 'knuckle bones' from deer. Evidently the Aclands ate a lot of venison. The 'deer room' has a ceiling of deer hide, and the two other rooms have woven matting decorated with fir-cones. Finally there's a very beautiful stained-glass window made from fragments of 16th-century Flemish glass. All this for a bear?!

A short walk away across a field is the nostalgic **Budlake Old Post Office** – or nostalgic for those who remember the 1950s. It is now a museum, but appears as a shop caught in a time warp: its shelves display biscuit tins with the new Queen's portrait, Brasso and Bluebell polish, Creamola rice pudding, Sunnyspread and Izal extra-strong toilet tissue. In the little garden is a pigsty, with instructions not to feed your pig with paper, soap or rhubarb leaves, and a cosy side-by-side privy. Recordings of local people talking about the old days can also be played.

The garden is open daily, year round, and the house most of the year (check times before you visit). The Old Post Office opens Monday, Tuesday and Sunday 14.00–17.00, as do Marker's Cottage and Clyston Mill.

Red Lion Broadclyst ☏ 01392 461271 🖥 www.redlionbroadclyst.co.uk. Located in a quiet spot next to the church, and serving typical pub food and local real ales.

Colebrooke, a gem of mid Devon

One of the Tarka Line Walks (see page 217) takes you from Yeoford station, through Penstone, past Colebrooke's church, and through the lovely little hamlet of Coleford before ending up at the next station, Copplestone. But of course you can equally well drive here, and I just hope you love the place as much as I did. Strictly speaking it's out of this locale but too special to omit.

It's Colebrooke's church and how it represents the village's past and present that makes the place so rewarding. Approaching St Andrew's you'll be walking up (and it is up – the church is on a significant hill) an ancient cobblestone path, one of the few remaining originals in the county. Inside you are struck by the fine barrel roof, and an unusual pulpit at floor level which seems more like a corral for the priest than a stage for his sermons. Nearby are two extraordinary carved bench ends, depicting a wildman or woodwose, clothed in feathers and holding an escutcheon for his master, and a more benevolent-looking and clothed man (although he has a pig's nose) wielding a club. They bear the coats-of-arms of the Coplestone and Gorges families who combined in marriage in 1472, so it is likely that the bench ends date from that time. Enclosed behind a very lovely screen is the Coplestone Aisle or Chantry, built by Philip and Walter Coplestone in memory of their father who died in 1457. In it is an ancient pre-dieu carved with the family coat of arms, and a bricked-up fireplace that will have kept the Coplestone family warm during winter services.

At the north end is something much newer: the Penstone Patchwork, created to commemorate the Millennium by the villagers of Penstone, a nearby hamlet of 22 houses. As the explanatory folder tells us, the hamlet is proud to be insignificant, a place where 'summer days pass unmarred by droves of tourists'. The book ends with the hope that the Penstone Patchwork 'will give you a flavour of this little place at this time in its history and perhaps an insight into the people who shared and relished its peaceful insignificance for a small fraction of its lifetime'. It does. Thank you Mary Stephenson for explaining what this delightful patchwork, depicting the history, flowers and wildlife of a Devon hamlet, is all about. It could represent so many 'insignificant' but much loved places in this county.

Coleford, just down the road, is an exceptionally picturesque village of crooked, whitewashed, thatched houses. The welcoming New Inn (01363 84242; www.thenewinncoleford) is 13th century and serves imaginative food.

The Exe Valley: Tiverton and Bickleigh

From its birth near Simonsbath, in Exmoor, down to Exmouth and the sea, the Exe has shaped the history of Devon. Though too shallow to carry much cargo, the river drove the wool mills at Tiverton and these days provides some very pleasant views and walks or bike rides along the Exe Valley Way.

The steep, sunny slopes also provide ideal growing conditions for vines, and the Yearlstone Vineyard, near Bickleigh, is a rewarding place to visit.

⑥ Tiverton

This pleasant town tends to escape the attention of visitors. It has a pedestrianised Fore Street, a covered market, an unusual church and perhaps the best museum in the county.

Textiles and faith have been the main movers and shakers here. The town's prosperity grew from its situation at the meeting of two rivers, the Exe and the Loman (the name means 'Town of Two Fords'). The water drove the textile mills and faith drove the construction of the many churches in and around the town. Two are notable: **St George's** on St Andrew Street (how confusing), an elegant Georgian church in the Wren style only open Tuesdays and Thursdays, and **St Peter's**, where you open the door to a blaze of colour. The kneelers, made by the church's Tappissers Group, are displayed as in an art gallery, resting on the shelf that normally carries hymn books. They encompass a whole range of subjects, from birds, flowers and butterflies to local landscapes, all meticulously stitched and a joy to see. I asked Jane Bonnick, a member of the group, how St Peter's came to have such distinctive and beautiful kneelers. 'They are made for a purpose, in memory either of a person, reflecting their lives and character, or of an event such as the Millennium, or Golden Jubilee. Or perhaps celebrating an organisation like The Mothers' Union. We are commissioned by the relatives or the group. For instance I'm making one for a silver wedding anniversary, and they wanted their spaniel, who had recently died, on the top and flowers all round the sides.' The whole church had the comforting feeling of a community centre rather than a museum. There's a large children's section and a basket full of lost gloves.

The museumy part of the church is the carvings on the outside of the Greenway chapel which Simon Jenkins in *England's Thousand Best Churches* describes as 'an encyclopaedia of English maritime history'. John Greenway was a wealthy 15th-century Merchant Venturer, widely travelled, who decorated the exterior of his chapel with carefully carved ships, all different, all armed. There is also an appealing pair of monkeys with very human bodies, and a gargoyle that is half man and half lion (or possibly what the carver imagined a lion to look like).

The nearby **castle** was built in 1106 by the first Earl of Devon, but was attacked and extensively damaged during the Civil War. In 1750, Richard Pococke reported seeing this inscription in the chapel attached to the castle:

Ho, ho, who lies here?
Tis I, the Earl of Devonshire,
With Kate my wife, to me full dear,
We lived together fifty-five year.
That we spent we had,
That we left we lost.
That we gave we have.

The castle is now privately owned, and open to the public only on the afternoons of Thursdays, Sundays and bank-holiday Mondays.

Lots of little museums in Devon depict rural life, so I was a bit sceptical when a visitor told me that the one at Tiverton was her favourite place in the county. But I can now see why. The **Tiverton Museum of Rural Life** is wonderful (www.tivertonmuseum.org.uk). You know it's exceptional as soon as you meet the enthusiastic volunteers who run it (the only paid members of staff are the curator and education officer) and I hope you'll willingly pay the small admission charge that helps keep it going. There really is something here for everyone: 15 galleries displaying a huge range of everyday things that our grandparents or great grandparents would have been familiar with. Steam train enthusiasts will spend a happy time sitting in the cab of *The Tivvy Bumper*, a Great Western Railway locomotive that once ran through pre-Beeching countryside round Tiverton, and those who like even older transport can examine Britain's most comprehensive collection of wagons. One of them has a horse story: in 1904 a man called Alf Wyatt won a bet that he could drive a wagon, loaded with barley, from Netherexe to Exeter, a distance of about seven miles. Nothing exceptional in that, you might think, but his team of three horses had no reins to guide or slow them. They responded to their master's voice, and arrived safely at the brewery despite the danger of the city's tramcars. That's in the outhouses. Inside there are toys, lace making, agriculture, cooking, public health… if it was used during the last few centuries, it'll be here. I was particularly taken by the barrel piano which, on request, will play a popular tune. These barrel pianos provided a nice little business for Canon Algernon Ogle Wintle, who bought them in the early part of the 20th century, renovated them, and resold them under his name. A visitor to the museum remembers Canon Wintle from his childhood near Bury St Edmunds. He recalls a rotund, grumpy man with a workshop full of barrel pianos. 'Ladies of the village used to trundle them up to his house, with the pins pulled out ready for him to put in the latest tunes.' The museum is open Monday to Friday, 10.30–16.30, and Saturday 10.00–13.00. Closed Sunday. When I was there the rooms rang with the excited cries of children: this is the perfect place to bring the kids, especially on a rainy day.

The **Grand Western Canal** joins the River Exe at Tiverton. Apart from the cycling route, already described, the canal offers gentle walks and also a horse-drawn barge which is about as slow as you can get. It takes 2½ hours to amble from Tiverton Wharf to East Manley. Here it pauses to let passengers see the aqueduct or just potter around, before returning to Tiverton. A commentary fills you in on local history and legends. With enquiries about this and boats for hire, contact the Tiverton Canal Company, on 01884 253345 or www.tivertoncanal.co.uk.

⑦ Bickleigh

Bickleigh is promoted in most guidebooks as being exceptionally picturesque. I was a little disappointed. Yes, its location at the junction of two rivers is lovely, and its five-arch bridge over the Exe, dating from 1630, is impressive. And the village is indeed quite pretty, though the thatched houses are spread out up steep hills or along the river, and there's no feeling of a village centre.

The church, some way from the river up a steep hill, has some interesting monuments, although it's probably best known for being the resting place of Bampfylde Moore Carew, the 'king of the gypsies' (see box on pages 58–9). Some more honourable

Carews are found in the church, and include a sad memorial to Elizabeth, who died in childbirth.

The focus for tourists used to be Bickleigh Castle, but this is now closed to the public. The owners have found that it's more profitable as a wedding venue. Across the river are the Devon Railway Centre and Bickleigh Mill, now called Devonshire's Centre. The former has a variety of attractions for children, including a narrow-gauge steam train, model railways and a model village. Devonshire's Centre is a craft shop and café.

The village is an excellent centre for walking, with one of the few stretches of the **Exe Valley Way** to be on footpaths rather than lanes, starting just beyond Bickleigh Mill and running to Tiverton, a distance of around four miles. From Tiverton there are frequent buses back to Bickleigh. The path runs close to the river, mostly through woods with stands of the invasive, but beautiful, Himalayan balsam. If there's been recent rain it will be very muddy; you will need boots. The path is well marked, though a map (OS Explorer map 114) or the *Exe Valley Way* booklet is useful. The booklet can be downloaded from www.devon.gov.uk/exevalleyway.pdf.

Two Devon impersonators

Bampfylde Moore Carew was born in Bickleigh in 1693, and buried there in 1759 after an exceptionally colourful life. A wild lad from a leading and reputable local family (his father was the Reverend Theodore Carew), he is said to have run away from home and ended up with a wandering group of gypsies. He quickly learned to live off his wits and was apparently a consummate actor. At the scene of a shipwreck, plunging into the waves as if swimming desperately ashore, he conned rescuers into giving him food, money and clothing; wrapped in rags, he feigned madness and received alms; and when a fire occurred locally he would sprint to the scene, elicit some facts from onlookers, then rub ash into his clothes and claim to be a needy survivor. He begged skilfully (sometimes dressed as a woman) and stole when he could. When the gypsy king died he was elected a successor – hence his nickname 'King of the Gypsies'.

He also had a good line in religious mania, spouting the scriptures wildly until some devout believer took pity on him and parted with cash. He was imprisoned, escaped, was recaptured, was shipped to the USA, escaped, was recaptured and fitted with a heavy iron collar, escaped again and took shelter with a native Indian tribe. Back in England, having tricked well-wishers into paying his passage, he evaded re-arrest by pricking his skin and rubbing salt and gunpowder into the wounds, to simulate smallpox.

After involvement with the Jacobite rebellion his exploits gradually lessened. He devoted himself to helping the gypsies, until illness forced him to resign his 'kingship'. Tales of his exploits – no doubt embroidered – were widespread in the West Country, and Thackeray refers to him in *Vanity Fair*.

Another story of impersonation involves a young woman who in 1817, walked wearily into a cobbler's cottage in Almondsbury (Gloucestershire), speaking an incomprehensible language but apparently asking to sleep there. She carried just a small bundle of possessions and her appearance and clothes seemed foreign. The cobbler's wife took her to the Overseer of the Poor who took her to the local county Magistrate who took her to the village inn... but she remained a mystery.

Yearlstone Vineyard

The vineyard (EX16 8RL; 01884 855700; www.yearlstone.co.uk), with its shop and café, is about half a mile from Bickleigh. The position is gorgeous, and the outdoor tables overlooking the sloping vineyard and miles and miles of mid-Devon invite you to linger. There are good snacks and, of course, wine. Yearlstone, owned by Roger and Juliet White, offers a variety of tours, from self-guiding to the full works, fully guided, with 'tutored wine tasting'.

SP Cadeleigh Arms Cadeleigh EX16 8HP ✆ 01884 855238
⊕ www.thecadeleigharms.co.uk. Good, locally sourced pub food, with some

Over the next few days various local worthies tried – but failed – to identify her country or language. She indicated that her name was Caraboo, and reacted to pictures of the Far East. Then a Portuguese seafarer claimed he could translate for her and an astonishing tale emerged. Her father was a wealthy Chinese and her mother Malayan royalty; she was thus a princess, and lived on an island named Javasu. Pirates had kidnapped her from her house, bound and gagged her, and carried her off to their ship. They sold her to the captain of a brig, which eventually reached England. She had jumped overboard in the Bristol Channel and swum ashore, then wandered for about six weeks before reaching Almondsbury.

After two months staying comfortably with the magistrate, enjoying the attentions of many fascinated visitors, she wandered off – and reappeared in Bath, once again being fêted as an exotic wonder. By now the newspapers were headlining her story, and this exposure caused her downfall. A boarding house landlady in Bristol recognised her as a former lodger, and a local lad claimed she'd shared a meal with him in a pub – speaking English – two days before her appearance in Almondsbury.

It turned out that the exotic Princess Caraboo, with her foreign manners and unknown language, was in fact a local Devon girl, Mary Baker; her father was a cobbler in Witheridge, a village a few miles west of Tiverton. So much for the Portuguese seafarer's translation! She had worked as a servant in various parts of England but never settled; presumably careful study of the employers and guests she'd encountered had enabled her to create this convincing *alter ego*. Also Witheridge held large fairs and cattle markets at the time, where Mary will have met foreigners. She may even have heard tales of the rôle-playing 'King of the Gypsies'. What is extraordinary is that she sustained the act so consistently, never stepping out of character, lapsing in her fake language or showing that she understood English. To spare the embarrassment of the many people she had fooled she was quickly packed off to America – where she soon found herself a comfortable place in society, once again fêted for her 'exotic past'. Eventually she returned home. She and Bampfylde Moore Carew would have had a whale of a time together, if ever they had met...

JB

innovative specials and gorgeous puddings.

Trout Inn Bickleigh ✆ 01884 855596 🖑 www.troutinn-bickleigh.co.uk. A beautiful, thatched family-friendly inn serving traditional pub food.

Sawday's Special Places to Stay

S7 Kilbury Manor
S8 Manor Farm
S9 Hooks Cottage

EXETER

M5

CHAPTER 1

CHAPTER 4

① Doddiscombsleigh

② Higher Ashton

③ Canonteign Falls

Wheal Exmouth

Trusham

A38

N

A382

BOVEY TRACEY

0   4 miles
0   5km

⑥ Stover Country Park

A380

DAWLISH

TEIGNMOUTH

A381

⑤ Orchid Paradise

S9

A38   A383   NEWTON ABBOT

CHAPTER 5

⑧ Buckfast Abbey

④ Ipplepen

Torbryan   S8

TORQUAY

BUCKFASTLEIGH

⑦   South Devon Railway

S7

A381

⑨ Pennywell Farm   A384

A385   TOTNES

PAIGNTON

THE EASTERN FRINGE
OF DARTMOOR

BRIXHAM

CHAPTER 6

3. THE EASTERN FRINGE OF DARTMOOR

The River Teign turns south at Dunsford, and gives map-makers the eastern border of Dartmoor National Park before its final journey to Kingsteignton and Teignmouth. Although technically some of the towns and villages in this section lie within Dartmoor National Park, their more gentle, leafy character fits better here. Along the river are some of the prettiest wooded areas of Dartmoor, splashed by waterfalls, and networked by footpaths and narrow lanes. Not surprisingly, the Teign river gives its name to many places here, with England's highest waterfall, **Canonteign Falls**, just one of them.

The surprising aspect of this locale is how remote some of the villages feel despite their proximity to Exeter and Newton Abbot. Try to find your way to **Doddiscombsleigh**, even with a good map, and you'll see what I mean. Within the **Newton Abbot triangle**, formed by the major roads of the area, lies a village lost in time, **Torbryan**, as well as Stover Park with its inspirational **Ted Hughes Trail**. Finally there's Buckfastleigh, which draws large numbers of tourists to its various attractions; these include both **Buckfast Abbey** and the enchanting miniature pigs at **Pennywell Farm**.

Getting there and around

Drivers will find this one of the most easily accessible locales, with all the places described lying near the A38. It's once you leave that dual carriageway to track down the little villages that you're in trouble without a sat nav.

The **bus** service down the A38 is frequent and fast, so it's easy to get from Exeter to Buckfastleigh, and there's a local bus to Doddiscombsleigh, but that's all, unless you plan to supplement bus services with a fair amount of walking. The *Teignbridge* bus timetable covers the area and, as always, Traveline (0871 200 2233; www.traveline.info) gives you the latest timetables.

The cream of the getting there options is the **steam train** which runs between Totnes and Buckfastleigh. See below.

South Devon Railway

This is one of those lovely dollops of nostalgia that Devon is good at. The scenic branch line of the Great Western Railway which runs along the River Dart was axed by Dr Beeching in 1958, but only 11 years later it was reopened – ironically by Dr Beeching himself – and is now run by a charitable trust and operated by volunteers (01845 3451427; www.southdevonrailway.co.uk).

The line between Totnes and Buckfastleigh is one of the prettiest in the county, following the river closely for most of its route. Steam locomotives run four times a day in summer (April to October) and on Sundays and occasional weekdays during the other months; diesel locos also operate.

Cycling and walking

This region has no off-road **cycle** paths, and its lanes are typically hilly and narrow, but with a bicycle you could see all its major sights in a day.

Compared with many other areas in this book, this isn't great **walking** country, but still some good possibilities can be devised using the *Teignbridge* bus timetable and the Ordnance Survey Explorer map OL110 (for the north of the region) along with Explorer map OL28. Access to Haytor on Dartmoor is achieved via the **Templer Way** (see page 97), which runs through this region, including Stover Country Park.

The northern Teign valley

Hidden in the hills of the east side of the Teign are two villages with exceptional churches, Doddiscombsleigh and Higher Ashton, while Canonteign Falls and its nearby mine are more closely associated with the river.

① Doddiscombsleigh

This little hidden village attracts both pub crawlers and church crawlers. 'Everybody knows the Nobody' they say, and indeed the Nobody Inn has been there for centuries, although prior to the mid 18th century it was a cottage. It's speculated that the mining boom brought enough thirsty customers to the village to merit opening a pub.

St Michael's Church has been providing spiritual refreshment for even longer: it has the finest medieval stained-glass windows in the county, and the original church probably predates the Norman Conquest. It's built from an aesthetically pleasing mixture of local stone of various colours, including granite from nearby Dartmoor. Inside, the famous windows can be observed at eye level since they and the roof are exceptionally low. This makes it easy for the visitor to appreciate their craftsmanship and imagination, and brings a feeling of intimacy. To quote the *Shell Guide*, 'the artist has looked at men without romanticising but with much charity.' Indeed. I loved the tired face of St Paul, shielding his right eye with one hand. And also St George's cute little horse, which looks more like a sheep. The saint is killing what appears to be a very large dragon indeed, though it's hard to make out whether we are looking at spines or claws. The most complicated window at the far end of the aisle is more difficult to see, but there are photos on the wall showing the detail.

Another interesting feature of the church is the array of stone floor memorials. There's one to three generations of William Babbs, who all lived to a fine old age: 90, 84 and 79. As the church leaflet points out, this stone was clearly carved well after the last William Babb, who was 'endowed with few words but many charitable deeds', died in 1667. The lettering is of a high quality and in excellent condition – despite being on the floor – but it is also mostly spelled in the modern way. So who ordered it to be carved and when?

The church is full of helpful explanations and snippets, including an illuminating explanation of the green man at the top of one of the columns, or capitals, and the very intriguing hare-lipped devil which would escape anyone's notice if it hadn't been pointed out by Dr Michael Tisdall (see box below).

Finally, it's touching to see the 1945 *Table of Fees* for burial services posted on the wall. A posh vault in the churchyard cost £7.17s.0d, whilst there was no charge for the burial of a still-born infant.

Surprisingly, given its remoteness, the 360 **bus** from Exeter runs here five times a day, so you can view the church and have lunch at the inn without the worry of either finding the place or parking.

The Nobody Inn ℡ 01647 252394 · 🖰 www.nobodyinn.co.uk. This has evolved from The New Inn (in the late 1700s) to The No Body Inn 'with reference to an unfortunate episode concerning a dead landlord'. Now it's Nobody. The restaurant has won many awards including, in 2009, Gold Awards from the Taste of the West for their steak-and-ale pie and West Country goat's cheese tart with pesto. Lovely traditional interior for cold days and a large beer garden for the summer.

The Devil's bite

Carved at the top of one of the stone capitals in St Michael's Church, Doddiscombsleigh, is a face. It's not a green man, nor a saint or angel. It has funny pointed ears, unusual foliage, and something strange about its mouth. Dr Michael Tisdall is a medical doctor with a passion for the unusual in Devon churches, so he has teased out the (probable) truth here. This carving is at the west end of the church, often called the Devil's End (indeed, some old churches have a little opening through which the devil can escape during services), and he has a hare lip. As a young doctor studying children's diseases, Dr Tisdall came across the expression 'devil's bite' to describe a hare lip. And the foliage isn't the usual rose leaves, it's *Succisa pratensis*, or Devil's bit scabious. So there we have it. A medieval carver portrayed the Devil in an instantly recognisable form – to the villagers of his day – but for us it takes the detective work of a knowledgeable enthusiast to get to the truth.

② Higher Ashton

About 1½ miles south of Doddiscombsleigh is Higher Ashton. The **church of St John the Baptist** is famous for its medieval rood screen, intricately carved to set off the 32 panels with their painted saints. You'll easily identify the well-known saints such as St Sebastian with his arrows, and a baby-faced St George killing a tiny, frightened dragon; the more obscure ones include St Apollonia (see box below) looking speculatively at a huge tooth held in the blacksmith's pincers. There is a conspicuous monument to smug Sir George Chudleigh (1657) who fathered nine sons and nine daughters, and a fascinating commemorative stone embedded in the floor, crudely carved, with September and October written as 7ber and 8ber – the first time I have seen this abbreviation.

St Apollonia and St Barbara

It's not clear to me why a woman who had all her teeth smashed with giant tongs becomes the patron saint of dentists. However, she appears on so many Devon rood screens that it's worth knowing something about her.

Apollonia lived in Alexandria in the 3rd century AD. She led an exemplary life, preaching the gospel during a time when this held considerable risks. Emperor Philip was none too keen on Christians, especially those like Apollonia who gave succour to his political prisoners. In AD249 she was arrested and, inevitably, tortured to persuade her to renounce her faith. All her teeth were smashed and then pulled out with iron pincers. When this had no effect her torturers piled up firewood, intending to burn her to death, but she leapt into the flames herself thus presenting the church with a dilemma: did she commit suicide (a crime) or was she a true martyr, dying for her faith? They chose the latter and sanctification.

Devon has 14 depictions of St Apollonia holding her torturer's pincers (the kind used by blacksmiths so not really suitable for dentistry). These are usually on painted rood screens or stained glass but one, in Stokeinteignhead, is carved into a stone capital.

If explosives are your thing, then St Barbara is your patron saint. Possessed of exceptional beauty and intelligence, she was kept locked in a tower by her father who had a rich suitor in mind. Here she converted to Christianity and managed to escape, only to fall into the hands of a shepherd. Before he could have his wicked way with her, divine punishment turned his sheep into beetles. Her father then contrived that she should be paraded naked throughout the region, but God supplied her with a robe. Frustrated, Dad then resorted to a variety of tortures before getting fed up and killing her with his sword, whereupon he was struck dead by a thunderbolt. So St Barbara is now the patron saint of artillerymen and their like.

③ Canonteign Falls and Wheal Exmouth

This is one of Devon's superlatives, the highest waterfall in England (220 feet), but it's also man-made which takes the gloss off a bit. Nevertheless it's worth a visit for the cool, ferny woodland and wildflowers. And for the enterprise of the ten generations of Lords of the Manor who have played their part in creating this tourist attraction (EX6 7RH; 01647 252434; www.canonteignfalls.co.uk). The house is on the site of a monastery owned by the canons of St Mary du Val in Normandy, hence the name Canonteign. After the dissolution of the monasteries it was converted into a manor house which was eventually bought by Admiral Edward Pellew, later Lord Exmouth. His descendants enjoyed a period of prosperity in the 19th century through the nearby lead and silver mines, respectively Frank Mills (named after its owner, a banker) and Wheal Exmouth (see below).

In the 1880s the mines fell into decline and the miners found themselves out of a job. But then the third Lady Exmouth stepped in with the idea of putting them to work again by diverting the leat that formerly serviced the mine to create a waterfall tumbling over natural rocks for the enjoyment of family and friends. After World War II there was no money to maintain the waterfall and it, and the nearby paths, became choked with vegetation and virtually disappeared. It was not until 1985 that the tenth Lord Exmouth rediscovered the walk and decided to open it to the public.

No buses run to Canonteign so you need a car or bicycle. It is well signposted from the A38, off the B3193 which hugs the River Teign. In the grounds are a couple of lakes with resident waterfowl, and a gentle path (Grandad's Walk) for those unwilling to tackle the climb up to the falls. The circular walk to Buzzard's View and the top of the falls

is lovely, and an Assault Course enables children to work off any excess energy. Helpful labels tell you what you're looking at, and there's a recreation of a Victorian fern garden complete with tree ferns.

To experience the full drama of the next attraction it's best to approach it on foot. Leave your car in the Canonteign car park and turn left at the road. In half a mile you'll come to an astonishing sight: the tall chimneys of the former **Wheal Exmouth** lead mine adjacent to the engine house, now a beautifully converted three-storey private home. There are two chimneys, one circular with finely-worked corbels, and other octagonal, topless, and with trees billowing out of its ragged opening instead of smoke The whole complex is both beautiful and historic, spanning the commercial history of the area, from mining to 'grand design' conversion.

If it's lunch time, take the green lane beyond Canonteign Manor, next to the golf course, to the **Manor Inn**. The walk takes around 20 minutes. For variety when returning to your car there's a footpath that runs parallel to the golf course (left at Byteign Lodge) through woods full of flowers and birdsong.

Cridford Inn Trusham TQ13 0NR ℓ 01626 853694 🖰 www.vanillapod-cridfordinn.com. The village (just south of Lower and Upper Ashton) has some pretty thatched cottages and this charming pub (also thatched, and containing what is thought to be Britain's oldest domestic window), whose Vanilla Pod restaurant serves seriously good food, if the fishcakes I had are anything to go by. Worth a detour.
The Manor Inn Lower Ashton EX6 7QL ℓ 01647 252304
🖰 www.manorinn.co.uk. Good food and a variety of ales served in beautiful surroundings by the river.

A wily parson

Parson Harris, who served the parish of Hennock, was known not only for his kindliness and fairness but also for his occasional recourse to a little white magic for the benefit of his flock. One day three fine fat geese were stolen from a farmer named Tuckett; and the following Sunday Parson Harris announced this from the pulpit, declaring also that he had cast a spell on the feathers of the birds so that three of them would stick to the nose of the thief. Immediately he spotted a member of the congregation raise his hand and anxiously touch his nose – so was able confidently to denounce him as the culprit! Other 'spells' that he cast tended to have similarly unmagical outcomes, but still served to impress his parishioners.

The Newton Abbot triangle

The A38, A380 and A385 trunk roads form a triangle with **Newton Abbot** roughly in the centre. Although the busy town itself is best avoided unless you have shopping to do (it has a big outdoor market on Wednesdays), there are places here that merit a slow visit. If you do find yourself in Newton Abbot, perhaps with time to spare in between buses, you could check out its little **museum** in St Paul's Road (01626 201121; www.devonmuseums.net). Open Monday to Saturday from March to late October, it has exhibits relating to (among many others) Isambard Kingdom Brunel, railways and the wreck-salvage pioneer John Lethbridge.

④ Ipplepen and Torbryan

Ipplepen is a surprisingly dreary village for this beautiful region, but if you're nearby is worth visiting for its church: it's huge and has a particularly beautiful rood screen, with inset saints and fan vaulting, and a 15th-century carved and painted pulpit resting on an old millstone. In the graveyard is the tomb of a coachman who took Sir Arthur Conan Doyle around Dartmoor to gain inspiration for a book. The man's name was Baskerville.

The tiny hamlet of **Torbryan** was described by Hoskins in 1954 as having 'perhaps the most uniformly attractive village church in Devon'. What makes it exceptional is that there has been no messing around with its interior since it was built in the 15th century. It has the lime-washed exterior characteristic of Devon, and clear glass windows that let in plenty of light to set off the carved, polychromed screen, pulpit and altar table. It is also redundant, cared for by the Churches Conservation Trust (the key-holder lives at the farm behind the church) and, sadly, I feel that its soul left with the last member of its congregation. The old church house, dating from the 14th century, is now an inn.

The Old Church House Inn Torbryan ☎ 01803 812372 ⌨ www.oldchurchhouseinn.co.uk. The meat served here comes from nearby farms, the fish from Brixham and the vegetables from local growers. This beautiful old inn is deservedly popular.

⑤ Orchid Paradise

Anyone who loves the variety and beauty of orchids might like a visit to Burnham Nurseries, to which is attached the permanent display that is Orchid Paradise. The 'growing area', housing plants that are for sale, is much larger, with a series of interconnecting greenhouses. One of the great pluses of this small attraction is that it is open seven days a week, all year, and is lovely and warm on a cold day. And dry on a wet day. Also, so I've heard, cool on a hot day, although Devon hasn't given me the chance to test that. Brown signs point the way to it at Forches Cross on the A382; 01626 352233; www.orchids.uk.com.

⑥ Stover Country Park

Whoever thought up the idea of linking poetry with nature in this lovely country park deserves an award. Stover (www.devon.gov.uk/stover_country_park.htm) is one of those agreeable places which has 'nothing to see' yet everything to observe. Within its 114 acres it brings you over heathland thick with gorse and heather, through deciduous trees and coniferous forests, along the banks of a river, adjacent to a tumbling stream and around a lake where herons stand sentinel among the reeds. A 100-yard, wheelchair-accessible aerial walkway was opened in 2003, looking over ponds and woodland. The interpretation boards are informative and the place is child-friendly in the right way. No coloured plastic, just an attention-grabbing introduction to the wonders of nature. The reason I came here, above all the similar country parks in Devon, was for the **Ted Hughes Poetry Trail**. Now I never thought that I particularly liked Ted Hughes. Too gloomy. But at the end of the two hours and 16 poems that it takes to complete the trail, I was a convert. This was evocative, accessible poetry, fitting perfectly to the location, about birds, fish and animals and the natural world in general. And not a crow in sight. Sadly, because of copyright problems, the centre has not been able to publish a booklet with all the poems.

The park is 300 yards south of the Drumbridges roundabout on the A382; it's linked by cycle routes to Bovey Tracey and Newton Abbot, and bus 39 (Exeter to Newton Abbot) passes by.

Buckfastleigh and area

⑦ Buckfastleigh

Buckfastleigh is a tourist hub which deserves its popularity. For one thing it has the best free town guide I have found anywhere; it's widely available at Tourist Information Centres. Buckfastleigh is also the terminus/start of the steam train that runs to Totnes, and has otters and butterflies, an abbey, and a restaurant with a difference.

The town's Tourist Information Centre is next to **The Valiant Soldier**, the town's best-known attraction. They call it 'The pub where time was never called'. When the brewery withdrew their licence in 1965 it seems that the landlords simply said 'sod this', locked up, and walked away. Mr and Mrs Roberts continued to live upstairs but, perhaps understandably, since they'd run the pub for 27 years, left their memories intact in the untouched pub area. It was only after the widow Alice Roberts sold the property in the mid 1990s that anyone realised what had happened, and Teignbridge council stepped in and bought the premises. It now offers the older generation a burst of nostalgia, with everything

just as it was, including the jumbled attic which has been recreated on a lower, safer floor.

The **South Devon Railway** (see page 61) is the perfect way to arrive in Buckfastleigh, easing you gently into the town via the **Railway Museum** and the **Otter and Butterfly Centre** (www.ottersandbutterflies.co.uk). The museum's focus is Isambard Kingdom Brunel, who decreed that this railway should be broad gauge. The line was later converted to standard gauge, but the only surviving broad-gauge engine is here. There is also a description of Brunel's 'atmospheric' railway from Exeter to Newton Abbot: literally atmospheric, since it used air pressure to drive the train (see page 41).

Riverford Field Kitchen Wash Barn, Buckfastleigh TQ11 0JU ☎ 01803 762074
🖰 www.riverford.co.uk. More than just a restaurant! This is part of the pioneering
organic farm which first introduced the concept of Veg Boxes, where seasonal
vegetables are delivered to local homes as well as hotels and restaurants. A tour of
the farm is part of the 'field to plate' experience. Lunch or supper consists of five
vegetable dishes and one meat dish, and diners sit together at a large table, so a
desire to be convivial should accompany a good appetite (you help yourself from the
communal dishes). Advance booking is mandatory. Closed Nov–Mar.

Buckfastleigh Caves

A visit to the little-known Pengelly Centre is a serious, but highly rewarding,
undertaking. Unlike Kents Cavern in Torquay there is no attempt here to provide
entertainment – the $1^1/_2$ to 2-hour tour is aimed at adults and bright children who
want to know about local history, geology and palaeontology. Most of the work
here is scientific, and volunteers from the William Pengelly Cave Studies Trust are
only available to give tours a few times a week, normally Wednesday and Thursday
in the summer, so check their website or phone before making plans. Bear in mind
too that there is quite a bit of walking along sometimes muddy tracks.

The caves were discovered by local boys exploring the disused quarries in the
1930s. On the floor of one cave they found some bones and took them to the
museum in Torquay. 'Nothing of importance – just pigs and cows' they were
told. Not satisfied by this explanation, they sent them to the Natural History
Museum in Kensington. This time the reaction was quite different, and the area
was cordoned off until the experts, who had correctly identified the fossilised
bones of elephant, hippopotamus and hyena, could take a look.

These huge animals, all larger than the species now found in Africa, thrived in
Devon during the warm period that preceded the last ice age – around 130,000
years ago – when the huge continent that contained Britain was in the southern
hemisphere.

The tour starts up a nearby green lane with a look at the local history, geology
and natural history including a description of the the greater horseshoe bats
which roost in one of the caves (see box on page 70). The nub of the tour is a
visit to Joint Mitnor Cave, now easily accessible via a system of boardwalks,
where the most exciting finds were made – over 3,000 bones, dug out of the
cave floor and walls. Some 120,000 years ago an earthquake opened a hole in the
roof of the cavern, and animals fell in.
Herbivores such as bison were followed by their
predators, hyenas. These two species provided
the majority of bones found, but there
were also wild boar, hippopotamus, bear
and rhinoceros, as well as four straight-
tusked elephants – two adults and two
babies. The adults, in fact, were too large to
fall through the hole but probably became

wedged and unable to escape. These elephants were far larger than present-day African elephants, the adults standing at around 15 to 20 feet high. Together with these monsters were found the bones of brown bears and animals familiar in the British countryside today: foxes, voles, badgers, red deer and fallow deer. Quite a few bones have been left in the cave to add interest to what is already a fascinating visit. There's a milk tooth of a baby elephant – but still an impressive size – and a leg bone gnawed by a hyena, as well as fossilised hyena droppings (the excavators could afford to leave some – they found five buckets full).

Eventually the cave filled up with animal remains and debris and was no longer a death trap. The last ice age, around 80,000 years ago, probably covered it completely until the quarry men opened it up in the mid 20th century.

William Pengelly Cave Studies Trust, Russets Lane, Buckfastleigh TQ11 0DY ☎ 01752 775195 🖳 www.pengellytrust.org.

Greater horseshoe bats

In Britain, this large bat is found only in the southwest of England and in Wales. The colony at the Buckfastleigh Caves is the largest in the UK, and particularly important since this species is in decline. It's a strange-looking animal with its large mobile ears and fleshy 'noseleaf' (looking like a horseshoe, hence its name) which amplifies the bat's calls; it makes these through its nose with its mouth closed, so that it can judge the distance of its prey. These bats have small eyes, but the expression 'blind as a bat' has little truth as bats can see fairly well, although only in black and white. However, in complete darkness they have to rely mainly on their echolocation 'sonar'.

Greater horseshoe bats are among the largest European species of bats; their impressive wingspan is about 16 inches. They can live for 30 years. These animals mate during the autumn but delay fertilisation until they have emerged from hibernation in the spring. Bats' wings are versatile. Apart from enabling them to fly – the only mammal that has evolved this way – the wings act as a cooling system in flight, since they contain innumerable blood vessels, and are a means of finding underground sites by detecting temperature changes from draughts emerging from entrances. Dozing bats wrap their wings right round their bodies. And when it comes to birth, the wings are more like an open umbrella, allowing the newborn baby to drop from its upside-down mother into safety. At times the baby hangs from a false nipple, positioned at the lower end of the abdomen, while the real nipples are near the armpit (or wingpit). The mother can fly with her infant thus attached, though she also parks it in the roost, hanging upside down, while she goes hunting. The young can fly and catch insects from about three weeks.

Bats emerge from their roosts about half an hour after sunset. Sit quietly and watch them, but do not disturb this protected species.

My thanks to Geoff Billington of Greena Ecological Consultancy for information.

⑧ Buckfast Abbey

This is an extraordinary place. The brochure says that Buckfast Abbey, founded in the 11th century and demolished in the 16th following the Dissolution of the Monasteries, is now 'home to a community of Benedictine monks who lead a life of prayer, work and study'. I don't doubt it, but somehow they have created a thriving commercial enterprise teeming with visitors willing to pay high prices at the Monastic Produce Shop, and who fill the modern abbey in numbers exceeding those to our great cathedrals. It's utterly commendable in the sense that the profits from tourism undoubtedly sustain the life of prayer. Nevertheless, something about it leaves me feeling a little uncomfortable.

That said, it's a beautiful setting and there's a wonderfully relaxed feeling about the place, with people strolling contentedly, quietly enjoying all it has to offer without any laid-on 'entertainment'. There's also the extraordinary achievement of the re-building of the Abbey church by just a handful of the monks themselves, starting around a hundred years ago. By hand they cut the great stones to shape, lashed wooden scaffolding together, hauled the stones up on rudimentary pulleys... it took them 32 years, and the beautiful and imposing St Mary's Church that you see today is the result.

Beekeeping here is also an interesting story, and Brother Adam, who worked with the Abbey's bees for over 70 years, is world famous for breeding a new strain which was a high honey producer, relatively gentle, and resistant to disease. During four decades he travelled some 100,000 miles to isolated areas of Europe, Asia and North Africa, persuading local beekeepers to give him queens from their indigenous strains; these he posted back to Buckfast. The result is known as the Buckfast bee, and its products are sold in the Monastic Shop - along with the famous Buckfast Tonic Wine, which has made headlines recently because of its apparent and rather incongruous popularity among young and anti-social drinkers. In Scotland it's affectionately known as Buckie.

There's also a lavender garden (when it's in flower, the perfume is wonderful) and sensory and physic gardens. The Grange Restaurant serves food at pleasant outside tables and has sensible little 'snack boxes' for children. Concerts are held regularly at the Abbey, and the monks also offer retreats.

If you arrive at Buckfastleigh by steam train, you can take a 'Heritage Bus' (a 1960s double-decker) from Buckfastleigh station to Buckfast Abbey.

Buckfast Abbey TQ11 0EE ✆ 01364 645500 🖰 www.buckfast.org.uk.

Tastes of Devon

Apart from its wonderfully varied local meats and seafood, Devon's local food shops and markets offer many smaller gastronomic pleasures. Top of my list is its **clotted cream**, thick, velvety and yellow, tasting quite unlike the thinner creams found elsewhere in Britain. The very best comes from Devon and Cornwall; there's no specific difference between the two counties, but the taste can vary according to the breed of cow and the preparation (milk is heated very slowly and then cooled, so that the cream rises to the top and can be skimmed off). A recent transatlantic visitor expected her 'Devon cream tea' to be a cup of tea with cream in it, but of course it's a far more sumptuous meal: freshly baked scones spread thickly with clotted cream and jam, accompanied by a pot of tea. In Devon, the jam usually goes on top of the cream, in Cornwall underneath. Various places sell clotted cream by mail order, for example Johns of Instow (01271 861387; www.johnsofinstow.co.uk) and Langage Farm, Plympton (01752 339712; www.langagefarm.com).

Then there are the **cheeses**, ranging from hard and nutty to soft and squashy, enriched with all manner of local herbs and flavours. Different areas have their own specialities. To pick just a few: Devon Blue is moist and crumbly, Exmoor Jersey Blue is rich and buttery with an elusive pepperiness, Beenleigh Blue made from ewes' milk is sweetish and tangy, Devon Oke is smooth and cheddary, Sharpham is similar to brie, Devon Smoake is – yes – smoky, and Tyning has a hint of toffee. For mail order try the West Country Cheese Co (01271 379944; www.westcountrycheese.co.uk).

With all the flowers of Dartmoor and Exmoor for bees to feed on, there are some excellent Devon **honeys**. The Quince Honey Farm in South Molton (EX36 3AZ; 01769 572401; www.quincehoney.co.uk) is entertaining to visit – describing itself as a 'hive of activity', it has good displays and demonstrations, and a wide range of bee-based products.

Finally there's the Devon **pasty** – and indeed the Cornish pasty too, because the taste depends more on the individual baker than on their county of origin. Generally a Devon pasty has its join or crimp along the top, a Cornish pasty along the side. You'll find them everywhere, and when a bakery is selling them hot from the oven, their rich, meaty smell wafting into the street... mmmmm! Of several good sources, Chunk of Devon from Ottery St Mary (01404 814401; www.takeachunk.com) have won a number of awards. I'm a fan of their homity pie, another West Country recipe.

Local fare can – indeed should! – be washed down with a good draught of Devon cider or scrumpy. Local pubs stock the particular ciders of their region; scrumpy is made from windfall apples and its potency can catch you unawares. Then head out on a long, slow walk across the moors to work off all those sinful calories...

JB

⑨ Pennywell Farm

Forget conservation and endangered species, this hands-on animal place is just that – its aim is to bring humans and animals as close together as possible and as such it offers perhaps Devon's most rewarding experience for children. Just look at the expression of a little girl gently stroking a tiny dozing piglet, and you'll see how well it works. Or sometimes doesn't: the squeals of disgruntled piglets can be heard from far off, but whenever a baby cries there are nursemaids – or nursemen – on hand to take it back for a soothing word or two.

Pennywell has been selectively breeding miniature pigs since 1992 (see box below), with the result that a piglet weighs just 250g (8oz) at birth and grows to about the size of a springer spaniel. It's not just the miniature piglets you can hug. Although I would challenge the statement that 'Pennywell animals love to be cuddled' (very few animals really enjoy being held), the rabbits and older piglets are remarkably tolerant of human attention, and selected ones are held in pens where visitors can join them for a stroke. As a pig enthusiast I was just as thrilled as the little kids around me when a piglet collapsed on its side in ecstasy as I scratched it under the chin.

Every half hour there is something different happening, such as ferret racing, bottle feeding or a falconry display, and there are plenty of non-animal activities for children too; much of it is under cover.

Pennywell Farm TQ11 0LT 📞 01364 642023 🖱 www.pennywellfarm.co.uk. Closed Nov-Feb.

Pennywell's miniature pigs

I talked to the ebullient Chris Murray about his miniature pigs. 'I've always loved pigs. I studied agriculture at Seale-Hayne in Exeter and got interested in breeding pigs then. They're ideal animals for selective breeding because they have two litters a year and up to 18 piglets per litter. Of course in those days we were breeding for improved meat, and we wanted our pigs to grow fast. Now it's the opposite – we want small, slow-growing pigs. All sorts of traditional breeds have been used in our breeding programme: Iron Age wild boar, Gloucester old spot and Tamworth for colour, Berkshire, middle white because they're small with smiley faces, kune-kune which have a nice temperament, and English lop, which are docile. We aimed for other small details too – for instance we wanted prick ears rather than lop. But not too small because tiny ears look mean. And we wanted a short snout, because it's more appealing, and the right mouth. It took us 16 years to breed the smile!

Yes, we sell them. As pets, of course. We have some lovely customers here! One lady has a pig that sits on the sofa and watches television with her and there's a man who takes his pig on bike rides.'

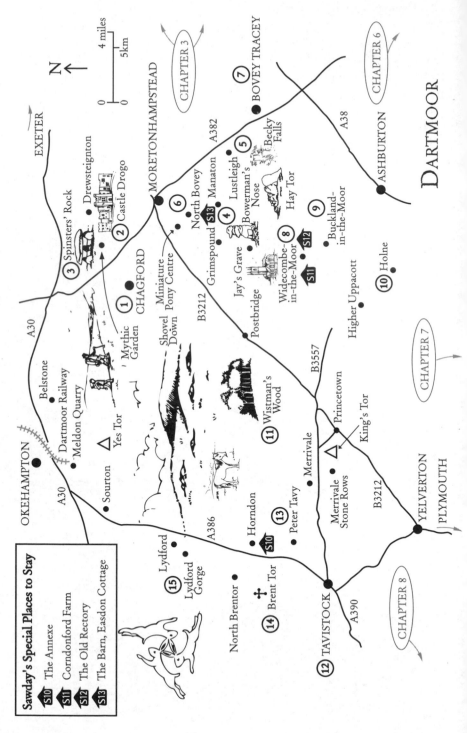

DARTMOOR

74

Sawday's Special Places to Stay

- S10 The Annexe
- S11 Corndonford Farm
- S12 The Old Rectory
- S13 The Barn, Easdon Cottage

N

0 — 4 miles
0 — 5km

CHAPTER 3

CHAPTER 6

CHAPTER 7

CHAPTER 8

EXETER

OKEHAMPTON

MORETONHAMPSTEAD

BOVEY TRACEY

ASHBURTON

CHAGFORD

TAVISTOCK

YELVERTON
PLYMOUTH

PRINCETOWN

Belstone
Dartmoor Railway
Meldon Quarry
Sourton
Yes Tor
Mythic Garden
Shovel Down
Miniature Pony Centre
Drewsteignton
Spinsters' Rock
Castle Drogo
North Bovey
Manaton
Lustleigh
Bowerman's Nose
Becky Falls
Hay Tor
Grimspound
Jay's Grave
Postbridge
Widecombe-in-the-Moor
Buckland-in-the-Moor
Holne
Higher Uppacott
Wistman's Wood
King's Tor
Merrivale
Merrivale Stone Rows
Peter Tavy
Horndon
Lydford
Lydford Gorge
Brent Tor
North Brentor

A30
A382
A38
A386
A390
B3212
B3557

1 2 3 4 5 6 7 8 9 10 11 12 13 14 15
S10 S11 S12 S13

4. DARTMOOR

Look at any map of Devon and you'll see the largely roadless blob that is Dartmoor. Literature and imagination give it an air of menace: *The Hound of the Baskervilles*, a bleak prison where the surrounding moor is the best security, and craggy tors emerging from heavy, disorientating mists. This national park is high – the highest land in England south of the Pennines – leaving the visitor exposed to raw winds sweeping in from the Atlantic. But there's a softer side to Dartmoor. On my last visit I missed the bus from Tavistock so hitched a lift with a man who'd retired to Walkhampton. 'When I tell people I live in Dartmoor, the first thing they ask is about the snowstorms. What they don't know is that this is a microclimate. I can look out of my window at snow on the hills, but around my house it's mild enough to go out without a coat'. So if you want Dartmoor bleakness you can find it. Once you cross a cattle-grid the hedges disappear, sheep and ponies raise their heads to watch you pass, and the wind catches your hair as you reach for a sweater. You can walk for hours without seeing a road – or a tree. And everywhere you see granite: rocks as large as cars scattered randomly or piled on top of hills to form the tors that define Dartmoor, quarried and dressed in the walls of the ancient village churches, or rough-hewn and arranged in circles or rows by the first humans to make the moor their home.

The low-lying perimeter is another world, however, networked by deep narrow lanes. Footpaths meander through gentle, flower-filled meadows or dark woodland, or along the banks of rivers. The Tavy, Teign and Dart dominate, but all have tributaries and you are never far from a brook. Hidden in the valleys are small villages, their church towers poking through the trees, and welcoming pubs. But no one visiting here would stay only in the valleys; Dartmoor *is* the high moor. You may regret venturing up there in mist and rain, but on a sunny day its wildness is alluring. It's aptly called England's last wilderness, and the feeling of space and silence, broken only by the trilling of skylarks and the scrunching of boots on stones, is intoxicating.

Dartmoor also has, uniquely, its visible prehistory in the monuments such as hut circles and stone rows that litter the moor. A newcomer might assume the tors are also the work of prehistoric people. The word comes from the Celtic *twr*, or tower, but these are the work of nature – erosion – not man. And in an area that has blessedly few 'tourist attractions' nature has provided children with some lovely scrambles and adults with hills to test their stamina, as well as giving Dartmoor its unmistakable horizon.

Dartmoor: the hand of man

There are more prehistoric sites here than anywhere in Europe, and Dartmoor is one of the easiest places in Britain to view the march of history, from Neolithic circles to the Neo-medieval Castle Drogo. In October 2009 a ceremonial site, which could date from as early as 6000BC, emerged when the Tottoford Reservoir near Bovey Tracey was drained. Archaeologists will take a while to decide on its age, but they all agree on its importance. At the time of writing most believe that the earliest remains on Dartmoor are **Neolithic**, around 4000BC, and that as true settlers these people had the most profound effect on the landscape by domesticating animals and cultivating crops. Then the Beaker people in the **early Bronze Age**, around 2200BC, built the Grimspound enclosed village and some two thousand other 'hut circles' on the moor. Bronze is an alloy of tin and copper so tin-rich Dartmoor was an obvious place to settle, the metal being easily extracted from rivers and surface deposits. Later, still a few centuries BC, came the **Iron Age**, whose most tangible heritage is the plethora of hill forts that are found in other parts of Devon, but not Dartmoor, and finally the two centuries of Christianity and its enduring symbol, the English country church, its fortunes tied to those of the tinners who continued to extract the valuable metal from Dartmoor until the mid 20th century. Wealthy tin merchants who endowed a church in a stannery (tin-workers') town were ensured a short cut to heaven.

Visiting Dartmoor today, you may find it puzzling that Neolithic and Bronze-Age people chose to settle in such an inhospitable region. Probably, in an age where finding enough to eat was the main preoccupation, the attraction was the abundance of game in the woodlands that at that time covered low-lying parts of the moor, and the good grazing for both wild and domestic animals in the higher areas. The climate was milder then, and the soil less acid; thousands of years of slash-and-burn agriculture impoverished the land and helped create the moor that we see today. The availability of granite for constructing durable, weather-proof homes and the mysterious stone circles and monoliths will have helped the inhabitants but frustrates archaeologists, since granite cannot be carbon dated. But that is part of the attraction: we just don't know what a lot of these structures were used for, nor even when they were built. We can simply enjoy them for what they are.

Moving forward to our known history, the **Norman Conquest** in 1066 resulted in tracts of land being set aside for the new King to indulge his enthusiasm for hunting. These areas, rich in game, were called **'forests'** although this did not mean woodland; the moorland of both Dartmoor and Exmoor were royal forests. In those times deer, wolves and wild boar were all plentiful. All have gone now, including the red deer. Penalties for harming animals in the royal forests were severe, and in the 12th century King John gave in to pressure and 'deforested' all of Devon apart from Dartmoor and Exmoor. In 1337 Edward III gave the Forest of Dartmoor to his son, the Prince of Wales and Duke of Cornwall. It remains the property of the Duchy of Cornwall – and the current Prince of Wales – to this day.

Dartmoor tin and the stannary towns

Dartmoor, with Cornwall, was the first known source of tin. Some 4,000 years ago, metal workers discovered that by mixing tin (10%) with copper (90%) they created a stronger but easily worked material: bronze. Because tin doesn't rust it is also used to coat other metals. Minerals containing tin are almost always associated with granite, hence tin's abundance on Dartmoor. The ore was originally collected from the streams and rivers, through the simple process of panning or 'streaming'. Once these deposits were exhausted – and streaming continued into the 17th century – the ore was extracted from the ground using pick and shovel, sometimes with the help of leats, or diverted streams, to wash away the debris. Millstones were used to crush the ore and extract the metal which was then smelted. Two smeltings generally took place, one at the site and the second, to produce pure tin, in one of the **stannary towns**. The Latin for tin is *stannum*, hence the term stannary.

Stannary towns in Dartmoor were mining centres where refined tin was collected, assessed for quality, then minted into coins or sold. The proceeds were passed to the Duchy of Cornwall. In 1305 King Edward I established Tavistock, Ashburton and Chagford as Devon's first stannary towns, with the right to organise their own political affairs through the Stannary Parliament and Stannary Courts. Other stannary towns such as Widecombe were established later as mining became more organised. Stannary laws were the first legal code of England, affording the miners considerable power.

Dartmoor ponies

In contrast to Exmoor, where all ponies on the moor are similar in appearance – as you would expect of a distinct breed – Dartmoor's ponies are much more varied. There are few true Dartmoor ponies left now, the result of generations of cross-breeding, there being no rules on what ponies may be grazed on this common land. Since no pony is truly wild, and many will be sold on at some point, there are commercial considerations. 'Coloured' (piebald or skewbald) ponies attract higher prices than bay or brown, the original Dartmoor pony colour, so they are replacing the less strikingly coloured animals.

Pony drifts, when the animals are rounded up and marked for ownership before being sold on, take place once a year in the autumn. The pony markets are held at Tavistock on the first Friday in October and Chagford the second Thursday in October.

The Dartmoor Pony Heritage Trust was set up to preserve the unregistered Dartmoor pony gene pool, and to maintain the traditional herds of native Dartmoor ponies. It aims to increase the value of the annual foal crop through handling, castrating colts not suitable for breeding and promoting the good temperament and versatility of these moor-bred ponies. Every year the Dartmoor Pony Heritage Trust, supported by Dartmoor Pony Society, assesses the quality and conformation of the foals and awards the cream of the crop Heritage status.

Dartmoor Pony Heritage Trust Contact Mrs Dru Butterfield, Charity Manager
☎ 01626 355314 🖥 www.dpht.co.uk.

Letterboxing on Dartmoor

In 1854, a Dartmoor guide named James Perrott placed an empty glass pickle jar by Cranmere Pool. He told hikers and other guides about it, and encouraged them – if they reached it – to put some record of their visit inside. People began to leave postcards and letters, addressed either to themselves or to others, which the next visitor would take and post: the Dartmoor equivalent of throwing a bottle into the sea containing an address. Gradually letterboxes were placed in other parts of the moor, each with a notebook and appropriate rubber stamp. Letterboxers now 'collect' these when they find them by marking the stamp into their own notebooks; when their total reaches 100 they can join the '100 Club'.

By the early 1900s the Cranmere pickle jar had been replaced by a tin box containing a more formal visitors' book, and in 1937 a granite box was erected there. Letterboxes around the moor today range from solid structures to jars and tins to plastic sandwich boxes, generally well concealed. There are strict guidelines about their maintenance, choosing sites considerately and not damaging the landscape; do read them on the website www.userfriendlydevon.com/100club/perface.html before placing a box of your own.

Remember, too, that a box placed in winter may be hidden by vegetation when you return to check it in the summer. A friend described how the growing bracken swallowed up not only the box but her smallest grandchild who was hunting for it: they found him when a little voice piped up from deep in the fronds 'Granddad, where are you?' Children love the challenge of letterboxing, and another friend told me that her three would be seriously grumpy in the car on the way home if they hadn't managed to find a box.

From Dartmoor, letterboxing has spread to other parts of Britain (Yorkshire, Isle of Man, Lundy, Scotland...). It caught on in the United States in 1998 and also exists in New Zealand, Germany and the Netherlands. A new version called geocaching, using GPS co-ordinates, is also gaining popularity.

So, if you spot an unexpected container on the moor, you may have taken the first step towards becoming a fully fledged Dartmoor letterboxer!

JB

Getting there and around

Despite my love of public transport, I have to admit that most people will choose to travel by car, especially off-season when the traffic is lighter and public transport to the heart of Dartmoor is less frequent. The national park authorities have been generous with the provision of parking areas, so most walks and places of interest are readily accessible, even in the busy summer months when an attempt to explore the minor single-track roads will result in more mileage done in reverse than forward. On summer weekends in July and August, stick to the wider roads and abandon your car as soon as possible.

Public transport

Dartmoor is a destination in itself, and some people will choose to spend their entire holiday there. It's perfectly feasible to do this using public transport, augmented by taxis if necessary.

In the summer months just about everywhere is accessible by bus, if only once a week, but initially most car-free people will use **trains** and **taxis** to reach their base. The nearest mainline train station is Ivybridge, at the southern tip of the national park, where there are at least two local taxi companies: Ivycabs (01752 895555) and Elite Cabs (01752 892222). Newton Abbot is a little further from the moor, but convenient for the eastern section; taxis from Station Taxis (01626 334488). From Exeter station you can catch the hourly X38 **express bus** to Ashburton (taxis: 01364 652423) or Buckfastleigh (01626 333333). Or, if you're basing yourself in the north of Dartmoor, take the 359 bus to Moretonhampstead, which leaves Exeter at two-hourly intervals, and book a taxi from John Chard in Chagford (01647 433219).

One of the most delightful ways of getting an overview of the moor is by **local bus**. The **Sunday Rover** gives access to both rail and bus services at low cost on Sundays between May and September, when scenic bus journeys are frequent and 'joined up' (see below). The service on Saturdays is almost as good, with the **Haytor Hoppa** (see box on page 80) taking a circular route through some of Dartmoor's most popular eastern places. There are other once-a-week offerings which are equally rewarding. On Wednesdays, for instance, you have the choice of the 671 from Okehampton to Newton Abbot, which stops at some of north Dartmoor's most delightful villages, Chagford, Manaton and Bovey Tracey, or the 672 between Newton Abbot and Buckland-in-the-Moor via Widecombe. Both give you ample time for exploration before catching the return bus.

The pick of the regular buses, in terms of scenery, is the Exeter–Plymouth Transmoor Link (82) which crosses Dartmoor on the B3212 from Moretonhampstead to Yelverton every two hours at weekends in the summer, and from October to May does the run twice on Sundays and the Easter holiday. So even in winter you can do a walk and still catch the last bus home.

The relevant bus timetables are *Teignbridge* and *West Devon* (www.devon.gov.uk/buses).

The Haytor Hoppa

The Haytor Hoppa (bus 271) was an instant success when introduced in 2009. It runs on a two-hourly schedule, summer only, and takes an hour to make the circuit from Bovey Tracey. Peter, at the tourist office, told me what a help it's been: 'When people came to ask about getting to Haytor we had to say 'It's a four-mile walk uphill' but now we just explain about the bus. Yes, it's a small bus but with large windows so you can see the view. And we won't leave you stranded on the moor; if the last bus is full, we'll send another one for you.'

When I caught the first bus of the morning (from outside Tesco) it was already half full of cheery locals who'd come from Newton Abbot. People chat to each other on the Haytor Hoppa, but it's hard to talk and look at the scenery. 'I love that', said my neighbour. 'It's the first glimpse of **Haytor**.' We passed close to the tor which was already crowned with children playing king of the castle. 'See – it looks different from every angle. I think it looks like a snail from here.' **Hound Tor** was soon visible to the right, and then we dropped down to **Widecombe** with glorious views all round.

The next sight to be pointed out to me was **Jay's Grave**. 'I haven't been there for a while but there always used to be fresh flowers laid there every day.' The grave belongs to Kitty Jay, a girl who took her own life after being seduced by a local lad. As a suicide she was buried outside the parish boundary, but exhumed in 1860 and reburied in a proper grave in its current position at a crossroads. Now I've visited it myself I can confirm that there were fresh flowers there – as well as some coins and an (empty) bottle of whisky. Then we were down in the trees and greenery of **Manaton** and past **Becky Falls** before reaching the main(ish) B3387 and back to Bovey Tracey. A delightful ride and a perfect overview of Dartmoor.

For bus walks off this route see page 89; information on the Haytor Hoppa and timetable: www.dartmoor-npa.gov.uk.

None of the county's heritage steam trains runs within the National Park, but the next best thing is a diesel train service operated by the **Dartmoor Railway** C-I-C from Okehampton. This uses a heritage 'Hampshire' diesel unit, lovingly restored by volunteers from the Dartmoor Railway Supporters Association to provide a tourist service to Meldon Quarry which has no public road access. Services operate mainly at weekends though, increasingly, extra trains are run during the week for walkers from The Manor House hotel in Okehampton.

Meldon Quarry station is currently the end of the line, but the track continues as the Granite Way cycle path to Lydford. And the good news is that a guard's van on the train can carry up to 20 bicycles as well as pushchairs. Walkers can return to Okehampton by train or on foot (downhill!) along the Granite Way, perhaps to **Sourton** to lunch at the extraordinary Highwayman Inn (see box on page 83). But even if you are not a walker, you shouldn't miss the two-minute stroll from the train to the Meldon Viaduct (now a scheduled Ancient Monument) which straddles the West Okement Valley. The viaduct was built in 1874 for the London and South Western Railway main line between Waterloo and Plymouth and is a striking example of Victorian engineering. The views as you walk across the viaduct are magnificent. At high season, some trains travel beyond Okehampton to Sampford Courtenay station, another pleasant walking area – and historically interesting (see box on page 177). Free leaflets describing local walks are available from Okehampton station.

The Dartmoor Railway

Dave Clegg

Railways are in my blood. As a toddler, I lived in North Wales and I remember my mother regularly taking me on the trams to Colwyn Bay. Then, like many boys I went train-spotting when I was old enough, and when I left school in 1960 I joined the Southern Region of British Railways at Woking. I enjoyed it, but was impatient to get on and so left the railways for other work. But while I was working for the Southern, I had an entitlement to free tickets and, thinking about it now, I suppose this really started my love of the Southern lines in Devon and Cornwall. Living near London, I'd travel down on the 1.10am newspaper train from Waterloo which got me down to Devon in the early hours. Here, on the mainly single-track lines west of Okehampton the pace of life was different. Modernisation hadn't reached this part of the railway system and it became known among enthusiasts as 'The Withered Arm'. I remember it used to take nearly an hour and a half for the 20 miles from Torrington to Halwill Junction – slow yes, but as I was sometimes asked up on the footplate it didn't matter!

Since retirement, I have had the time to work as a volunteer, and I must say it's much better working because I love to, rather than because I have to! I believe it was 2003 when I turned up at Okehampton one day and asked if I could get involved. The Dartmoor Railway was run by paid staff at that time and the management weren't too keen on taking on volunteers. But I was allowed to paint an old van used for cycle storage and as I kept turning up, I was soon manning the bar on the evening dining trains. Now volunteers are very actively encouraged and recruitment of new people forms a large part of what I do.

But my main activity and interest have been working with colleagues to refurbish our two-coach diesel train that currently runs the services. It took us about a year to restore the unit and you can imagine the tension when the day came to start her up after a year without moving a wheel. Would it start? Would all our efforts be in vain? What a relief, what joy when the engine finally burst into life. I will never forget that moment!

At the moment, we are only allowed to run at a maximum of 25mph. However, once the rebuilding of a disused platform at Yeoford has been completed in 2010, Dartmoor Railway services will be extended to that station using more modern trains – and at higher speed. Passengers will then be able to connect there with Exeter and Barnstaple trains. There is also a hope that the line could eventually be reinstated to Tavistock and Bere Alston where it would connect with the Tamar Valley Line to reach Plymouth again.

The journey to Meldon Quarry may take only ten minutes but there is plenty to see. There is an unbeatable view of Okehampton Castle, with its leaning eastern wall, down below in the valley, alongside the West Okement river. The castle was the seat of the Sheriff of Devon and was built soon after the Norman Conquest. The train then passes through a wooded area – carpeted in bluebells each May – before tunnelling underneath the A30 and immediately into the Dartmoor National Park and Meldon Quarry. There are so many aspects to running a railway – train crews, catering, station maintenance, tending flower beds, running tombolas to raise funds, and so on. Volunteers are involved in all of these activities, and speaking as a 'regular', I can say how heart-warming it is when the public give positive feedback about what we are achieving. Personally, I want to see Okehampton plugged back into the main railway network as soon as possible; but meanwhile it's great fun and as we're a fairly small outfit of like-minded people, it's easy to get to know everyone and make strong friendships. The enthusiasm is infectious! My wife says it has given me a new life. For once I think she's right!

Cycling

The lanes around the moor are too steep and narrow for all but the most sturdy and courageous cyclists. There are, however, few restrictions to cycling off-road as long as you stick to bridle paths and designated cycle tracks. Many of these follow dismantled railway lines with easy gradients but you need a proper mountain bike to cope with the rocks and loose stones. The popular bike-bus service, the **Dartmoor Freewheeler**, was suspended in 2009 but may be reintroduced in 2010; it helpfully transported you and your bike to the high moor so you could more or less freewheel back. The national park authority has comprehensive cycling information and maps on www.dartmoor–npa.gov.uk.

Among the several dedicated cycle paths is **The Dartmoor Way**, a 90-mile circuit around the perimeter of the national park, some of it along abandoned sections of railway. Though strenuous in parts it's perfectly manageable. An easier ride is **The Granite Way**, an 11-mile route between Okehampton and Lydford, which follows a disused railway so gradients are gentle and you can take your bike on the Dartmoor Railway. The Princetown railway track is also a popular route for mountain bikers. Easiest of all is the four-mile circuit round Burrator Reservoir in western Dartmoor.

Bikes can be hired at **Devon Cycle Hire**, Bridestowe, Okehampton (01837 861141) at the start of The Granite Way, at **Dartmoor Cycles** in Tavistock (01822 618178) and **Bikus** in Bovey Tracy (01626 833555). **Let's Go Biking** (www.letsgobiking.com) will do a holiday package for you which includes luggage transfer so you can enjoy the Dartmoor Way unencumbered.

The Highwayman Inn and Cobweb Hall, Sourton

Philip Knowling

Putting the lie to the idea that follies are useless is the Highwayman Inn at Sourton, on the bleak west side of Dartmoor.

Sourton is the sort of place you could pass through without noticing if it weren't for the late Buster Jones. Over a 40-year period Buster transformed two of Sourton's key buildings into fabulous, fascinating architectural wonders.

What makes this pub a folly? Well, for a start it's a pub that sells very little beer and has hardly any regulars. Then, it's the most lavishly and imaginatively decorated inn you could ever visit. Inside and out there's wit and whimsy, imagination and inspiration – plus a little macabre kitsch. The Highwayman is a fantasy blend of pirate ship, church, museum, junk shop and fairy-tale.

The Highwayman is testimony to the hard work, imagination and enthusiasm of one man – John 'Buster' Jones. In 1959 Mr Jones moved his family to Devon and took over the New Inn, Sourton – a small, run-down pub in a 13th-century building. Buster and his wife Rita changed the name to the Highwayman Inn and to promote it, Buster acquired the old Okehampton to Launceston stage coach and set it up as a lobby at the front door of the pub.

He hauled pieces of bog-oak off the Moor and used them as bar tops; the dartboard is fixed to a tree-stump set into the wall. There are bits of ship (a carved door from an old whaling ship called *Diana*) and pieces of church (from Plymouth).

One room has a nautical theme – it's below decks on an 18th-century sailing ship cum bric-a-brac shop with bar facilities. Elsewhere, there's an indoor grotto full of stuffed animals (an inventive use of road-kill). Cartwheels and lanterns and sewing-machines also feature.

Buster also turned the former Sourton village hall into a fairytale Gothic *cottage orné* – despite a certain amount of conflict with the planning authorities. Today Cobweb Hall is a holiday let, standing on the edge of rising moorland. It's a novel and intriguing place to stay – and there's a rather special pub just across the road...

The two buildings are now in the good care of Buster's daughter, Sally. The Highwayman is world-renowned – and rightly so. Visit it – your local will never seem quite the same.

Walking and backpacking

Until I came to live in Devon I avoided walking on Dartmoor, imagining waist-deep bogs negotiated in driving rain, and being lost for days in landmark-obscuring mists. So I've been excessively pleased by the reality – strolls along tumbling brooks, walks through bluebell woods, striding out along a disused railway with the knowledge that it won't suddenly take me up an energy-draining hill, and grassy paths up to tors with a 360° view.

The walks described here are mostly easy, two- or three-hour affairs, but die-hard hikers can get their teeth into the real thing by tackling the 102-mile-long **Two Moors Way** which runs from Ivybridge on the southern edge of Dartmoor (accessible by train) across the roadless area of the southern moor, before revisiting civilisation at New Bridge and continuing north to Exmoor. The first stretch is 18 miles of moorland, so a serious undertaking, but the feeling of being utterly alone in one of the most densely populated countries in the world makes it worth the effort. It also allows you access to **The Dancers**, a group of stones at the head of perhaps the longest prehistoric line of stones anywhere (over two miles), and to an ancient clapper bridge (a somewhat timeless design of all-stone span that appears in various parts of Devon and Cornwall; all Dartmoor's clapper bridges are medieval) that has never seen motor traffic. After Holne the path frequently crosses roads so can be walked as part of a circular route if you are not planning to do the whole thing to Exmoor.

The **West Devon Way** runs for 37 miles between Okehampton and Plymouth, skirting the western edge of the moor, and the **Templer Way** (see box on page 97), running from Teignmouth to Haytor, is only 18 miles long and accessible in many places by public transport. Most people will be looking for a variety of **day or half-day walks**. With the help of the OS Explorer map you can safely plan your own route according to energy, weather and interests. Some 'bus walks' which allow you to walk from A to B without returning to your starting point are described later, but otherwise just spread out a map and get planning. If you have children a route taking in a few tors is ideal since these provide excellent scrambling as well as views for the grown-ups and are perfect picnic spots. They will be less rewarding – or even downright dangerous – on a wet and misty day, however. River valleys are perfect in inclement or warm weather, being protected from driving rain and affording the chance to cool off if it's hot. The disused railway line and quarry tracks make for easy, safe walking even if the weather closes in, and are firm underfoot, and if you check out pub locations on the national park website or in the *Dartmoor Guide* you can build in a well-earned meal or drink.

The National Park runs **guided walks** throughout the year, varying in length from two to eight miles and covering every area and aspect of the moor. Led by knowledgeable and enthusiastic guides, these are a great way of getting under the skin of Dartmoor. There is a small fee for the walks, but they are free for those arriving by public transport. Another good reason to take the bus! **Llama walks**, based near Widecombe (01364 631481; www.dartmoorllamawalks.co.uk) offers guided walks where your luggage and picnic are carried by llamas. The cost of these varies from £30 to £45.

Dartmoor is one of the few places in England where true **backpacking** – carrying all your needs for a few days in the wilderness – is both possible and sensible. Camping is permitted almost everywhere, providing you avoid farmland, prehistoric sites and enclosed areas. If you'd prefer not to carry your own tent there are a dozen youth hostels and bunk houses scattered around the moor. However, to my mind once you've experienced the freedom of wild camping, and if you're strong and fit enough to carry a pack, there's no contest between it and dormitory accommodation. See the Dartmoor National Park website (below) for more information on where you can and can't camp.

Walking maps and guides

The OS Explorer map OL28 is the best walker's **map** – at 1:25,000 scale, double sided, and showing all the national park, and all field boundaries. The rights-of-way network on it doesn't initially look that impressive, but once you've worked out that there's free access to much of the open land, and that the little black dashed lines on the map are usually workable paths, things get a lot easier. If you're driving or cycling, the 1:50,000 Landranger maps 191 and 202 give you just the right level of detail.

Harvey's map of *Dartmoor* at a scale of 1:50,000 is perfect for planning walks though not really detailed enough to use without the backup of the OS Explorer. It doesn't mark churches.

Even if you're an expert map reader it's well worth buying a **walking guide** so you can get a feeling for what's achievable. The Bossiney guide, *Shortish walks on Dartmoor*, is easy to follow with clear maps. Cicerone's *Walking on Dartmoor* by veteran walker John Earle is well written and comprehensive but, maddeningly, has neither a location map showing all the walks nor an index. I have been assured that this will be corrected at the next printing, however.

Ten Dartmoor Tors and *Ten Dartmoor Rivers*, both by John Earle and published by Halsgrove, are illustrated guides detailing short walks on the moor and valleys, and *Dartmoor; Walks into History* also by John Earle (Halsgrove) puts Dartmoor into its historical context.

Riding

Climbing the hills on someone else's legs has an obvious attraction, and riders will have an experience far superior to a normal hack along rural bridleways. There are several riding stables on Dartmoor, and all offer a variety of rides ranging from one hour to all day.

I did an hour's ride at the Skaigh Stables, run by the delightful octogenarian Rosemary Hooley. 'Go to that horsebox and put a coal-scuttle on your head.' she said. 'Health and safety; can't let riders go out without a hat.' My horse was a perfect gentleman and the variety of scenery and terrain we were able to experience in an hour was extraordinary. We rode through woodland, forded the river twice, and then climbed up on to the high moor for wonderful views before dropping down to Belstone. At my request we had a trot and canter, but I would have been as happy to stick to a walk and just admire the view. I was told that riders who could count themselves experienced at home, because they rode regularly in an enclosed school, were sometimes unprepared for a hack in such rugged terrain. It's better to underestimate your proficiency. Complete beginners are welcome – the ride will be tailored accordingly and the horses are used to taking care of such people. If you are riding fit, an all-day ride is superb, allowing you to experience a variety of countryside and have a good pub lunch.

All the stables listed below offer similar rides at a similar cost: about £18 for an hour to £60 or so for all day.

Babeny Farm Riding Stables Poundsgate ✆ 01364 631296.
Cholwell Riding Stables Mary Tavy ✆ 01822 810526.
Shilstone Rocks Riding Centre Widecombe-in-the-Moor ✆ 01364 621281
⌂ www.dartmoorstables.com.
Skaigh Stables Belstone ✆ 01837 840429 (eve) or 01837 840917 (day)
⌂ www.skaighstables.co.uk.

Prehistoric Dartmoor

It's thrilling to come across the signs of early human habitation on the moor, particularly when we really don't know why these people, living up to four thousand years ago in a warm, forested place which provided for all their basic needs, went to the trouble of moving huge hunks of granite into geometric patterns. It is also a sobering reminder of the effect of deforestation and climate change on a once green and fertile land. Here is an assortment of easily visited examples of Neolithic and Bronze Age sites.

The most impressive Neolithic site (built between 3500 and 2500BC) is **Spinsters' Rock**, a chambered tomb or cromlech on the northern outskirts of Dartmoor not far from Castle Drogo. It would once have been visible only as a mound of earth which has either eroded away or been removed to reveal the 'chamber' (now more like a shelter) comprising three upright stones forming a tripod, capped by a huge domed piece of granite.

Spinsters' Rock stands nonchalantly in a meadow full of buttercups and, from time to time, cows. Take the A382 off the A30, pass the sign to Venton on the left, and at the next crossroads you'll see it signposted. The gate leading to the site is opposite the yard of Shilstone Farm (a shilstone is the 'lid' of a cromlech). The sign tells us that it was allegedly built by three spinsters one morning before breakfast. Most of the monuments on Dartmoor date from the Bronze Age, and it's hard to choose between the huge number of **stone circles and rows**. An easily reached stone circle is the unimaginatively named Nine Stones at **Belstone** (I counted 21), which is actually a cairn, a burial place within a circle of stones. Or, it's a circle of nine maidens who were turned to stone for dancing on the sabbath. Your choice. It is easily reached from the village, and is marked on the OS Explorers map 28. Once you're through the gate at the end of the road, follow the track to the end of the stone wall, then head uphill and you'll see the stone circle.

Equally accessible are the splendid dual lines of stones at **Merrivale**, thought to date from between 2500 and 700BC. They're near the road and can also be incorporated into an enjoyable 'bus walk' (see page 89). There are two double rows of stones, with a third single row at an angle to the others. A standing stone, or *menhir*, marks each end of the rows and there's also a small burial chamber.

Finally, **Grimspound** is the best-preserved Bronze Age pound, or walled enclosure, on the moor and only a short, though steep, walk from the road, about four miles north of Widecombe. The rather fanciful speculations that this massive circle of stones was a Druid temple or Phoenician settlement were quashed when excavations in the late 19th century concluded that the large external wall was nothing more exciting than a corral for cattle, and the smaller stone circles within it the remains of huts, some of them dwellings and others food stores. Considering their age, the huts were quite sophisticated: you can still see the stone beds, which were probably covered with bracken or animal skins.

I had some trouble finding Grimspound by car. The road is unsigned and the ruins are not obvious from below. Look for the sign to Headland Warren Farm and park at the lay-by just to its north. Opposite you'll see a couple of stone steps and a path that leads up to the site. Alternatively, walk there from Widecombe, taking the Two Moors Way; it runs above the site, thus giving you the best view of the circle and huts in this wild and desolate place. Imagine the time it would have taken to haul all those stones into position. Then visualise the hillsides covered in trees, providing cover for wildlife and edible plants, and the cattle safe inside the compound. Maybe it wasn't so harsh a life after all.

For a total immersion in prehistoric sites, try **Shovel Down** near Scorhill, at the end of tiny lanes west of Chagford. It has a bit of everything – clapper bridge, stone circle, stone rows, hut circles, Kestor Rock (a splendid tor) and Round Pound (an Iron Age animal enclosure).

To boldly go...

If this chapter tempts you to explore Dartmoor, beware! It's a place of many and fearsome hazards. Take the pixies, for a start. They're friendly little beings on the whole, but if you mock or disbelieve in them they turn distinctly nasty. Visitors who are 'pixie-led' can lose all sense of direction and wander alone for days through the mist or be drawn to their death in marshes. Be particularly careful not to trample foxgloves or stitchwort, as these are their special flowers. If you do feel threatened, quickly turn your jacket inside out (or your pockets, if you're not wearing a jacket) as this will appease them.

Then there's the Devil. Despite its many beautiful churches, Dartmoor is one of his favourite haunts. In 1638 he caused consternation in Widecombe when he tethered his horse to the church tower, bringing it crashing down as he galloped away. Today he and his Wisht hounds, huge and fearsome black creatures with eyes like glowing coals, hunt at dead of night by Dewerstone and Hound Tor; you may hear the thud of their ghostly hooves in the distance. Should you catch the appetising scent of bacon frying near Mis Tor, don't be tempted to go closer; his frying pan is there and he'll be cooking up his breakfast.

Witches are another risk. To mix her potions, the Witch of Sheepstor uses the water from Crazywell Pool, where at dusk a ghostly voice whispers the name of someone in the parish who is about to die, and Bowerman the Hunter was turned to stone (Bowerman's Nose) because he and his hounds accidentally disturbed a coven of witches when they were making spells. In fact there's a serious danger of being turned to stone for some misdemeanour or other, so watch your step, particularly on Sundays: it happened to the Nine Maidens at Belstone Tor and The Dancers in the Erme Valley because they danced on the sabbath.

If you're driving or cycling along the moor's roads, keep a careful lookout for the Hairy Hands: they'll grab the steering wheel or handlebars and try to force you off the road. Mostly they're on the B3212 near Postbridge, although they've been spotted near Exeter too. Making the sign of the cross is said to discourage them. If you do encounter them and you run to the nearest cottage for help, be aware that it may vanish; some travellers near Buckfastleigh were approaching one at dusk, attracted by the lights in its windows, when suddenly it wasn't there. UFO encounters have been reported on Dartmoor too, so watch out for aliens.

A headless coachman drives Lady Howard's coach and horses across the moor from Okehampton; Benjamin Gayer, a former mayor of Okehampton who was hanged on Hangingstone Hill, appears as a black pony; and the black pig that haunts Lydford Castle is actually the infamous Judge Jeffries. Less threatening are the sad little piglets of Merripit Hill, thin and starving, which trot desperately to and fro in search of food. If you've survived all these, then be careful in Ashburton: the goblin-like Cutty Dyer, who lives by King's Bridge, accosts drunks and other undesirables and throws them in the river. Normally he tolerates tourists, but one never knows...

JB

Dartmoor by bus and on foot

There's something smug-making about combining a bus trip with some walking. You feel complacently green, and there's none of the hassle of parking your car and returning to your starting point. Here are a few such walks, but there are lots of other possibilities. Bus timetables may change so check the latest schedules.

A Sunday itinerary

This is a terrific circular trip using the Sunday Rover. It runs anticlockwise round the perimeter of Dartmoor via Lydford Gorge to Tavistock, then to Merrivale from where you can walk to Princetown in time to catch the last Transmoor bus back to Exeter.

We started at Exeter bus station, boarding the X99 express to **Okehampton** station; here you're transported straight back to the days of chatty ticket officers, wooden luggage trolleys piled high with trunks and leather suitcases, old railway posters and baskets of flowers. There's also a café and a shop crammed with stuff to make any railway enthusiast reach for his wallet. Time for a cup of coffee before catching the 187 bus to **Lydford** where we had time to walk the length of the gorge before catching the next bus to **Tavistock**, then the 272 heading towards Ashburton. We got off this at **Merrivale**, and made our way up to the stones (see page 87); then continued north to pick up the disused railway line which runs around Kings Tor. This involves a certain amount of cross-country walking, but there are two handy landmarks: the television mast which supplies Princetown, and Kings Tor. Start at the car park and head in the direction of the mast, and you should locate the first of the stone rows without difficulty. The second row is just beyond it, running parallel, and the small burial chamber is about halfway along. Next, head to a standing stone adjacent to a wall, then set your sights on Kings Tor. The disused railway track circles round it, so you can't really go wrong. After that it's easy – just follow the track to Princetown You are walking on a nice piece of history here. The Plymouth and Dartmoor railway was built in the 1820s to transport granite from the quarries. When this became uneconomical in the 1880s the route was sold to the Great Western Railway. The last passenger service ran in March 1956. The track passes the disused Swell Tor Quarry, and if you have the time and energy it's worth investigation; look for the stone corbels that were cut in 1903 for the widening of London Bridge but never used.

The last Transmoor bus (82) to Exeter left **Princetown** in the early evening giving us plenty of time for the walk and a quick browse in the museum.

Between Moretonhampstead and Dunsford, the road is as beautiful in its lushness as the trans-moor route is for wilderness. It runs through the oaks of Bridford Wood, clinging to an almost vertical hillside abutting the Teign and ending at Steps Bridge.

Two Saturday walks using the Haytor Hoppa

I tested out two Haytor Hoppa walks and found the timings spot on. For the first

I did the full bus circuit, for the pleasure of it, and got off at **Parke**, near Bovey Tracey, to walk through the woods and along quiet lanes to **Lustleigh**, and then up to the beautiful mossy woodland of **Lustleigh Cleave** and down to **Manaton**. There's a particularly lovely bit close to Manaton where you cross the river on the boulder stepping stones known as Horsham Steps in the National Nature Reserve of Bovey Valley Woodlands. It would have been a perfect place for a picnic, surrounded by trees and birdsong, and with water to cool off in. This walk took four hours but I lingered over lunch.

The other, shorter, walk is from **Jay's Grave** to Manaton, via the famous landmark of Bowerman's Nose. There's a signed footpath to the right which runs over a grassy hill to Hayne Down from where you can see **Bowerman's Nose**.

A footpath runs south of the Nose and brings you out to **Manaton**. It's an easy walk and the rocky face of the unfortunate hunter does not look unhappy despite having been turned to stone. Indeed, he has the expression of a twitcher who has just spotted a rare bird. After all, he has a beautiful view of patchwork fields to look out on for eternity, and his faithful hounds are nearby, also turned to stone, on Hound Tor.

Two hours is sufficient for this walk. For both walks you'll need a good map (OS or Harvey's) which shows the footpaths.

Further information

Dartmoor National Park ⚲ www.dartmoor-npa.gov.uk. An exceptionally good website, easy to navigate and bang up to date. The *Dartmoor Guide*, published by the National Park, is a tabloid-sized publication which repeats the information found on the website. It's free, widely available in shops and tourist information centres, and invaluable.

www.DiscoverDartmoor.co.uk Straightforward website with answers to frequently asked questions.

Bus and train timetables Traveline ☎ 0871 200 2233 ⚲ www.traveline.co.uk, or www.devon.gov.uk/buses.

Chagford, Castle Drogo and the north

This is one of the prettiest areas of Dartmoor, with more than its share of river gorges, tors and prehistoric ruins, as well as the delightful **Mythic Sculpture Garden**, which is close to **Spinsters' Rock** (see page 86). Chagford makes a perfect base for exploring the region, and you can dispense with your car since this village can be accessed by public transport in both summer and winter. The 173 bus runs several times a day from Exeter, stopping at Drewsteignton and Castle Drogo, and the 179 runs three times a day from Okehampton, so all the places described here can be seen on a 'bus walk'.

① Chagford

The first time I came here it struck me as almost too perfect, and a little complacent with it. Perhaps it was the ideal location, sandwiched between the River Teign and Chagford Common, cluttered with prehistoric remains, or the satisfactory shape of the village with a defined centre dominated by the 'Pepper Pot' market house. But when I returned it took on a more comfortable personality. A sale of work was under way in the village hall, full of old-timers talking about their ailments, which contrasted nicely with the new-age art galleries and shops. I drifted in to **The Big Red Sofa** (01647 433883; www.thebigredsofa.co.uk) for a coffee and a map, and became transfixed by a conversation between two customers discussing the relative merits of strimming and scything. Very Chagford. This bookshop cum art gallery cum coffee shop gives you the feel for the village as well as anywhere. I asked Alan McGeorge, the owner, how he came to set up such an innovative business. 'I had been thinking about a semi-retirement strategy that somehow linked art, books, coffee and a gentler pace of life. The Big Red Sofa concept evolved from there. And Chagford can be a wonderful place to live and work. I have an unconventional take on the world and there are like-minded people here. It is also a sensationally creative place. It feels like home.'

This was a stannary town and shows its former tin wealth in its church which has, like Widecombe, some 'tinners' rabbits' on one of the bosses. Although much restored, with some very modern additions, the church has great appeal; its fine features include a 400-year-old stone carving of an archangelic St Michael with luxuriant locks, slaying a 'nasty little demon'. The modern carved wood pews and pulpit are especially fine. Look out, too, for the lovely needlework hanging in the south aisle; showing the history of the region, this was made by the Chagford Women's Institute.

Gidleigh Park near Chagford TQ13 8HH ☏ 01647 432367 🖰 www.gidleigh.com. Set in its own 45 acres, yet near Chagford, this is a seriously posh hotel with a two-star Michelin restaurant. Come here for that very special treat when you don't care how much you spend.

⑤ Sandy Park Inn Sandy Park, Chagford, TQ13 8JW ☏ 01647 433267 🖰 www.sandyparkinn.co.uk. Located at Sandy Park, a couple of miles northeast of Chagford at the western end of the Teign gorge, this is the place for a treat after a long day's walking. Imaginative, locally sourced food (puddings a speciality). Closed Sunday evenings.

22 Mill Street Chagford ☏ 01647 432244. Top-quality dining at a slightly lower price than Gidleigh Park. Highly thought of by locals and visitors.

② Castle Drogo

'It looks like a Stalinist gulag!' a visitor remarked. 'And the tapestries look like old bedspreads,' his wife added. Indeed, some find it hard to warm to this monument to 20th-century extravagance and megalomania. But warm I did, and I think it's worth the effort.

Drogo was conceived by Julius Drewe, who retired at the age of 33 and, needing a way to use up his money, decided without any evidence that he was descended from the Norman Baron Drogo de Teign who had given his name to Drewsteignton. Now he needed an ancestral home; so he bought the Drogo estate in 1910 and employed Edwin Lutyens to make his dreams reality. Not a bad commission, even for the most renowned architect of the 20th century.

I never thought that granite could look identical to concrete, but that's the impression given by the precisely cut blocks of stone. Inside, the plasterless walls are the same austere grey and even the furniture is all right angles. The feeling of incarceration is not helped by the muted light. But as you make your way through the house, things soften and brighten, and, coaxed by the enthusiasm and knowledge of the National Trust volunteers, I started to appreciate what I was seeing. The drawing room is almost cosy, for instance, a light, bright room with windows on three sides allowing you to appreciate the castle's magnificent location: ahead lies craggy Dartmoor, and to the side is the Teign Valley. The Dining Room is quite intimate since the Grand Design was never completed. Indeed, the original plans show a castle of, as the brochure puts it, 'heroic size', which must have made Sir Edwin very, very happy.

The human side of this story is what makes a visit to the castle ultimately rewarding, and this is found in the small room called Adrian Drewe's room. Adrian was the first-born son who died in 1917 at Ypres, at the age of 26, having been married for just one year. As the oldest boy he had been involved in the planning of Castle Drogo from the beginning. It's clear from the lovingly displayed memorabilia in the room how deeply missed he was, and one imagines that his father's enthusiasm for the great castle died along with his son. The reduction of the original plan by two-thirds could not have been purely for financial reasons.

Lutyens' ingenuity is found throughout the house. Electricity, for instance, was a relatively new thing, and there are all sorts of electrical gadgets including an electric tablecloth to keep plates warm, and an electric cup-and-saucer warmer. The shower unit incorporated with the bath wouldn't be out of place in a modern bathroom and the loo has a state-of-the-art flush.

The enthusiasm of the National Trust volunteers is infectious. Ginnie Woolfe has been working here for seven years. 'I love it not only because the castle is in such a stunning position, but because it's filled with all the interesting items that the Drewes brought back with them from their travels and from their previous home, Wadhurst Hall. Chatting with the visitors is my favourite part of the job.

They come from just about anywhere in the world, and I don't think I've ever talked to a visitor who hasn't loved the place.'

The castle was cutting-edge in its use of hydro-electric power from the Teign, and plans are afoot to reinstall this, as well as firing the boiler with woodchips, which would make the castle close to self-sufficient for its energy needs.

Castle Drogo is served by bus 173 between Exeter and Moretonhampstead (weekdays) or the 274/279 on Sundays and bank holidays.

Fingle Bridge and the Teign gorge

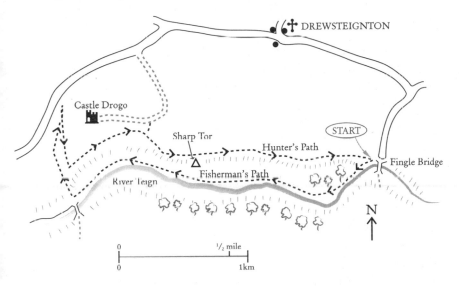

One of the most popular walks on Dartmoor, this 3½-mile 'circular' (oblong really) walk takes you from the picturesque Fingle Bridge, south of **Drewsteignton**, along the Fisherman's Path which hugs the north side of the River Teign, passing through beautiful deciduous woodland and mossy rocks. The return is along the high-level Hunter's Path over open moorland, with gorse, heather and stands of silver birch. There are opportunities to access the Castle Drogo estate at the western end of the circuit, and the walk can begin from the Castle's car park instead of Fingle Bridge (where the parking is limited); here you can pick up the National Trust's booklet *Walks in the Teign Valley and Castle Drogo Estate*.

Variations of the walk can be done by taking the bus 173 to Drewsteignton and catching it again at Castle Drogo.

✂ **The Drewe Arms** Drewsteignton ☎ 01647 281224 🖰 www.thedrewearms.co.uk. This 17th-century thatched pub, right next to the church, serves good food and local ales in an assortment of small rooms, and has a history tied to Castle Drogo. It was

Julius Drewe (who else?) who persuaded the landlord to change its name from The Druid Arms and provided his coat of arms for the inn sign. The Mudge family took over in 1919 and Mabel Mudge was reputedly the oldest landlady on record, retiring in 1994 at the age of 99 having run the pub for 75 years. She was 101 when she died. **Fingle Bridge Inn** Fingle Bridge, Drewsteignton EX6 6PW ☎ 01647 281287. The beautiful location by the river is the main draw here.

③ Spinsters' Rock and Mythic Sculpture Garden

The carved stones in these two sites may span 5,000 years, but in their own way they are equally mysterious and appealing. So how convenient that they are within walking distance of each other (less than two miles), and accessible by the 173 bus, although of course most people will drive.

Spinsters' Rock, a Neolithic burial chamber, is described on page 86. If coming by bus you will need to ask the driver to let you off at the turnoff, half a mile beyond Venton. It's a lovely walk up the hill to Shilstone Farm. The lane is shaded by huge beech trees straddling a stone wall, something you often see in Dartmoor. The trees would originally been a hedge providing additional shelter for livestock, but no one told them to stop growing.

After looking at the tomb, continue up the lane to the T-junction and turn right, then right again, and you'll soon see the 'car park' for Mythic Garden on your left (you would be forgiven for supposing it to be a farm yard). **Stone Lane Gardens/Mythic Garden** (01647 231311; www.stonelanegardens.com) are about 200 yards further down the road. On quiet days an 'honesty box' collects your £4 fee, there are maps to guide you round the woodland paths and a printed list of the sculptures, and you're on your own to enjoy this perfect blend of the work of man and nature. Because what's special here is that this is not just five acres of woods and water, with some intriguing sculptures popping up in unexpected places, but a nationally important collection of birch and alder trees, collected by horticulturist Ken Ashburner from all over the world. I met his wife June up to her neck in shrubbery, yanking out weeds, and learned that 'we've been here since 1962, gradually buying up the land so we could start the garden. We now have about 40 species of birch and slightly fewer of alder. I change the sculptures every year. Yes, they're by different artists, and as you can see, there's lots of variety. Have you seen the spiders? They're rather fun – follow that path and you'll see them on the right.'

There was no way I was not going to like this place, since I love this sort of secret, woody garden and dabble at sculpture myself, but June and Ken have made something exceptional here. Go and see for yourself. The garden is open year round but the sculpture exhibition is only in the summer: May to October.

The east

In the triangle formed by the northern apex of the A382 and the B3212 is one of Dartmoor's few paying attractions, contrasting with some of the most remote-feeling yet accessible valleys in Dartmoor and two of its prettiest villages. One of the gateway towns to the high moor is also here.

The Miniature Pony Centre

A friend who lives in Doccombe finds this the ideal place to bring her grandchildren; it has enough child-pleasing attractions inside and out to happily fill a sunny or rainy day. The first decision is between seeing the new baby ponies and donkeys in the open barn, or pedalling around on the tractors, then we might go to the outdoor activity area with tunnels, slides, rope climbing frame, and a small climbing wall, and then on to pat the ponies in the large paddock. Whatever the weather the wooden indoor activity area gets them excited with more sophisticated forms of climbing and scrambling apparatuses.' There are other animals – Kune Kune pigs, pygmy goats and rabbits to pet, and a falconry display, but the tiny ponies are the main attraction. 'At the end of the afternoon the children can join in rounding up the ponies into the barn where they are allowed to help feed them and put them to bed.'

The Transmoor Link (82) bus stops at the Miniature Pony Centre.

④ Manaton and Becky Falls

Manaton was once two villages, Manaton Magna and Manaton Parva, which explains its fragmented nature. Upper Manaton, around the church, is perfection: a spacious green sets off the fine church of St Winifred, dressed in traditional Devon white, with a row of thatched houses behind it. One splendid house, Wingstone Manor, was, for a time, the home of John Galsworthy, who wrote *The Forsyte Saga*. The village green was bought in 1928 from its previous owner, Lord Hambledon (who owned a huge swathe of the region in the early 19th century), for £75 collected from parishioners.

The interior of the church has some rather splendid pillars of Devon granite and a fine wooden screen which was literally defaced during the reformation. Every carved saint and angel has had its face chiselled away. A helpful explanatory sheet tells us what we would be seeing, if we could: for instance St Margaret of Antioch being swallowed by a dragon, with just her red dress visible as she disappears down its throat. She cut her way out of its stomach with her handy sword, so has become the patron saint of women in childbirth. Sadly, I have to admit that I couldn't find her. The view from the churchyard across the moor to Haytor must be one of the best in Dartmoor.

A little over a mile to the southeast are **Becky Falls**, a delightful place for pottering although the waterfall itself is pleasant rather than dramatic in the summer. There are three walking circuits of varying difficulty so you can suit your visit to your abilities. It's quite pricey, at £6.95, so it's worth spending half a day here to enjoy the birdwatching (we saw a dipper bobbing about on the rocks) and the mossy quietness. It's a great place for children, too, with opportunities for boulder scrambling, and some tiny ponies and enormous pigs to pet.

The Haytor Hoppa bus runs to Manaton and Becky Falls on Saturdays (summer only), and the 671 makes a single journey on Wednesdays all year. The timing allows you to explore Becky Falls and Manaton and have a meal at the Kestor Inn before catching the return bus.

Kestor Inn Manaton ☎ 01647 221204. This is actually in a little hamlet called Water, a half mile outside Manaton. Nice views from the conservatory area, and a mix of locals and hikers. Serves Otter real ale and homemade bar food.

⑤ Lustleigh and ⑥ North Bovey

Here are two classically picturesque villages of thatched cottages, cut off from mainstream traffic by the nerve-rackingly narrow approach lanes, but each with a good pub and interesting church.

Lustleigh sits at the base of the Lustleigh Cleave escarpment (see page 90) which makes it an excellent place to stoke up on carbohydrates before tackling those hills. Fortunately the Primrose Cottage Tea Rooms can do the job nicely. The church is worth a visit for its finely carved screen, and pew ends whose subjects include a rather jolly lion and an elephant. They are by Herbert Read, a fine wood carver who contributed to the beauty of several Devon churches at the end of the 19th century.

North Bovey's grassy green is shaded by oak trees of different sizes, all planted to commemorate an event: variously Queen Victoria's Jubilee, George V and Queen Mary's Silver Jubilee, various coronations, and, smallest of all, a Millennium tree. The pub serves food that's good enough to make you want to linger and the church is delightful, with worm-eaten pews and mainly clear glass to let Dartmoor in. There's an elaborate carved pulpit, and a good screen (no painted saints, however). The floor of the nave is almost covered with crudely lettered memorial stones to parishioners who died in the 1700s, and a little harmonium sits waiting to rouse the small congregation to song. Above the approach to the altar are some brightly painted roof bosses; look for the 'tinners' rabbits' (see box on page 108) above the altar rail.

The Cleave Lustleigh ☎ 01647 277223. A 15th-century thatched pub with a quiet garden, ideal for a mid-walk lunch.
Primrose Cottage Tea Rooms Lustleigh ☎ 01647 277365. Traditional cream teas in a primrose-coloured thatched cottage.
Ring of Bells North Bovey ☎ 01647 440375 🖥 www.ringofbells.net. Another 15th-

century thatched pub, with several small rooms and a sunny beer garden. High-quality food with an extensive evening menu and very good lunches. Otter and St Austell Tribute beers plus guest ales.

Templer Way: the granite tramway

This 18-mile trail is more than just a long-distance footpath from Teignmouth to Haytor, it is an extraordinary example of using a local material – granite – in hitherto unimaginable ways.

James Templer was born in 1722. An orphan, he ran away to sea and made his fortune in India. On returning to England he bought the Stover estate (see page 67) and built Stover House.

In the 1820s his grandson, George Templer, had bought a granite quarry on Haytor, Dartmoor, and needed to find a way of moving the blocks of stone to a seaport so they could be transported to London (Dartmoor granite was used for many buildings and even London paving stones). So he built a granite tramway, using grooved granite instead of metal rails. Even the points and sidings were made out of granite. Teams of up to 19 horses pulled the huge, flat wooden trucks. The braking mechanism for going downhill was primitive, to say the least, but history does not tell us about the accidents that must surely have happened.

The granite tracks are still visible along parts of the Templer Way; on Dartmoor you can see them near Haytor and near Bovey Tracey.

⑦ Bovey Tracey

I didn't much care for Bovey Tracey when I first saw it, largely because I found the **House of Marbles** disappointing. Perhaps I expected too much. Marbles are such beautiful things, so I was hoping for more art and less commerce. That said, the marble run – the biggest in the world – is fascinating. I could happily have spent an hour watching the giant marbles progress along an intricate maze propelled by nothing more than gravity. And it's free.

I found my art, however, in Bovey's wonderful gallery of the **Devon Guild of Craftsmen** (see below), and in some beguiling craft shops, and the positive impression was reinforced by the very helpful and enthusiastic staff at the Information Centre opposite.

With all those sheep on Dartmoor, it's not surprising that there are two shops whose business depends on wool. Most of the wool, however, does not come from local sheep. I learned why from Cat Frampton, a farmer (and jeweller – farmers need a second income these days). 'All our wool has to go to the Wool Board' she said. 'And there's almost no money in it. It barely pays the cost of shearing. In the old days the woolclip paid for all of the winter feed. Not any more.' I asked if she resented the Wool Board's control. 'Ha! The Wool Board is a pesky fly compared to DEFRA's charging rhino!' We left it at that.

Of all of Dartmoor's 'gateway towns', this is where I'd choose to spend a rainy day. And if the rain stopped, I would head for **Parke**, one of the National Trust's unsung pleasures, about a mile out of town on the B3387. The house is used as National Trust offices, but the 205-acre estate is open to the public and includes a walled garden in which a variety of fruit trees are being grown to demonstrate different cultivation techniques such as cordons, fans and espaliers. The information board adds: 'In time we hope to add examples of food that could be grown in our changing present climate, such as kiwi fruit, olives, citrus fruit, tea, pepper etc.' This felt optimistic on the chilly July day of my visit, but who knows… and if the experiment succeeds they will supply the cafés and restaurants of Devon's NT properties so it will have wide-ranging benefits.

The rest of the estate is given over to a selection of well-signposted woodland and river walks. And it's free.

Basics and shopping

Tourist Information Centre Car Park, Station Rd ✆ 01626 832047
🖰 www.boveytracey.gov.uk.

Bikus St John's Lane ✆ 01626 833555🖰 www.bikus.co.uk. Open 10.00–17.00. Cycle hire as well as sales and repairs. Some of Dartmoor's most attractive places are a few miles from Bovey: Haytor is just four miles away, while the pretty villages of Lustleigh and North Bovey are within easy cycling distance.

Bovey Handloom Weavers 1 Station Rd ✆ 01626 833424
🖰 www.boveyweavers.com. I spoke to Stuart Gregory who is the weaving side of the business. His wife, Liz, runs the shop. It was Liz's father who started the business over 70 years ago, having learned his trade in Scotland. The two looms that you can see being operated in the workshop are the Harris tweed type – beautiful old things that were as interesting as the material being woven: tweed, rugs, and material for ties, headscarves, etc. I asked about alpaca and other fine wools. 'Weaving wool always has to be worked at a greater tension; it has to be twisted much harder so it doesn't pull apart. Knitting wool such as alpaca is too loosely spun to use on a loom.' That's why, I realised, Joyce in Spin a Yarn has such a huge range of wools. Knitters have far more choice.

Cottage Books Fore St ✆ 01626 835757. A small independent bookshop with a good selection of maps and local guides.

Devon Guild of Craftsmen Riverside Mill ✆ 01626 832223
🖰 www.crafts.org.uk. Open 10.00–17.30 daily. This is seriously good stuff, with all manner of crafts in a shifting exhibition, from jewellery and stained glass to sculpture, pottery and ceramics. In addition to the exhibitions there are a variety of events and workshops including some aimed at children. Upstairs, the Terrace Café sells homemade food in spacious surroundings, inside or out.

House of Marbles Pottery Rd TQ13 9DS (near the roundabout on the Newton Abbot road) ✆ 01626 835285; www.houseofmarbles.com. Shop and tea room, glass-blowing demonstrations, museum.

Spin a Yarn 26 Fore St ✆ 01626 836203🖰 www.spinayarndevon.co.uk. Stocks a kaleidoscope of yarns from round the world, enough to make a knitter's mouth water. Or fingers itch. Joyce Mason sells yarn that is not available elsewhere in the country, and attracts visitors from far and wide. She also hosts two-day courses on knitting, crochet, felting and spinning. 'People love to have the opportunity to sit and knit and chat while learning new skills,' she says. 'It's the perfect switch off from a hectic world!'

Food and drink

SD **The Rock Inn** Haytor Vale TQ13 9XP ✆ 01364 661305 www.rock-inn.co.uk. A 300-year-old inn standing high on Dartmoor. Run by the same family for over 20 years, it offers convivial surroundings and local produce. Beer garden for fine summer days.

Central Dartmoor

With Widecombe-in-the-Moor as its focus, this region offers the most variety and therefore the most appeal to visitors. It has bleak, open moorland, craggy tors, farms and wooded valleys sheltering villages accessible by steep, narrow lanes. Some of Dartmoor's oldest prehistoric sites are here, including Grimspound (see page 89), and iconic sites such as **Jay's Grave and Bowerman's Nose** (see page 90).

⑧ Widecombe-in-the-Moor

To most visitors this village is the capital of Dartmoor, with a cathedral to boot. Its popularity as a tourist honeypot stemmed originally from the traditional song about Widecombe Fair (Old Uncle Tom Cobley and All): it's the one place in Dartmoor everyone's heard of. And once the tourists came they needed to be provided for; Widecombe must, for its size, have more tearooms and car parking space than any other village in Dartmoor. Despite the coaches and crowds its charm is undiminished, making it an excellent base for exploring the moor and the valleys even without a car. With your own transport – car or bicycle – you have all of Dartmoor within easy reach.

The village sits in a hollow, with the extraordinarily high tower (350 feet) of the church visible from the surrounding hills and giving it the popular name of the Cathedral of the Moor. Much of the **church** dates from the 14th century, but the tower was added later and paid for by tinners: Widecombe was a stannary town. The church is dedicated to St Pancras, and I thought I'd find out something about this saint – partly to get the image of a London railway station out of my mind, and partly because I was curious about the significance of the painting of Abraham and Isaac which hangs near the south door. It turns out that this young orphan was beheaded in AD304 as a 14-year-old for proclaiming his faith. He is patron saint of children, which explains the painting, and can also do his bit for headaches – well, he would, wouldn't he? – and cramp. And, to tell the truth, for perjury, although I'm not sure how that works… Quite a few of his relics ended up in England which explains why there are several churches dedicated to him.

There is plenty of interest in the church; it has a granite pulpit, brought down from the moor, and a good rood screen. The painted bosses on the chancel ceiling are easiest to look at via the information sheet which describes the legends attached to each of them. They include a Green Man and a pelican-in-her-piety, as well as the 'tinners' rabbits' found in most stannary town churches (see box on page 108).

Mixed up with all the legends of Widecombe is the fact that during a dramatic thunderstorm on 21 October 1638, the church was struck by lightning and four people were killed, and many injured, when the tower crashed through the roof. Very little happened in the 17th century that wasn't the work of God or the devil. In this case, an innocuous-looking gentleman had popped into a Poundsgate inn for a glass of ale and asked the way to Widecombe. The landlady remembered afterwards that she heard his drink hiss as it went down his throat. In Widecombe the devil, for it was he, tethered his horse to a pinnacle of the tower while he went about his mischief with some local lads. Some say he was involved in a tussle to gain a soul, others that he simply forgot that his black steed was still tethered, and galloped away, toppling the tower. The pious congregation disregarded the fact that God had, perhaps, selected a time when a service was being held to do a bit of smiting, and the church records their gratitude and praise.

Next to the church is the original **Church House**, which was once an ale house to refresh travellers, and then a poor house. It is now the village hall and headquarters of the local National Trust, with a good bookshop and information centre. On the spacious green is a **Millennium Stone** under which are buried photos of every house and every family in the parish. However, they are on CD/DVD so whether the people who unearth it centuries hence will be illuminated or puzzled remains to be seen.

Try to time your visit to Widecombe to fit in with a tour of the town by Tony Beard (see box opposite). He will greatly extend your knowledge and appreciation of his home village.

The Old Inn ✆ 01364 621207. Conveniently situated in the centre of the village, it is indeed old (14th century) and has a spacious car park. The food is simple but good, and reasonably priced.

⑤ Rugglestone Inn ✆ 01364 621327 ⊕ www.rugglestoneinn.co.uk. This small and very popular inn on the outskirts of Widecombe has been a favourite with locals and visitors for many years. The food is very good and the location sublime. Open all day at weekends. Reservations essential.

A Dartmoor man

From an interview with Tony Beard, the 'Wag from Widecombe.' Tony's Sunday lunchtime broadcasts on Radio Devon (www.bbc.co.uk/devon) have a following worldwide. In 2009 he was president of the Devonshire Association, founded in 1862.

My mother was in service at a house in Dartmoor, which is where she met and married my father, a local lad. One story she often told was how she was invited to Sunday lunch at Higher Uppacott, the longhouse*. Dinner was cooked in the traditional manner in the huge fireplace, on a covered metal plate surrounded by the hot coals. She said it was one of the best meals she'd ever eaten.

I went to the local primary school in Widecombe and then got a scholarship to Plymouth College. My parents raised dairy cattle and needed help on the farm so for many years I delivered milk in the area. In the early days people would come and collect the milk, then we had a van and sometimes delivered the milk in churns. Bottles with cardboard tops gave way to metal tops. In the end we were supplying virtually the whole parish. When they brought in regulations saying milk must be pasteurised, the equipment was too expensive and we had to give up the dairy and go into beef. Delivering milk was a community service. I think I did everything except deliver a baby! For instance I would change light bulbs and replace a fuse. I would collect 10 or 12 pension books, go to the post office, pick up the pensions and deliver the money the next morning. That's all gone now. People had known me since the day I was born so they trusted me completely. It's been ruined now by red tape and mistrust. I think it's an honour to have lived through those times.

Our local history group has written a book on Poundsbury, looking at one century, 1900–2000. And the changes that have taken place! In those days the village was completely self-contained: dairy, butchers, bakers, carpenter, shoemaker, undertakers, builder, wheelwright – and a couple of shops. Now there's only a red phone box (which is scheduled so they can't take it away) and all the rest of the village is holiday homes. What a contrast!

When electricity came to Widecombe in 1963 everybody bought a television. But we soon got fed up with watching that and started a little drama group. We did a pantomime and I used to compère it and sing a few songs. Eventually that led to my slot on Radio Devon. I do a Sunday show from 12.00 to 2.30, chatting about the countryside and nature, and play some requests.

I've got the right voice for radio because of my accent, but dialect goes further than that. There are lots of different words in the Devon dialect, and these can even vary from region to region within the county. For instance that little creature the woodlouse has several different names; round here it's called *granfer grigg*. A blue tit is an *ackermail* and a wren is a *tit-e-tope*. We call a thistle a *daishel*, and sometimes we swap letters around so a wasp is a *wapse*.

* Regular escorted visits take place to Higher Uppacott. Phone 01626 832093, or check the website (www.dartmoor-npa.gov.uk) or the Dartmoor Guide.

Widecombe Fair

Widecombe Fair, the popular market that enticed Bill Brewer, Jan Stewer, Peter Gurney, Peter Davy, Daniel Whiddon, Harry Hawk and Old Uncle Tom Cobley and all to borrow Tom Pierce's grey mare to transport them from their homes in north Dartmoor to the fun and revelry, is always held on the second Tuesday in September. Originally a livestock show, it has now evolved into more of a tourist attraction, with exhibitions and a funfair. The recently restored Uncle Tom Cobley model with its working parts, which was last exhibited 50 years ago, made its first appearance in 2009.

⑨ Buckland-in-the-Moor

The pretty thatched cottages are the main attraction here, along with the clock on the **church of St Peter**; the numerals have been replaced by the words 'MY DEAR MOTHER' in gothic lettering. But the church is so much more than the clock. For one thing it is clearly loved. Jam jars containing bunches of wild flowers adorn every available surface and a note rests by a pair of reading glasses: 'Spectacles kindly left by a visitor for the use of other visitors'. And, yes, there's plenty to read here. A framed description of the church suggests: 'The church on its sloping site looks as if it were carved from a natural granite outcrop or perhaps risen over time fully formed from the rock of Dartmoor.' Before entering, look for the tomb of a soldier who died 'succouring a foeman'. It's touching how proud the community obviously was of this demonstration of humanity. Once inside, you can appreciate the contrast between the rough-hewn granite pillars and the intricately carved wooden rood screen. Its narrow uprights end in fan vaulting – a characteristic of Devon churches. There's a 12th-century font, but no stained glass – it's not needed when the windows look out on to a green and yellow landscape of trees and daffodils.

East of the village, beyond the cluster of thatched cottages, is **Buckland Beacon** from where, they say, you can see the English Channel. It is anyway one of the most beautiful views on Dartmoor, a mixture of woods, river and moorland. Nearby are two granite slabs on which are carved the Ten Commandments. These were provided by the same benefactor as the unique church clock: William Whitely. Mr Whitely was one of many Devonians who felt strongly about the attempted introduction of a new prayer book in the 1920s. The proposal was rejected, and the Ten Commandments remind parishioners of God's unchanging laws – and landowner Whitely's influence.

⑩ Holne

In contrast to chocolate-box Buckland, Holne's attraction is its feeling of community – and the lovely walk there with an option to cool off in the river. Park (or get off the bus) at New Bridge and take the footpath south through National Trust property for about a mile. The track initially follows the River Dart through flower-filled woodland and then meanders uphill, crossing a field or two before emerging near the village. As the main track leaves the river you can take a small path to the swimming area where flat slabs of rock channel the stream into deep, cool pools.

Holne feels like a lively place with plenty happening. There is a 14th-century pub, the Church House Inn, and a village shop which doubles as a tea room. I was so impressed at the efforts of the owners to promote it, having followed a trail of posters since New Bridge, that I had lunch there, bypassing the obvious attractions of the pub. I didn't regret it. Although the building is new there are nice touches like the bird feeder just outside the window and a bird book on the table to help with identification.

Charles Kingsley, who wrote *The Water Babies* and *Westward Ho!*, was born here. His father was vicar, and Charles is commemorated in a stained glass window in the church, which is worth visiting in its own right. A splendid lightning-blasted yew stands in the graveyard, so hollow it resembles scaffolding rather than a solid tree. The church entrance is a little wonky – it seems to lean to the left – but inside all is as it should be. A lovely rood screen similar to the one in Buckland depicts 40 saints of varying obscurity, and a helpful loose-leaf binder explains who's who and what they were patron of. The pulpit, carved in 1480 from a single block of oak, is awaiting restoration so parked tidily at the side of the building.

Another nice touch is the leaflet *Walks around Holne*, available in the church. Both Holne and Buckland in the moor can be reached by the 672 bus, which runs on Wednesdays.

Church House Inn ✆ 01364 631208 🖰 www.churchhouseinn-holne.co.uk. As the name indicates, this was once a church house, providing rest and sustenance to weary parishioners. It was built in 1329, and serves good food.
Holne Village Store and Tearoom ✆ 01364 631135. A good selection of homemade snacks.

⑪ Wistman's Wood

'It's straight out of Tolkien,' a friend remarked. 'You wouldn't be surprised to meet a hobbit there.' This small grove of stunted oaks is one of the few remaining examples of the forest that once covered much of Dartmoor, and is not to be missed. Perhaps I'm biased, having visited it on an intermittently sunny day in April, when the banks of the approach track were covered with primroses and the vanilla-scented gorse was in bloom. It's a two-mile walk to the grove, first up a farm track and then across the moor where you scan the barren hillside ahead for anything resembling a tree. Suddenly there it is, a green-coated fairyland of gnarled and twisted boughs, festooned in epiphytes, ferns, liverwort and moss, the oaks finding footholds between moss-covered boulders. It's as though some fanatical knitter has been at work with miles of green wool. In early spring the low sun gave the leafless green branches an almost golden outline.

The west

Much of the western moor, north of the B3357, is used by the Ministry of Defence as a firing range (no doubt under the watchful eye of St Barbara – see page 64). If a red flag is flying, you can't go there. This uncertainty restricts the number of visitors to this part of the moor, which perhaps gives it extra appeal for those who like to be alone. One of Dartmoor's most interesting and popular ancient sites is here, but outside the 'danger area': the **Merrivale stone rows** (see page 87). The stones are easily accessed from the road; park at the car park just east of Merrivale village. **Tavistock** is the gateway town to the region, with the other villages described here mostly lying to its north, on or west of the A386. The two Tavy villages, **Mary Tavy** and **Peter Tavy**, sound like a cosy married couple. They are named after their church saints, however. Mary Tavy was the centre of a copper boom in the 19th century, leaving Peter Tavy with the rural charm. One of Dartmoor's dramatic, steep-sided canyons, or cleaves, is here, providing western Dartmoor's best river walk.

As you continue to follow the A386, England's highest church at **Brent Tor** should not be missed, nor should **Lydford Gorge**.

⑫ Tavistock

This fine town is a convenient gateway to Dartmoor for those using public transport, and worth visiting in its own right. The first building of significance here was the Benedictine abbey, built about a hundred years before the Norman Conquest on the banks of the River Tavy. *Stoc* is old English for a farm or settlement. The abbey became wealthy, and the town's success was cemented when it was made one of the first stannary towns. On the dissolution of the monasteries the abbey's land and the nearby town were bought by the Russell family who later became the Dukes of Bedford. The tin ran out, but a burgeoning cloth industry filled the gap and financed the fine church of St Eustace, before that too failed. However, just when the town seemed destined for oblivion, large deposits of copper were found at Mary Tavy at the end of the 18th century, and the new wealth of Tavistock was assured.

William Marshall, travelling in 1796, thought Tavistock had the potential to 'rank high among the market towns of the kingdom', adding: 'at present, though meanly built, it is a tolerable market town'. His prediction came true. It is now one of the most architecturally homogenous towns in the West Country, thanks to the money lavished on it by the 7th Duke of Bedford.

The Victorian Gothic architecture is most evident in Bedford Square, which is the centre of the town, and site of the covered **Pannier Market** (Tuesday–Saturday) which has been held since 1105. Forget picturesque visions of horses with panniers: there are tables and stalls as in any other market. The highly recommended **Farmers' Market** is held in the morning of the second and fourth Saturday of each month. Once a year there is a **Goose Fair** (the second Wednesday in October) along Plymouth Road. You can buy just about anything there – except, possibly, geese. Historically these markets will have been just as their names suggest. The Reverend Stebbing Shaw, writing in 1788, describes the approach road to Tavistock: 'This being market day we met numbers of the people flocking hither with grain, a few sheep, and an abundance of Michaelmas geese. The common vehicles in this country are panniers and horses; nor did we meet a single carriage the whole day.' The little **Tavistock Museum** (Bedford Square; 01822 612546; www.tavistockhistory.ik.com) is open from March to October and has changing exhibits on the town's history.

If you have time to spare in Tavistock, take a stroll along the **canal**. Built to transport copper ore to Morwellham Quay (see page 191) it runs for 1½ miles before going underground. You can also walk across the viaduct, which is such a prominent landmark in the town.

As you would expect for a town of this size, Tavistock is easily reached by **bus** from Plymouth, and also by the 118 and 187 from Okehampton.

Basics

Tourist Information Centre Bedford Sq ☎ 01822 612938
📮 www.discoverdartmoor.com.
Book Stop 3 Market St ☎ 01822 717244📮 www.bookstoptavistock.co.uk. Books, maps and a relaxing coffee shop.
South West Crafts Church Lane ☎ 01822 612689
📮 www.southwestcrafts.co.uk. A large assortment of high-quality crafts by various artists and craftspeople.
Tavistock Cycles Paddons Row, Brook St ☎ 01822 617630
📮 www.tavistockcycles.co.uk. Mountain bikes for hire – ideal for a day or two on Dartmoor.

Food and drink

Robertson's organic café 4–8 Pepper St ☎ 01822 612117
📮 www.robertsonsorganic.co.uk. 'Best pizzas in Devon' as well as other goodies.

⑬ Peter Tavy and walks on the western moor

Tucked away in a valley with the high moor to its east, Peter Tavy does not feature in most tourist itineraries, but has its own quiet charm, and is a base for some pleasant walks. Its church, with four exceptionally large pinnacles on the tower, is much maligned. Hoskins, the most respected chronicler of Devon, describes it as 'abominably restored' and indeed it is more notable for what has been removed (such as the rood screen) than for what remains. However, it does have some fascinating carved oak panels, probably former pew ends, which are now fixed to the wall for easy viewing. The lively carvings are of a green man and some Tudor knights with feathers in their helmets, perhaps representing the members of the Drake or Cole families (the grave of Roger Cole, who died in 1632, is in the large and flower-spattered graveyard). All in all this church belies its negative reputation.

An interesting walk is to take the track, Twyste Lane, which runs from Peter Tavy up into the moor, passing the unsanctified grave of John Stephens who, spurned in love, committed suicide in the 18th century. A mile or so beyond is a tall standing stone, the **Langstone**. Over 10 feet tall, this menhir is at the head of a stone row, but the stones aren't easy to see. It was used as target practice by American soldiers in the lead-up to D-Day; you can still see the bullet marks.

John Earle, who founded and still helps run the Dartmouth Expedition Centre (www.dartmoorbase.co.uk), recommends the three-mile **Tavy Cleave walk**. Park at Lanehead, northeast of Horndon (itself northeast of Mary Tavy), and follow the track east to Nattor Farm. At the end of the drive, look for the gate to your northwest. There's a concrete bridge here over the leat, but don't cross it, turn right and follow the path alongside the leat which leads to the Tavy River. Follow it upstream and you'll enter 'one of the really impressive deep valleys on Dartmoor. There are also some lovely swimming pools here.' Full details of this walk are given in John's *Ten Dartmoor Rivers*, published by Halsgrove.

Before embarking on either of these walks you should check whether there is firing on the Willsworthy ranges.

⑤ Elephant's Nest Inn Horndon PL19 9NQ ✆ 01822 810273
⌂ www.elephantsnest.co.uk. An isolated inn, renowned for its food and wide range of beers.
Peter Tavy Inn ✆ 01822 810348. A 15th-century inn full of charm and locals.

⑭ Brentor (Brent Tor)

The conical hill topped with its proud little church is a landmark throughout western Dartmoor, and the view from the top is, as you'd expect from the highest church in England, magnificent. On a clear day you can see Bodmin Moor and Plymouth Sound. The church is old, some say it was finished in 1130, and stands at an altitude of 1,130 feet, but that sounds a little too neat. There are many legends about why it was built at such a height. One explains that the original intention was to build the church at the base of the tor nearer to the village. However, the devil feared this might encourage all the villagers to go regularly to worship, so he sent his imps to move the foundation stones to the top of the hill each night after work had finished. At first the builders rolled the stones back to the bottom again, but soon got fed up with this and decided to let the devil have his way. They named the church after St Michael, who is patron saint of grocers, mariners, the police and other emergency services, paratroopers (that must surprise him...) and the sick. The saint came to visit his newest church, and took great exception to the fact that the devil had engineered its position outside the village. St Michael then engaged in a fearsome battle with the devil, finally hurling a great boulder at him and knocking him head over heels to the base of the tor. The boulder still lies there today, as a reminder of this saintly victory.

It's only a ten-minute climb to the church for a fit person, up a rough path lined with foxgloves, through cow-grazed pasture, dodging cowpats. The church itself is tiny and utterly simple inside. It's the location that makes it so special; and the fact that it celebrates evensong every Sunday in the summer.

⑮ Lydford Gorge and Lydford

Hidden away off the A386, this is one of those happy places with plenty to see and a regular bus service. People have always loved waterfalls, and **Lydford Gorge** has been enticing visitors to its White Lady Waterfall for around 300 years, although it was the arrival of the railway in 1865 that put it within reach of holidaymakers. Now owned by the National Trust, the 1½-mile stretch of river deserves its popularity – it really does live up to expectations.

The gorge walk is designed as a 'circular' (oblong) route, and follows a one-way system so you walk west along the southern bank of the river and return the other side. This is a three-mile walk with some steep sections. If you don't want to do the whole thing, I would recommend the Devil's Cauldron circuit accessed from the main entrance. Here the river is forced through a narrow space between rocks, with the path an eyrie overhead, pinned against the steep fern-clad rock face so you look down on the churning white water.

The other end, with the White Lady Waterfall, is drier and less ferny than the eastern section, and the descent to the falls is quite steep – although there is a longer, 'easy' path as an alternative. The waterfall is just that – a waterfall – so unless there has been a lot of rain it is not that spectacular though certainly beautiful in its wooded environment. The Reverend Stebbing Shaw, who visited Lydford in 1788, was moved to paroxysms of delight. '…you are presented with the finest milky streams imaginable, neither too perpendicular to be one confused heap, nor too much divided to be ungraceful; but one continued silvery chain of 200 feet [actually it's 90 ft]; towards the bottom the rock projects so favourably as to fill the air with aqueous particles, and to imitate the effect of a real fountain, softly falling in a silver shower… This surprising waterfall pleased me altogether more than any in the North of England or Scotland, and being a greater rarity in these parts it is more valuable and striking.' Perhaps I should take another look.

The paths between the two focal points are lovely, with a variety of trees and flowers, including bluebells in May, and a chance to see the different moods of the river, from quiet pools to mini-waterfalls.

Lydford Gorge attracts large crowds so if you have a choice, avoid the busy summer months. Early spring is a perfect time to be there, when the water is high and the woods are touched with green. Autumn, with its yellows and russets, is equally appealing. Some of the trails are closed in winter, but access to the waterfall is open year round.

If you are coming by bus you can halve the walk but still follow the full length of the gorge. The southern section from the main entrance is the most varied, so, if you get off at the War Memorial in the centre of the village and stroll a quarter of a mile down to the gorge, you can walk to the White Lady and emerge to catch the bus outside the Waterfall Entrance; the bus stops are just to the left up the hill.

Lydford is more than just the gorge. The village is steeped in history, with the remains of a Norman fort (now visible only as a grassy mound) and a little square Norman 'castle' that looks as if it were built by a young child out of Lego bricks. This was used as a stannary court and jail, infamous for the harsh judgements meted out in the 17th century. Lydford's position between two ravines gave it a natural defence so the village has prospered since before the Norman Conquest when it had its own mint, producing silver 'Lydford pennies' from 973. Then came the tin boom at the end of the 12th century, when it became a stannary town (see page 77). It was also Dartmoor's biggest parish, necessitating the transport of decaying corpses across Dartmoor, from as far afield as Bellever, to be buried at Lydford. **The Lych Way**, running from Powder Mills (between Postbridge and Two Bridges) to Lydford, is the ancient route that they used to take.

Castle Inn ✆ 01822 820241 ⬥ www.castleinnlydford.co.uk. Lydford's pub in the centre of the village has plenty of unforced charm (it has a darts board and a beer garden) as well as two exceptionally fine stained-glass panels. I wasn't able to find out the history of these, but they may have come from a church since one shows a Green Man, and another the 'tinners' rabbits' or 'three hares' which feature in most stannary town churches (see box).

S) The Dartmoor Inn Lydford, EX20 4AY ✆ 01822 820221 ⬥ www.dartmoorinn.com. A classy inn with accommodation as well as seriously special meals for non-residents. Closed Sun eve and Mon lunch.

The tinners' rabbits

In several places in Dartmoor you can see depictions of three rabbits or hares, so designed that they appear to have two ears each while actually sharing the second ear with their neighbour. No one really knows their significance. Some say they are a symbol of the Holy Trinity, others that they are a secular symbol of the three elements of the tin trade: tin, market, wealth. One thing is certain: they are not unique to Dartmoor, a similar design being found in Iran, Mongolia and along the Silk Route. So this curious emblem has been favoured by Muslims and Buddhists as well as Christians.

My feeling is that artists have always played with clever designs like this, and it may be no more than Escher's tricks with fish and birds gradually reversing their shapes: a creative play with 'now you see it now you don't'.

The Snaily House: tracking down a legend

Staying in Widecombe recently I remembered reading, long ago, about a house nearby known as the Snaily House, where two old spinster sisters had existed for a while on a diet of snails. My enquiries provoked a variety of reactions. Our B&B landlady pondered the nutritional value and wondered whether eating the shells as well would add sufficient roughage – well, she had just given us a very good breakfast! Staff in the information centre discussed the probable chewiness and decided they would taste much like whelks; and a keen gardener enjoyed the idea of snails being eaten rather than eating.

Gradually more versions of the story started to emerge, some brief and others clearly stretched to many times their true length by the teller's or writer's imagination. That's how it is with legends!

The small two-storey cottage, whose proper name was Whiteslade, did exist, and the crumbled lower part of the ruin is still visible today. The vegetation is tangled now, and gorse and nettles grow among the stones, but once it was a working farm. The snail legend seems to date from some time before 1840 and probably referred to the thick black slugs that thrive in damp areas; locally they are sometimes known as snails. They may have been pickled or salted, as was done long ago in the Hebrides to provide food during the bleak Scottish winters. Perhaps some snails were involved too; the wild garlic growing nearby would have added flavour.

As the story goes, the two sisters were negligent farmers, producing poor crops, yet they appeared healthy and well fed even when times were hard; some villagers suspected them of stealing sheep or other livestock, while others whispered furtively of witchcraft. Few visited the isolated cottage. Then one day a neighbour peered through the window as the sisters were sitting at their meal and saw what was on their plates. One version of the legend has the women feeling so ashamed that they became complete recluses and 'just faded away'; but it seems likely, knowing the good-heartedness of Devon people, that some gifts of more appetising food then appeared on their doorstep. For the story to have survived over almost two centuries, the discovery must have caused considerable local gossip, and yet there are records of slugs being eaten in other parts of Dartmoor when food was short.

I realise that in the interests of accuracy I should have procured some slugs and experimented with various methods of cooking and eating them before writing this account; but, dear reader, there are limits to my dedication. I leave you with the picture of the two old ladies in their isolated cottage, hunched together over their dining table, by the light of a smoky oil lamp, tucking in to something that may or may not have been a greater delicacy than you or I have ever tasted.

JB

The Snaily House lies a few hundred metres from the Bellever Forestry Commission car park, on the opposite side of the river Dart, reached by a rough path along the river bank: quite squelchy after rain. It's shown on the OS Explorer map of Dartmoor. Bellever is a mile or so south of Postbridge, via a turning off the B3212.

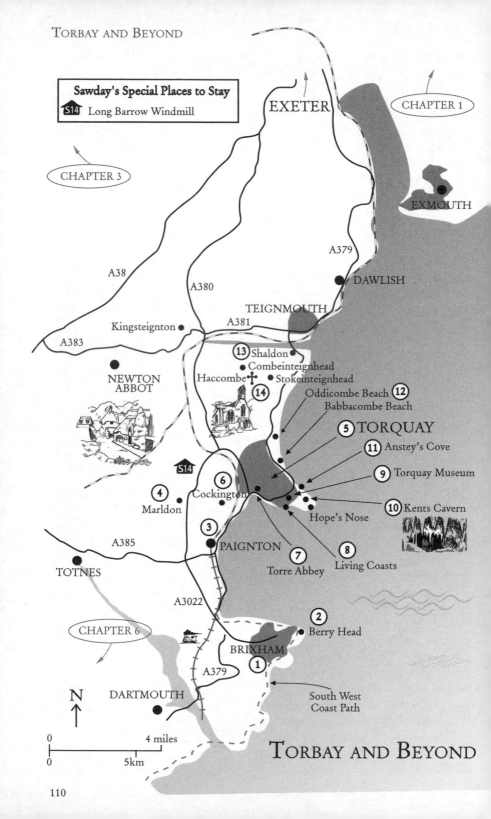

Sawday's Special Places to Stay

S14 Long Barrow Windmill

CHAPTER 1

CHAPTER 3

EXETER

EXMOUTH

A379

A38

A380

DAWLISH

TEIGNMOUTH

A381

Kingsteignton

A383

13 Shaldon

Combeinteignhead

NEWTON ABBOT

Haccombe

Stokeinteignhead

14

Oddicombe Beach **12**

Babbacombe Beach

5 TORQUAY

11 Anstey's Cove

9 Torquay Museum

S14

6

Cockington

4

Marldon

10 Kents Cavern

Hope's Nose

3

A385

PAIGNTON

7

Torre Abbey

8

Living Coasts

TOTNES

A3022

CHAPTER 6

2 Berry Head

BRIXHAM

1

N

DARTMOUTH

South West Coast Path

0   4 miles

0   5km

TORBAY AND BEYOND

5. TORBAY AND BEYOND

The wide, curved deep-water harbour of Tor Bay has played a regular part in history, as well as attracting more recent visitors to its mild climate and sandy beaches. W G Maton, writing in 1794, reported: 'The bay appears to be about twelve miles in compass [four miles as the gull flies], and is reckoned one of the finest ... for ships our coast can boast of. It was the general station for the English fleet during the whole time of William III's war with France, and here it was that this monarch arrived, when Prince of Orange only, on the memorable fifth of November, 1688.' The Napoleonic Wars (1799–1815) elevated the area still further, partly because the Channel Fleet was anchored in Tor Bay for a while, with Napoleon on board *en route* to exile on St Helena, and partly because the war in Europe prevented the nobility from doing the Grand Tour abroad so some used the Devon coast as a substitute. Indeed, Napoleon may have inadvertently promoted the area as a holiday destination. On seeing the bay for the first time he is said to have exclaimed: 'Enfin, voilà un beau pays!' Suddenly, **Torquay** was fashionable and once the Great and the Good started coming here, they never really stopped.

The bay area with its linked towns is officially known as Torbay, but the marketing people prefer 'the English Riviera'. It can come as a shock to find yourself in **Paignton** and see how dreary an English seaside resort can be, or to be stuck in one of Torquay's traffic jams. But take heart: if you know where to go and what to see, there are some excellent art exhibitions, the spookily interesting **Kents Cavern**, and surprisingly rural lanes folded into the hills behind the town. In fact Torquay has more peaceful walks and picnic places than you could justifiably expect. Nearby are the craggy projections of **Berry Point** and **Hope's Nose** as well as the small, pebble-and-sand coves that characterise the section of coast north of this headland.

Continuing north you leave the razzmatazz behind and enter the deep tranquillity of the countryside around **Stokeinteignhead**; here you're never more than a few miles from a major town but feel in the middle of nowhere.

Getting there and around

It's horrid **driving** and parking in Torquay, and you can manage perfectly well here without a car. The **bus** service in the town and along the coast is excellent and will leave you with a far more positive feeling towards Torbay. There's even a twice-a-day bus service within the pocket of wildness around Stokeinteignhead, with a good linking service to Torquay.

Paignton and Torquay are accessible by **rail** from a branch line from Newton Abbot. The stretch from Exeter to Newton Abbot is one of the most beautiful in Devon, running close to the sea and the red cliffs of Dawlish. An equally picturesque alternative is the **steam train** which runs between Kingswear, on the River Dart, and Paignton, a lovely route for window gazing even without the time-warp livery of the stations and their staff. A 'Round Robin' ticket enables you to include a cruise on the River Dart to Totnes, and return to Paignton in an open-top bus.

Ferries run regularly between Torquay and Brixham, and also from both Brixham and Torquay to Dittisham and Greenway on the River Dart. The refurbished *Fairmile* (ex-*The Western Lady*) operates on some of these routes. Check the Tourist Office or Greenway Ferry for the latest timetable (0845 4890418; www.greenwayferry.co.uk).

Cycling and walking

In Torbay itself a **bicycle** is an efficient means of transport rather than enjoyment; it's ideal for covering the long, bleak stretch of waterfront between Torquay and Paignton, and gives you quick access to Cockington. Only around Shaldon and Stokeinteignhead does cycling become a pleasure (for those with strong legs and good gears) and the perfect way to explore the region's small villages. Bicycles can be rented in Torquay and Paignton.

For such a populated area there is a good selection of long-distance walking trails. Wending its way round the area for 35 miles, the **John Musgrave Heritage Trail** starts at Maidencombe, north of Torquay, heads inland following paths and lanes to Cockington, then continues to Totnes. The most rewarding section of the **South West Coast Path** is round Berry Head and the stretch south of Shaldon, though it cuts across the grain of the land, so to speak, so there are many ups and downs. If you only want to walk a short way there are plenty of exits to the Teignmouth Road where you can pick up one of the frequent buses. Shaldon is also the starting point for the **Templer Way**.

Brixham and Paignton

Brixham is generally considered the most picturesque of Torbay's three towns, and Paignton the least, but beyond that they simply appeal to different tastes.

① Brixham

Brixham pushes out towards Berry Head, the southern prong of Tor Bay, and the start of one of the South West Coast Path's most spectacular sections: to Kingswear. In the mid 1500s John Leland described it as 'a praty Towne of Fischar Men, caullid Brixham'. It's still pretty, though in a rather self-conscious way, and still has the fishing trade.

Among its visitor attractions are the two Napoleonic-era forts, and a replica of Sir Francis Drake's *Golden Hind*. Then there's the Coffin House, set back from the quay in King Street and thought to date from around 1640. It gets its name from its shape: that of a coffin standing on its end. The story goes that a young lady of the town had set her fancy on a young man who in no way met with her father's approval; in fact he had told the suitor that he'd sooner see him in his coffin than married to his daughter. So the young man bought the 'coffin house' and showed it to his sweetheart's father – who apparently relented in the face of such ingenuity and gave his blessing to their marriage.

Ferries run from Brixham to Torquay and beyond.

② *Berry Head National Nature Reserve*

The ecosystem of thin limestone soil and a mild but breezy climate favours both flora and fauna in this reserve (01803 882619; www.countryside-trust.org.uk). There's a breeding colony of guillemots, which can be seen in the spring and early summer, and watched in close-up on the CCTV cameras at the Visitor Centre. The caves beneath Berry Head are also an important roost for greater horseshoe bats, and cattle have been introduced, indirectly to provide the dung beetles which are a favoured part of bat diet. Over 500 species of limestone-loving plants have been recorded here.

Brixham Tourist Information Centre The Old Market House, The Quay ☎ 01803 211211.

Poop Deck Restaurant 14 The Quay, Brixham ☎ 01803 858681 ⌖ www.poopdeckrestaurant.com. Small fish restaurant. Large portions.

The Grove

A Torquay resident, Jon Pressling, responded to my request to reveal his favourite 'secret place' with the following: 'A hidden spot where I always take friends who've never visited before is the woods [The Grove] leading up from Churston Cove, near Brixham. Here you will find wood carvings in the tree stumps and up in the trees themselves, which were created by pupils at a local Brixham school. Very few people know about this and I only discovered it by going on a run around this area. In the springtime the fields nearby are also full of bluebells making it even more special. An area of tranquillity which is increasingly hard to find in Torbay.' These woods are at the start/finish of the John Musgrave Heritage Trail.

③ Paignton and Marldon

It's hard for me to find a reason to linger in Paignton except for the steam railway, the sandy beach (if you have children) and the zoo. The long stretch of sand hemmed in by the traffic-clogged main road and holiday complexes is not my scene, but some people come here every year so it clearly works for them. For a bit of aesthetic therapy take yourself off to **Oldway Mansion** which is now used as council offices and a wedding venue. It's open all year: check hours on 01803 207933. The original mansion was the creation of sewing machine magnate Isaac Merrit Singer, remodelled in the style of the Palace of Versailles by his architect son, Paris, who made it as magnificent as possible. In 1909 he invited his lover Isadora Duncan, the dancer and darling of US society, to Oldway, making much of its splendour. She went expecting, as she said, 'a glorious time'. It didn't happen. She wrote to a friend: 'I had not reckoned on the rain. In an English summer it rains all day long. The English people do not seem to mind it at all. They rise and have an early breakfast of eggs and bacon and ham and kidneys and porridge. Then they don mackintoshes and go forth into the humid country until lunch, when they eat many courses, ending with Devonshire cream.'

Meanwhile Paris had suffered a stroke; under the care of a doctor and nurses, he spent most of his time in his room on an invalid's diet of rice, pasta and water. Isadora was banished to the opposite end of the building for fear of 'disturbing' him. Isolated from her lover, she practised her dancing and entertained herself as best she could, soon ending up in the arms of the conductor and composer André Caplet. Shortly afterwards she returned to France, with very few happy memories of Paignton.

Paignton Zoo

This distinguished zoo, one of England's best, is the big sister of Living Coasts in Torquay (see page 119) and is the only reason that I would revisit Paignton. What I love about it is the feeling of space and greenery. It was the country's first combined botanical and zoological garden, not always an easy relationship: 'I hate animals,' the former head botanist once said, 'They eat all my plants.'

Paignton Zoo has solid conservation credentials, helping projects in Nigeria, Zimbabwe and Malawi among others. It has some impressive African primates, including Hamadryas baboons and lowland gorillas. 'They're all males,' I was told. 'Because gorillas live in complex social groups, these chaps need to learn how to be gorillas here, before going to other zoos where they can breed.' Their spacious enclosure is as natural an environment as can be achieved in a zoo.

A new exhibit is the Crocodile Swamp which is as attractive to humans on a cold day as it is to warmth-loving crocs. The plan is to have a demonstration of crocodile feeding, showing how these normally immobile animals can leap from the water. I trust it won't be like the demonstration that used to take place in Madagascar's zoo: the over-enthusiastic keeper now has only one arm.

Basics

Paignton Tourist Information Centre Apollo Cinema, The Esplanade
☎ 01803 211211.
Cycle Hire 20 Dartmouth Rd ☎ 01803 521068.
Paignton & Dartmouth Steam Railway Queens Park Station, Torbay Rd
☎ 01803 555872 🖰 www.paignton-steamrailway.co.uk.

Food and drink

The Harbour Light Restaurant Paignton Harbour ☎ 01803 666500
🖰 www.theharbourlight.co.uk. Family-run for over 55 years, with great views across
Tor Bay or Paignton Harbour. Fish is bought daily from Brixham market.

Horizons South Devon College, Long Rd, Paignton ☎ 01803 540505 (main college
number)🖰 www.southdevon.ac.uk/horizons-restaurant. Relatively unknown except by
locals and regulars; you are served by students on the College Hospitality and
Catering courses. Lunches and evening meals are at affordable prices and the menu
changes constantly.

Occombe Farm Preston Down Rd ☎ 01803 520022 🖰 www.occombe.org.uk. Farm
shop with great variety of organic produce, both meat and vegetables, and a variety
of local ales and cider. Café particularly recommended for breakfast. Nature trail,
regular events. Open (almost) every day, all year round. Hourly bus service: 60/61.

The pudden' eaters of Paignton

Paignton's inhabitants got that nickname after a giant pudding was made in part
payment for the granting of the town's charter by King John, back in the 13th
century. For a while the pudding was made annually but then the custom lapsed,
and it was made only once every 50 years or so, if that. It was said to be seven years
in the making, seven years in the baking and seven years in the eating, although the
last of these sounds less likely! It was also called a 'white pot pudding' or 'bag
pudding' – boiled in a cloth, with a recipe of flour, suet, raisins and eggs.

One such pudding was made in 1819 for the annual show; described as 'a messy
pudding', it took 64 hours to boil and was paraded round the town on a wagon
drawn by eight oxen. The largest – weighing one and a half tons – was made in
August 1859 as part of a great feast to celebrate the coming of the railway to
Paignton. It was shaped like a giant pyramid, 13ft 6in at the base and 5ft around the
apex. Around 18,000 people turned up hoping for a piece, and fights broke out. As
the crowd surged forward, the police tried valiantly to protect the pudding but were
outnumbered: soon only the crumbs remained. Post-office workers reported that a
number of squashy, greasy little parcels were dispatched the following day.

Smaller puddings continued to be made from time to time. One in 1968
commemorated the granting of the town's charter and almost 1,550 portions of it
were sold for charity. In 2006 there was another, to mark the 200th anniversary of
Isambard Kingdom Brunel's birth. Finally, in August 2009, one was made for the
annual Paignton Regatta. A solid, seven-tiered pyramid weighing 70 kilos, it was
chuffed into the town by the Paignton & Dartmouth Steam Railway then paraded
in a 1947 Bedford lorry, as the town crier called on the inhabitants to come and eat.

Present-day pudden' lovers take note! If your mouth's already watering, keep an
eye on websites such as www.thisissouthdevon.co.uk to see when you too can
sample Paignton's 700-year-old delicacy.

JB

Redcliffe Hotel

Philip Knowling

On the sea front where Paignton ends and Preston begins, the Redcliffe Hotel was built as a private residence in 1856 by Colonel Robert Smith. He had found success in India, and to mark the fact he built in the Indian style – or a fantasy version of it, known as Hindoo. It's a great grey confection of Eastern arches, exotic turrets, pointed windows and Arabesque crenellations. The Hindoo style stems from the Mughals of central Asia, descendants of Ghengis Khan who founded a golden age of science, arts and architecture; one of their greatest achievements was the Taj Mahal. Mughal architecture uses columns and courtyards, marbles and mosaics, arches, domes and turrets. To the Western eye it is romantic, evocative and elegant but in Torquay Smith's creation must have shocked and bemused the locals – the effect would have been like building a city skyscraper in Widecombe.. When Robert Smith started work on his grand design in the 1850s Paignton was a small fishing village. He took an early 19th-century coastal defence tower set on an outcrop of red sandstone among the dunes and marshes and turned it into a sumptuous new home, Redcliffe Towers, with 23 bedrooms and five acres of gardens.

After Smith died aged 86 in 1873 the property changed hands; it was owned for a time by Paris Singer, whose father built nearby Oldway Mansion, and it took in troops during the Boer War. Redcliffe Towers was converted to a hotel in 1904. Author Dick Francis famously stayed here every year since 1952, so they must be doing something right. A new wing echoing the original style was added in 1986.

Smith lived an exotic life and left us an exotic legacy. A Torquay amusement arcade is perhaps the only other local example of the Hindoo style. Its proximity is surely no coincidence.

The Redcliffe is arguably the largest folly in Devon. The first important buildings in the Indian style were Sezincote House (1803) and the Royal Pavilion, Brighton (1804), so Redcliffe Towers wasn't a first – but it's Devon's own version of these great buildings and a place that deserves to be cherished.

④ Marldon

Marldon merits a mention because of the welcome speed with which you can lose yourself in the little lanes leading to it, and for Compton Castle, a splendid fortified manor house. The village celebrates an **Apple Pie Fair** each July.

Compton Castle (open end March to end October; Monday, Wednesday and Thursday; 01803 661906) is sometimes cited as the finest building of its kind in Devon. It certainly makes a dramatic impression when you round a corner and find yourself suddenly upon it, its huge castellated walls towering above you in an appropriately threatening way. The house belonged to the Gilbert family from the 1300s to 1800, and again in the 20th century. There are connections here with Sir Walter Raleigh – Katherine Gilbert married Walter Raleigh in 1550, after her first husband Otho Gilbert died, and gave birth to the little Sir Walter. The run-down estate was purchased by a descendant of the original Gilberts in 1930 and painstakingly restored before being handed over to the National Trust. Only part of the house is open.

SP Church House Inn ☎ 01803 558279 🖰 www.churchhousemarldon.com.
This ancient inn, adjacent to Marldon's church, originally housed the artisans who worked on the church, and now serves locals and visitors who appreciate its ambience and food.

Torquay and around

⑤ Torquay

Visitors have been holidaying in Torquay for hundreds of years. Until recently, no one had a bad word to say about it. Dr W G Maton wrote happily in 1794: 'Torquay far exceeded our expectation in every respect. Instead of the poor, uncomfortable village that we had imagined, how great was our surprise at seeing a pretty range of neat, new buildings, fitted up for summer visitors, who may certainly here enjoy convenient bathing, retirement, and a most romantic situation.' A visitor burbled to Bishop Phillpotts that Torquay was like Switzerland, to which he replied: 'Yes, only there you have mountains and no sea, and here we have sea and no mountains.' There are, however, hills which give the upper town its attractive, layered look, and some splendid mansions overlooking the bay. The seafront and marina are attractive, and there is a sandy beach – at least until the high tide chases the sunbathers on to the esplanade.

Perhaps it all started to go wrong with the arrival of the trams, as predicted by Charles Harper in 1905. 'Presently there will be electric tramways at Torquay! Conceive it, all ye who know the town. Could there be anything more suicidal than to introduce such hustling methods into Lotus-land?' The hustling methods of the modern motor-car have anyway done for Lotus-land, but stick with it because there are plenty of escapes.

The most attractive and interesting area of Torquay is the knob that includes Hope's Nose, north of Living Coasts. The 32 bus runs to, or near, all the places in this area.

⑥ *Cockington*

I had a resistance to Cockington. With all the lovely villages in Devon it seemed pointless to go to one that was more or less manufactured for tourists, especially one whose brochure claims it as 'South Devon's Best-Kept Secret' followed by

'Known the world over, the famous…'. However, I was wrong. Yes, Cockington is chocolate-box pretty, yes, it's packed with coach parties and tourists, but Cockington Hall is also full of interest and to be able to escape Torquay within minutes and walk through spacious parkland beside a brook is not to be sneered at.

Although you can drive here there are much better alternatives: the Cockington bus runs every 20 minutes from outside the Princess Gardens. Cockington Lane is opposite Livermead Beach; the lane crosses the railway line and Old Mill Road, then you'll see the Watermeadow Walk on the right, running parallel to the lane almost all the way to the village less than a mile away.

In 1935 Torquay Corporation bought Cockington and the town has owned it ever since, preserving the thatched cottages and forge as in a time warp. Even the Drum Inn, designed by Sir Edwin Lutyens in 1934, is perfectly in keeping. Cricket is still played on the pitch with its traditional pavilion, an ideal place to listen to the thwack of ball on willow. But the main interest here is **Cockington Court** and its church. This elegant mansion was once owned by the Cary family, but for the last 300 years of its private ownership belonged to the Mallocks. It is now a crafts centre, and very good crafts too. In the galleries upstairs are some seriously fine jewellery and other 'light' crafts, whilst in the old stable yard there are seven craft workshops including glass-blowing. They were giving a demonstration while I was there, and turning out impressively good stuff in front of the clicking cameras.

When you've finished with the crafts there are the gardens to stroll in and the church to visit. The latter's ornate and unusual pulpit is said to include decorated timbers taken from the Spanish flagship *Nuestra Señora del Rosario*, which was captured by Sir Francis Drake during the Armada (see below). It consists of various pieces of screenwork, some from the 15th century, others possibly from the early 16th and the book-rest from still later. Parts may be from the front of a rood gallery. The whole effect is colourful and a little bizarre. There seem to be cherubs with wings sprouting from the sides of their heads, bringing the disconcerting mental image of heads flapping around the Devon countryside. It is said that the originals may have been portraits of captains or clergymen with huge ears to show that they 'heard all', but were converted to something more appropriate for their new home. Maybe.

⑦ *Torre Abbey*

A great deal of thought, time and effort have gone into the restoration of Torre Abbey (01803 293593; www.torre-abbey.org.uk) and it has succeeded admirably.

The abbey was founded in 1196 and at the time of the dissolution of the monasteries was the wealthiest Premonstratensian house in England. Some of the ancient monastic buildings remain, including an early 14th-century gatehouse and a tithe barn, now known as the Spanish Barn because it rather improbably played a part in the Spanish Armada. In 1588 Sir Francis Drake, on board the *Revenge*, captured the 1,000-tonne Spanish man-of-war *Nuestra Señora del Rosario.* An oil painting of the Spanish captain surrendering to Drake is in Buckland Abbey. The crippled *Rosario* was towed into Torbay, where almost 400 of her crew were held prisoner in the tithe barn while she was repaired enough to be used as a floating prison. These prisoners are said to have included a young woman who had disguised herself as a sailor so that she could go to sea with her beloved husband. During their two weeks of imprisonment in the barn she caught a chill and died; her ghost can sometimes be seen and heard there, lamenting her fate.

After the Dissolution, the abbey passed through many hands before being bought by Sir George Cary in 1653. It remained in the hands of this Catholic family until 1930 when it was bought by Torquay Corporation to be used as a museum and art gallery.

Most of Torre Abbey is now a museum, housing a very good collection of art, including ceramics. There is something here to appeal to everyone, well displayed and free from crowds. Treasures include William Blake's engravings for the *Illustrations to the Book of Job*, and paintings by Holman Hunt and Burne Jones. Other rooms are preserved as they were when it was the Carys' private residence, with some of their loaned furniture. You can also see the secret chapel, used regularly through the times when Catholicism was banned.

Take time, too, to visit the peaceful and beautifully kept gardens, where there's a Palm House and Cactus House.

⑧ *Living Coasts*

The surprise here is not that there should be such a good marine wildlife collection in a seaside resort but that it hasn't been done elsewhere. Living Coasts (Beacon Quay; 01803 202470; www.livingcoasts.org.uk) is a good enough excuse to visit Torquay – which otherwise can dampen the spirits with its traffic jams and department stores. It admirably achieves what it set out to do when it was first opened in 2003: conservation and education. One of the world's rarest species of seabird is here, the bank cormorant from Robben Island. Compared with the puffins and penguins it's pretty boring to look at, but that's not the point; the influx of tourist development on Nelson Mandela's former prison home is pushing its endemic wildlife towards extinction, and Wild Coasts has teamed up with the South African conservation group Sanccob to save these birds and other endangered species.

The place is full of surprises. The puffins are not the usual ones seen in Britain but exotic tufted puffins from the Pacific, and in addition to the familiar African penguins often seen in zoos there are flamboyant macaroni penguins which, with their golden headdresses, live up to their name (macaroni has nothing to do with pasta, it means 'dandy'). Mammals are represented by fur seals and – until recently – a colony of the common brown rat in a happy ship habitat. Apart from humans, it is probably the animal that's had the most impact on coastal wildlife.

A recent addition to Living Coasts is the mangrove swamp. This is where you can see one of the marvels of evolution, the four-eyed fish, and it's worth describing what is so special about *Anableps anableps* in some detail. This little fish hails from Central and South America where it spends much of its time floating near the surface of the water, thus rendering it vulnerable to predators from both above and below. Evolution has come up with a neat solution: eyes that can see both above and below water at the same time. Each eye has two lenses and two retinas, to give perfect vision whether through water or air, and the fish is as happy breathing air for short periods as it is in the water.

But that's just the start of its peculiarity. Whereas most fish have pretty unexciting sex lives, releasing eggs which are fertilised outside the female's body, the four-eyed male fish has an impressive reproductive organ called a gonopodium. But this can only move in one direction – sideways. The female has an appropriate genital opening, but with a sort of hinged lid to it, so she can only be penetrated from one side. Thus for a successful coupling to take place, *Anableps anableps* has to find a compatible mate, either right-sided or left-sided. That accomplished, she pulls off a final trick: the birth of live young rather than the laying of eggs.

⑨ *Torquay Museum*

There's a miscellany of exhibits here (529 Babbacombe Rd; 01803 293975), including a reconstructed Devon farmhouse, some artefacts excavated from Kents Cavern and an Agatha Christie gallery. The 32 bus stops outside the museum.

⑩ *Kents Cavern*

I'd convinced myself I wasn't going to like this well-publicised attraction (89 Ilsham Rd; 01803 215136; www.kents-cavern.co.uk). I've had too many depressingly commercial and dumbed-down cave experiences and expected this to be all entertainment and no education. Well, I was wrong. It's wonderful! We were lucky to be on the last tour of the day, with only one interested and enthusiastic family, so our excellent guide was able to match his commentary to our interests. He told us that they can have as many as 30 people, which would not only make it hard to hear the explanations but also diminish the genuine feeling of awe at being in a place inhabited by our human ancestors and animals for around 350,000 years, and where modern man, homo sapiens, sheltered some 30,000 years ago. The prize find at the cavern was a fragment of homo sapiens jaw bone which was recently dated to almost 40,000 years ago; making it the oldest fossil of modern man found in Britain. There is also speculation that it's not *homo sapiens*, as the information boards tell us, but Neanderthal, which would make it even more remarkable.

We learned about William Pengelly, the first cave scientist, and his work excavating and identifying the bones found here. There's a model of the great man, frock coat and all, which highlights the difficulty of maintaining Victorian decorum in these conditions. Among the animal remains found in the cave were the teeth of woolly mammoth and scimitar-toothed cat, as well as a large number of hyena bones. Recent evidence suggests that the humans using the cave may have been cannibals: marks from flints used to butcher animals were found on human bones.

The stalactites and stalagmites make Kents Cavern visually superior to the caves at Buckfastleigh. And knowing that it took them 60,000 years to get that way adds to one's appreciation. There was once an almost complete pillar of stalagmite and stalactite. Now it's just a stub next to its taller companion. Charles Harper (see box on page 122) describes how this happened: 'It began to be formed when the world was young. It grew and grew with the drops of water, charged with lime, percolating from the roof, and being met by its fellow stalagmite with equal slowness rising from the floor. And stalactite and stalagmite had nearly met, and only wanted another three or four centuries to bridge the remaining interval of an eighth of an inch, when a visitor, falling accidentally against them, broke them off! "What did you say?" one asks the guide. "What *could* you say?" says he.'

Basics

Tourist Information Centre (English Riviera Tourist Board) 5 Vaughan Parade ℓ 01803 211211 ⬚ www.englishriviera.co.uk.
Simply the Bike 101–102 Belgrave Rd ℓ 01803 200024. Bicycle sales and hire.

Food and drink

Angels Tea Room Babbacombe Downs Rd ℓ 01803 324477. A traditional tea room offering some of the best coastal views in the southwest. The jam and scones are excellent, and there is a good selection of teas. The ideal place to relax and watch the world go by.

Blue Walnut Café Walnut Rd ℓ 01803 605995 ⬚ www.bluewalnutcafe.com. A fully licensed continental café which is also home to an original 25-seat nickelodeon, making it one of the smallest functioning cinemas in the world. They also host regular alternative live music and art displays. Their Saturday morning breakfast and film showing is the perfect start to the weekend.

Orange Tree Restaurant 14–16 Parkhill Rd ℓ 01803 213936 ⬚ www.orangetreerestaurant.co.uk. With prices on the high side this is not a place to rush; true Slow Food of the highest quality, and the wine list is very well chosen. The favourite restaurant of one resident who recommends it 'for a romantic evening and to sample the best Torbay has to offer'.

Steps Bistro 1 Fleet St ☎ 01803 200770 🖰 www.stepsbistro.co.uk. Tucked away up a side street, and serving very good food at a reasonable price.

The explorers of Kents Cavern

There's nothing secret about Kents Cavern (except, perhaps, when and why the apostrophe was dropped). Humans have been living there, on and off, for around 40,000 years, and tourists have been visiting the caves since at least 1571. We know that because William Petre carved his name and the date into the soft limestone walls, and another visitor followed suit in 1615. 'Robert Hedges of Ireland' added his name and village in 1688 (the hamlet of Ireland is near Dartmouth).

By the time Dr W G Maton paid a visit in 1794 there was a guardian to prevent such abuses. Maton describes 'Kent's Hole' as 'the greatest curiosity in this part of the country'. He was guided by two women with candles and tinder-boxes. 'The lights, when viewed at a distance, gleaming through the gloomy vaults, and reflected by the pendant crystals, had a most singular effect. We began to imagine ourselves in the abode of some magician, or (as our companions were two ancient females, and not the most comely of their years) in the clutches of some mischievous old witches...'

Although William Pengelly is the name associated with scientific excavation of the caves, he wasn't the first to take an educated look. In 1824 a Mr Northmoore broke through the lime deposits on the floor to the clay below and recognised the bones of extinct animals. The following year the chaplain of Tor Abbey, the Rev J MacEnery, finding himself with time on his hands, started three years of excavation and discovered 'the finest fossil teeth I had ever seen!' He also collected many bones and some flint implements. Both these men paved the way for William Pengelly's scientific exploration of Kents Cavern between 1865 and 1880, and his conclusion that 'man was, in Devonshire, the contemporary of the mammoth and other extinct cave-mammals; and that, therefore, his advent was at a much earlier period than has commonly been supposed; or that his extinct brute contemporaries lived much nearer to the present day than has been generally believed; or that both propositions are true'.

After Pengelly had enlarged the caves and sparked worldwide interest, more people wanted to make a visit. Charles Harper took a look in 1805 or thereabouts. 'A limestone bluff, shaggy with bushes, trees and ivy, rises abruptly to the right of the road, and in the side of it is a locked wooden door, upon which you bang and kick for the guide, who is guide, proprietor, and explorer in one. When he is not guiding, he is engaged in digging ... The freehold of the famous cavern which ever since 1824 has been the theme of more or less learned geological treatises was recently sold at auction for a trifling sum; not to an institution or a scientific society but to the guide, who has conducted many geological pundits over it, and by consequence has acquired an air of greater omniscience than the most completely all-knowing of those not remarkably modest men of science.'

Walk to Daddy Hole and Hope's Nose

A quick escape from Torquay is provided by taking the footpath to Daddy Plain and, if you have time, to Hope's Nose.

The path starts at the Imperial Hotel, on Parkhill Road, uphill from Living Coasts. Go through the hotel gate and you'll see the path on the left. It's a most agreeable walk, with good sea views, benches to rest on, plenty of wild flowers, and peeps into the gardens of the millionaires' homes that overlook the sea.

Above the curiously named Daddy Hole (Daddy was a colloquial name for Devil or Demon who was allegedly responsible for the landslip which created the hole) is Daddy Plain, an expanse of flat grass, popular with families and their dogs, backed by a row of picturesque houses. It's a shortish walk back down the road to Torquay, or there's the bus.

The path continues round the Nose, briefly joining Meadowfoot Sea Road, before climbing above it to pass through Lincombe Wood on the South West Coast Path. Soon it splinters off to take you to the tip of the Nose where you can look across to the other horn of the bay, Berry Head.

⑪ Anstey's Cove

This tiny bay is an unexpected delight so close to Torquay and seems to have changed little, if at all, since 1907 when Charles Harper described the steep path leading to the beach and the café.

Perhaps the walk from the car park deters visitors. Even on an August Bank Holiday, admittedly drizzly, we were the only people there until joined by an old fisherman and his dog, checking for mackerel. He told us that the nearby Redgate Beach, now closed because of the danger of rock falls, used to be connected to Anstey's Cove by a wooden bridge. Mind you, adventurous souls can still get round at low tide, or swim round at high tide, to enjoy a beautiful beach backed by high red-and-green cliffs with the dramatic spike of Long Quarry Point at its northern end. It's man-made, our fisherman friend told us, the result of quarrying in Victorian times for the high-quality limestone, similar to marble, which was used to build some of Torquay's finest houses.

The beach at Anstey's is composed of the most beautiful pebbles, as colourful as marbles, red and white mixed with greens. At high tide it disappears and no doubt, being so small, gets crowded on a sunny summer day. But it's worth taking a look.

⑫ Babbacombe and Oddicombe beaches

Charles Harper found the walk down to the beach too challenging for comfort: 'There are winding walks down to Babbacombe, but for all their circumbendibility they are so steep that by far the easiest way to descend would be to get down on to your hinder parts and slide… the walking down jolts the internal machinery most confoundedly.' Now, fortunately for those worried about their internal machinery, there is a cliff railway to transport visitors up and down the steep cliff – at least in summertime (it is closed from early October to Easter). This deposits you on Oddicombe beach, which was once lovely but now is dominated by a fast-food outlet; it still has good swimming off the pebble-and-sand shore, however. The more up-market Babbacombe is reached via a delightful walkway, hugging the jungle-clad cliff, with access to slipways and rocks for adrenaline-fuelled jumps into the sea. The refurbished Cary Arms (01803 327110; www.caryarms.co.uk), which has been there for several hundred years, has an excellent menu, and there is also a more humble café.

The northern pocket

From Babbacombe you can drive, take the bus, or walk the South West Coast Path north to Shaldon and its nearby villages. It's only eight miles and the bus runs every 20 minutes or so, so if you decide to walk and then get discouraged by all the hills, it's easy to give up and bus the rest of the way.

⑬ Shaldon

This appealing small village looks over the Teign estuary at its much larger partner, Teignmouth, and has several attractions. There's a pleasant, sandy **beach** (though covered at high tide) which you approach through a tunnel – lots of fun for children – often called the Smugglers' Tunnel though I doubt if that was its actual purpose; it's a little too well built.

Towering over the beach is a red headland, Ness Point, and on this high ground is a delightful little zoo, the **Shaldon Wildlife Trust**. They sensibly specialise in small animals such as marmosets and tamarins from South America, meerkats from Africa, and lemurs from Madagascar. There is also a small collection of reptiles and invertebrates. The enclosures are well designed and spacious and the animals well cared for.

For such a small village there's a surprising amount going on: an international music festival in June, a horticultural show in July, and a water carnival in August. The number of the helpful **Tourism Centre** is 01626 873723, or check out www.shaldon-village.co.uk.

Sheldon can be reached via the train to Teignmouth and then the ferry across the estuary, or by the 321 bus from Torquay.

If you take the road to the west, walking along the estuary, you'll see a tiny church tucked away at the end of an alley with its back to the Teign. This is the **church of St Nicholas**, and it's officially in Ringmore, but only about half a mile from Shaldon village centre. I'd read that it has a Saxon font, though the writer Hoskins dismisses it as containing 'nothing of note'. It was early evening, well after closing time, but the cleaners were busy hoovering. And Hoskins was right, there's really nothing of note inside the church, but one of the cleaning ladies couldn't wait to show me a special gravestone. It's to William Newcombe Homeyard, the inventor of Liqufruta, a garlic-based cough remedy which was revered as a cure-all in the early part of the 20th century. When he died in 1927 his widow wanted the brand name of his great achievement to be put on his gravestone, but it was vetoed by the vicar as inappropriate advertising. She then asked if she could put a Latin inscription instead and that was approved. So forget the Saxon font and seek out the three-tier commemorative cross with Gothic letters proudly spelling out ATURFUQIL on the top stone, in the 'unfading' memory of its creator. No, it's not Latin, just Liqufruta spelt backwards!

The splendid **Homeyards Botanical Gardens** in Shaldon were created by Maria Laetitia Kempe Homeyard with the money made from her husband's invention. They're free of charge and have all sorts of things to look at, including an Italianate garden and a summer house designed to look like a castle.

⑭ Stokeinteignhead, Combeinteignhead and Haccombe

The alternative spellings, Stoke in Teignhead and Combe-in-Teignhead, give a clue to the pronunciation, although I have also heard 'Stokeeintinny' and Combaintinhead'. These two pretty villages, deep in the countryside yet a stone's throw from Teignmouth and Newton Abbot, have good pubs, thatched cottages, and interesting churches. Arch Brook, which runs into **Stokeinteignhead**, gives the village some extra charm which it has in bucketfuls anyway. There's a particularly pretty row of white houses lined up along the combe and the church has the oldest screen in the country. Certainly it seems to be a simpler design than usually seen, and there's a brass dated 1375 which makes it the oldest in Devon.

Combeinteignhead also has an absolute treasure in its church, which you'd never guess when approaching its shocking pink door and seeing the even more inappropriate pink wall-tiles inside which make it look like a municipal swimming pool. It's only when you get to the north transept (to the left of the altar) that you see the carved bench ends. These date from Elizabethan times, and are fascinating in their subjects as well as the bold carving and beautiful dark oak. There are saints galore, including St Catherine with a big crown and her wheel, a very serious St Peter with exuberant flowing locks and a giant key, St George in full armour spearing a tiny, dog-like dragon, and one of those really obscure saints that turn up in Devon churches from time to time: St Genesius, dressed in a fool's costume of cap and bells. Two strange men, side-by-side, seem at first glance to be dressed in densely-pleated costumes, but it's much more likely to be fur (the lion's mane is done the same way). Each is holding a club, or escutcheon, and has a mop of unruly hair. These are probably 'wild men' or wodwo (woodwose), which appear quite frequently in old church carvings, perhaps representing untamed nature. There is a recognisable lion, but what are we to make of the animal which looks like a lion until you notice its long back legs and huge feet clutching a branch? Could it be a baboon? An animal the carver had never seen but had described to him? There is also an utterly indefinable animal, or possibly it's a fox, carrying off a goose flung over its shoulder – an image sometimes seen in churches. These are the most interesting carvings I've seen in any Devon church, so it's well worth braving the pink.

Near the church are the lovely almshouses built of red sandstone, given to the village by William Bouchier, Earl of Bath, in 1620.

Haccombe is worth the diversion, but only on a Wednesday afternoon (14.00–16.00), from April to September, when the little, peach-coloured church is open, or for a service (09.15) on Sunday mornings. Since medieval times the church of St Blaise has been associated with the adjacent manor, originally lived in by the de Haccombe family and later by the Carews. The original mansion was replaced by the present Georgian building at the end of the 18th century. Approaching the imposing house down the narrow lane, you have an uncomfortable feeling of trespass and expect His Lordship to emerge with a musket. However, it has long since been converted to flats.

The horseshoes nailed to the door of the church – only one and a half of them now, although there used to be four – are said to be relics of an ancient wager between a George Carew, Earl of Totnes, and Sir Arthur Champernowne of Dartington as to which of them could ride his horse furthest out to sea in Torbay. Carew won, and afterwards nailed his steed's shoes to the door saying that the brave beast should work no more but live out its life in pasture. The church's tiny interior is a treasure-trove of memorials to erstwhile owners of Haccombe and other ecclesiastical goodies. To put you in the right frame of mind, there's a 'wool-comb' with fearsome nails; St Blaise was martyred by being flayed with a carding comb used to process wool, and then beheaded. Despite this, as a physician he managed to dislodge a fishbone from a child's throat, so is now patron saint of the wool trade and of throat ailments. He is also the patron saint of Dubrovnik, where a reliquary supposedly contains some of the saint's body parts – and a fish bone.

The biggest memorial is for Sir Hugh Courtney who died in 1425 and his wife Philippa, and nearby is a miniature alabaster memorial, possibly of their son, Edward, who died while a student at Oxford. Sadly the hands are missing, but the sculpture is otherwise in very good condition, including the charming dog on which his feet rest. The size suggests that this was a 'heart burial' and that the rest of the body was interred elsewhere. Had he not died the estate might not have passed to the Carews, for it was his sister who married Sir Nicholas Carew. Sir

Stephen de Haccombe, the knight who built the church in gratitude for his safe return from the Crusades in 1233, is also there along with his wife Margaret. The stone carving was originally covered with plaster, and painted. Traces of the paint and plaster remain, most notably in the moulding of a chain. His crossed feet rest on a rather cute lion. Beneath the carpet by the altar is a fine set of Carew brasses. There's some good medieval stained glass in the windows, some from Haccombe Manor; the east window is 17th-century Flemish. Note, too, the lovely uneven, medieval floor tiles.

Sir George Carew, who captained the Mary Rose and died when she sank in 1545, was one of the Haccombe Carews. When the *Mary Rose* was raised in 1982, two small pieces of her timber were given to the church and are now incorporated in the processional cross.

The church is unusual in having an archpriest rather than a vicar. The office of archpriest was set up by Bishop Odo of Bayeux, half brother of William the Conqueror, who was shocked at the low standards of the English clergy. Originally the archpriest had considerable powers, reporting to the Archbishop of Canterbury rather than the local bishop. These days little is left of the office except the name, which is fiercely defended by the parishioners, and the entitlement to wear a fur stole. One of the archpriests at Haccombe was the renowned botanical artist, the Reverend W Keble Martin. He was appointed to the church when it was delapidated and covered in ivy, with visiting birds the only congregation present to listen to his services. One such bird was a wren that nested in the pulpit. The nest is there today, and if you poke your finger into the obvious hole in the stone carving, and wiggle it to the right, you can still feel it. No one would dream of removing it! Keble came to Haccombe from a busy industrial parish and is reported to have been advised to find something else to do after complaints by his parishioners that he had visited all of them twice in one week. His great work, published in 1965 when he was 88, was *Concise British Flora in Colour*, which was anything but concise, containing 1,400 meticulous watercolours.

Church House Inn Stokeinteignhead, TQ12 4QA ☎ 01626 872475. Spacious dining room serving an imaginative menu with unusual wild ingredients, such as chanterelle mushrooms and samphire. Closed for lunch at 14.00.

The Coombe Cellars Combeinteignhead, TQ12 4RT ☎ 01626 872423 ⬠ www.thecoombecellars.co.uk. Every old guide to Devon mentions this inn, even Harper's 1907 account where he quotes Keats as writing: 'And Coombe at the clear Teignhead/ Where close by the stream/ You may have your cream/ All spread upon barley bread.' It was then called Ferry Boat Inn, and the 'Cellars' were fish cellars. Recently taken over, it has been substantially modernised and serves food all day; the waterside position is fantastic, and the Keats verse is on the wall.

Sawday's Special Places to Stay

- **S15** Riverside House
- **S16** End Cottage
- **S17** The White House
- **S18** Nonsuch House

CHAPTER 5

NEWTON ABBOT

CHAPTER 3

BUCKFASTLEIGH

CHAPTER 4

A38

A384

② Dartington Hall

A385

South Devon Railway

③ Staverton

TORQUAY

A381

④ Berry Pomeroy

PAIGNTON

① TOTNES

A385

River Dart

⑥ Ashprington

⑤ Stoke Gabriel

Paignton and Dartmouth Railway

BRIXHAM

S15

S16

Tuckenhay

Cornworthy

Greenway

S17

⑧

⑦

Dittisham

South West Coast Path

A3122

⑨

DARTMOUTH

S18

⑫ Blackpool Sands

⑪ Coleton Fishacre

A381

⑩ Kingswear

CHAPTER 7

CHAPTER 6

South West Coast Path

N

TOTNES AND THE RIVER DART

0   4 miles

0   5km

6. TOTNES AND THE RIVER DART

The **Dart** is arguably the loveliest river in England and, like the three other great rivers, the Exe, the Plym and the Taw, has played an important part in shaping the history of Devon. **Totnes**, at the upper navigable end of the river, has been a prosperous town since at least the 10th century, and continues the trend thanks to the energy and creativity of its inhabitants. Of all the larger towns in Devon, this is the most rewarding to visit, so provides a perfect starting or finishing point for a walk or cruise down/up the Dart. Although Totnes is as far inland as you can go by passenger boat, the Dart is still a significant presence north of the town, and Dartington Hall, with its focus on sustainability and the arts, perfectly complements the spirit of Totnes. The **South Devon Railway** follows the river upstream as far as Buckfastleigh.

As the river snakes its way south, it passes small villages or grand houses which flourished as a result of their location and then subsided into tranquillity when water transport ceased to be viable. Now they are an ideal base for exploring this exceptionally beautiful part of Devon, and for refreshment while walking the Dart Valley Trail. At the river mouth is **Dartmouth**, and its twin town **Kingswear**, which have been enchanting travellers for centuries, and to the east and west stretches the South West Coast Path. If there's one locale that I would choose above others in this book, it would probably be this one because of the variety and something-for-everyone aspect.

Getting there and around

This region is easy to access by car and particularly well served by public transport, including river boats, as well as having one of the best short(ish) walking and cycling trails in the county.

Public transport

Totnes is served by frequent **buses** from all parts of Devon, and is also on the mainline **railway** from Exeter to Plymouth. If you come from Exeter by train you're in for a treat since this line is one of the most scenic in the county, running very close to the shore from Powderham right down to Teignmouth. Sit on the left to enjoy the view of the red cliffs and surf. Once at Totnes there's a choice of (occasional) buses, steam train, river boat and even river taxi.

The bus timetable covering the region is *South Hams*. Very few **local buses** serve the villages along the Dart, but Berry Pomeroy and Stoke Gabriel have a reasonable service, and Dartmouth and Kingswear are well covered. As always, specific bus information is available from Traveline (0871 200 2233;

www.traveline.org.uk) and the website www.devon.gov.uk/buses.

The region is blessed with two **steam train lines**, the South Devon Railway between Totnes and Buckfastleigh, with a stop at Staverton, and the Paignton and Dartmouth Steam Railway. Both run close to the river, but the SDR is particularly scenic. The original trains lost money so regularly that the line was closed in 1958 even before Dr Beeching axed his way through all the little unprofitable railways of Britain. It was reopened as a preserved steam line by Beeching himself in 1960. The volunteer-operated trains run from late March to the end of October; the trip takes 30 minutes (0845 345 1420).

The River Link **river cruise** runs regularly (times depend on the tides) between Totnes and Dartmouth, and from Greenway to Dartmouth (01803 834488; www.riverlink.co.uk). The same company also operates the **Round Robin** transport package which combines river cruise, steam train, ferry and bus between Paignton, Totnes, Kingswear and Dartmouth.

Cycling

Totnes is full of enthusiastic cyclists, and using the bicycle as a means of transport is accepted practice. For recreational cycling, the River Dart cycle path, part of the still-to-be-completed NCN2 Coast to Coast Route, provides some lovely river views along largely traffic-free paths. The Totnes–Dartington stretch is 3½ miles in total, going to Dartington and on to Hood Barton in the direction of Staverton and Buckfastleigh. The three-mile ride from Totnes to Ashprington is largely traffic free, but quite hilly. Much of it runs along the old Sharpham carriage drive, and crosses the estate on the way to Ashprington.

Cycle hire in Totnes

Hot Pursuit 26 The Stables, Ford Rd, Totnes Industrial Estate ☎ 01803 865174.
B R Trott Warland Garage, Totnes (at start of Ashprington Cycle Path)
☎ 01803 862493. Closed Thursdays.

Walking

There's a wonderful variety of walks here, mostly with views of water: either the river or the sea. **The Dart Valley Trail** is described on page 142, and the **South West Coast Path** options on page 152. You can also walk the **John Musgrave Heritage Trail**, from Totnes to Torbay. A look at the OS Explorer map OL20 will suggest many other walks and for those who prefer to be guided there's the annual **South Devon Walking Festival** (01803 861384; www.southdevon walkingfestival.co.uk). The **South Devon Area of Outstanding Natural Beauty** website, www.southdevonaonb.org.uk, has details of many walks in the area which can be downloaded.

Totnes and around

① Totnes

A few years ago a hand-painted addition to the town
sign summed up the image of Totnes perfectly: 'Totnes,
twinned with Narnia.' But Totnes is no fairy tale. Its success in creating a genuine
alternative to 'clone towns' is built on the knowledge that the world's supply of oil
is dwindling, and that a different, less consumerist life-style is not only inevitable
but enjoyable. Transition Town Totnes, or TTT, is the result, outlined in *The
Transition Handbook*, by Rob Hopkins. One initiative linked to this is the Totnes
Pound, which helps keep local businesses at the forefront of the local economy.

Symbols of this 'Yes we can' philosophy are the two Indian motorised
rickshaws which were brought to the town in 2007. Everything was right: they
ran on bio-fuel made from discarded cooking oil, and there were plenty of
potential customers in the visitors who arrive at the river ferry terminal and then
face the long uphill walk to the top of the High Street. But the scheme hit a snag:
the rickshaws couldn't be licensed to take paying passengers since they didn't
comply with the Hackney Carriage law. The engines were not sufficiently
powerful and there weren't enough doors. Rather than give up, the rickshaws are
now offering a free service (though donations are appreciated) and raising
money through advertising.

Totnes is blessed with a perfect position. Its location at the navigable limit of
the River Dart ensured its place in early history, with Brutus of Troy (see box
on page 132) making a rather giant leap for Britain here. Even the Totnes Pound
isn't a new idea – the town minted its own coins in the 10th century. It grew rich
on the cloth trade and in Tudor times was second only to Exeter in the wealth
of its citizens. Daniel Defoe described it as having 'more gentlemen in it than
tradesmen of note' and an 18th-century visitor wrote with approval that Totnes
'abounds in good shops to supply the country.' There are said to be more listed
buildings per head of population here than any other town in England. This has
helped ensure that it still abounds in good shops, mostly individual and quirky,
since large chains look for large premises.

Apart from the shops there is plenty to engage visitors. The circular,
crenellated **Norman castle** sits, like a child's drawing, on a hill, and the 15th-
century red sandstone **church of St Mary** competes for attention. The rood
screen here was carved from Beer stone, rather than the more usual wood, at the
command of the town corporation who wanted it to rival Exeter Cathedral.
The Guildhall started life as the refectory of the Benedictine Priory, but was
rebuilt during the height of the town's wealth in the mid 16th century, for the
Guild of Merchants. It has been the home of the town council ever since.

One of the Tudor houses on Fore Street contains the **Elizabethan House
Museum**, whose little rooms overflow with an eclectic mix of furniture, local
history and childhood. Charles Babbage, credited with the invention of the first
computer (see box on page 136), has his own room here.

Brutus of Troy – and Totnes: a new take on an ancient tale

As one version of the rather complicated legend goes, Aeneas (hero of Troy and of Virgil's *Aeneid*) had a son named Ascanius who had a son named Silvius who struck up an illicit affair with the niece of a princess, Lavinia, whom his grandfather had claimed in conquest. When the local soothsayer learned that the young woman was pregnant, he beat his not inconsiderable breast and launched into full prophetic mode, foretelling that the child would cause the death of both its parents and would then wander through many lands before gaining great honour. The mother did indeed die in childbirth, and the boy, named Brutus, later killed his father with an inadvertent arrow, mistaking him for a stag while out hunting.

For this misdemeanour Brutus was exiled to Greece, where, as he reached adulthood, he was lauded for his wisdom as well as for his courage and skill in battle. He engaged in various campaigns, particularly in support of a group of Trojans who had been enslaved by the Greeks after the fall of Troy, and forced the King, Pandrasus, to give him 324 ships, well stocked with food, so that he and the Trojans could journey onward. The king's daughter, Ignoge, was part of the bargain too, and wept bitterly as Brutus's ship bore her away from her homeland.

After sailing for two days and one night they came to a green and wooded island, rich in game. At its heart was an abandoned city with a shrine to the goddess Diana, where Brutus and his crew offered the appropriate libations and prayed for guidance. That night, the goddess appeared to Brutus in a dream. She told him of an empty island far away beyond the sunset, once peopled by giants, where he and his group could settle. They would breed a race of kings there, whose power would extend to all the earth.

Onward they sailed, westward and then north, fighting and pillaging as they went. On the Italian coast they were joined by Corineus, a fearless warrior, who became Brutus's right-hand man. Many were their conquests together. But the earlier dream remained vividly in Brutus's mind, and after a successful battle in the area of Tours he bid his men prepare to leave. They piled their booty on board and set sail again in search of their promised island.

Many weeks and many storms later their sails were tattered and their stomachs empty. Waking one day to sunlight and a calm sea, they saw ahead of them a rocky shoreline, with grey cliffs towering above sandy bays. It was the coast of Cornwall, in the country then known as Albion. The breeze bore them softly northeastward until they came to a river mouth. They eased their ships up-river on the high tide,

Basics

Markets are held on Fridays and Saturdays opposite the Civic Hall, and in summer there's an Elizabethan market on Tuesdays (when there is also a guided walk) with the stallholders dressed fetchingly in Tudor costume.

Totnes Information Centre The Town Mill (in front of Morrison's), Coronation Rd ☎ 01803 863168 🖰 www.totnesinformation.co.uk.

past low hills and wooded headlands, until they reached a narrow bay (now that of Totnes) overlooked by a higher peak. Leaping from the deck, Brutus set off up the hill to survey the area. A boulder on which he placed his foot as he climbed can be seen in Totnes to this day, in Fore Street; it's known as the Brutus Stone. (Later versions of the legend tell a slightly different story – believe what you will!) Satisfied, he called his people ashore and they set up camp.

Despite the goddess's earlier assurance that the area was free of giants, they were still a problem. At night the ground would shake and the rumble of deep voices echoed around the hills. Some do say that the narrow lanes of Devon were first scratched in the rich red soil by their fingers, and that the hilltops and valleys were shaped by their trampling feet. For a while they kept their distance, but gradually drew closer. Brutus's fighters chased them back into caves in the hills and finally wiped them out – the biggest and nastiest of them, Gogmagog, a full 12 feet tall, was slain by Corineus in single combat.

Brutus began to divide up his new kingdom among his followers. Corineus got what is now Cornwall and echoes his name. Then Brutus decided to build a capital, and searched far and wide for a suitable location. Coming upon the Thames, he walked its banks for a while before deciding upon the site for London. There he built the rough wooden structures that would later become a city No longer Albion, his kingdom was now called Britain after his own name.

By now Brutus and Ignoge had three sons. Twenty-three years after landing in Totnes, Brutus died, and his sons split his kingdom between them. Locrinus, the oldest, inherited what is now England. Kamber received Wales – hence 'Cambria'. Albanactus, the youngest, inherited Scotland. It's said that Brutus was buried in London, in around 1100BC, no doubt with due ceremony and pomp. And here, with his death and the accession of his sons, the Totnes connection to the story ends.

Remember that this has been the stuff of legend. But, mythically speaking, think back to the goddess Diana's prophecy. A far-off island... a race of kings... power extending over all the earth... And that's taken straight from Geoffrey of Monmouth, writing more than eight centuries ago. Doesn't it make your spine tingle just a little...?

Source: Geoffrey of Monmouth's History of the Kings of Britain *(Historia Regum Britanniae), completed in around 1136 and based on some earlier source(s); plus a dollop or two of 2009 imagination.*

JB

The Totnes Rickshaw Company ✆ 01752 698101 or 07943 854157.
Totnes Bookshop 40–42 High St ✆ 01803 863273 🖰 www.dartington.org/cider-press-centre/books.

Food and drink
Although two of these three restaurants are vegetarian, a resident is keen to point out

that 'Totnes has no fewer than three butchers, so any illusion that it's made up of tofu-munching hippies is misplaced'.

Fat Lemons Café 1 Ticklemoore Court, Ticklemore St (off The Plains) ☎ 01803 866888. A fine selection of teas and coffees as well as good vegetarian food.
Rumour 30 High St ☎ 01803 864682. A popular, well-regarded place with a good range of dishes. Reservations advised.
Willow Vegetarian Restaurant 87 High St ☎ 01803 862605.? A popular place serving a wide range of veggie dishes.

Special events

Tudor Totnes Guided Walk Each Tuesday 'Mistress Alice', a costumed guide, takes visitors (and local residents) on walks around town, putting it in its historical (16th-century) context. From June to August there's no need to book. Meet at Market Square at 11.30 and 13.00. Cost: £5.
Totnes carnival Mid August. Traditional stuff: fancy-dress parades, competitions etc.
Orange race Mid August, after the carnival. To make a change from eating the things, you can chase them down the hill. Sir Francis Drake started the ball rolling, so to speak, and it's now an annual event. There are races for all age groups, from four to 60+. A stalwart supporter was Mrs Pope, who ran her last race when in her late 90s.
Totnes Festival September. Music, performance literature and, this being Totnes, complementary therapies.

Living and working in Totnes

Nigel Jones, Manager, Totnes Bookshop

You ask why I moved here? Basically to end my career. Well at least to stop making the advancement of my career my *raison d'être*. I have always been looking for a place to live where I can work locally, shop locally and live locally and Totnes is definitely that town. I also wanted to start a family and have enough spare time to spend with my children, not be out of the house before they wake and back when they are in bed. By making my world smaller I spend less time travelling, or waiting on platforms, or stuck in traffic jams.

At the Totnes Bookshop I feel we are part of the community and offer our customers something more than a raft of celebrity memoirs and trashy novels – although we do stock the odd trashy novel and celebrity memoir. Many people in Totnes are striving towards more sustainable ways of living, both for themselves and for communities, and we have vibrant Current Affairs and Green Living sections to reflect their interests. Having worked in bookshops in England, Scotland and Wales I think the Totnes customers are a bit different – ready to try reading something interesting and always keeping us on our toes about new authors and books they have discovered. Maybe it's because some have chosen, like myself, to live life at a slightly slower pace and have more time for reading.

② Dartington Hall

A footpath/cycle path runs close to the river at Totnes Bridge, heading to the Cider Press Centre and then up a little-used road to Dartington Hall. It makes a delightful walk of less than two miles; almost immediately you are under shady trees with the bustle of the town seeming far away.

Dartington Hall is a centre for the arts, mainly music, and if you visit during the International Summer School you're likely to hear the strains of singing or a concerto seeping through the walls and open windows.

The estate dates back at least a thousand years. The FitzMartin family owned it in the 12th century and probably built the church, now ruined apart from the tower. By the mid-14th century it had reverted to the Crown and Richard II granted it to his half-brother John Holand who built the first great country house here.

In 1559 a prominent Devon family, the Champernownes, bought the estate and owned it for nearly 400 years. By the beginning of the 19th century, however, the family fortunes, and the buildings, were in ruins. Leonard and Dorothy Elmhirst saw Dartington's potential and bought it in 1925. He the son of a Yorkshire clergyman and she an American heiress, they shared a vision of rural regeneration through the arts. Leonard had done missionary work in India and studied agriculture in order to improve farming methods there. It was on his return to India that he became secretary to Rabindranath Tagore, the writer and social reformer, who had won the Nobel Prize for Literature in 1913, sowing the seed for the establishment of Dartington Hall as a place for 'experiment and new creation'. His wife shared his enthusiasm for radical causes, and together they aimed to bring 'economic and social vitality back into the countryside' as well as restoring the Hall to its former glory and creating one of the finest gardens in Devon. They also founded the progressive Dartington Hall School (now closed) and their interest in the arts made their house a magnet for artists and musicians from around the world.

The Dartington Hall Trust (www.dartington.org) continues the Elmhirsts' work. There are two annual summer festivals, literature followed by classical music, and a continuous programme of lectures, films and theatre. It is a wonderfully gentle, peaceful place to visit, just to stroll around the gardens, take a look at the Great Hall and any other buildings which are not being used, and eat at the award-winning White Hart Bar & Restaurant or the two (healthy) snack-vans parked outside.

The **Cider Press Centre** is the commercial wing of Dartington, but all profits from the shops and restaurants go to furthering the Trust's aims. The crafts on offer include a wide range of high-quality glass, pottery and jewellery. After your visit, woodland walks will take you back to Totnes or on to Staverton from where you can catch a South Devon Railway steam or diesel train to Buckfastleigh or Totnes.

Bus 165 runs every two hours from Totnes to Dartington Hall.

Two mobile snack bars park outside the White Hart Bar: **Van Rouge** for 'Hand-made ice-creams' and other goodies; and the **Smooth Booth** (www.smoothbooth.co.uk), a take-away van with smoothies and freshly squeezed orange juice (yummy!). There are picnic tables and benches nearby in the peaceful gardens of Dartington Hall.

S) The **White Hart Bar & Restaurant** Dartington Hall ✆ 01803 847100. Very good food using, as you would expect, organic and locally produced ingredients.

Charles Babbage, inventor extraordinary

Charles Babbage hated music, and was tormented by the barrel organs, buskers, fiddlers and other rough-cast musicians who enlivened London's 19th-century streets. He bombarded *The Times* with angry letters, and engineered a parliamentary bill to curb the noise. The objects of his fury retaliated by playing for hours outside his house; in his obituary in 1871 *The Times* commented that he had 'reached an age, [in] spite of organ-grinding persecutors, little short of 80 years'.

Street musicians apart, his interests were wide-ranging. Statistics fascinated him. His writings covered such subjects as how to lay the guns of a battery without exposing men to enemy fire, the causes of breaking plate-glass windows, and the boracic acid works of Tuscany. However, he is best known for the **Difference Engine** he invented in the 1820s: a massive calculating machine, designed to produce accurate results for logarithmic and other mathematical tables. For lack of funds it was never built in his lifetime, but a version built from his plans by London's Science Museum in 1991 worked as he had forecast. In the 1830s he followed it with his **Analytical Engine**, based on a punched-card system and the precursor of today's computers.

Born in 1791, Charles was from an old Totnes family, and Totnes proudly claims him as one of its 'sons'. The Elizabethan House Museum in Totnes (see page 131 and www.devonmuseums.net/totnes) has a room devoted to him.

Apart from his 'engines' he invented – among many others – a prototype submarine, an Occulting Light a system for deciphering codes, and more prosaically the cow-catcher on the front of American trains. In 1828, he was appointed to the Lucasian Chair of Mathematics at Cambridge, and in 1831 founded the British Association for the Advancement of Science. He was also instrumental in founding the Royal Astronomical Society and the London Statistical Society.

In 1833 he met Ada Byron, Countess of Lovelace (see page 264); she was fascinated by his 'engines' and contributed to his work on them – but died in 1852.

In 1864, the ageing and increasingly grumpy Charles wrote his obsessive *Observations of Street Nuisances*, recording 165 of them in less than three months, but achieved little else before his death. However, his name lives on in several university buildings and the Babbage crater on the moon. Since he loved trains, he might be happy that in the 1990s British Rail named a locomotive after him; also perhaps that his lunar crater is well out of reach of noisy street musicians...

JB

③ Staverton

The village has a good pub, The Sea Trout (01803 762274), but its main attractions are the railway station and the ancient packhorse bridge nearby. The bridge, built in the early 15th century, is considered the best medieval bridge in the county.

The South Devon Railway between Buckfastleigh and Totnes stops at this beautifully preserved station. It is how people like to remember the 1950s, although I doubt if the busy station in those days had so many flowers and so much birdsong. It is cared for by volunteers from the Staverton Preservation Group, and there is also a wagon repair workshop here to keep the rolling stock on the rails.

Trains run frequently enough for you to alight here and stroll up to the Sea Trout, or take a brisker walk to Dartington and thence to Totnes.

④ Berry Pomeroy

The village has been in the possession of only two families since the Norman Conquest. The Pomeroys (Ralf de la Pommeraye) and Seymours (Wido Saint Maur) both came over with William the Conqueror. Ralf or Ralph Pomeroy was given the baronial estate by William I, and his family owned it until 1548 when his fortunes collapsed and he was forced to sell it to Edward Seymour, Duke of Somerset.

The Pomeroys built a defensive castle in the late 15th century, ideally situated in a deer park so hunting could be enjoyed as well as a lifestyle appropriate to their station. The Seymours considered themselves even more elevated, not without reason, since the Duke of Somerset was the brother of Jane Seymour, the third wife of Henry VIII, and the only one of six wives to bear him a son. Jane died shortly after giving birth and Edward VI, the boy-king, ascended the throne when he was only nine. His uncle was appointed Protector until the boy reached maturity but Edward died at the age of 15. The Duke, being Protector of the Realm and king in all but name, was a man of immense power and wealth, but his rise in fortune was followed by an abrupt fall: he was overthrown as Protector by political enemies in 1549 and beheaded two years later.

His son, also Edward, made Berry Pomeroy his home and set about building the finest mansion in Devon within the walls of the original castle. His ambitions were continued by his son, another Edward, and grandson, a further Edward, so four generations of Edward Seymours have left their mark on the village, its church and its castle.

Royalists like the Seymours had a difficult time in the civil war (see box, page 143) but their fortunes were restored, along with the monarchy, and the 6th Duke welcomed William, Prince of Orange, to Berry Castle after he had landed at Brixham in 1688.

The present Duke and Duchess of Somerset still live in the village.

Getting there on foot or by bus

The tiny village lies only a mile from Totnes, with the castle a further mile away, so although there is ample free parking at the castle it's more rewarding to walk there, using part of the area's long-distance footpath, the **John Musgrave Heritage Trail**, and the ancient paths through woodland leading to the castle. This also gives you the opportunity to visit the church in its context as part of the Pomeroy/Seymour history. Or, if you want a shorter walk, catch the hourly bus 111 to the village. Walkers using the John Musgrave trail start at Bridgetown and follow Bourton Road. Thereafter you'll mostly be walking along green lanes until you reach the footpath that follows Gatcombe Brook which once powered a corn mill for the Pomeroy estate. After a pretty area of open water and a bridge you'll pass through a gate and up to the Wishing Tree (see page 140) and the castle.

To continue the circular route, take the footpath through the woods to the road, and on to the village. After visiting the church you can either take the **bus** back (there's a timetable for the 111 in the porch) or continue down the lane to the main Totnes-to-Paignton road at Longcombe Cross where there are frequent buses to Totnes.

Berry Pomeroy Castle

I initially had a slight problem with the castle because my expectations were so high. I'd read various descriptions of this romantic ruin, starting with an account by W G Maton writing at the end of the 18th century: '...the principal remains of the building... are so finely overhung with the branches of trees and shrubs that grow close to the walls, so beautifully mantled with ivy, and so richly encrusted with moss, that they constitute the most picturesque objects that can be imagined.' Hoskins (1954) describes it as 'one of the most romantically beautiful ruins in Devon, almost buried in deep woods on the edge of a cliff.' Quite a bit of clearance must have been done by English Heritage to have brought it to its present rather austere state. So it's worth taking the time to explore properly, with the audio guide, to bring the ruin to life and imagine it in its heyday when a succession of Sir Edward Seymours were striving to make it the grandest mansion in Devon before running out of money, or enthusiasm, and abandoning it to the elements.

Berry Pomeroy is also famed as being one of the most haunted castles in Britain, and almost yearly there are reports of someone seeing a ghost here, usually the White Lady. For some first-hand accounts check out web: www.ghost-story.co.uk.

The **café** at the castle serves very good snacks.

Sir Edward Seymour, a Worthy of Devon

John Prince was vicar of Berry Pomeroy from 1681 to 1723, during which time he researched the history of Devon's noble families. His book *The Worthies of Devon* was published in 1701 and makes delightful reading. Here are some extracts from his description of the life of the third Sir Edward Seymour.

Sir Edward Seymour Baronet was born in the Vicaridge house of Berry-Pomeroy (by this Gentleman's generous Presentation, the Author's Present Habitation) a mile and quarter to ye East of the town of Totnes in this County, about the year of our Lord 1610. The occasion of his being born there (as I have heard it from his own mouth) was this, for that Berry Castle (the Mansion of this Honble family) was then a rebuilding: and his Lady-Mother, not likeing the Musick of Axes and Hammers (this Gentlemans great delight afterward) chose to lay down, this her burthen in that lowly place.

He had no sooner passed the care and inspection of the Noursery, but that he was put abroad to School (it enervates youth to keep it too long at home under the fondling of a Mother) first at Shireburn, after that at Blandford in the County of Dorset. At which last place, he met with a severe Master, tho a good Teacher: the Memory of whom, would often disturb his sleep long after he was a Man. However, he met there with Excellent Improvements in School-Learning; Especially in the Classicks. Which were so deeply rooted in his Memory while a youth that he rememberd much of them, even in his old age. Insomuch upon occasion, not long before his Death he would repeat you 20 or 30 verses of Virgil or some other Author, Extempore, as if he had conned them over but just before.

... it pleased almighty God, in just Punishment of a Nation whose sins had made it ripe for Vengeance, to let loose upon it, a most dreadfull Civil Warr. A War founded upon the glorious pretences of Liberty, Property, and Religion: which yet in effect soon subverted them all. And when matters brake out into open violence between the King and Parliament, this Gentlemans native Principles of Loyalty soon instructed him which side to take.

[Sir Edward, then a colonel, was taken prisoner at Modbury] ...the noble Colonel, was carried by Sea to London: and Committed to Winchester House in South-Wark. Out of which he made a desperate Escape, by fileing Off the Bars of the Window, and leaping down, upon the back of the Centinel that stood under; who being astonished by so unexpected a rancounter, the Colonel wrested his Musket out of his hand, and gave him such a sound Rebuke as hindered him, for the present, from following after him, or making any Discovery of him.

...This Honble Barronet submitted to the Arrest of Death on the fourth of December in the year of our Lord 1688 and near about the Seventy Eighth of his Age. And lyeth interrd in the north Isle of the parish church of Berry-Pomeroy among his Ancestors, without any Sepulchral Monument.

My thanks to the vicar of Berry Pomeroy, Peter Bellenes, for introducing me to the writings of John Prince.

The Wishing Tree

I visited Berry Pomeroy with a friend who used to take her children to the Wishing Tree. 'We had to walk backwards – very tricky with three little children in wellies. They kept falling over. One year we made a special journey [from Guildford] because all three were about to take exams.' There is now no sign indicating the magical powers of this mighty beech, but it's still there, by the footpath that leads down to Gatcombe Brook, so we clambered round it, forwards, and made our wishes. Just in case. Later I found this description in a 1963 Devon guide: 'According to local tradition, to walk backwards round this tree three times will bring the fulfilment of any desire… [but] as the earth has fallen away from the far side, the slope is now too steep to admit of perambulation round the tree – either backwards or forwards.'

The church

The church stands on its own, overlooking a glorious view. The first thing you notice is the vaulted porch, with some interesting faces carved on the bosses. Inside, the exposed brickwork is unusual, and the finely carved gilded screen stretching the full width of the nave catches the eye. The saints painted on the panels have been literally defaced, presumably at the time of the Reformation, leaving their eloquent hands to do the talking.

There's a memorial stone to the Reverend John Prince, author of *The Worthies of Devon* (see box), but the glory of the church is its Seymour chapel with the memorial to Lord Edward Seymour, son of the Protector, and his son (another Edward) with his wife Elizabeth Campernowne. All are lying uncomfortably on their sides, with their heads propped on one hand. Elizabeth has two of her 11 children with her: a baby in a cradle at her head and at her feet a little girl, described as 'an imbecile child', sitting in a chair. Her features do, perhaps, look like Down's syndrome. Lined up below are the kneeling figures of the nine surviving children.

The lower River Dart

The claim that the Dart is the loveliest river in England is not misplaced. Ancient oak forests (the name Dart is derived from the Old English for Oak) line the banks, drooping their gnarled trunks towards the water. Where the trees end the hills begin, chequerboard fields of red earth and green pasture sloping steeply up to the horizon. Sometimes the river widens so it feels more like a lake, and at other times it's so narrow you could throw a stone to the other side. Small villages of whitewashed cottages hide along the arms of creeks, and splendid mansions are just visible through the trees. Clusters of sailing boats lie moored at Dittisham and Stoke Gabriel, and a variety of passenger-carrying vessels use the river as a highway. The perfect way to get to know the river is to walk from Totnes to Dartmouth, and take the River Link boat back.

Cruising the River Dart

The hour-long River Dart Cruise, operated by **River Link** (01803 834488; www.riverlink.co.uk), enjoyably combines getting from Dartmouth to Totnes, or vice versa, with an overview of the sights along the river. It takes an hour, and you'll see a reasonable amount of birdlife, including cormorants and herons, as well as learning about the history of the houses and villages *en route*. River Link also do trips to Sharpham Vineyard, and jazz cruises. There's a snack bar on board and dogs are welcome. Other, more intimate ways of exploring the river include canoeing and sailing. See below.

Paddling the Dart

To get to know the river at its own level, so to speak, you need to be in a small boat or canoe. I spent a few hours in one of the three-man canoes operated by Essential Adventure, and loved it. Graham Cary, Andy Miller and their team introduce you not only to the basics of paddling a canoe but also to bushcraft and survival skills. Or, if you want to go beyond the river, there's caving, abseiling and even archery.

We started our trip at Stoke Gabriel and, with the tide with us but the wind in our faces, we paddled energetically to Tuckenhay for an early lunch. Birds were plentiful: cormorants, egrets, shelduck and mallard. And if we were lucky, Graham said, we might see a seal, although they tend to linger in the upper river until the tide has turned.

On the way back to Stoke Gabriel we stopped on a beach to become familiar with bushcraft, including lighting a fire without matches and learning what wild foods are safe to eat.

Boat hire

Canoe Adventures ☎ 01803 865301 ⟨ www.canoeadventures.co.uk. Guided tours exploring the Dart aboard Voyager 12-seat canoes.

Dittisham Sailing School Contact through Anchorstone Café, Manor St, Dittisham; Jasmine Harvey ☎ 01803 722365. Sailing tuition and hire, as well as motor-boat hire.

Essential Adventure ☎ 01803 862570 or 07900 583676 ⟨ www.essential-adventure.co.uk. See box above.

John Haggar Self-drive canoe and kayak hire ☎ 01803 866257.

Marshall's Sailing School Dittisham; Kate Marshall ☎ 01803 770246 or 07973 520515 ⟨ www.marshallsailing.com. Boat hire and tuition.

River taxi ☎ 07814 954869. **Tim Burke** has two boats, the *River Rat* (10 people) and the *Otter* (12), which he operates as taxis, taking you wherever you want to go on the river for a very reasonable price. His main business is transporting people from the steam train station in Totnes to Vire Island and Totnes Town Bridge. However, he will pick you up at any of the riverside places described in this chapter, depending on the tides. He can only operate in a three-hour window each side of high tide.

Totnes Kayaks Baltic Wharf, Totnes ☎ 01803 864300

⌂ www.totneskayaks.co.uk. Courses range from one-day introduction for beginners to certification courses for experienced paddlers. Also rentals.

The Dart Valley Trail

This lovely walkers' trail links Dartmouth to Totnes, and Greenway to Kingswear. In total it's 17 miles, but is linked to buses, ferries and the steam train so is easy to do in sections. With some planning, you can take in all that is typical of the area: river views (of course), small villages with impossibly narrow streets (you'll be glad you're on foot) and ancient oak woods. The main options are: the lower Dart from Dartmouth to Dittisham and Greenway, then back to Kingswear (9 miles); ferry from Dartmouth to Dittisham and walk back on either side of the river (4–5 miles); Totnes to Dittisham, taking in the villages of Ashprington, Cornworthy and Tuckenhay, and take the ferry back (8–9 miles). If these seem too long, the river taxi (see above) can drop you off or pick you up at any point along the river providing you plan for the tides.

⑤ Stoke Gabriel

A village of confusingly winding lanes funnels traffic down to the riverside car park, where the salmon fishermen used to mend their nets. The church is large and, for Devon, relatively uninteresting apart from the striking wooden pulpit which is partly painted in green and gilt, and the beautiful rood screen with its intricately carved leaf design. The glory of the church is the yew tree that stands – or rather sprawls – in the graveyard. It is reckoned to be between 800 and 1,300 years old and is feeling its age. It stands hunched and droopy, with every limb supported on a pillar or draped across a tombstone. In early May the graveyard was full of cowslips with a fine view down to the river.

The village is not on the Dart Valley Trail so driving is the easiest way of getting here. It's served by bus 25 from the main Paignton–Totnes road, or the Friday-only bus 2 from Totnes.

Church House Inn ☎ 01803 782384. Nicely chatty and welcoming medieval pub with a splendid ceiling; decent bar food.

The Rivershack The Quay, Stoke Gabriel ☎ 01803 782520

⌂ www.therivershack.co.uk. A café in a lovely location, with very good local food and large portions.

⑥ Ashprington and the Sharpham Estate

The picturesque village of **Ashprington** sits at the top of a hill, the tall, slender tower of its church dominating the scene and its pub a welcome sight for those who've walked or cycled the three miles from Totnes.

The church of St David was thoroughly done over in the 19th century, but still retains some interesting features. Even before entering the graveyard I was struck by the lychgate which has a resting slab for the coffin – often considered to be a medieval feature, although this one dates from the 19th century. The tower, too, is unusual. Probably dating from the 13th century, it is constructed in four sections, each slightly smaller than the last, giving it a tapering appearance, and there's an external staircase to the belfry. On entering, the first thing you notice is the beautiful wooden pulpit. This is by the noted Devon woodcarver Herbert Read (or his son, also called Herbert), and is intricately carved with all manner of flora and fauna: vines, birds and even a snail, as well as the Virgin Mary and other biblical Marys (it was given in memory of Mary Coltam Carwithen of Ashprington House). The monuments are eye-catching. Three generations of Bastards are commemorated without shame: it was the surname of the family that inherited Sharpham Estate in the 19th century, following the death of Captain Philemon Pownall whose monument is in the church (see box on page 144).

Captain Pownall's former house and estate, enfolded in a loop of the river, are now owned by the **Sharpham Trust** which runs weekly **Buddhist Meditation Retreats** at The Barn (01803 732661; www.sharphamtrust.org). There could not be a more beautiful place to experience the inner stillness that the Go Slow movement is all about.

Sharpham Vineyard

Open from March to December, Sharpham Vineyard (01803 732203; www.sharpham.com) offers a variety of tours in addition to a shop selling wine and cheese. The estate is not generally open to the public so this is one way of taking a proper look at the glorious landscape. Tours range from a self-guided or guided walk round the vineyards followed by an 'instructed' wine tasting, to a full-blown half-day Sharpham Wine Experience.

The views over the Dart from the long, steep lane down from Ashprington are such that drivers will need real concentration to stay on the road. **Walk** or **cycle** there from Totnes (about three miles) and you'll be enjoying the most beautiful trails in the Totnes area. Both the Dart Valley Trail and NCR2 pass the entrance to Sharpham Estate before reaching Ashprington. Walkers have two unusual transport options for returning to Totnes if they don't want to retrace their steps. The Harbourne Shuttle bus (01803 732092) runs on Wednesdays and Fridays, taking villagers from Cornworthy, Tuckenhay and Ashprington to Totnes for their shopping. The timetable is flexible, but it usually returns from Totnes around noon, so works for an afternoon walk from any of these villages back to Totnes. Alternatively, if the tides are right, the river taxi operated by Tim Burke (see page 141) can drop you or pick you up at Sharpham.

Durant Arms Ashprington ☎ 01803 732240 ⌂ www.durantarms.co.uk. Decent food and St Austell ales.

The Vineyard Café ☎ 01803 732178 ⌂ www.thevineyardcafe.co.uk. Light meals in a super location overlooking the River Dart. Local produce from the Sharpham Estate, mostly free-range and organic.

Waterman's Arms Bow Bridge (between Ashprington and Tuckenhay) ☎ 01803 732214 ⌂ www.watermansarms.net. An upmarket hotel and restaurant in an idyllic riverside setting.

Captain Philemon Pownall

Philemon Pownall (or Pownoll, or Pownell) was born in 1734 in Plymouth, the son of a master shipwright, so he naturally went to sea to seek his fortune. At the age of only 28 Philemon struck gold – literally. War between Britain and Spain broke out in January 1762 and His Majesty's sloop *Favourite*, to which he had recently been promoted captain, was one of several warships despatched to guard Cape St Vincent. On 15 May, *Favourite* and the frigate *Active* spotted the Spanish man-of-war *Hermione* returning home to Cadiz from Lima; she responded to their challenge with a broadside, so they let loose their guns and took her. It then emerged that Hermione was no simple warship: she had set sail from Lima before the outbreak of war and was carrying bags of dollars, gold coins, ingots of gold, silver and tin – and, more prosaically, a large stock of cocoa.

The prize money from this capture was a record for the time: in total over £500,000, of which Pownall's share was £64,872. Even the ordinary seamen from the two ships received around £480 each, a sum it would have taken them over 30 years to earn. More than 20 wagons were needed to carry the booty to London.

Pownall and his fellow captain from the *Active*, Herbert Sawyer, had earlier been courting the two daughters of a merchant from Exeter, who had refused their suits because of their inadequate financial status. Now they rapidly married their sweethearts and even settled an annuity on the merchant!

Pownall spent his money lavishly. He had his portrait painted by Sir Joshua Reynolds, and started building his manor at Sharpham. The estate has a river frontage of nearly three miles, with gardens designed by Capability Brown. He also commissioned the decorative Sharpham shellwork recently on the antiques market valued at £250,000, as a gift to his wife Jane. It was their daughter, also Jane, who married the unfortunately named Edmund Bastard. They had no sons, so the Bastard line ended there.

Pownall remained in the navy. In 1776 he was wounded in a skirmish off Brittany and lived the rest of his life with a musket ball lodged in his chest. In June 1780 he was killed by cannon fire while engaging a French privateer, and Admiral John Jervis wrote in tribute that he was 'the best officer, & most excellent kind hearted man in the Profession'.

JB

⑦ Tuckenhay and Cornworthy

The tiny, elongated village of **Tuckenhay**, squeezed between the River Wash and a steep hillside, makes an agreeable and peaceful base for exploring the middle section of the river. It's hard to believe that until 1970 this was an important industrial centre, with the paper mill providing local employment, and ships plying the river to transport its high-quality paper throughout the realm. It was used, among other things, to make banknotes. During wartime, when the raw materials were hard to get, local people were asked to save their rags and printed paper for the factory. They had to divide them into three bags: wool, cotton and paper – an early version of today's coloured bins. The mill and its outbuildings have been converted into luxury self-catering accommodation (0870 442 2515; www.tuckenhaymill.co.uk).

I stayed at Riverside House and woke to find an Egyptian goose making a speech from a river bollard. Within an hour of leaving the guesthouse I knew that this was the essence of Go Slow Devon. Crossing the river on a tiny bridge, I followed a well-used footpath along Bow Creek, past benches for the weary, picnic places for the hungry, and a rope swing suspended from a high branch for energetic youngsters. The tide was low and kelp looked incongruous piled against the red earth of the river bank. In April, primroses brightened the footpath and the hazel catkins suggested rich nutting in the autumn.

A steep track took me to **Cornworthy** which is bypassed by most tourist traffic because it has 'no places of interest': a huge advantage. It has a great feeling of community and village pride. Notices were pinned on the board outside the church, and the houses and gardens were tended with love.

The church is a rewarding mixture of old and new. There's a beautiful, simple screen, all worm-eaten, and a parish book detailing the history of the village and the Tuckenhay paper mill. Representing the present day are two modern sculptures: an angel's wing by Jilly Sutton and the feet of Christ, pierced by nails, by Robin Williams, son of a church warden. They are a walker's feet, with skinny shins and knobby, crooked toes. On the prayer board was a note 'Please help Mirabelle get her other leg strong again.' Adding, as an afterthought, 'My tortoise'.

On the way back to Tuckenhay I passed the ruined Augustinian priory of St Mary, reportedly founded for seven religious women. It was a victim of the Dissolution of the Monasteries and abandoned in 1539. Nothing much remains except the gatehouse with its rather splendid arch, large enough to allow the passage of horse-drawn carriages, framing Cornworthy in the valley below. Nearby is a more humble doorway for pedestrians.

⑧ Dittisham and Greenway

The river is at its narrowest between these two places, and a motorboat acts as a **ferry** from one to the other. There's no particular schedule, you just ring a large bell when you're ready to cross and by and by the boatman will appear.

The sailing centre of Dittisham is reminiscent of Cornwall, with a hillside of tightly packed, steeply stacked white cottages with slate roofs. If you arrive here by car, avoid heading down to the quay; you'll regret it – there's no parking and your car may end up in the Ferry Inn or the river. Look for the car park in the upper town (the Ham) which overlooks the river. Once you have admired the cottages and speculated which one changed hands for over eight million pounds, there's not a whole lot to see here. The church is unexceptional, but has an interesting 15th-century stone pulpit, intricately carved, gilded and painted, entwined with fruit and foliage, with some very gloomy saints or apostles in the niches. This caught the eye of Richard Pococke, travelling in 1750:

'I...crossed the river Dort to Ditsham, a village with a little street in it, and a large ancient church new modelled, where I first saw one of those carved stone pulpits, of which sort there are many in this country'.

Agatha Christie

Dame Agatha Christie – born Agatha Miller in Barton Road, Torquay, in September 1890 – is the best-selling novelist of all time, with sales of her work (novels, plays, short stories) topping two billion, in more than 60 languages; only Shakespeare, the Bible and the Koran have achieved higher figures. Her play *The Mousetrap*, which opened in London's West End in 1952, is now the longest-running theatre play in history. One actor from its early days was the young Richard Attenborough.

The play came about because the late Queen Mary, a devoted Christie fan, was asked by the BBC how they might best celebrate her 80th birthday on radio. She requested something by Agatha Christie – who obliged by writing a short sketch, *Three Blind Mice*, which was broadcast in 1947. Christie then adapted it, as the stage version of *The Mousetrap*.

Christie had no formal education; she was taught reading by her mother, arithmetic by her father and French by a governess. On Christmas Eve in 1914, as World War I was breaking, she married Captain Archibald Christie of the Royal Flying Corps; they honeymooned in Torquay's Grand Hotel. During the war Torquay Town Hall was turned into a hospital and she worked there, thus gaining useful information about poisons and meeting many Belgian refugees, the blueprints for Hercule Poirot. Her Torquay connections are commemorated in the Christie Gallery in Torquay Museum (see page 120), or you can track various landmarks by strolling the one-mile Agatha Christie Trail around the town. It starts from the Tourist Information Centre and even, in true Christie fashion, contains a puzzle for you to solve.

The marriage was not happy, and in December 1926 Britain's newspapers were buzzing with the news that she had 'disappeared'; a massive search was mounted and, for the first time in Britain, planes were used to back up the efforts of police and the public. There were murmurs of foul play, and rewards were offered for information leading to her return. Ten days later she was spotted: it turned out she had abandoned her car near her home in Surrey, travelled by train to Yorkshire and checked in to the

Alastair Sawday's
Special Places to Stay

We have been building our collection of Special Places to Stay since 1994 and are delighted to dish up a small selection for you here.

How do we choose our Special Places?

It's simple. There are no rules, no boxes to tick. We choose places that we like and are fiercely subjective in our choices. We also recognise that one person's idea of special is not necessarily someone else's so there is a huge variety of places and prices on our website and in our books. Those who are familiar with our Special Places series know that we look for comfort, originality and authenticity and reject the insincere, the anonymous and the banal.

Inspections

We visit every place to get a feel for how it ticks. We don't take a clipboard and we don't have a list of what is acceptable and what is not. Instead, we chat with the owner or manager and then look carefully and sensitively round the house. It's all very informal, but it gives us an excellent idea of who would enjoy staying there. Once chosen, properties are re-inspected every few years to keep things fresh and accurate. In between inspections we rely on feedback from our army of readers, as well as from staff members who are encouraged to visit properties across the series. This feedback is invaluable to us and we always follow up on comments, so do let us know how you get on in these places. You can do this and find out more about each of those Special Places at **www.sawdays.co.uk**.

Disclaimer

We make no claims to pure objectivity in choosing our Special Places. They are here because we like them. Our opinions and tastes are ours alone; we hope you will share them. We have done our utmost to get our facts right but apologise unreservedly for any mistakes that may have crept in.

You should know that we don't check such things as fire alarms, swimming pool security or any other regulations with which owners of properties receiving paying guests should comply. This is the responsibility of the owners.

We hope you enjoy your stay with our owners, all of whom can deepen your understanding and experience of Devon & Exmoor.

⌂ West Colwell Farm

Devon lanes, pheasants, bluebell walks *and* sparkling B&B. The Hayes clearly love what they do; ex-TV producers, they have converted this 18th-century farmhouse and barns into a cosy, warm and stylish place to stay. Be charmed by original beams and pine doors, heritage colours and clean lines. Bedrooms feel self-contained, two have terraces overlooking the wooded valley and the most cosy is tucked under the roof. Linen is luxurious, showers are huge and breakfasts (Frank's pancakes, lovely bacon, eggs from next door) are totally flexible. A pretty garden in front, beaches nearby, peace all around. Bliss.

Frank & Carol Hayes
Offwell,
Honiton, Devon EX14 9SL
- From £75.
  Singles £55.
- 3 doubles.
- Restaurants 3 miles.
- 01404 831130
- www.westcolwell.co.uk

⌂ The Gallery Townhouse

What a gem of a place Beer is. The hill drops down to the pretty village street and ends at a spectacular pebbled bay. Behind a smart clothes shop is a contemporary, light-filled holiday house. On the ground floor is a snug with a sofa and a TV, on the first are three bedrooms (with lambswool mattresses, eco paints, crisp white linen) and a super family bathroom. And, up tall stairs in the 'loft', is a spacious open-plan living space with sage-green beams, exposed stone, a well-equipped kitchen and windows overlooking the rooftops. Take the stunning cliff path to Branscombe, return to a crab sandwich at the local pub.

Liz & Malcolm Robinson
Fore Street,
Beer, Devon EX12 3JB
- £300-£900 per week.
  Short breaks available.
- Townhouse for 6.
- Self-catering.
- 01297 20307
- www.devonretreat.com

S3 The Sea House and Rosie's Cottage

Twelve paces from the sea is an inspired renovation of two ferryman's cottages. Natural materials combine with deceptively simple touches to create warm and harmonious interiors. The Sea House has its living area downstairs and its bedrooms up, absolutely every room has a sea view and, from the decking, you can see small fishing boats chug in and out of harbour – watch young children though. Rosie's Cottage has watery views too, and a balcony that overlooks the river. The sunny character of the rooms reflects Pepita's personality and the overall impression is one of creativity, generosity and space. Bliss.

Pepita Collins
Axmouth,
Devon EX12 4AB
- Sea House £1,600 per week (all year). Rosie's Cottage from £450 per week.
- Sea House for 6. Rosie's Cottage for 4.
- Self-catering.
- 07941 464989
- www.harbourdetail.com

S4 The Devon Wine School

Alastair and Carol run their wine school from this delightfully rural spot where the night sky still twinkles, and look after you to perfection. Chill out in an open-plan sitting/dining room with wooden floors, smart chesterfields, Xian terracotta warriors and claret walls. Choose from bedrooms in the house, or brand new ones in a separate building; all are light, unfussy and elegant with swish bathrooms. Work up an appetite on the hard tennis court: food is taken seriously and sourced locally, the wine is a joy and reasonably priced, the atmosphere is house-party style; relaxed and friendly.

Alastair & Carol Peebles
Redyeates Farm, Cheriton Fitzpaine, Crediton, Devon EX17 4HG
- From £80. Singles by arrangement.
- 5: 1 double, 1 twin. Old Milking Parlour: 3 doubles.
- Dinner, 3 courses, from £29.50. Occasional lunch. Pub 1 mile.
- 01363 866742
- www.devonwineschool.co.uk

A glorious and much-loved estate of 700 acres, woods, pastures, parkland and house. Stay in the huge Park Wing, deliciously elegant and generously furnished – the sitting room once formed part of a medieval Great Hall. Or book the Garden Wing, stylish in the nicest possible way, with Farrow & Ball tones, coral sofa and checked cushions, books and antiques. Both wings have open fires, garden, parkland or moor views. There are swings, grass tennis courts, paddocks with Shetland ponies, and a barbecue for warm nights. Village pubs (two with good food), shops and a farm shop are two miles off, Exeter ten.

Right beside the main street in the village – but the full impact of this stunning house doesn't hit you until you are inside. Dating from 1154 it was originally an Augustine priory; now Dawn has swept through with a fresh broom while keeping all the lovely architectural features – there's even a 30-foot well in the drawing room. Bedrooms are spoiling and peaceful with deep mattresses on large beds with organic cotton sheets, herbs and fresh flowers; bathrooms are sumptuous. Dawn runs courses in textiles, food history and gardens. You are incredibly well looked after here.

Catriona Fursdon
Cadbury, Thorverton, Exeter, Devon EX5 5JS
- £340-£820 per week.
  Short breaks available.
- Park Wing for 6. Garden Wing for 3.
- Self-catering.
- 01392 860860
- www.fursdon.co.uk

Dawn Riggs
Halberton, Devon EX16 7AF
- £150. Singles £90.
- 2 doubles.
- Light supper, 2 courses, £25.
  Dinner, 4 courses, £40. Restaurant 8 miles.
- 01884 821234
- www.theprioryhalberton.co.uk

🏠 S7 Kilbury Manor

You can stroll down to the Dart from the garden and onto their little island, when the river's not in spate! Back at the Manor – a listed longhouse from the 1700s – are four super-comfortable bedrooms, the most private in the stone barn. Your genuinely welcoming hosts (with dogs Dillon and Buster) moved to Devon to renovate a big handsome house and open it to guests. Julia does everything beautifully so there's organic smoked salmon for breakfast, baskets of toiletries by the bath, the best linen on the best beds and a drying room for wet gear – most handy if you've come to walk the Moor. Spot-on B&B.

Julia & Martin Blundell
Colston Road, Buckfastleigh, Devon TQ11 0LN
- £70–£90. Singles £45–£60.
- 4: 2 doubles. Barn: 1 twin/double;
  1 double with separate bath.
- Pubs/restaurants 1.5–4 miles.
- 01364 644079
- www.kilburymanor.co.uk

🏠 S8 Manor Farm

Capable Sarah is a keen gardener, and produces vegetables that will find their way into your (excellent) dinner, and raspberries for your muesli. She keeps bees and hens too, so you can have honey and eggs for breakfast, served in a smart red dining room. The farmhouse twists and turns around unexpected corners thanks to ancient origins, and the good-sized bedrooms, one with its own bathroom, both painted light yellow, are reached via two separate stairs – nicely private. The lovely village is surrounded by apple orchards and has two good pubs for eating out.

Sarah Clapp
Broadhempston, Totnes, Devon TQ9 6BD
- From £70. Singles £45–£50.
- 2: 1 double;
  1 twin with separate bath/shower.
- Dinner £17–£23. Packed lunch £5.
  Pubs 500 yds.
- 01803 813260

🏠 S13 The Barn, Easdon Cottage

Difficult not to use the word 'hideaway': the setting is magical, secluded and entirely peaceful... sit and watch the sun go down from your little terraced garden. Hugh and Liza have converted with solid good taste: pine floors and good modern rugs, a corner kitchen cleverly fitted out, and maximum use of space. There's a Rayburn for winter warmth, a wicker sofa, a double futon to sprawl on and gorgeous views to the moors. The bathroom is cork-tiled, the double bed is king-size, a brocade curtain hugs the door for cosiness on winter nights, and the bedspread comes from Anokhi – an Indian touch.

Liza & Hugh Dagnall
Long Lane,
Manaton, Devon TQ13 9XB
- From £225 per week. Short breaks available.
- Cottage for 2.
- Self-catering.
- 01647 221389
- www.easdoncottage.co.uk

🏠 S14 Long Barrow Windmill

Views from this white windmill stretch 20 miles across the glorious South Hams to Dartmoor. A hand-built staircase curls up the four levels – all smart and shipshape in maple, oak and teak – to a top-floor lookout with glass for walls, a comfy sofa and central heating. A modern bathroom lies below; down again is an uncluttered bedroom with Victorian bed, down duvet and feather pillows; on the ground floor is a simple kitchen with cupboards custom-built to follow the curved walls. Buzzards soar overhead; your neighbours below are foxes and badgers. A romantic spot for a balmy summer evening or a stormy winter's night.

Vince Hallam
Moles Lane,
North Whilborough, Devon
- £350–£650 per week. Short breaks available.
- Windmill for 2 plus sofabed.
- Self-catering.
- 01803 316191
- www.devonwindmills.co.uk

S15 Riverside House

The loveliest 17th-century cottage with wisteria and honeysuckle growing up its walls and the tidal river estuary bobbing past with boats and birds; in summer you can dip your toes in the water while sitting in the garden. Felicity, an artist, and Roger, a passionate sailor, give you beautiful bedrooms, fresh flowers, thick towels and pretty china. No need to stir from your fine linen-and-down nest to use the binoculars: bedrooms have long views over the water and wide windows. Wander up to the pub for dinner – in fine weather they have quayside barbecues and live music.

Felicity & Roger Jobson
Tuckenhay,
Totnes, Devon TQ9 7EQ
- From £75. Singles from £60.
- 2: 1 double; 1 double with separate shower.
- Packed lunch £6. Pubs 100 yds.
- 01803 732037
- www.riverside-house.co.uk

S16 End Cottage

Beyond the very pretty front garden (Penny is a garden designer), the house, last in a terrace of three, faces south to the village. Inside, light pours into every room; curtains are ceiling-to-floor and the beds have beautiful linen; bathrooms are generous and up-to-date. The sitting room is big and cosy with a red sofa, log stove, books and games, and there's more space for lounging in the charming farmhouse kitchen; this feels like staying in a friend's house. Step out to the pretty village of Cornworthy with its award-winning pub, or try one of the circular walks from the door. Perfect.

Penny Smith
Mount Pleasant,
Cornworthy, Totnes TQ9 7ES
- £450-£900 per week.
- Cottage for 6.
- Self-catering.
- 07961 322710
- www.endcottage.com

S17 The White House

Gaze on the sparkling estuary from the comfort of your bed in this very friendly, very relaxing house at the top of the hill – filled with books and art. There's classical music and Hugh's homemade bread at breakfast, and a real fire for your sitting room in winter. Fresh, pretty bedrooms have sherry, chocolates, bathrobes and opera glasses for views; more village and estuary views from the garden terrace. A ferryman transports you to Agatha Christie's house just across the river: shake the bell opposite the Inn! Another ferry takes you to Dartmouth – catch the river boat on to Totnes.

Hugh & Jill Treseder
Manor Street,
Dittisham,
Devon TQ6 0EX
- From £85.
  Singles from £55.
- 2 doubles.
- Pubs a short walk.
- 01803 722355

S18 Nonsuch House

The photo says it all! You are in your own crow's nest, perched above the flotillas of yachts zipping in and out of the estuary mouth: stunning. Kit and Penny are great fun and look after you well; Kit is an ex-hotelier, smokes his own fish fresh from the quay and knocks out brilliant dinners. Further pleasures lie across the water: a five-minute walk brings you to the ferry that transports you and your car to the other side. Breakfasts in the conservatory are a delight, bedrooms are big and comfortable and fresh bathrooms sparkle.

Kit & Penny Noble
Church Hill, Kingswear, Dartmouth, Devon TQ6 0BX
- Low season from £95.
  High season from £125.
- 4: 3 twins/doubles, 1 double.
- Dinner, 3 courses, £35. (Not Tues/Wed/Sat.)
  Pub/restaurant 5-min walk & short boat trip.
- 01803 752829
- www.nonsuch-house.co.uk

S19 Turtley Corn Mill

The mill has six acres sloping down to a lake – space for a multitude of picnic tables: order a hamper in advance. Ducks too... boules, jenga and a huge chess set. Inside is a spacious bar with slate floors; a wooden-floored 'library'; and a mill room (turning wheel right outside) with wood-burner and newspapers. Dine on homemade and local game terrine, beef in red wine or seafood cassoulet. A menu is printed each day. Swish new bedrooms come with light chunky furniture, excellent beds dressed in crisp cotton and goose down, and spacious showers. The South Hams is close, as is Dartmoor; the perfect stopover on the A38.

Samantha & Scott Colton
Avonwick,
South Brent, Devon TQ10 9ES
- £89–£110.
- 4 doubles.
- Main courses £9.75–£16.95.
  Bar meals from £5.25.
- 01364 646100
- www.avonwick.net

S20 Annapurna

Rural bliss: the garden of this pretty, cream-painted longhouse surrounded by munching cows and happy hens looks down the folded valley to the steeple of Modbury Church. Inside, Carol and Peter spoil you with blueberry pancakes, organic home-baked bread, home-laid eggs and charming bedrooms with a fresh, country feel. Choose independence in the annexe with your own sitting room, or sleep in the main house; each room is lovely with garden flowers, good beds and sparkling bath or shower rooms. Fabulous walking starts from the door and you are close to the watery delights of Salcombe and Dartmouth.

Carol Farrand & Peter Foster
Mary Cross, Modbury, Devon PL21 0SA
- £65–£75. Singles £30–£40.
- 4: 1 twin/double; 1 single with separate bath.
  Annexe: 1 double & sitting room
  (small single room let to same party only).
- Pubs/restaurants 1 mile.
- 01548 831299
- www.annapurna-devon.co.uk

S21 Washbrook Barn

Hard not to feel happy here – even the blue-painted windows on rosy stone walls make you want to smile. Inside is equally sunny. The barn – decrepit until Penny bought it six years ago – rests at the bottom of a quiet valley. She has transformed it into a series of big light-filled rooms with polished wooden floors, pale beams and richly coloured walls lined with fabulous watercolours: the effect is one of gaiety and panache. No sitting room as such, but armchairs in impeccable bedrooms from which one can admire the rural outlook. The beds are divinely comfortable and the fresh bathrooms sparkle.

Penny Cadogan
Washbrook Lane, Kingsbridge, Devon TQ7 1NN
- From £80. Singles from £50.
- 3: 1 double; 1 double, 1 twin, each with separate bath/shower.
- Dinner occasionally available in winter. Pubs/restaurants 10-minute walk.
- 01548 856901
- www.washbrookbarn.co.uk

S22 South Hooe Count House

It's lovely here, so peaceful in your own private cottage perched above the river; steep steps lead to canoes for the intrepid. Delightful Trish leaves you homemade bread and marmalade, deep-yellow yolked eggs from her chickens and local bacon for you to cook. Choose a spot on the cushioned window seat or write your novel on the sheltered terrace which catches the sun; Martha the aged donkey may drop in for tea. There's a soft sofa and a wood-burner in the sitting room, and a large double bed in the light-filled bedroom. Live by the tide and emerge refreshed.

Trish Dugmore
South Hooe Mine,
Hole's Hole,
Bere Alston,
Yelverton, Devon PL20 7BW
- £4450-£595 per week.
- Cottage for 2.
- Self-catering.
- 01822 840329

Biscuits, scones, fresh flowers. Breakfasts are courtesy of their own Tamworth pigs with homemade bread, jams and marmalade, eggs from their hens; wellies and waxed jackets on tap. Rupert and Kim are busy farmers and artist/designers who choose to give guests what they would most like themselves. So... you have the whole of the stables, tranquil, beautifully restored and with field and sky views. Downstairs is open-plan plus kitchen; upstairs, sloping ceilings, warm wood floors, big bed, soft towels. It's cosy yet spacious, stylish yet homely, and the Atlantic coast is the shortest drive.

Rupert & Kim Ashmore
Woolsery,
Bideford,
Devon EX39 5PY
- £80.
  Singles £60.
- Barn: 1 double, sitting room & kitchen.
- Pub 3 miles.
- 01237 431140

The moment you arrive at the whitewashed farmhouse you feel the affection your hosts have for the place. Richard is a lover of wood and a fine craftsman – every room echoes his talent; he also created the pond that's home to mallards and geese. Ann has laid brick paths, stencilled, stitched and painted, all with an eye for colour; bedrooms and guest sitting room are delectable and snug. Open farmland all around, sheep, pigs and hens in the yard, the Tarka Trail on your doorstep and hosts happy to give you 6.30am breakfast should you plan a day on Lundy Island. Readers love this place.

Ann & Richard Dorsett
Buckland Brewer,
Bideford, Devon EX39 5EH
- £70. Singles by arrangement.
- 2: 1 double, 1 twin.
  Self-catering cottages available
- Pub 1.5 miles.
- 01237 451666
- www.bearafarmhouse.co.uk

S25 Old Post Cottage

Back in the 1830s this neat white cottage was the post office. Its thick stone walls have seen centuries of history, but the only signs of antiquity inside are wood beams and an inglenook; the rest is bang up to date. Fresh white paint and comfy taupe sofas, a fitted kitchen with all you need to rustle up breakfast or crack a lobster claw. After a day at the coast, shower and rest in calm uncluttered bedrooms. Then choose... dinner inside or out, in the garden, or in one of the village's pubs or little restaurants? You barely need to use the car: there's a shop for croissants and you can stroll downhill to Woolacombe.

Emma Knight
Mortehoe, Devon EX34 7DS
- £375–£695 per week.
- Cottage for 4.
- Self-catering.
- 020 8538 3834
- www.oldpostcottage.com

S26 Beachborough Country House

A gracious 18th-century rectory with stone-flagged floors, lofty windows, wooden shutters, charming gardens. Viviane is vivacious and she spoils you with seemingly effortless food straight from the Aga, either in the kitchen or in the elegant dining room with twinkling fire. Chickens cluck, horses whinny but otherwise the peace is deep; this is perfect walking or cycling country. Ease any aches and pains in a steaming roll top; bathrooms are awash with fluffy towels, large bedrooms are fresh as a daisy with great views – admire them from the window seats. Combe Martin is a short hop for a grand beach day.

Viviane Clout
Kentisbury, Barnstaple, Devon EX31 4NH
- From £70. Singles £45.
- 3: 1 twin/double, 2 doubles.
- Dinner, 2-3 courses, from £19. Pub 3 miles.
- 01271 882487
- www.beachboroughcountryhouse.co.uk

🏠S27 North Walk House

Come for the organic, local food: jazz-enthusiasts Kelvin and Liz are passionate cooks, serving candlelit dinners in the large bistro-style dining room at one convivial table; try Appledore sea bass or braised Exmoor beef. Bedrooms, all with sea views, have brass beds, stripped floors, local art, modern pine and TVs; bathrooms are brand new with tiles from Provence – all is clean, comfortable and informal but not state of the art. A paved terrace at the front is fine for a cup of coffee, or a glass of wine, and a look at the view. Great for coastal path walkers and foodies.

Kelvin Jacobs & Liz Hallum
North Walk, Lynton, Devon EX35 6HJ
- From £78. Singles from £44.10.
- 5: 4 doubles, 1 twin.
- Packed lunch £7. Dinner, 4 courses, from £24.95. Pub/restaurant 0.25 miles.
- 01598 753372
- www.northwalkhouse.co.uk

🏠S28 St Vincent House & Restaurant

Jean-Paul and Lin do their own thing brilliantly; boundless kindness and fabulous food are the hallmarks. Find stripped floors, warm rugs, gilt mirrors and polished brass in front of an open fire. Spotless bedrooms have good beds, warm colours and super little bathrooms. Aperitifs are served in the front garden in summer; hop back into the restaurant for scallops cooked in butter and lemon, filet mignon with roasted garlic, lavender and vodka ice cream. John-Paul is Belgian, so are his beers, chocolate and waffles; the latter are served at breakfast with free-range eggs and local sausages.

Jean-Paul Salpetier & Lin Cameron
Market Street,
Lynton, Devon EX35 6JA
- £75-£80.
- 5 twins/doubles.
- Dinner £24-£27 (not Monday or Tuesday).
- 01598 752244
- www.st-vincent-hotel.co.uk

Pootle through the vibrant green patchwork of Exmoor National Park and bowl down a pitted track to land in Blyton-esque bliss – a classic Somerset farmyard, crackling with geese and hens, round which is the gentleman farmer's house. Bedrooms are airy and calming with grand views, books, fresh flowers and small, but neat-as-a-pin bathrooms. Bring children and they will be in heaven, with eggs to collect and pigs to pat, or come just for yourself and a bit of indulgence. Food is 'River Cottage' style and much is home reared, the walking is fabulous for miles and kind Rachael sends you off with a thermos of tea.

Five miles south of Minehead, as the pheasant flies, is Luxborough, tucked under the lip of the Brendon hills. From September to February the low-beamed, log-fired, dog-dozed bar buzzes with members of the Chargot shoot. Often they stay to dine, very well: on potted ham hock; fish from St Mawes; and beef, lamb and venison that's almost walked off the hills. A shelf heaves with walking books and maps; James and Siân lend them freely, all are returned. For those lucky enough to stay, bedrooms ramble around the first floor (one below has a private terrace) and are individual, peaceful, homely and great value.

Rachael Abraham
Wheddon Cross, Somerset TA24 7EX
- £70-£80. Singles £37.50.
- 3: 1 double, 1 twin/double;
  1 single with separate bath.
  Self-catering barn available.
- Dinner, 3 courses, £20.
- Cold/hot packed lunch £6.75-£9.75.
- 01643 841791
- www.northwheddonfarm.co.uk

James & Siân Waller
Luxborough,
Watchet, Somerset TA23 0SH
- £75-£100.
  Singles from £55.
- 10: 7 doubles, 3 twins/doubles.
- Main courses £11.95-£16.95.
  Bar meals from £4.95.
- 01984 640319
- www.theroyaloakinnluxborough.co.uk

Across the river at **Greenway** is Agatha Christie's former holiday home, now owned by the National Trust and opened to the public in 2009. She didn't do any writing here, but the sloping grounds, with glimpses of the river through the trees, provided settings for some of her murder mysteries. Perhaps you need to be an Agatha Christie fan to get the most out of a visit to the house, then you'd marvel that you were looking at the actual Steinway piano she played, or appreciate the papier-mâché tables because she collected them. Or an archaeology fan, since Christie's husband, Max Mallowan, organised digs in Iraq and other Middle Eastern sites and his collections are more interesting than her bits and pieces. Perhaps the lasting impression was of coupledom. The Mallowans clearly loved doing things together and Agatha was an enthusiastic helpmate on Max's archaeological trips. And it would be hard not to be happy in such a beautiful setting.

Swan Hydro Hotel in Harrogate, using the surname (Neele) of a woman who was currently her husband's mistress. She claimed amnesia, but it emerged much later that she had more probably been reacting to her husband's affair. After some months they separated, and divorced two years later.

In 1930 Christie married archaeologist Max Mallowan, who was later to be knighted, and for the next 30 years travelled happily with him to and from his various excavations in the Middle East. *Murder on the Orient Express* was inspired by her experiences on that train during one of these trips. Asked by an interviewer what marriage to an archaeologist was like, she is said to have replied 'Wonderful – the older you get, the more interested he is in you'. In 1938 they bought the Greenway estate (see above) on the River Dart which became their much-loved holiday home.

Burgh Island Hotel in Bigbury Bay (see page 170) is the setting for her best-selling novel (and the world's best-selling mystery) that started life in 1939 as *Ten Little Niggers*, but later appeared as *Ten Little Indians* and/or *And Then There Were None*. Political correctness dogs even crime writers! The 'writer's hut', reputedly built for her there in the 1930s, is now called the Beach House and is available for guests. Kents Cavern in Torquay also appears in one of her novels, as Hempsley Cavern in *The Man in a Brown Suit*. Her father helped to finance excavations at Kents Cavern and was an enthusiastic volunteer on William Pengelly's dig there (see page 120).

Agatha Christie died in 1976, but since then has reached an even wider audience through the many new television adaptations of her plays and books. In 1991, Royal Mail commemorated her with a special Agatha Christie stamp book. An Agatha Christie week and Agatha Christie Festival are held annually in Britain and typically feature plays, films, readings, mystery weekends and a host of other activities. For more details see www.agathachristie.com (she would have been quite tickled to have her own official website!). Like *The Mousetrap*, the 'Queen of Crime' is nowhere near her final curtain...

JB

The garden is worth a visit for its peacefulness and some unusual plants.

Greenway is open Wednesday to Sunday, from the end of February to late October. Because parking is limited, and the approach lanes are narrow, the National Trust insist that parking is prebooked (01803 842382). Visitors are encouraged to come to Greenway a green way if possible: on foot, bike or boat. This is no great hardship when a large part of the house's attraction is its position overlooking the river and gorgeous surrounding scenery. The walk here from Dartmouth or Kingswear is particularly rewarding, passing as it does through the oaks of Long Wood. Alternatively you can park on the approach lane and follow the well-signposted Greenway Walk, or take the steam train to Churston and walk from there. Or there's the ferry from Dartmouth, or Tim Burke's river taxi (see page 141). In fact, you're spoilt for choice.

⑤ The Ferry Boat Inn Dittisham ☎ 01803 722368. Renowned for its location, right on the waterfront, with views across to Greenway, and good pub food. The gents' loo is in a converted chapel, inviting patrons to 'spray and pray'.

Dartmouth and Kingswear

It is rare for a town to combine a rich and interesting history with present-day beauty. Usually the accidents of geography that gave it strategic importance a few hundred years ago also caused its later industrialisation. Dartmouth and Kingswear have escaped this fate and the mouth of the River Dart is exquisitely picturesque. The writer W G Maton, although sometimes given to hyperbole, describes his arrival in the late 1700s in words that could still be used today:

We were in some measure prepared for the enchanting scene which our passage across the Dart opened to us… On our left appeared the castle, which stands at the mouth of the river, surrounded by a rich mass of oak, and the steeple of an adjoining church just peeps above the branches. Opposite to us was the town, situated on the declivity of a craggy hill, and extending, embosomed in trees, almost a mile along the water's edge. The quay and dock-yards project into the river, and cause an apparent curvature in its course which had an effect inexpressively finished and beautiful. Some ships of war, and several small vessels, floating in different parts of it, broke its uniformity. The rocks on either side are composed of a glossy purple slate, and their summits fringed with a number of ornamental plants and shrubs. Enraptured with so lovely a scene, we arrived insensibly at the quay of Dartmouth.

Kingswear is equally attractive in a smaller way, and the walk from here to **Coleton Fishacre**, or to **Brixham** if you can manage the 11 miles, is one of the best on the South West Coast Path.

⑨ Dartmouth

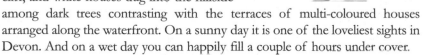

Present-day visitors should endeavour to arrive, as Maton did, by water, or via the coastal path or steam train to Kingswear, for the enchanting view across the Dart. Arrival by car will only result in frustration and the inevitable backtracking to the park-and-ride car park which, in summer, may be the only place you can leave your car for longer than four hours. Seen across the river, the view is much as Maton describes it, with the castle at the furthest point of the cliff, and white houses dug into the hillside among dark trees contrasting with the terraces of multi-coloured houses arranged along the waterfront. On a sunny day it is one of the loveliest sights in Devon. And on a wet day you can happily fill a couple of hours under cover.

At the time of the Domesday Book (1086) the River Dart was under the control of the Lord of Totnes, Dartmouth coming into its own only with the arrival of decked sailing ships. The Second and Third Crusade sailed from here in 1147 and 1190, and, for the 300 years that Bordeaux was under English rule, trade was brisk between the two countries, with wine the main import, and wool, carried down the river from Totnes, the export. John Hawley (see box below) built up his business through this two-way trade. Royal favour was guaranteed to this maritime town when privateers could fight the King's battles for him and enrich both themselves and their monarch. Richard II, a weak, effete king, if we are to believe Shakespeare, seems to have been particularly grateful for the services of Hawley and his followers to protect the shores from French invasion.

England lost Bordeaux in 1453, and Dartmouth's prosperity declined; but the great explorers of the Elizabethan era revived it, and from 1580 it profited from the cod fishery in Newfoundland. The Civil War took its toll, and the town sank into relative obscurity until the building of the Royal Naval College in 1899–1905. Its strategic importance in World War II ensured that it was extensively bombed; the town sent 485 ships to Normandy for D-Day. The planned railway never reached Dartmouth so industrialisation also passed it by. We can be thankful for that.

Much of the Dartmouth you see today is on reclaimed land. Even before John Hawley's time the industrious inhabitants were harnessing the tides to provide power to their mill. Sea water ran into an inlet, known as the Mill Pool, through an artificially narrow entrance. Then at high tide a sluice gate was dropped, diverting the receding water to turn the mill wheel. The former Mill Pool now provides the only flat land in town. Dartmouth lost some of its most beautiful medieval buildings in a road-widening scheme in the 1800s, but the timber-framed Butterwalk, dating from 1635, is still there, slightly askew on its granite pillars and rich with carvings. It now houses the little **museum** which is well worth a visit (01803 832923). Staffed, as are many Devon museums, by volunteers it contains a variety of maritime exhibits. Model ships illustrate the history of Dartmouth from the wine trade to Drake's *Golden Hind*, and the *Mayflower* which put in for repairs before taking the Pilgrim Fathers to America. Look out, too, for the exquisitely carved ivory boat from China and the even more amazing man-of-war carved from bone by Frenchmen incarcerated in Dartmoor Prison during the Napoleonic Wars. There is also an extensive collection of ships in bottles.

Dartmouth was the birthplace of **Thomas Newcomen** (1663–1727), whose Atmospheric Engine was one of the forerunners of the Industrial Revolution. It was used to remove water from flooded mines, which hitherto had been hauled out by teams of horses. The museum has some Newcomen exhibits, but more interesting is the reconstructed engine near the tourist office. And if you really want to understand how it worked, look at the neat animation on the Wikipedia website.

If you do no other sightseeing in Dartmouth, go to **St Saviour's Church** and look at the door inside the south entrance. It's thought to have been made in 1372 but the vigour and artistry of the ironwork would be amazing even for 1972. Two slinky lions leap through leafy branches, claws out, eyes bulging, mouths snarling. Equally impressive and dramatic are the huge brasses near the altar, sometimes hidden under the carpet but often on display. A print taken from a brass rubbing is on the west wall, so you can examine them as a whole. They commemorate John Hawley and his two wives. He is in full armour, with his feet on a feisty lion, chastely holding the hand of one wife (he outlived them both). Often church brasses and memorials are of people whose deeds have been forgotten, but not so John Hawley. Privateer, pirate, MP and 14 times mayor of Dartmouth, he shaped the history of the town (see box opposite) and paid for 'his' end of the church.

Other notable features are the splendid screen, with its fan vaulting, painted in muted gold and charcoal grey, and the early 16th-century painted Devonshire carved stone pulpit covered with bold clumps of foliage. The figures of saints were hacked off during the Reformation, to be replaced by secular emblems of the Kingdom: England, Scotland, Ireland and Wales.

Other sights are **Bayard's Cove**, a picturesque cobbled quay, and **Dartmouth Castle**, built in 1488 on the site of one of John Hawley's fortifications, to guard the narrow opening to the estuary. The church of St Petrock is incorporated within the castle grounds. The castle, owned by English Heritage, is open daily except between November and March when it's open weekends only. It's a pleasant one-mile walk from the centre of town, or there's a ferry.

The imposing **Britannia Royal Naval College** (where the Queen first met Prince Philip) is open daily for group tours (01803 677787; www.brnc.co.uk).

River Link ferries connect Dartmouth and Kingswear. You can take the

Lower Ferry or the Higher Ferry less than a mile upriver, designed to carry cars from the A3122 to the A379, its continuation on the Kingswear side. The Lower Ferry carries both cars and passengers, or there's a smaller passenger boat. River cruises to Totnes or to the castle are booked at one of the kiosks along the quay.

John Hawley, a 'Schipman of Dertemouthe'

John Hawley was one of those hugely successful entrepreneurs who shaped the history of England and who ensured that their name lived on in brass. Born around 1340 into a prosperous Dartmouth family, Hawley built up his ship-owning business until he had about 30 vessels, an asset which came to the attention of King Edward III who was involved in the interminable wars with France which later became known as the Hundred Years' War. He was granted a privateer's licence by the king in 1379. This meant that he could attack enemy ships, which might just happen to be carrying valuable cargo, and share the proceeds with the king. The arrangement worked well on both sides, and Hawley clearly gained the respect of his fellow citizens, since he was elected mayor of Dartmouth a total of 14 times, and also served twice as the town's MP.

Of course sometimes the line between 'enemy' and 'valuable' became a bit blurred and, as the description of Hawley in St Saviour's notes, 'There seems little doubt that he was also a pirate.'

Hawley is believed to be the inspiration for Chaucer's 'schipman of Dertemouthe', a somewhat shady character. He will have met Chaucer when the latter was customs officer for Edward III. Any illegal business of Hawley's was far outweighed by the benefits he brought to Dartmouth, however, during his tenures as mayor. He successfully kept the strategic port safe from enemy attack by building fortresses on each side of the mouth of the Dart and stretching a huge chain across the harbour to repel enemy ships.

The story goes that after a particularly successful sortie into French waters, from which he returned laden with booty, he declined to accept any personal reward, asking that the King's generosity be visited on his native town instead. Hence Dartmouth has a particularly charming coat of arms: King Edward III, flanked by two lions, all perched precariously on a very small boat.

Hawley's last battle was fought in 1404, not on sea but on land, on Blackpool Sands just south of Dartmouth. England was having a little war with the Bretons at that time, under the leadership of William du Chatel. He had an army of 2,000 knights and their support troops, whereas Hawley's force was mostly farm labourers armed with bows and arrows, plus their wives who were expert with the sling-shot, yet they routed the French in a Shakespearian triumph against the odds. King Henry IV was so delighted by this victory that he ordered a *Te Deum* in Westminster Abbey.

Hawley died in 1408, in his late 60s. His huge, elaborate memorial brass in the chancel of St Saviour's is not excessive given his larger-than-life contribution to the town's prosperity and status. And anyway, he built the chancel.

Basics

Dartmouth Tourist Information Centre The Engine House, Mayors Ave
📞 01803 834224 🖰 www.discoverdartmouth.com.
Paignton and Dartmouth Steam Railway Queens Park Station, Torbay Rd, Paignton
📞 01803 555872 🖰 www.pdsr.co.uk.
River Link Dart Pleasure Craft Ltd, 5 Lower St, Dartmouth 📞 01803 834488
🖰 www.riverlink.co.uk.

Food and drink

The Dartmouth Festival of Food An annual event in October.
🖰 www.dartmouthfoodfestival.co.uk.
The Seahorse Restaurant 5 South Embankment 📞 01803 835147
🖰 www.seahorserestaurant.co.uk. Terrific seafood from Mitch Tonks. Very popular, so
book ahead.
The Singing Kettle Tea Shoppe 6 Smith St, Dartmouth 📞 01803 832624. Seriously
good cream teas, and lunches too.

⑩ Kingswear and the South West Coast Path

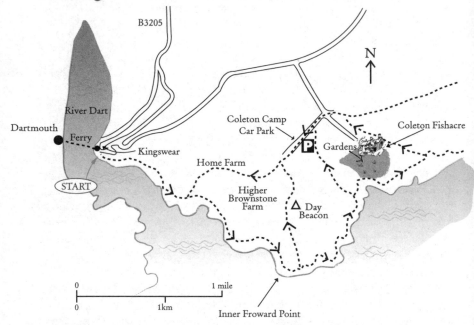

Kingswear is little more than the ferry terminal, a pub, and a car park for those
sensible enough not to try to bring a car into Dartmouth. Nevertheless, it has
the same multicoloured terraced houses backed by green cliffs up which the
road towards Brixham climbs in a series of hairpin bends. It is also the starting
point for a particularly lovely, though strenuous, stretch of the coast path. When
I did it in April the cliffs were splashed with purple and yellow from violets,

primroses and gorse, and new-born lambs were gambolling in the fields. But any time of year it would be lovely if you're fortunate with the weather.

From Kingswear the path plunges almost immediately into woods, past Kingswear Castle, now Landmark Trust self-catering accommodation, and on round the coast as far as Brixham if you have the stamina. You can make this a circular walk by following the coast for two miles to Inner Froward Point, then taking the track inland that leads past the Day Beacon, or Day Mark Tower. This looks like an unfathomable folly, but in fact it was built in 1856 as a 'day lighthouse', providing a 'mark' or 'beacon' for ships that otherwise might miss the concealed Dartmouth harbour. You return to Kingswear by turning left at the T-junction and taking the footpath that runs past Higher Brownstone Farm and Home Farm. The total distance is a bit over four miles, but it will feel more because of the up-and-down nature of the path.

The best walk of all is to park at the Coleton Camp car park, and visit Coleton Fishacre house and gardens (and café) before walking back to Kingswear. You'll be bowled over by the view of Dartmouth as it gradually appears through the trees, particularly if the sun is shining on those multicoloured houses. The sign at the entrance of Coleton Fishacre says there is no access to the coastal path but it crosses the bottom of the gardens.

⑪ Coleton Fishacre

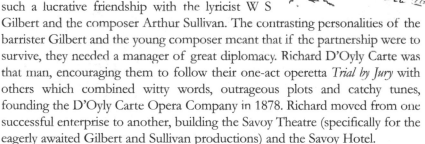

The National Trust acquired this house and garden in 1982, initially to link the unconnected sections of the South West Coast Path which now runs through the lower garden. It was built in the 1920s as a holiday home for Sir Rupert D'Oyly Carte, the son of Richard D'Oyly Carte who struck up such a lucrative friendship with the lyricist W S Gilbert and the composer Arthur Sullivan. The contrasting personalities of the barrister Gilbert and the young composer meant that if the partnership were to survive, they needed a manager of great diplomacy. Richard D'Oyly Carte was that man, encouraging them to follow their one-act operetta *Trial by Jury* with others which combined witty words, outrageous plots and catchy tunes, founding the D'Oyly Carte Opera Company in 1878. Richard moved from one successful enterprise to another, building the Savoy Theatre (specifically for the eagerly awaited Gilbert and Sullivan productions) and the Savoy Hotel.

Richard D'Oyly Carte died in 1901 a very wealthy man, and that inheritance allowed his son Rupert, who took over the business, to continue to make money – and to build Coleton Fishacre. His architect Oswald Milne, formerly assistant to Sir Edwin Lutyens, was influenced by the Arts and Crafts movement which, at the turn of the century, highlighted the skill of individual craftsmen as an antidote to mass production.

You need to be something of a connoisseur to fully appreciate the inside of the house. Only the built-in features are original – Bridget D'Oyly Carte, who inherited the house from her father and sold it in 1949, left very little furniture, and the replacements are unremarkable, though authentically Arts and Crafts style. It's worth taking time to read about the fixtures that remain from the original house – like the Art Deco Lalique uplighters in the dining room, the tide-indicator in the hall, and the splendid Hoffman painting of Coleton with an accompanying wind-dial in the library. The polished limestone fire surround in the sitting room is also fascinating: the stone comes from Derbyshire and is impregnated with fossils. I was also intrigued by the 1930s map of the Great Western Railway network in the butler's pantry: it would be the job of a Gentleman's Gentleman to look up the guests' trains.

The garden of Coleton Fishacre is absolutely gorgeous. It slopes steeply down in a series of terraces to Pudcombe Cove, where the D'Oyly Cartes had their private bathing pool and jetty. Stone was quarried from the grounds to use in the building of the house, allowing for the dramatic use of level areas and steep descents. Lady Dorothy was a keen gardener and plant enthusiast, and the grounds are an appealing mixture of native, untended vegetation and exotics such as tree ferns and the Persian ironwood. A stream runs down to the sea, providing a natural water feature. Even in rain this garden is lovely; in the spring sunshine, when the bluebells are out and the trees have that misty haze of green, it is magical.

The house (01803 752466; www.nationaltrust.org.uk) is open Saturday–Wednesday Easter–November and weekends in February and March, but is not directly accessible by bus; the 22, 24 and 120 run along the main Brixham–Kingswear road, a 1½-mile walk away.

South of Dartmouth

The South West Coast Path lures you away from the town to the castle, and then along the cliffs to a pretty little shingle beach, Compass Cove, where you can swim. Continue round the cliffs or take the short cut via Little Dartmouth, until you pass the delightfully named cluster of rocks, the Dancing Beggars. Stoke Fleming is the next village then the surprisingly named beach of Blackpool Sands, scene of John Hawley's last battle.

The walk here from Dartmouth is about six miles – but only three by the road. Bus 93 runs hourly back to Dartmouth.

⑫ Blackpool Sands and Gardens

Blackpool Sands (01803 770606; www.blackpoolsands.co.uk) is a deservedly popular privately owned beach. Like Slapton, the 'sands' are actually fine shingle, but there is a sandpit for children with the real stuff. The bay lies framed in a semicircle of woods and green pasture. There are no junk-food outlets here, just the Venus Beach Café, which serves quality food under cover. Toilets, showers, watersports, lifeguards… this is firmly geared towards holiday-makers, and does it extremely well. No dogs allowed in the holiday season.

Behind the beach is a sub-tropical garden of the type that grows so well on Devon's south-sloping shores. Sir Geoffrey Newman, owner of Blackpool Sands, understands the allure of a secret garden: you enter through a green door, overhung with fuchsia. Subtropical plants from the southern hemisphere thrive in this sheltered place, as does native vegetation. The gardens are open from April to the end of September.

Brixham to Dartmouth by sea: a guide for birders

Tony Soper

A pleasure-boat cruise of Devon's south coast from Torbay (Torquay or Brixham) offers a great opportunity to observe seabirds and other wildlife, even if the cruise is for general interest. If you are a birder, don't forget your field guide, and a pair of binoculars is recommended for everyone

As you leave Torbay behind you, the massive limestone cliffs of Berry Head loom on your starboard hand. Perched on the outermost clifftop you'll see the diminutive tower of the highest lighthouse in the British Isles. Tucked in around the corner and behind a few sentinel islets is a stretch of near-vertical cliff, some 200 feet high, pierced by seabird ledges and a fine cave: it's home to a thriving colony of kittiwakes and guillemots. Keep a sharp eye open for a possible peregrine power-diving on a hapless newly fledged chick. Many years ago puffins bred on the cliff slopes here; now we see just the occasional solitary one paddling a few miles offshore. Shags will keep station as you cruise. On a calm day there may be swarms of jellyfish decorating the surface of the sea, there may be the lazy fins of a basking shark cruising for plankton, there may even be a turtle. On a wild day clouds of gannets will be looking for shelter and a shoal of mackerel to indulge their plunge-diving. This open-sea part of the cruise may offer anything from a healthy slice of discomfort to a Mediterranean-style tan.

Dartmouth is guarded by a typically shaped mewstone, a giant lump of rocky cheese, as you approach its entrance. On the exposed seaward side the steep slope is colonised by cormorants, a secret cove is a favoured seal pool and the jungle of sea-kale is home for herring gulls. Great black-backs favour the very top of the island. A chain of rocks, some barely submerged, leads across to the mainland

Your final approach takes you between the much-photographed twin castles of Dartmouth and Kingswear as you enter the sheltered harbour. Now you have the choice of jumping ship to join one of the River Link ferries which will take you up the winding waterway to Totnes; crossing the harbour by way of the Lower Ferry to Kingswear and the steam railway back to Paignton; or getting a quick cream tea and reboarding for the return passage to Brixham. The perfect day.

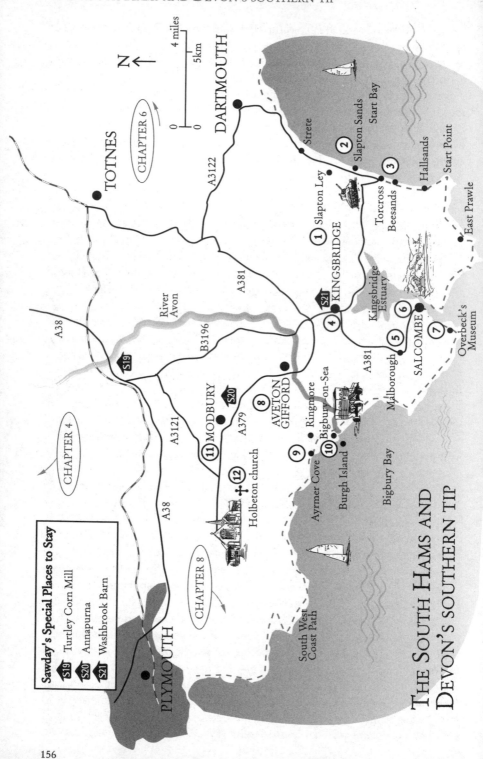

7. THE SOUTH HAMS AND DEVON'S SOUTHERN TIP

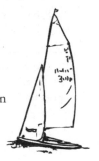

The name **South Hams** probably derived from the Saxon *hamm* which meant peninsula but also a homestead or village. Some take it literally, and there are plenty of piggy references in the coastal landscape here: Pig's Nose, Ham Stone, Gammon Head.

The extreme south of Devon described here has its roots planted firmly in the sea; the coast and all it can offer is the magnet for visitors here, with **Salcombe** its epicentre. From here you can hire a boat and putter around the estuary, select some of the most scenic stretches of the South West Coast Path, or spend the day on some of the prettiest sandy beaches in the county. With sea and sand and endless rock pools to investigate, it's an ideal family destination.

Coming from Dartmouth in the east, the first place of special interest is **Slapton**, with its long beach that played the part of Normandy during the war. But hereafter visitors gravitate south, beneath an imaginary horizontal line drawn through Kingsbridge. Here, in the South Hams, Devon points two knuckles towards Brittany, bifurcated by the estuary up which a weekly steamer used to carry merchandise to and from Kingsbridge, and which is now served by a passenger ferry.

Among a clutch of likeable and highly photogenic villages on the west coast are **Thurlestone** and enchantingly named **Inner Hope**. Finally there's the River Avon, with its trick pronunciation (see page 172), to cross before you reach **Bigbury-on-Sea** and walk or take the sea tractor to **Burgh Island**.

Getting there and around

There is really only one main road in the region (the A379 from Dartmouth to Kingsbridge and on to Plymouth, connecting with the A381 to Malborough and Salcombe). The narrow lanes that link the villages south of this line evolved through foot and hoof traffic and are not designed to transport holidaymakers. If you are visiting the area in July and August you would do well to leave your **car** at home, or at least drive as little as possible. You can access the area by public transport by taking the **train** to Totnes or Plymouth and then **bus** X64 from Totnes to Kingsbridge, the 'capital' of the region, or the 93 from Plymouth to Kingsbridge or Slapton; the X64 also runs from Exeter. From Kingsbridge there are regular buses to Salcombe, and much of the western part of its peninsula. The most satisfying mechanised way of arriving in Salcombe is by ferry from Kingsbridge: the *Rivermaid* runs several times a day from June to October, dependent on the tides (01548 853525).

Public transport

This is not a good area for users of public transport since buses rarely venture south of the A379. When they do, they are utterly delightful, and can be used for bus walks as well as just the pleasure of riding in them. There's a bus from Kingsbridge to Malborough and Hope Cove which gives walkers the opportunity to take the coastal path to Salcombe; the same one runs to Thurlestone, opening up another stretch of coastal path. Full details are given in the relevant sections.

The bus timetable for the area is *South Hams*, which you can pick up at Tourist Information Centres or from www.devon.gov.uk/buses, or contact Traveline (0871 200 2233; www.traveline.info).

With so few buses available, you may need to use taxis if you are without a car. Local firms include **Arrow Cars** Kingsbridge; 01548 856120, **Moonraker Taxis** Malborough; 01548 560231, **John Edwards** Modbury; 01548 830859 or 07967 374502 and **Tim Craig** Holbeton; 01752 830225.

Cycling and walking

A maze of small lanes meander up and down the relentlessly hilly, switchback South Hams, and the gradients can make it tough and slow-going for **cycling**. The National Cycle Network barely covers this area, although it's planned that NCN2 will go from Salcombe to Plymouth. However, the section from Ashprington, south of Totnes, to East Portlemouth is finished. It runs via Blackawton, using quiet lanes.

You can take your bike on the passenger ferry between East Portlemouth and Salcombe, and cycling is the best way of exploring the East Portlemouth prong thoroughly since there's no public transport. A bicycle is also ideal for exploring the other southern lumps and bumps which are isolated between river estuaries connected only by bike-carrying passenger ferries.

Most **walkers** will head for the South West Coast Path and this southern stretch is certainly one of the very finest, being far from a main road yet with enough accessible refreshments to keep body and soul together, and enough accessible beaches, some sandy, to ensure that you carry your swimsuit. The coast path between Thurlestone and Hope Cove is broad and pushchair-friendly, whilst sections by Bolt Head and Soar Mill Cove, and around Prawle, have significant ups and downs. Fewer walkers do the more isolated rugged stretch of the coast path west from Thurlestone, partly because of the lack of public transport. There are no buses until you reach Newton Ferrers, a tough 13 miles or so away. The additional challenge on this part of the path is working out the timing so that you cross the rivers when the ferries are running or, in the case of the Erme, at low tide when you can paddle across. Carry a tide table.

If you prefer to learn more about the area through a guided walk, check out the **South Devon Walking Festival** (01803 861384; www.southdevonwalking festival.co.uk) which takes place in early October and has something for almost everyone.

Walking maps, guides, information and websites

The two-sided OS Explorer map OL20, scale 1:25,000, covers all of this region. For coastal walks generally, see *The South West Coast Path* official guide; www.southwestcoastpath.com, and *Shortish walks: the South Devon Coast* (Bossiney Books). Other useful publications are *Classic Walks in Devon* (Norton Publishing) and *Holiday Times*, a free A3-format magazine listing events in the South Hams (available in most Tourist Information Centres). The Tally Ho bus company lists some good bus walks on www.tallyhocoaches.co.uk, as does www.southdevon aonb.org.uk.

The Slapton area

First impressions are not that exciting: a long stretch of coarse sand/fine shingle and slate on one side and a lagoon on the other. But the interest here is what it *is* rather than what it seems, for not only is **Slapton Ley** one of Devon's most prized nature reserves, but **Slapton Sands** played a pivotal role in World War II.

John Leland, travelling in the mid 16th century, described Slapton as having 'a very large Poole 2 Miles in length. Ther is but a Barre of Sand betwixt the Se and this Poole; the fresch Water drenith into the Se thorough the Sandy Bank, but the Waite of the Fresch Water and Rage of the Se brekith sumtime this Sandy Bank.' And so it is today. The A379 runs along a narrow spit of land between the 'large Poole' and the sea, and is breached from time to time despite modern engineering providing an outlet for the lake water. In 2001 a severe storm destroyed the road, and isolated the village of Torcross and its neighbours for four months. Now Natural England, which shares responsibility for the area with local councils, says that next time may be the last; it's just too expensive to repair.

① Slapton Ley

A hundred years or so ago the Ley was of commercial and sporting interest, providing reeds for thatching, and waterfowl and fish for shooting and angling. When it looked as though it was going the way of so much of Devon's coastal landscape, with holiday development taking precedence over scenery and wildlife, it was bought by the conservationist Herbert Whitley, founder of Paignton Zoo, as a wildlife sanctuary. The Ley, the largest freshwater lake in Devon, is now leased to the Field Studies Council by the Whitley Trust.

The nature reserve is well known amongst bird watchers for its rare species. With luck you could see a bittern or a great crested grebe. There are two bird hides looking out over the reed beds, with information on the species most commonly spotted as well as a check list of recent sightings. For those who like to spot their wildlife while on the move, a trail runs through the reserve, sometimes along boardwalks, with a choice of exit points so you can decide on your preferred length. The maximum, if you want to include Slapton, is about three miles. Starting at the car park at Slapton Bridge, the path runs round the northern shore of the lake, then gives you a choice of two short routes to Slapton or a longer one via Deer Bridge. Watch out for the beautifully carved handrail on the wooden viewing platform during the early part of the walk. The Field Centre runs a variety of guided walks, courses and events: 01548 580685; www.slnnr.org.uk.

You will enjoy **Slapton** far more if you walk into it, rather than try to drive; the narrow road forms a fearsome bottleneck in the summer. It's an attractive village and both its pubs offer a warm welcome. The Chantry Tower dates back to the religious foundation set up in 1372 by Sir Guy de Brian. He bore the standard of Edward III at the siege of Calais, to encourage six priests, a rector, five fellows and four clerks to pray for him and his family. The foundation was dissolved in the Reformation, and the stone of the associated chapel was used to build the house, also known as The Chantry, in whose garden the tower stands. You can't visit the tower, but can see it from outside the pub. It is home to a noisy congregation of jackdaws and herring gulls.

S Kings Arms Strete ☎ 01903 770377 🖰 www.kingsarms-dartmouth.co.uk. Northeast along the coast from Slapton, this Edwardian place is full of delicious smells wafting temptingly from the kitchen; there's a garden, and the views over Start Bay alone justify a visit here.

Queen's Arms ☎ 01548 580800 🖰 www.queensarmsslapton.co.uk. A traditional one-room village hostelry with good honest food, and fish and chips on Friday. It has an intimate walled garden, plus the ultimate prize in Slapton, a car park.

S Tower Inn ☎ 01548 580216 🖰 www.thetowerinn.com. A little grander than the Queen's Arms, with a garden overlooked by the Chantry Tower and complete with wandering cockerel and hens and a rooftop view of Slapton. The 14th-century flower-bedecked building has low beamed rooms and flagstones, and the food is excellent. Parking is awkward.

② Slapton Sands

The 'sands' are not that inviting, being fine shingle so not the sort of stuff you can build sandcastles from. Swimming is 'bloody cold' according to a resident, because the shore shelves steeply so you are quickly out of your depth and the sun has little effect. All in all there are better beaches in the area, though the northern part of the Sands is popular with naturists. It's perfect browsing territory for beach pebbles, with plenty of flat stones good for skimming.

Near the middle car park is a monument presented to the people of South Hams by the US army as a thank-you to the 3,000 villagers who vacated their homes to allow for the military exercises that led up to D-Day (see box opposite).

The Sherman tank at the **Torcross** end is a memorial to the American troops killed during Exercise Tiger; it was retrieved from the sea in 1984 through the tireless efforts of Ken Small, a local hotelier.

Exercise Tiger

In November 1943 the inhabitants of nine villages in the Torcross area were ordered to leave their homes for an indeterminate period. Slapton Sands was similar to a beach in Normandy, codenamed Utah Beach, which would be used for the D-Day landings, and the American troops needed to practise. The locals, however, were told only that the area was needed for 'military purposes'. Just imagine what was being asked of these 3,000 villagers: Torcross, Slapton, Stokenham, Chillington, Frogmore, Sherford, Blackawton, East Allington, and Strete were farming communities, their winter and spring crops had been planted, winter fodder was stored in the barns, and their ration of coal in the shed. They had to decide what to do with their cattle or sheep, and how to move heavy farm machinery. Then there were the churches to worry about. The little village church has always been at the heart of the rural English community, and in those days most villagers will have been churchgoers. Church valuables, including the carved wooden screens, were dismantled and removed to a place of safety, those that couldn't be removed were sandbagged, and in each church was pinned the following notice:

To our Allies of the U.S.A. This church has stood here for several hundred years. Around it has grown a community, which has lived in these houses and tilled these fields ever since there was a church. This church, this churchyard in which their loved ones lie at rest, these homes, these fields are as dear to those who have left them as are the homes and graves and fields which you, our Allies, have left behind you. They hope to return one day, as you hope to return to yours, to find them waiting to welcome them home. They entrust them to your care meanwhile and pray that God's blessing may rest upon us all.
Charles, Bishop of Exeter.

Various exercises were held from March to April, all involving heavy bombardment of the beach area. To replicate as closely as possible the Normandy landings, live ammunition was used. Exercise Tiger took place between 26 and 29 April 1944, as a full rehearsal for Operation Overlord planned for June. The first exercise went without a hitch, but during a routine patrol of the English Channel German E-boats discovered the vessels preparing for the second assault and fired on two ships with torpedoes, setting fire to one with the loss of at least 749 lives. The radio message that could have summoned help in time to save some of them was delayed because a typing error gave the wrong frequency. Accounts suggest that a thousand or so Americans were killed during the months of exercises, some through 'friendly fire'.

Everyone involved in Exercise Tiger was sworn to secrecy; Operation Overlord was imminent and proved to be the beginning of the end of the war. The villagers started to trickle back to their damaged and rat-infested homes a few months later. Some never returned.

Further reading
The American Forces at Salcombe and Slapton during World War Two (Orchard Publications).
Exercise Tiger: the D-Day Practice Landings Tragedies Uncovered by Richard T Bass (Tommies Guides).
The Forgotten Dead by Ken Small (Bloomsbury).
The Invasion before Normandy: Secret Battle of Slapton Sands by Edwin P Hoyt (Scarborough House).
The Land Changed its Face: the Evacuation of the South Hams 1943–44 by Grace Bradbeer (Harbour Books).
Torcross and Slapton Ley: a Pictorial Record (Orchard Publications).

③ From Torcross to Beesands and beyond via the cliff path

This short but varied and scenic walk takes you over the cliffs with good views of Start Point lighthouse, through some woods, and to the long shingle beach at Beesands. The beach is beloved of mackerel fishers, and families seeking seclusion.

Charles Harper, writing at the beginning of the 20th century, described the villagers keeping chickens in upturned decaying boats. 'They are the most trustful cocks and hens in the world, and follow the fishermen into the inn and cottages like dogs.' He goes on to describe the Newfoundland dogs of Beesands, and neighbouring Hall Sands, which were trained to swim out through the surf to meet the incoming fishing boats. The dogs would grab the end of the rope and bring it to the beach so the boats could be hauled on shore.

Harper describes Hall Sands (**Hallsands**) which, when he visited (probably 1905), was beginning the process of falling into the sea. Half of the only inn had already gone 'while the landlady was making tea' and it was only a matter of time before the rest of the village met the same fate. This entirely preventable disaster was caused by the commercial dredging of shingle for the construction industry (Plymouth breakwater), with the result that the beach was about 12 feet lower by the time they stopped in 1902. Without their natural defences, the cottages were exposed to every storm and by 1917 they had almost all gone. You can see what's left of them below the cliff path, but a Hallsands resident reports that two fishermen's cottages remain standing and privately owned: 'No electricity, only kerosene lamps and an outside shower. Water pouring down the chimney on rough days!'

Beyond Hallsands is the lighthouse of **Start Point**, about four miles from Torcross. The name comes from Saxon *steort* which means tail, as for example in redstart.

><><><><

Britannia Beesands ☎ 0845 0550 711 www.britanniashellfish.co.uk. Run by fisherman Nick Hutchings and his wife Anita, this is better described as a shack than a restaurant. It's right on the beach and Nick's recent catches are kept alive in a 'holding pool' so you know the food is totally fresh. You can choose from a wide variety (depending on what's been caught recently), from shellfish to crab and lobster, skate, etc.

S Cricket Inn Beesands ☎ 01548 580215. Very good food (mainly fish) in a capacious restaurant with dog-friendly tables near the bar.

S Pig's Nose Inn East Prawle ☎ 01548 511209 www.pigsnoseinn.co.uk. Good pub food and a lively atmosphere.

St Andrew's Church Beesands. Refreshments every Sunday with the proceeds going to charity.

S The Start Bay Inn Torcross ☎ 01548 580553. Walk here to build up a hearty appetite for outstanding fish and chips at this 14th-century beachside tavern.

East Prawle

Mike Harrison

East Prawle is one of my favourite places. This is the southernmost village in Devon, far from anywhere and approached by miles of narrow lanes. Prawle Point is a significant corner on the coast where there is a daily watch on shipping (which visitors can often join – there is a small museum here, and sometimes access to the main lookout room). The village is perched some 370 feet above sea level, and six paths radiate like spokes to different parts of the coast offering a great selection of short or long circular walks. Within a short range you can explore soaring cliffs, ragged rocky headlands, secluded coves and picture-perfect small sandy beaches, conveniently facing south. As a taster try Gammon Head with adjacent Maceley Cove (low tide best) or walk further to other beaches.

East Prawle village also offers useful facilities including the Pig's Nose pub, an excellent shop/café, parking, toilets and basic camping. There is the charm of old buildings and a slow-changing history with a real sense of community. However, before making the pilgrimage be warned that amenities tend to the simple end of the spectrum – many are caught out with the frugal opening hours – and the magnificent views are only achieved by walking. It's rarely level and of course the rain often lashes in from the ocean. Authentic Devon, in other words.

Kingsbridge, Salcombe and area: the southern tip of Devon

This most southerly part of Devon is the honey pot of the South Hams, with all the attractions that holiday-makers need: sandy beaches, boats, fishing, walking, and the mildest climate in Devon.

④ Kingsbridge

These days the only shipping that calls here is the *Rivermaid* which plies the estuary between Kingsbridge and Salcombe, but in the early 20th century a 'market packet' steamer ran between Kingsbridge and Plymouth, calling at Salcombe on the way. Limestone was brought by ship from Plymouth, and its by-product, quicklime, produced in the limekilns that are still to be found between Kingsbridge and the sea.

Kingsbridge retains a lot of charm, its steep Fore Street the very antithesis of Clone Britain with varied and interesting shops. There's also a museum, a cinema, and regular happenings throughout the year. I found the tourist information centre at The Quay (01548 853195; www.kingsbridgeinfo.co.uk) exceptionally helpful, and they publish a comprehensive (free) guide to the area which lists all the major events and attractions. A farmers' market is held on The Quay on the first and third Saturday of the month.

The **Cookworthy Museum** is a restored 17th-century grammar school, still in use in the early 1900s, which gives insights into what life was like in Kingsbridge and area over the centuries. It's named after William Cookworthy, who discovered china clay in Cornwall and went on to develop porcelain manufacturing in England.

⑤ Malborough

This must be one of the most frequently misspelled village names in Devon. It's an attractive village with a good number of thatched cottages, including one painted an eye-popping blue, and at least two pubs. The large church, with its spire, dominates the view from miles around and makes a handy landmark for walkers. I found it too austere for my taste, but there are some nice touches inside such as the informative map of the village drawn by a member of the WI and a floor-stone in memory of William Clark with a misspelling and some letters seemingly inserted as an afterthought.

Malborough's post office sells OS maps and a leaflet *Footpaths in Malborough Parish* which details all the car parks in the area as well as a selection of footpaths connecting to the most glorious section of the South West Coast Path between Bolt Head and Bolt Tail. Thus car drivers can avoid the hassle of parking in Salcombe.

⑥ Salcombe

Like Dartmouth, Salcombe deserves to be entered on foot or by water. The views of the boat-flecked harbour and the opulent houses clinging to the wooded hillside should not fight with negotiating hairpin bends and trying to find somewhere to park. If you do drive in, use the park-and-ride facility on the A381.

Walkers can park in the vicinity of Malborough and take the coast path to South Sands and then the ferry into town, perhaps stopping at Overbeck's Museum on the way, and returning to the car by bus (see Bus Walk).

Salcombe *is* boats. The town has always looked seawards, building its prosperity from fishing and maritime trade and, in recent times, from hobby sailors. Most people who come here regularly love messing about in boats, and just about everyone will take an estuary cruise or at least one of the ferries, to either Kingsbridge, East Portlemouth or South Sands. Do-it-yourself sailors can hire a sailing boat, a self-drive motor boat, a rowing boat or a kayak. As befits this book, there is a speed limit in the estuary, so forget about hiring a speed boat. And it's actually not a real estuary since there's no river; it's a flooded valley, or 'ria'.

You can also learn to sail. The Island Cruising Club runs courses for all ages, either living aboard the old Mersey Ferry, *Egremont*, or ashore, going out daily for tuition on a variety of dinghies. Typically the courses run for a week but can be adjusted to need.

If you want something a little extra with your estuary cruise, try the Eco-Estuary trips run by Whitestrand Boat Hire. I went out with Anna, who runs the company with her husband Chris. 'My degree is in biology, and then I went to work as a researcher at the Natural History Unit in Bristol, so it's wonderful to be able to bring some of my knowledge to this business.' Wildlife here does not come when it's called, so although I knew there was a small chance of seeing grey seals or even porpoises, I was not too disappointed when they didn't appear. I was happy to look at herons, egrets and shags, and the smartly dressed shelducks which, surprisingly, nest in old rabbit burrows. And to learn what lay under the water – huge fan mussels, for instance, and even sea horses. Their relatives, the pipe fish, are sometimes found in rock pools, along with cushion stars, brittle stars and anemones. 'Did you know,' asked Anna, 'that limpets move around but always find their way back "home" by following their own pheromone trail?' No, I didn't. 'And that barnacles have the largest sex organ in relation to their size in the animal kingdom?' Um, yes.

Anna and Chris also follow the guidelines of The Green Blue programme (www.thegreenblue.org.uk) to minimise their impact on the estuary. The town itself is a maze of little streets, alleys and tourist shops, and has a good **Maritime Museum** (open summer only). This and the Overbeck's Museum have photos of the old sailing ships, built in the 19th century, both in Kingsbridge and Salcombe. Many of these are of the schooners, designed for speed, which carried pineapples from the Bahamas and oranges and lemons from the Azores, for the markets in London. However, ships had been built in the estuary, on any convenient foreshore, for centuries.

The remains of Salcombe Castle, **Fort Charles**, still guard the entrance to the estuary. It was the last Royalist stronghold in the West Country and was under siege in early 1646 when the Cromwellian forces during the Civil War set up a battery on Rickham Common, on the opposite shore.

A ferry trip from Salcombe: East Portlemouth and Mill Bay

Across the water, at **East Portlemouth**, are some beautiful sandy coves. Most of the sand is covered at high tide so a tide table is handy if you want to spend time here building sand castles.

One of the most rewarding adventures, possible only at low spring tides in the early afternoon, is to walk along the foreshore all the way to a sand bar called 'the Hipple' at the harbour's entrance. This can be exposed for a couple of hours and provides opportunities for all the family; wave jumping, body boarding – and a wonderful place for a picnic! If the tide is not quite low enough there is access from the cliff path which provides some lovely walking whatever the tide, with an easy circular trip if you return via the 'high path' from Gara Rock.

On the way you will cross **Mill Bay**, where the Americans were based during World War II, bringing a sparkle to the eyes of local girls. They had a workshop there, and the remains of the big concrete slipway are still on the beach. During the preparations for D-Day, in 1944, the estuary was full of American ships, with landing craft concealed under the trees along the shores of the estuary. Over in Salcombe, Normandy Way and the Normandy Pontoon are named to commemorate their embarkation.

Back at the ferry a cannonball was very recently discovered in the foundations of a wall; maybe the Royalists spotted a Cromwellian platoon queueing for the ferry!! It is now proudly on display in the Village Hall.

Stop at the **Venus Café** for refreshment before climbing the steps behind the ferry landing to the village. As you go through the five-barred gate at the top of the path, look to your left and enjoy one of the most spectacular views. The estuary lies below you, right up to Kingsbridge. On a fine day the southern fringe of Dartmoor can be clearly seen. Pass the cottages on your right and, at the top of the hill, you will find the 12th-century church of St Winwaloe (St Guénolé), whose followers came over from the Abbey at Landévennec in Brittany. He is also patron saint of at least six churches in Cornwall. The medieval screen, with its panels of saints and beautiful carving, was restored in the 1930s.

There is no shop in East Portlemouth, but pubs can be found at **East Prawle** (see box on page 163) and at South Pool, both within walking distance.

Basics

Salcombe Tourist Information Centre Market Street, Salcombe ☏ 01548 843927 ⚲ www.salcombeinformation.co.uk.

Island Cruising Club ☏ 01548 531176⚲ www.icc-salcombe.co.uk. Sailing holidays and instruction from the age of 5 upwards.

Salcombe Dinghy Sailing Whitestrand Quay ☏ 01548 511548 ⚲ www.salcombedinghysailing.co.uk. Dinghy hire for experienced sailors or tuition for beginners.

Singing Paddles Kingsbridge ☏ 07754 426633 ⚲ www.singingpaddles.co.uk. Canoeing and kayaking tuition.

South Sands Sailing South Sands Quay ☏ 01548 843451 ⚲ www.southsandssailing.co.uk. Sailing and kayak tuition and rentals. Taster trips on catamarans. Discount offered if staying at the nearby youth hostel.

Tallyho buses ⚲ www.tallyhocoaches.co.uk.

Whitestrand Boat Hire Whitestrand Quay, Salcombe ☏ 01548 843818 ⚲ www.whitestrandboathire.co.uk. Self-drive boat hire, from rowing boats to a wide variety of motor boats, plus fishing trips and estuary cruises including the 90-minute Eco-Estuary tour.

Food and drink

Dick and Wills Fore St ☏ 01548 843408 ⚲ www.dickandwills.co.uk. A favourite with discriminating locals, this waterside brasserie is under new ownership (2009) and 'serves great food, with a New England style feel inside'. Go here for a special treat.

SP Fortescue Arms East Allington ☏ 01548 521215⚲ www.fortescue-arms.co.uk. East Allington is a village off the A381, a few miles north of Kingsbridge, so if you're heading for Salcombe at lunchtime, or are looking for a real treat for dinner, it's worth the detour. Run by Werner Rott (Austrian) and Tom Kendrick (Canadian), its food is well above average; a real treat, in fact.

SP Millbrook Inn South Pool ☏ 01548 531581 ⚲ www.millbrookinnsouthpool.co.uk. Anna, from Whitestrand Boat Hire, says that this pub in South Pool, at the end of the southeast prong of the estuary, is accessible at high tide by boat. 'It's always magic on a summer's evening, and the lanes there are perfect for seeing glow worms and bats in late evening in July/August.' If you haven't a boat it can also be reached by road.

Salcombe Yawl Sandwich Shop off Fore St ☏ 01548 842143. Good crab sandwiches.

Venus Café East Portlemouth ☏ 01548 843558 ⚲ www.venuscompany.co.uk. Delightful location overlooking the estuary, close to the ferry. Whenever possible they use local and environmentally friendly produce.

SP Victoria Inn Fore St ☏ 01548 842604. Busy little town-centre pub near the water's edge, with generous portions of bar food that includes a daily fish special.

Bus walk: Inner Hope to Salcombe

This walk is around seven miles and takes you along some of the most dramatic coastal scenery in south Devon, much of it owned by the National Trust. The bus trip, on the glorious 162 operated by Tallyho, is as scenic and interesting as the walk.

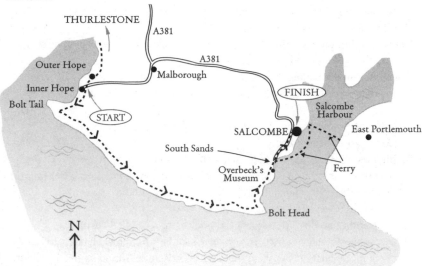

Park at Kingsbridge or Malborough and take the 162 bus to Inner Hope. The early morning departure goes straight from Kingsbridge to Malborough before passing through Galmpton to Hope, but the early afternoon one takes the little lanes through the villages of Thurlestone (see *Bus walk* on page 172) and South Milton before Malborough. It was full of locals when I took it, chatting happily with the driver whom they obviously knew well. He paid scant regard to bus stops, dropping them off at their homes, or in one case the pub.

Of the two Hopes, Inner Hope is the pretty one, and the view from the bus terminus overlooking the bay will make your spirits soar. There are thatched cottages hugging the curve in the road, a steep hill down to the sea, the Sun Bay hotel in case you decide just to potter in the area, and a forested cliff where the trees have been forced into retreat by the wind, creating a natural amphitheatre. Then it's simply a case of abandoning Hope (sorry) and following the coastal path to Salcombe, via Bolt Tail where you can admire the view towards Burgh Island. Bolt Head is six miles away past splendid scenery.

Around Bolt Head and Sharpitor the landscape really surpasses itself, with craggy rocks high above you and poking out from the sea below. Sailing boats indicate that that you are nearing Salcombe and soon you'll have a spectacular view of the harbour surrounded by wooded hills. Look out for signs to **Overbeck's Museum and garden**, a National Trust property, which offers a well-earned break in its tea room (and a free cup of tea if you arrive without a car) as well as an eclectic collection and a beautiful garden (see page 170).

From Overbeck's you descend steeply to the South Sands beach from where there is a ferry to Salcombe, with a café by the quay. Or you can walk into town along the road.

Buses back to Kingsbridge via Malborough run hourly until the early evening or, if the tides are right, you could get the ferry to Kingsbridge.

Some like it hot

If you use your satnav to take you from Exeter to Salcombe, you'll follow increasingly narrow lanes until you reach the village of Loddiswell. Shortly before the village a sign on the left announces 'South Devon Chilli Farm'. Stop and take a look – it's a great place. And unique.

Jason Nickels and his business partner Steve Waters started the chilli farm in 2003. How did someone who used to work for a large London travel agent end up growing chillies in Devon? 'Well, because I'd travelled a lot I had a taste for hot chillies, and we just realised that there was a gap in the market'. They began by renting some land down the road, and planted a few chillies. The farm was an immediate success (I noticed an *Entrepreneur of the Year* certificate in the shop) so they were able to buy more land as well as an orchard, which will make them self-sufficient in apples for the chilli apple jellies and other products. 'We both like gardening, but neither of us has any horticultural training. But chillies are easy, they grow fast and don't need any special care'. Except, I noted, from snails. Jason pulled a few from his nursery plants. 'Snails can't taste the hotness in a chilli' he explained, 'and they go for the fruit rather than the leaves. Apparently there's calcium in the centre of the chillies which they need for their shells'.

There are around 70 varieties of chilli at the farm, with perhaps 6,000 plants growing in greenhouses and poly tunnels. Visitors are welcome to visit the show tunnel and see the different varieties. The shop sells plants and chilli products including chilli chocolate, made on the premises, which is addictive after the initial shock. 'We do a good mail order service, especially in seeds, but we don't mail out plants – but people come from all over the country to the shop'. The plants are labelled in detail: where they come from, what they look like when mature (so the decorative side) and – most important – the degree of hotness. The very hottest is Bhut Jolokia from India, and there are plenty of mild ones with the encouragement 'a good plant for inquisitive children'.

South Devon Chilli Farm, Wigford Cross, Loddiswell, Devon TQ7 4DX; 01548 550782; www.sdcf.co.uk. The shop, selling a huge range of chilli products from sauces and chutneys to jellies and soft drinks – and of course the famous chocolate – is open year round except for weekends from January to Easter. The best months to visit are September and October, when the chillies are ripe.

⑦ Overbeck's Museum

Otto Overbeck was an eccentric chemist of Dutch ancestry, and an insatiable collector. His former house (01548 842893) is full of objects collected during his travels, a maritime room with model ships, and a mini natural-history museum with cases of mounted butterflies, beetles, stuffed animals including an armadillo, and a monitor lizard's foot. And there are cases and cases of birds' eggs. In 2006 the museum received a mysterious parcel. It contained a little bustard's egg, stolen by a teenager in 1963 and returned by the remorseful adult who had rediscovered it when clearing his late parents' home.

Pride of place is given to the Overbeck Rejuvenator, a rather alarming collection of cables, combs and cylinders which passed an electric current from the head to the affected part of the body. It could cure most ills, Overbeck claimed, and its rejuvenation qualities were proved by photographs of the young-looking inventor: 'My age is 64 years, but I feel more like a man of 30'. His book, *Overbeck's Electronic Theory of Life*, was published in 1931.

One room is dominated by a polython, a sort of giant music box, and the predecessor to the gramophone. I requested the *Hallelujah Chorus* and considering it's all done by mechanically plucking metal struts it sounded pretty impressive.

The sub-tropical gardens are exceptionally beautiful, dropping down the hillside in a series of terraces, each with its own character and plants, and with lovely views over the Salcombe Estuary.

The easiest means of getting here is by the ferry to South Sands.

River Avon, Bigbury-on-Sea and Burgh Island

It's confusing, to say the least, that this small river that rises in Dartmoor has the same name as the much larger one that flows through Bath and Bristol. A few hundred years ago it was called the Awne or Aume, and local people still pronounce it Awne. When and why it changed its name is open to conjecture.

The river is very scenic, with sandy shores, gnarled oak trees overhanging the eroded banks, plenty of birdlife, and quite a few boats. There's a marked Avon Estuary Walk which was misdescribed in an old guidebook (admittedly 1980s) as following the edge of the river at low tide from Aveton Gifford right down to Bigbury. Nice idea, but after floundering around in sinking mud and slippery rocks for an hour we threw in the towel and drove to Bigbury. However, the walk does indeed exist and is well signposted once you accept the notion that it mostly follows paths high above the river.

To do justice to this area you need a tide table, both to enjoy the tidal road at Aveton Gifford and know whether you will walk to Burgh Island or take the sea tractor. The only bus into Bigbury-on-Sea is on Fridays, and the timing doesn't work out for a bus walk. So all walks need to take circular route.

Wrecks in Bigbury Bay

In February 1760, the tall, 90-gun warship *Ramillies* set sail from Plymouth to join the channel fleet blockading the French sea ports. But then a fierce storm blew up and forced the elderly ship to drop back to repair her leaking hull. The storm worsened, blowing her eastward up the Devon coast; her old timbers creaked and her captain feared for her survival. Passing a small island in the darkness, he identified it as Rame Head just west of Plymouth, where he could run for shelter into Plymouth Sound. Too late, he realised the storm had blown him further up the coast: in fact it was Burgh Island in Bigbury Bay, which offered no shelter but instead a line of sheer, forbidding cliffs. He attempted to drop anchor, but the cables fouled and the anchors could not hold the pitching vessel in the huge seas. She lurched landward and smashed into the cliffs just beyond Bolt Tail.

For her 700-odd men there was little hope in the churning water. Only 26 survived. The *Ramillies* broke up, and one survivor described her as 'drove into such small pieces that it appears like piles of firewood'. With the coming of dawn, watchers on shore saw Hope Bay littered with bodies, and more drifted in on every tide.

Bounty from the sea was a bonus in a hard existence, and word of the tragedy spread quickly. Even while the bodies were being gathered in, looters were at work. It's said that several of the old houses in the area still incorporate timbers and other fittings from the *Ramillies*.

She was by no means the only ship to end her days beneath the waters of Bigbury Bay: the remains of the *Chanteloupe* lie near Thurlestone Rock, where she was wrecked in 1772 with a cargo of rum, Madeira wine, sugar and coffee from the West Indies. There was only one survivor. A sad story tells of a woman washed ashore wearing finery and many jewels, presumably in an attempt to keep them safe when abandoning ship, who may have survived the wreck but had then been killed on the beach for her riches. Even a century later, it was said that a local woman still had a piece of her fine muslin apron. The victim's identity was never known and no murder was proved, but villagers had strong suspicions. Earlier, in 1588, during the rout of the Spanish Armada, the *San Pedro el Major* had gone down with the loss of 40 lives. Tin ingots from a wreck possibly dating as far back as the Iron Age (although this is unverified) have been found in the estuary of the River Erme, and a wreck dated to 1671 lies nearby. Others sank in the 19th and 20th centuries. But it's the *Ramillies*, with her dramatic end and her tragic loss of life, that features most strongly in the area's history.

JB

⑧ Aveton Gifford

The pleasant village of Aveton Gifford (pronounced Awton Jifford), with its Fisherman's Rest pub (01548 550284), is a convenient starting point for riverside walks including the 7½-mile Avon Estuary walk described (along with lots of other walks in the area) on www.southdevonaonb.org.uk, which uses paths along both banks and the ferry across the river mouth. If it's low tide you can walk along the tidal road from Aveton Gifford which brings you eye to eye with swans, and is slippery with seaweed. There's a sign at the far end: 'Caution: these fish are lesser spotted Amazonian piranha. Do not feed by hand.' Yes, the water covers the road at high tide and piranhas abound. If you are beginning the walk here and continuing down the west side of the estuary to Bigbury-on-Sea, keep a keen eye out for a turning where the path leaves the shore and turns right up some concrete steps. We went straight on into ever-deepening mud, as had a fair number of other people judging by the footprints.

Bus walk: Aveton Gifford to Thurlestone

This four- to five-mile walk takes you down the well-marked Avon Estuary Walk, following the eastern bank of the river to Bantham and then to Thurlestone along the coastal path.

Park in Kingsbridge and take bus 93 to Aveton Gifford; there's a regular summer service from around 09.00, though not on Sunday. Walk down to the main roundabout (where you can park if you prefer this free car park to Kingsbridge) and follow the main road in the direction of Kingsbridge. Just after the bridge there's a small road to the right which leads to the signed Avon Estuary Walk. After that it's quite straightforward until you reach **Bantham**, but if you need detailed directions you'll find them on the Tallyho website. At Bantham, where the Sloop Inn (01548 560489) can provide a welcome pub break, you have a choice: either follow the South West Coast Path, hugging the coast until you see **Thurlstone's** famous pierced sea rock, then head up to the village, or take a short cut across the golf course along a signed public footpath. Your choice probably depends on how much time you have to catch the 162 bus back to Kingsbridge; it stops outside the village shop and there's a pub nearby. The last bus leaves late afternoon and takes a scenic hour (nearly) to reach Kingsbridge, whilst others take a mere 15 minutes.

⑨ Ayrmer Cove and Ringmore

Ayrmer Cove is a beautiful secluded cove with enticing tide pools, flanked by craggy silvery-grey cliffs. It's owned by the National Trust so utterly unspoiled (apart from a surprising amount of litter when I was there) and is also only accessible on foot which keeps the crowds away. The cove can be visited using the car park at Ringmore, making a short but steep circular walk. Descend to the beach down Smugglers Lane, and return along a section of the coastal path towards Bigbury-on-Sea before heading back to Ringmore via a footpath; or you can park in Bigbury and make a day of it.

In either case, take the opportunity to visit one of the region's prettiest villages, **Ringmore**, and its Journey's End Inn. This is a classic Devon village with lots of thatch and tall, crooked chimneys. The church has a funny little spire plonked in the middle of the tower like an afterthought. If the name of the pub sounds familiar to theatre-goers it's not surprising: the playwright R C Sherriff wrote his play in the 1920s while staying there, and the pub was named after it. In its colourful past the inn was thick with smugglers and they say there was a false wall behind which their booty was stashed.

More innocently, the pub hit the headlines by nurturing a piglet called Incredible. Born prematurely just after the war, Incredible's dad was a champion, and the pub's owner was not prepared to let him die like his siblings. During his infancy he consumed three bottles of brandy mixed with glucose and milk, and was kept snug by the Journey's End stove. He flourished but there was, for a while, a downside: he was addicted to alcohol and refused his unfortified feed.

If coming from Bigbury-on-Sea, take the coastal path through the Challaborough Holiday Park and keep walking along the coastal path to the blessed seclusion of Ayrmer Cove, then up Smugglers Lane to Ringmore. From there you could extend the walk to Bigbury (and its pub), visit the church (see below) and then pick up the Avon Estuary Walk back to Bigbury-on-Sea. Or take the shorter route from Ringmore to Bigbury-on-Sea. Either way you will be walking along a section of road leading down to the bay which gets busy in the summer.

⑩ Bigbury-on-Sea and Burgh Island

The names Bigbury and Burgh both derive from the original name of the island, Borough. This seems to have been in use at least until the early 20th century, perhaps later. Almost as old is the general disapproval of Bigbury-on-Sea by visitors looking for 'unspoilt Devon'. Writing in 1907 the author of *The South Devon Coast*, Charles Harper, describes the estuary thus:

Wide stretch the sands at ebb, but they are not so wide but that the prints of footsteps have disfigured them pretty thoroughly; for where the land slopes down to the shore in grassy fields, the Plymouth people have built bungalows, and are building more. Burr, or Borough, Island is tethered to the mainland at ebb by this nexus of sand. It is in these circumstances a kind of St Michael's Mount, and like it again in that it once owned a chapel dedicated to St Michael. The chapel disappeared in the lang syne, and when the solitary public-house ceased business, civilisation and Borough Island wholly parted company.

Let me state straight away that I don't share the disapproval of **Bigbury-on-Sea**. When I was there on a sunny(ish) July day the broad sands were full of children playing and their parents relaxing. Across the water at **Bantham** there were black specks of surfers on the waves. Everyone was having a thoroughly good time, and that's what a car-accessible beach is all about. It's also a beautiful location, with secluded bays within walking distance for those of a more solitary nature. If you decide this is the time to learn how to **surf**, check out the South Devon Discovery Surf School (07813 63962; www.discoverysurf.com).

The comment that 'Borough Island' has 'wholly parted company with civilisation' is particularly ironic given that the Devon's most exclusive hotel is here, along with the once-closed pub which now does a thriving business serving the numerous visitors who stroll across the sand to the island or take the historic sea tractor there.

Burgh Island

When I started planning this book I was in two minds as to whether to include Burgh Island. A hotel that can cost as much as £600 per night (all inclusive) seemed the antithesis of Go Slow. But I thought I ought to see it for myself and I absolutely loved it! And it is as true to the spirit of this book as anywhere listed because to stay at the Burgh Island Hotel you must step back in time, to the 1930s, when life was indeed much slower.

First, some history. **The Pilchard Inn** has been serving ale to visitors, on and off, since 1395. In its smuggling heyday there was supposedly a tunnel running from a cave on the beach where Tom Crocker, the king of smugglers, hauled his booty to the pub where it could be safely stored. Apart from a few fishermen's cottages, the first accommodation on the island was a wooden summer house built by a famous music-hall artist, George Chirgwin, who bought the island in the late 19th century as a retreat from his adoring fans. Known in those non-PC times as 'The white-eyed Kaffir' he performed in black greasepaint with a white diamond around one eye. The summer house is still there in the grounds of the hotel, and is now used as a staff house.

The **hotel** was built in 1929 by Archibald Nettlefold, who bought the island in 1896 and commissioned the architect Matthew Dawson to design him a 'Great White Palace'. Less was known in those days about the effects of severe weather on a steel and concrete building – corrosion of the steel has brought many problems to subsequent owners. But that was to be in the future. Until the war, the luxurious hotel drew the rich and famous from all over Britain. Among its visitors were Amy Johnson, Agatha Christie (who wrote *And Then There Were None* here), Noel Coward, Winston Churchill, and royalty: the Mountbattens stayed here, as did the Prince of Wales with Wallis Simpson. The hotel closed in 1955 but continued as self-catering accommodation. New owners from 1985 to 2001 ran it again as a hotel, but with little investment, so when Deborah Clark and Tony Orchard bought it in 2001 it took years gradually to restore it to its full Art-Deco-style glory, and make Burgh Island itself a visitor-friendly place.

What is so special about the hotel these days is not just that the place itself is in the 1920s style, but that everything about it is in period. So, for instance, there are no TVs in the bedrooms (although one has been allowed into the lounge) and the library only has books, mainly Penguin paperbacks with the classic orange and maroon covers, dating from that era. The background music is, of course, 1930s, and guests dress for dinner as they would in its heyday. That means black tie. 'You should never worry that you might be overdressed, as this is simply impossible' states the information leaflet. If your budget doesn't run to staying here, the restaurant is open to non residents for Sunday lunch, and in the evenings providing the dress code is observed.

Much of the island is open to non-guests, so the walk across the causeway – or more fun, crossing by sea tractor at high tide – is recommended. The view from the top of the island is stunning; even the cliffs around Ayrmer Cove seem to be in the Art Deco style.

Darren the Forager

Darren Dickinson has an unusual job. He's a forager, and regularly supplies the Burgh Island hotel with wild food.

'My interest began when I met my partner, who is from the Czech Republic. They have a culture of foraging which we really don't have in this country. Then I met Connor and realised that there was a market for foraged food, and I began to take it seriously. My main foods are mushrooms – chanterelles, ceps, hedgehog fungi, and some other unusual ones – and sea greens such as sea beets, sea lettuce [which is the 'crispy seaweed' served in Chinese restaurants] and sea kale. Those are the mainstay, although I may also gather fruits such a bilberries and blackberries, and some flowers are good too. Gorse blossoms can be eaten and the flowers of sea kale are like little nuggets of nectar. But mushrooms are my main source of free food. I don't go for the field mushrooms because they're too similar to commercial ones; I like to get down on my hands and knees and seek out the more challenging ones, like chanterelles. I remember one time I met a Russian woman with three children, carrying a basket of about three kilos of chanterelles. It was on one of my usual places so I was determined not to be beaten. I was crawling around under rhododendrons in the rain but I managed to find two kilos.

Mostly there's very little competition for foraging, but eastern Devon's a problem because of Hugh Fearnley-Whittingstall. He uses a lot of wild foods and has helpers to do the foraging and also hosts foraging days.'

Is he ever tempted to trespass? I asked. 'Well, I must admit that once I did pop into a garden for some particularly alluring red-cracking bolete. But I knocked on the door first and there was no reply.'

What's the greatest allure? 'Foraging is, in many ways, a getaway from day-to-day life. It gives you an extra appreciation of the countryside and the elements. A rainy day is as good as a sunny one because of what nature can yield. I think it's our harvesting instinct coming to the fore. And you only pick what you need because you can return next week. And the following season. It's just one big treasure hunt.'

Burgh Island Hotel Burgh Island ✆ 01548 810514 ⊕ www.burghisland.com.
Wonderful food!

S♥ Pilchard Inn Burgh Island. Owned by the Burgh Island Hotel, so same phone and website. It's age and history is evident everywhere. Tiny bar – punters queue at the door – cheery service, simple bar food (sandwiches etc). Gets very busy in the summer.

Modbury and area

⑪ Modbury

Modbury has become known nationwide and beyond for being the first plastic-bag-free town in Britain. They're not banned, but there is a charge for them so people think before asking for one. You can buy the special Modbury bag in most shops. It's a pleasant town, with a good selection of shops, and an exceptionally helpful Tourist Information Centre.

South of Modbury is a network of steep, narrow lanes ambling down to the coast, then turning around because they're blocked by the unbridged River Erme. This is the attraction for walkers or cyclists. To the east of the river are **Kingston** and **Ringmore** (described earlier), with paths and lanes running down to meet the South West Coast Path. At low tide it's possible to wade across the river using the old ford. Unless it has been raining heavily this should be only knee deep and more of a paddle than a wade.

Tourist Information Centre 5 Modbury Court ✆ 01548 830159
⊕ www.modbury.org.uk.

Food and drink

Bistro 35 35 Church St ✆ 01548 831273. Recommended for intimate dinners.

Crab Pot Café 4 Poundwell St, Chene Court ✆ 01548 831647
⊕ www.thecrabpot.co.uk. The best seafood in Modbury. Unlicensed so bring your own wine.

Top o' the Steps 5 Church St ✆ 01548 830072. Gift shop and coffee room. Recommended for coffee and light lunches.

White Hart Hotel Church St ✆ 01548 831561⊕ www.whitehart-inn.co.uk. Good for early family dining.

⑫ Holbeton church

This appears in Simon Jenkins' *England's Thousand Best Churches*, so any Jenkins devotee will want to see it, although it's quite a way from the main A379 route to Plymouth and the 94 bus only comes once a day. What makes it remarkable is that it's an example of Victorian restoration that has enhanced a church rather than spoiled it. The restoration was done by J D Sedding in the 1880s and is typical of the Arts and Crafts movement. The elaborate lychgate and porch and doors give you an idea of what is to come, and my impression on entering was that someone had gone wild with a chisel. Every possible surface of stone or wood is carved. The stone pulpit is dense with apostles, vine leaves, and ears of wheat. The bench-ends are a tangle of flora and fauna, and the screen is so intricate that it needs concentration to take it all in. It's beautifully done but, to me, lacks the surprises and primitive appeal found in older churches; realism is everywhere, with creatures and plants correct in every detail so leaving little to speculation.

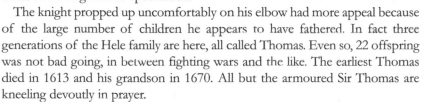

The knight propped up uncomfortably on his elbow had more appeal because of the large number of children he appears to have fathered. In fact three generations of the Hele family are here, all called Thomas. Even so, 22 offspring was not bad going, in between fighting wars and the like. The earliest Thomas died in 1613 and his grandson in 1670. All but the armoured Sir Thomas are kneeling devoutly in prayer.

The church is perched on a hillside overlooking the village, its 120-foot steeple heralding its presence as you descend the suicidally steep hill. The views from the graveyard down to the Erme valley towards Mothercombe are splendid and all in all it's worth the diversion.

The Prayer Book Rebellion

As part of the Protestant reforms instigated under Edward VI, the familiar prayer book in Latin was declared illegal and, from Whit Sunday 1549, churches in England were required to adopt the new *Book of Common Prayer* in English. Resistance to this was particularly strong in Devon and Cornwall, as people saw their traditional methods of worship under threat. At Sampford Courtenay (near Okehampton) parishioners likened the English prayer book to a 'Christmas game' and persuaded their priest to retain the Latin version; the authorities moved in to enforce the change and in the consequent fracas a local man was stabbed with a pitchfork.

Villagers in their thousands, generally armed with no more than farm implements and staves, then rose in support and marched to Exeter, demanding the withdrawal of the English version. They were no match for the well-armed military force sent to quell them: more than 1,000 died at Crediton, 900 at Clyst St Mary, 300 at Fenny Bridges and 1,300 in a final stand at Sampford Courtenay. The militia continued into Cornwall; by the time the rebels were crushed, some 4,000 from both counties had died – and to little purpose, as when Edward's half-sister Mary (a devout Catholic) succeeded him in 1553 she re-legalised the Latin version anyway.

JB

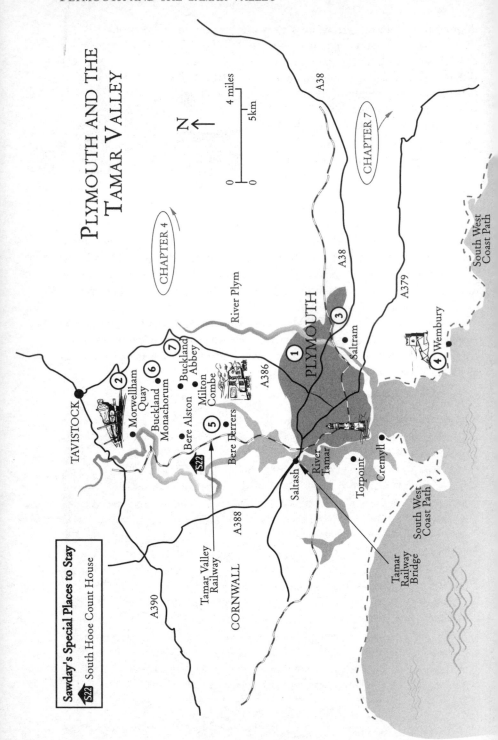

PLYMOUTH AND THE TAMAR VALLEY

CHAPTER 4

CHAPTER 7

N

4 miles

5km

A38

A38

A379

South West
Coast Path

River Plym

PLYMOUTH

Saltram

Wembury

①

③

④

A386

Buckland
Abbey

⑦

Milton
Combe

Morwellham
Quay

Buckland
Monachorum

⑥

②

Bere Alston

⑤

Bere Ferrers

S22

TAVISTOCK

Saltash

River
Tamar

Torpoint

Cremyll

South West
Coast Path

Tamar
Railway
Bridge

A388

Tamar Valley
Railway

CORNWALL

A390

Sawday's Special Places to Stay

S22 South Hooe Count House

8. PLYMOUTH AND THE TAMAR VALLEY

Plymouth in the last century was a poor village inhabited by fishermen. It is now so increased in buildings and population, that it may be reckoned among the best cities of England...This great advantage it derives from the capaciousness and convenience of a large bay, which, extending itself inland between two promontories, not only admits ships to a tranquil and secure sheltering place, but conveys them with the tide, which is here very powerful, into two other bays still further inland, being the spacious channels of two rivers.
Cosmo III, Grand Duke of Tuscany 1669, as recorded by Count L Magalotti.

More than 400 years before the Duke's appreciation of Plymouth, one of the 'spacious channels' he mentions, the River Tamar, was carrying tin, lead and silver ores seaward from the mines on and around Dartmoor. Then copper was discovered and, by the 19th century, the Tamar valley was Europe's largest source of copper ore. Visiting the peaceful Tamar valley today, it's hard to believe that for a short while Morwellham Quay was England's busiest port. Plymouth, on the other hand, has 'increased in buildings and population' still more, and the Elizabethan seafarers who once knew every nook and cranny would have a hard time finding their way around. It has one of the most spectacular estuarine positions of any British city, and there's plenty both here and in the river valley for visitors to enjoy.

Getting there and around

By car and public transport
The A38 links Plymouth and the surrounding area to both Cornwall and Exeter. Plymouth has **rail** connections from most parts of Britain, and regular direct daytime services from London. From Exeter, sit on the left-hand side for a beautiful stretch along the shore of the Exe estuary. Locally, the Tamar Valley line covers the 15 miles between Plymouth and Gunnislake. Countrywide **buses** and long-distance National Express **coaches** serve Plymouth, often with a change at Exeter, and there's a good network of local buses. Try to avoid lingering at Plymouth's Bretonside bus station; it's deeply unappealing.

Cycling and walking
The Tamar valley offers great **cycling** possibilities, from moorland on Dartmoor's fringes to the deep lanes near the river. The traffic-free **Plym Valley Cycle Trail**, part of the Devon coast-to-coast route, runs for seven miles along an old railway line from Plymouth to Clearbrook near Yelverton. The ride begins

at Laira Bridge or Marsh Mills, where the Plym Valley Railway is being restored. It follows the Plym estuary past Saltram House and through bat-hung tunnels, ferny railway cuttings and shady woodland, then on to Bickleigh Vale and Clearbrook. From there you're ideally placed to explore the Tamar Valley and Bere peninsula.

The most rewarding named **walking** trail in the area is the **Tamar Valley Discovery Trail**, a 30-mile route from Tamerton Foliot, on the outskirts of Plymouth, ending up at Launceston in Cornwall (leaving Devon as it crosses the River Tamar to Calstock); the first part can be walked only between February and September since it uses some permissive paths which are closed in winter. If you're starting from Tamerton, check the tide table beforehand: you'll be crossing the Tavy at Lopwell Dam by a causeway, and it's above water only for two hours each side of low tide. Once on the Bere peninsula you can follow the trail as it skirts the east bank of the Tamar, or choose any of the little lanes that confound car drivers entering this cul-de-sac. And since you're right on the Cornish border, it's highly tempting to stray out of Devon by taking the foot passenger ferry across the estuary from Plymouth to **Cremyll**: from there the peninsula offers wonderful walking, along the coast path to the remarkably unspoilt conjoined villages of Kingsand and Cawsand, and on to Rame Head; or wander at will through **Mount Edgcumbe Country Park** (where there's free access).

① Plymouth

Cities don't generally offer much chance of being 'slow', but big bustling Plymouth has its gentler side too. Sometimes at dusk, looking out seaward from the historic Hoe, it's easy to imagine great high-masted ships turning gently at anchor in the bay, their sails curving to some ancient evening breeze. Sir Francis Drake sailed from here, along with Raleigh, Grenville, Hawkins and so many other Elizabethan seafarers; the Pilgrim Fathers finally set off for their 'promised land' from here, and England's battle-fleet of galleons sailed from the harbour to defeat the Spanish Armada. Captain James Cook began his voyage around the world here, in 1772, as did Sir Francis Chichester in 1966.

Today's cosmopolitan city originated as the 'littel fishe towne' of Sutton, owned by the monks of Plympton Priory until the 15th century. Its deep harbour (still known as Sutton Harbour) offered safe anchorage to the English fleet during the Hundred Years' War. In 1439 it became the first town in England to receive its charter by act of Parliament, and it was a prosperous naval and trading centre in Elizabethan times. The Royal Naval Dockyard at next-door Devonport was completed in 1698 and brought further prosperity to the town. Stroll around Plymouth and you're strolling through history.

Severe bombing during World War II destroyed some 20,000 buildings in Plymouth, including 100 pubs, 42 churches and 24 schools, so massive post-war reconstruction took place. This did introduce some characterless architecture, but enough old buildings remain or have been restored, and in the centre the overall impression is pleasant and spacious. Now the wide, traffic-free Armada Way stretches from near the railway station down to the Hoe, studded with gardens, benches, pavement cafés and small shops, and the city has won several awards for its floral displays. The historic Barbican area below the Hoe retains a strong flavour of its Elizabethan origins. Readers of this guide might not choose to spend a night in Plymouth but it deserves at least a day visit.

Getting around the city

Plymouth has several **car parks** but they do get busy. Three **Park and Ride** bus services run from the outskirts (Coypool near Marsh Mills roundabout, the George Junction near Derriford, and Milehouse) to the city centre, linking with the convenient network of **Citybuses**. There are Citybus stops directly outside the railway station, including one for their open-top tourist bus (01752 662271) which visits the city's main attractions; the tour takes about an hour if you stay on board, but once you've bought your ticket you can get on and off at will. For a quick chuff on a **steam train** – possibly pulled by a little red engine named Albert – check out the Plym Valley Railway (Marsh Mills Station, Coypool Rd PL7 4NW; www.plymrail.co.uk) that starts from opposite the Coypool Park and Ride; the line is less than a mile long at the time of writing but is being developed.

You might well not choose to **cycle** around Plymouth, although the Plymouth City Council encourages it and has produced a leaflet *Enjoy Plymouth by Bicycle*. Maps and information are available on www.plymouth.gov.uk; click on *transport and streets*, then *cycling*.

Various designated **walks** cover the main points of interest, with leaflets available from the Tourist Information Centre in the Barbican and interpretation boards at specific sites. The interesting places are pretty much all within walking distance of each other and the steepest hill you'll need to climb is up from the Barbican to either the Hoe or the centre.

What to see and do

The surviving cobbled streets and quaysides of the **Barbican** were once the heart of ancient Plymouth, the stamping ground of sea captains, sailors, merchants and even pirates. Now speciality shops, workshops and restaurants jostle together among the old port buildings and alleyways. A spot of slow browsing is in order. Pause at a café, and you could be sipping your coffee on the spot where Elizabethan explorers planned their next voyage over a glass or three of fine French brandy. For bibliophiles there are second-hand bookshops bursting at the seams with temptations; the Tudor House in New Street, built in 1799, sells Liberty prints (as in Liberty of London's Regent Street); while in Parade Antiques (also New Street) I spotted a dalek, a shark, an aircraft propeller, a stuffed mongoose fighting a cobra, various copper warming pans, masses of militaria, an old gramophone, shelves full of miscellaneous knick-knacks – and more books. The Barbican Pasty Co bakes its own fresh pasties daily, and the various galleries display local art and crafts.

At 60 Southside Street in the Barbican is the **Black Friars Distillery**, the working home of Plymouth Gin since 1793 and before that a private home and even a debtors' prison. Tours will take you through the gin-making process and you can sample it in the striking refectory bar, said to be where the Pilgrim Fathers spent their last night before embarking on the *Mayflower*.

The **Mayflower Steps** are reputedly close to the spot where the Pilgrim Fathers started their voyage (see box on page 194), and the **Mayflower Exhibition** in the Tourist Centre building, using displays, film and interactive graphics, tells the story of the ship, the harbour, and the people who have lived and worked there down the ages. Most fascinating are facsimile pages from William Bradford's original handwritten journal *Of Plimoth Plantation*, written between 1630 and 1647; the history of the first 30 years of the colony, it's the single most complete authority for the Pilgrims' story and the original was a great treasure. The exhibition is open all year and is a good wet-weather option too, as is the Marine Aquarium.

And if, on the quay nearby, you should spot a giant prawn (or perhaps cod) clinging to the top of a pillar, don't worry: you're not hallucinating. It's happy up there. On the base of the pillar are descriptions of other sea creatures.

At the **National Marine Aquarium**, across a small footbridge from the Barbican, you'll meet the partially sighted loggerhead turtle named Snorkel, found stranded on a Cornish beach in 1990. She couldn't survive in the wild, but is clearly thriving here and delights visitors. The two little puffer fish, Nigel and his best friend Colin, are fun too.

Don't be misled by the cute names: the aquarium was the first in the UK to be set up solely for the purpose of education, conservation and research. It acted as an adviser to the BBC's 'Blue Planet' TV series, among other productions. Around 400 different species are on show, in realistic habitats from coral reefs to local shorelines. In the Coral Seas viewing area, where I saw Snorkel and the puffers, more than 70 species of colourful exotic fish cruise or flip by, somehow keeping to invisible lanes like swimmers in an indoor pool so that they don't bump each other. The glass wall is concave, with visitors standing within the 'cave' so there's a feeling of being right among the fish.

Other viewing tanks include Shallow Water (marine life of Plymouth sound, including an octopus that can open a jar to get at food), Weird Creatures, and

Mediterranean Sea where the largest sharks (including three sand tiger sharks) are kept, and swim lazily above watching visitors.

The 25 bus stops nearby. If you're driving, follow the brown signs. Just up from the Barbican area, the **Merchant's House** is Plymouth's largest and finest 16th-century home. It was 'modernised' in the early 17th century by seafaring adventurer William Parker, who later became Mayor of Plymouth; he'd raided the Spanish treasure fleet in the Caribbean in the 1590s, which no doubt helped to pay for the work. The seven rooms each have a specific theme – for example one is a pre-war chemist's shop, another a Victorian schoolroom – reflecting aspects of Plymouth's past. **The Elizabethan House**, with its low ceilings and creaky sloping floors, was the home of some Elizabethan sea captain or merchant; the rooms have been atmospherically restored to recreate the conditions of the time.

Nearer to the railway and bus stations, the **City Museum and Art Gallery** in Drake Circus is open all year (closed Sunday and Monday) and admission is free. The 11 galleries cover a wide range, from Maritime Plymouth (of course!) through porcelain, sculpture, silverware, natural history and 'Artists of St Ives and the South West' (including Dame Barbara Hepworth). There's a small tribute wall to Beryl Cook, one of Plymouth's best-loved artists.

St Andrew's Church dates in its present shape from the 15th century, although there's evidence of a Christian community there since the 8th century and the first vicar, Halphage, was named in 1007. Elizabethan seafarers including Drake, Grenville and Hawkins worshipped there, as did Catherine of Aragon and (it is said) Charles II. War is no respecter of history, however, and a single night of heavy bombing in 1941 left it a burnt-out shell. The next morning, a local schoolmistress placed a wooden board over the north door with the inscription RESURGAM, meaning *I will rise again*. For some years it remained a roofless 'garden church' with services held in the open air, but then was indeed rebuilt, with stained-glass windows in gloriously rich colours designed by John Piper. On the feast-day of St Andrew in 1957 a moving service of re-consecration was held, attended by around 2,000 people. Imagine the singing, echoing up into the new roof!

Awarded minster status in 2009, St Andrew's is peaceful and lovingly cared for, its size is impressive, and it has good displays illustrating its past. No historically interesting architecture remains, but some of the surviving (or restored) old monuments have enjoyable inscriptions. Look out for the 1665 one to Mrs Mary Sparke, starting 'Life's but a Sparke...'

Behind St Andrew's is the **Prysten House**, dating from 1498; it was built by Thomas Yogg or Yogge, a wealthy merchant involved in the French wine trade. 'Prysten' (priest's) seems to have been a misnomer attributed to the house in the 19th century. At the time of writing it's not regularly open; ask in the church about seeing inside. Next to the church, the impressive **Guildhall** with its tall, landmark tower is a relative newcomer: completed in 1874 and then restored after bomb damage sustained in World War II. If you like neo-gothic carvings, it has them aplenty.

Plymouth's must-visit attraction is of course the historic **Hoe** (the name comes from a Saxon word meaning *high place*), where Sir Francis Drake is said to have been playing bowls when told of the approach of the Spanish Armada. When I was there on a sunny September day, people were strolling, walking their dogs, flying kites, picnicking on the grass, and gazing out across Plymouth Sound from helpfully placed benches. The large island in the bay is now known

Sir Francis Drake

'Drake he's in his hammock an' a thousand miles away' as Sir Henry Newbolt's poem, *Drake's Drum*, goes. In fact it's a bit off track, as it continues that Drake is 'slung atween the roundshot in Nombre Dios Bay' – considerably more than a thousand miles away, on the coast of Panama. He had set off from England in August 1595, with a fleet of 26 ships, hoping to take both Nombre de Dios (where he had already captured a treasure-laden mule train in 1573) and the city of Panama; but the well-prepared Spanish force proved too strong. While retreating by sea to Puerto Bello, Drake contracted dysentery and died, in January 1596; he was buried at sea, off Panama. It was a sadly inglorious end for a sailor and adventurer who had made a great contribution to the England of his day.

Born around 1540 in a small leasehold farmstead just south of Tavistock, Drake first 'went to sea' some ten years later when his parents travelled by boat from Plymouth to Kent, and found lodging in one of the old hulks moored in the Medway estuary near Chatham. The young Francis was now surrounded by maritime life, from small fishing and cargo vessels to the towering men-o'-war in the naval dockyard. In his teens he was apprenticed to the captain of a small merchant boat trading across the channel, and inherited her some years later when her owner died. His cousin, the wealthy Plymouth shipowner John Hawkins (see page 189), had set up lucrative trading links with the New World; seizing the opportunity, Drake sold his boat and enlisted in his cousin's fleet.

In 1569 Drake married his first wife, Mary Newman, in Devonport's St Budeaux Church. She came from nearby Saltash in Cornwall, where her restored 15th-century cottage can be visited.

Drake's father Edmund, a farmer, was an ardent Protestant lay preacher in turbulent religious times, so the young Francis probably acquired strong anti-Catholic attitudes. He encountered (Catholic) Spaniards on a voyage to the West Indies and the contact wasn't friendly; dislike turned to hatred after a Spanish attack in 1568 in which three English ships were lost. From then on, he sought revenge against Spain.

With the Queen's blessing, he became a thoroughly successful pirate, capturing Spanish vessels and bringing home rich spoils. In 1577 he embarked on his famous circumnavigation of the globe (pausing to raid the Spanish harbours in Cuba and Peru on the way); he then claimed California for England, arranged a treaty with the as Drake's Island; it isn't open to the public, but the various harbour cruises (see below) will take you past and tell you about its history.

The **Citadel** at the Hoe's eastern end, with massive 70-foot walls, was built in 1665 by Charles II and remained England's most important coastal defence for around 100 years. Today it's used by the military but tours are available from March to September. **Smeaton's Tower**, 72 feet high, was built in 1759 as the

sultan of the Moluccas for the trading of spices, sailed home with a glittering amount of treasure – and was knighted. Arise, Sir Francis. He also became Mayor of Plymouth, and bought himself Buckland Abbey, as well as other manors and businesses. Never reticent about his abilities, he also entered parliament, as MP for Bossiney in Cornwall.

In 1585 the Queen sent him off – to his delight – to raid Spanish settlements in the Caribbean. The Spaniards prepared to counter-attack, but in 1587 Drake sailed into Cadiz harbour and did immense damage, 'singeing the King of Spain's beard'. Spain retaliated the following year with its Armada, a massive fighting force of 151 warships and almost 30,000 men. The high-born Lord Thomas Howard was appointed Admiral of the opposing English fleet, the lowlier but more flamboyant Drake a Vice-Admiral. For almost a week fierce battles raged along the English Channel. In a nutshell, England outmanoeuvred the Spaniards, 'drummed 'em up the channel' and routed them, to huge popular acclaim. Drake was lauded in prose and poetry, and souvenir-makers produced a crop of commemorative items. However, his star was waning and his final voyage – to Panama, with John Hawkins, who also died on the trip – was a failure. In his will, Hawkins had left Drake his 'best jewell which is a Cross of Emerodes', but Drake survived his cousin by less than three months.

To the public Drake was a hero; to his peers less so. An arrogant, flamboyant, self-made man of relatively lowly birth, he was looked down on by some sectors of the aristocracy. His courage and skills as a seaman were in no doubt, but his judgement could be faulty. He was a favourite of the Queen, and revelled in his glittering social status, yet one of his main land-based undertakings was the very practical construction of a leat (channel) to bring fresh water to Plymouth from the River Meavy. An old legend tells that he rode off to Dartmoor and searched until he found a suitable spring, then turned his horse about, spoke some magic words to the spring, and galloped back to Plymouth with it bubbling along obediently behind him. Such was his public image.

Queen Elizabeth called him 'my pirate', a Spanish ambassador called him 'the master-thief of the unknown world', and the Elizabethan historian John Stow wrote 'He was more skilful in all points of navigation than any'. Tristram Risdon, writing 20 years or so after Drake's death, went even further: 'Could my pen as ably describe his worth as my heart prompteth to it, I would make this day-star appear at noon-day as doth the full moon at midnight'. And reputedly he also played a mean game of bowls...

JB

Eddystone lighthouse, but was moved (apart from its base) from the Eddystone rock to the Hoe in the 1880s because of sea erosion. Its interior has been restored and is open to visitors year-round (closed Sunday and Monday). From 1937 until decimalisation, its image appeared behind Britannia on the English penny coin.

The Hoe has various **war memorials**: the large naval memorial, in Portland stone, contains dozens of plain, neatly lettered bronze panels recording the names of the 22,443 (yes, that many) men and women of the Commonwealth navies who lost their lives at sea during both World Wars.

At the seaward end of the Hoe there's a huge open-air lido, the Tinside Pool. It's open daily, May to September. To its east, between the Hoe and the Barbican, is a small, shingly beach, as well as the possibility of swimming off the rocks. For more fresh air and exercise, **Central Park**, beyond the railway station, is Plymouth's largest open space, with good views across Plymouth to the Sound.

For market fans, **Plymouth City Market** at Frankfurt Gate (closed Sundays) has a mass of family-run stalls selling everything from Devon lamb, fresh vegetables, pasties and locally caught fish to household goods, clothes, crafts and toys. Many of the food stalls have the label 'own grown'. A **farmers' market** with yet more fresh local produce is held in Armada Way's Piazza, on the second and fourth Saturdays of the month.

Annual events in Plymouth include a half-marathon and Lord Mayor's Day in May, the British Firework Championships in August and 'Meet the Navy' days in September. The 2009 programme at the **Theatre Royal** included productions from the National Theatre, Chichester Festival Theatre and Glyndebourne. Big national sporting events (including Wimbledon tennis) are shown on the big screen in the Piazza.

Basics

Plymouth Tourist Information Centre 3–5 The Barbican (opposite Mayflower Steps) ☎ 01752 306330 www.plymouth.gov.uk/homepage/leisureandtourism and www.plymouthcitycentre.co.uk. Note that some of the listed attractions are open in the summer months or on certain days only, so it's important to check beforehand.
National Marine Aquarium ☎ 01752 600301 www.national-aquarium.co.uk.
Plymouth City Museum and other museums ☎ 01752 304774 www.plymouthmuseum.gov.uk.
Summer Festival events www.plymouthsummerfestival.com.
Theatre Royal ☎ 01752 267222 www.theatreroyal.com.
Tinside Swimming Pool ☎ 01752 261915 www.plymouth.gov.uk/tinsidelido.

Eating and drinking

England's 17th-largest city – as Plymouth proclaims itself to be – has no shortage of bars, cafés and restaurants. Below are some close to its main attractions. Those in the Hoe area have great views across the bay. You'll spot many others as you stroll: try them, and do tell us for the next edition.

Barbican area

Barbican Kitchen Brasserie 60 Southside St (in Black Friars Distillery) ✆ 01752 604448 www.barbicankitchen.com. Run by the Tanner brothers, Chris and James, of Tanners Restaurant (below) and TV fame, this upmarket brasserie is open daily for lunch and dinner.

Cap'n Jaspers Whitehouse Pier ✆ 01752 262444 www.capn-jaspers.co.uk. On the old Fish Market Quay with a view over the harbour, quirky, practical, cheap – a much-loved Plymouth institution, with outdoor tables whose legs are made of chains, intriguing gadgets, a pirate-ship mural, and hot, filling, banger-and-burger-style food. You can have half a yard of hot dog, a quarter-pounder on lettuce with North Atlantic prawns... and watch life go by as you eat.

Piermasters Restaurant 33 Southside St ✆ 01752 229345 www.piermasters restaurant.com. Claims to be Plymouth's oldest seafood restaurant and is very strong on fish; also uses locally sourced meat, poultry and game.

Platters 12 The Barbican ✆ 01752 227262. A popular, unpretentious restaurant known for its good, very fresh seafood (the chips are good too). Look for the 'catch of the day' specials. Busy at peak times.

The Watering Hole Quay Rd ✆ 01752 667604. A wide choice of good-value dishes.

Hoe area

The Terrace Café/Bar Madeira Rd ✆ 01752 603533 www.theterracecafebar.co.uk. A busy, cheerful place at the base of the Hoe.

The View Restaurant Madeira Rd ✆ 01752 664327 www.rpcyc.com. The restaurant of the Royal Plymouth Corinthian Yacht Club; open Tue–Sat for reasonably priced bar lunches, all-day snacks including cream teas, and an evening bistro.

The Waterfront Restaurant/Bar 9 Grand Parade ✆ 01752 226326 www.thewaterfront.org.uk. At the western end of the Hoe, the upmarket Waterfront opens daily 12.00–23.00. It was once the home of the Royal Western Yacht Club, where Sir Francis Chichester first stepped ashore after circumnavigating the world in 1967.

St Andrew's area

Tanners Restaurant Prysten House, Finewell St ✆ 01752 252001 www.tannersrestaurant.com. A treat! This restaurant in the historic Prysten House (page 183) was opened in 1999 by young celebrity chefs James and Chris Tanner (BBC TV's *Saturday Kitchen* and *Ready Steady Cook*, Good Food Channel's *Great Food Live*). The menus, strong on fresh, local food, don't come cheap – but why should they? Samples and prices are on the website. Open Tue–Sat for lunch and dinner; booking often essential; parking available outside the Guildhall.

Devon's globetrotting sons

As well as Drake, Grenville and Raleigh (pages 28, 184 and 200 respectively), other Devonian seafarers and explorers have made their mark on history. **Robert Falcon Scott**, known for his ill-fated Antarctic expedition in 1912, was born in 1868 in Devonport, and **William Bligh** of *Bounty* fame was born in 1754 in St Tudy near Plymouth.

John Hanning Speke was born in Bideford in 1827 and **Sir Richard Francis Burton** in Torquay in 1821. They set off to Africa together in 1856 to discover the source of the Nile, and in 1858 became the first Europeans to reach Lake Tanganyika. Burton fell sick and returned home; Speke continued and discovered what was then thought to be the Nile's source, naming it Lake Victoria.

Back in the 16th century several swashbuckling seafarers were distinguishing themselves in the eyes of Queen Elizabeth I, whether by advancing her acquisitions in the New World, bringing home glittering booty from their sacking of Spanish ships and possessions, or defeating the Spanish Armada. Less glamorously, many profited from the slave trade. **Sir Humphrey Gilbert** (1539–83), from Compton near Plymouth, was Raleigh's stepbrother and cousin of both Drake and Grenville. Fascinated by America, which he believed was the lost continent of Atlantis, he sought to discover a 'northwest passage' to China via its northern waters. He backed three exploratory voyages by Frobisher (below) and his *Discourse of a discoverie for a new passage to Cataia* (Cathay) was published in 1576. In 1583 he reached Newfoundland and claimed St John's for the Queen, founding a colony there: the first English colony in North America.

Plymouth from the water

Various small cruise companies enable you to experience Plymouth from the sea. It's a very pleasant way of spending an hour or more. Running boats is a pricey business so the cruises aren't necessarily cheap; also remember that schedules can be upset by the weather. The various ferries also offer you good views of the bay – the Torpoint Ferry is the only one that carries cars.

Cruises

Fish 'n' Trips ☎ 07971 208381 🖰 www.fishntrips.co.uk. Fishing trips of various lengths, on purpose-built 28-seater fishing/passenger boats *Ronnoch Moor* and *Iolaire*. Partnered with Plymouth Hoe Cruises (below).

Plymouth Boat Cruises (Sound Cruising) ☎ 01752 408590 or ☎ 07813 980833 🖰 www.soundcruising.com. Ticket kiosk: Phoenix Wharf, Barbican ☎ 01752 671166. This company is strong on wildlife. Their Calstock Cruise (see page 190) takes you past the Dockyard and Brunel's rail bridge, and up through the beautiful Tamar valley to visit Calstock. The Dockyard and Warship Cruises show you Plymouth Sound

Sir Martin Frobisher (c.1535–94) was a Yorkshireman, but died in Plymouth; he captained the *Triumph* valiantly during the Armada attack. He'd been less successful in 1576, when he believed he had discovered the much-sought northwest passage and a source of gold-bearing ore; after heavy investment, some by the Queen herself, it turned out that the ore did not contain gold, and his 'passage' was in fact what is now known as Frobisher Bay on Baffin Island in Canada.

Plymouth-born **John Hawkins** (1532–95) was a shipbuilder who introduced important changes to the design of England's warships, making them more manoeuvrable than any before. This helped England greatly in her defeat of the Spanish Armada, during which Hawkins was rear-admiral of the English fleet. He was also an effective Treasurer of the Royal Navy and an MP, but was at heart an adventurer and enthusiastically embraced the piracy prevalent at the time. Sadly his speciality lay in human cargo and he is remembered as the chief pioneer of the English slave trade. Between 1562 and 1569, sometimes accompanied by Drake, he trafficked many hundred souls and amassed huge profits for himself and his backers; in 2006, almost 450 years later, his descendant 37-year-old Andrew Hawkins publicly apologised for his ancestor's actions.

John Davis or **Davys**, born in Sandridge near Dartmouth around 1550, was a friend of the Raleigh and Gilbert families. He made a number of exploratory voyages and brought back useful geographical information; his manual *The Seaman's Secrets* was published in 1594, and the 'backstaff' (for finding the altitude of heavenly bodies when at sea) and double quadrant that he invented remained in nautical use for a century or so after his death.

JB

(including Drake's Island) as well as Devonport Naval Dockyard. Other cruises follow the Devon coast or take you up the River Yealm. Their cruise to Morwellham Quay is currently in doubt: see page 191. Joint 'Saver' tickets are available, for your cruise plus the Maritime Museum.

Plymouth Hoe Cruises ☎ 07971 208381 ⌂ www.plymouthhoecruises.co.uk. Partners of Fish 'n' Trips, above, these operate small-boat harbour, wildlife and eco-cruises including Mount Edgcumbe Country Park and Devonport Dockyard.

SeaTrek ☎ 01752 266420 or ☎ 07982 591649 ⌂ www.seatrek-plymouth.co.uk. More adventurous than the above are SeaTrek's coastal treks in their 12-passenger, rigid inflatable boat, with a hydrophone, underwater viewing boxes, and a colour screen that shows up underwater objects located by echo-sounder. Cruises run all year (weather permitting). SeaTrek are linked to the Marine Aquarium and their ticket office is there.

Tamar Cruising ☎ 01752 822105 ⌂ www.tamarcruising.com. This established company, which also operates the Cremyll Ferry, runs regular River Tamar, Dockyards & Warships cruises; a cruise including entry to Edgcumbe House in Cornwall; a scenic River Tamar & Calstock cruise; and occasional special Tamar Birdwatching Cruises.

The Tamar Estuary: a guide for birders

Tony Soper

Sailing from Phoenix Wharf on the four-hour Calstock Cruise offered by Plymouth Boat Cruises will reveal the astonishing variety of scenery and birdlife on the Tamar Estuary. These are general-interest cruises, so if you're a birder don't forget your field guide and, whatever your interest, binoculars are highly desirable.

As you pass the imposing Citadel and see the grassy expanse of the Hoe, the sheltered anchorage of Plymouth Sound opens on your port hand. Maybe you'll spot a fleet of racing dinghies or yachts; certainly there will be some naval warships or auxiliaries, for you are about to enter the Hamoaze, the deepwater anchorage that serves the Naval Base. Check the upper rigging of any laid-up vessels, for cormorants delight in colonising ships that sit here for more than a season or two. This part of the trip showcases the marine industrial history of the city, from its 18th-century slips and dry-docks to the nuclear facility.

The twin suspension bridges mark the beginning of the wildlife-rich middle section of the estuary. As you work up on the rising tide there will be exposed mudflats on either side. Shorebirds with short legs probe the soft mud for lugworms and assorted invertebrates, those with long legs wade in the shallows and pounce or sweep for shrimps. It's along these wet mudscapes that the elegant avocets show up in early winter.

In early summer parties of young shelducks hoover their way across the mud, finding sustenance in the uncountable numbers of tiny *Hydrobia* snails. Herons, jealously guarding the riparian rights to their allotted stretch of foreshore, stand knee-deep in water and wait patiently for the fish to come to them. Cormorants jack-knife to chase an eel or a flatfish on the muddy bottom. As the tide rises and covers the mud, the birds find a safe roosting place ashore until the ebb reveals their hunting grounds again. The herons, solitary fishermen, now enjoy some sociable company. Check the waterside trees as you sail higher into the narrower reaches to find a communal cormorant roost. And at each end of the summer comes the time when an osprey, passing by on migration, may stop for a week or two to plunge for a takeaway mullet.

The upper reaches of the tidal Tamar offer fine reed beds, alive in summer with the chatter of warblers. There will be otters here as well, but you'll be lucky to see one. Devonians call them 'dim articles', a reference to their invisibility not their intelligence. And around the Cotehele bend at last you reach the waterside village of Calstock. There's time to stretch your legs ashore and go for a cream tea before you return down a high-water scene, totally transformed from that of the upward journey.

Incidentally, if you want to be a proper Devonian please say Tamar as 'tamer'!

Ferries

Cawsand Ferry ☏ 01752 822784 🖰 www.cawsandferry.com. A seasonal (summer) service that carries people, prams, bicycles and dogs between the Barbican and the beach by the strikingly unspoilt Cornish village of Cawsand on the Rame peninsula.

Cremyll Ferry ☏ 01752 822105 🖰 www.tamarcruising.com. This year-round service, between Admiral's Hard in Plymouth and Mount Edgcumbe in Cornwall, carries passengers, bicycles, small packages – and walkers on the South West Coast Path. There has been a ferry here since 1204; the city council now owns the ancient right to run it. Times vary seasonally.

Mount Batten Ferry ☏ 01752 408590 🖰 www.mountbattenferry.com. This is more of a **water taxi** service: two yellow boats shuttle between the Barbican and Mount Batten. The half-hourly service operates year-round, and rides from the Barbican to other points around the bay can also be arranged. It's run by Sound Cruising (see *Cruises*, above).

Tamar Passenger Ferry ☏ 01822 833331 🖰 www.calstockferry.co.uk. This seasonal passenger ferry (Apr–late Sep) links the attractive riverside village of Calstock with the National Trust's historic Cotehele Quay in Cornwall. It's useful for walkers on the Tamar Valley Discovery Trail.

Torpoint Ferry ☏ 01752 812233 🖰 www.plymouth.gov.uk/torpoint ferry. This large car ferry, running across the Tamar between Plymouth and Torpoint in Cornwall, also takes buses and lorries. It's a regular, 24-hour, 7-day, all-year service, with ferries only ten minutes apart at peak times.

Escapes from Plymouth

If you've been staying in Plymouth you may feel like a short trip out into the country, or just want to explore the nearby area from elsewhere. Here are some suggestions to start you off.

② Morwellham Quay

This World Heritage Site is an amazing re-creation of the past – and, sadly, its future is in doubt at the time of writing. It went into receivership in September 2009, when Devon County Council withdrew its funding. The trustees are actively seeking a rescue package; if they succeed, the site could reopen to tourists – in some form or another – in 2010. Even without the quay's activities, you can enjoy the surroundings, with their combination of tranquillity and history.

Morwellham Quay is on the River Tamar, four miles west of Tavistock. The nearest rail stations are Calstock and Gunnislake. You'll need to check the current transport possibilities if the site reopens. For drivers, there's a massive car park.

UNESCO designated the quay a World Heritage Site in 2006. Looking at the silent site today – a broad, flat area of riverbank with some sheds, a few cottages, large pieces of machinery and an old sailing ship – it's hard to imagine that when Queen Victoria visited it in 1856 it was known as 'the richest copper port in the Queen's Empire'. Originally built by the Cistercian monks of Tavistock Abbey, around the 10th and 11th centuries, as a means to transport goods and themselves to and from Plymouth, it quickly developed; by the late 12th century ships came to load up with locally mined tin, lead and silver ores. Later, the Industrial Revolution caused a huge demand for metals of all kinds; the hills of west Devon and east Cornwall were rich in tin, lead, copper, arsenic and manganese, and these were shipped via Morwellham to north Wales, with its substantial coal supplies, for smelting. It was said that Morwellham's quayside sometimes held enough arsenic to poison the entire world! A canal was laboriously dug from Tavistock, to facilitate transport.

In 1844 Europe's largest known copper lode was discovered just four miles from the quay, and Morwellham became a busier port than even Liverpool. Vessels from Europe and further afield came to collect their loads of gleaming ore. But – then the copper began to run out. Eventually the company running the mine was forced to close, with huge loss of employment. The Great Western Railway's arrival at Tavistock superseded river transport; the great quays gradually fell silent, machinery rusted and the waterways silted up. After 1,000 years of activity, Morwellham Quay slept. In 1933 the canal was bought by the West Devon Electric Supply Company, and the hydro-electric plant they built there still provides power to the National Grid.

Restoration began in 1970. By 2009, costumed staff were manning the quay's exhibits and helping to recreate its 19th-century heyday. A riverside tramway carried visitors deep into the heart of the old copper mine; children could dress up in period costume; various traditional crafts were demonstrated. The 100-year-old ketch *Garlandstone*, built on the Tamar, was moored at the quayside. Echoes of the past were everywhere. It could be one of Devon's most unusual, atmospheric and historic sites; how sad if it closes permanently.

Morwellham Quay Tavistock PL19 8JL ☎ 01822 832766
🖱 www.morwellham-quay.co.uk and www.tamarvalley.org.uk

③ Saltram

The park around Saltram, perched high above the River Plym on the outskirts of Plymouth, is one of the city's valuable 'green spaces'. Citybus 22 from Plymouth will drop you at Merafield Road half a mile away; cycle path NCN27 and the West Devon Way run along the bank of the Plym (in the park) from Plymouth's Laira Bridge. For drivers there's a spacious car park.

The magnificent Georgian house – it played the part of the Dashwoods' home, Norland Park, in the film of *Sense and Sensibility* – has exquisite Robert Adam interiors, original furnishings and fascinating collections of art and memorabilia. It has been the home of the Parker family for 300 years and one-time owner Lord Boringdon was a close friend of Sir Joshua Reynolds, so naturally the latter's paintings are featured.

The landscaped gardens attached to the house are beautiful, with their follies and fine array of shrubs and trees, but the real delight is the surrounding park: open daily from dawn to dusk and offering a range of walks, cycle rides and gentle strolls, whether inland or along the river. Maps are available from reception or you can follow your nose and the signs. Dogs are allowed in parts of the grounds only, but there's a considerate little fenced-off 'dog corral'.

Saltram Plympton, Plymouth PL7 1UH ☎ 01752 333500 🖰 www.nationaltrust.org.uk.

④ Wembury

Wembury's **beach** is the perfect seaside escape. With shale/shingle at high tide and a wide expanse of sand at low tide, it offers safe, clean bathing and paddling. Views are stunning, of sea and cliffs. There are rock pools to explore, shells to collect, a café, a small Marine Conservation Centre, and a shop selling basic beachy things. From Plymouth, bus 48 goes to Wembury village, a short walk from the beach, or you can follow the South West Coast Path from Bovisand in the west or (via a summer ferry) Newton Ferrers and Noss Mayo in the east. For drivers, there's a car park outside St Werburgh's Church and another, near the café, belonging to the National Trust which owns the whole area.

The **Marine Conservation Centre** (Church Road; 01752 862538; www.wemburymarinecentre.org) is open from roughly Easter to October, with good, family-friendly explanations of flora and fauna, illustrations of local sea life, hands-on exhibits, quizzes and leaflets about nearby attractions. Rock-pool rambles are held in the summer; these promote the gentle approach of looking carefully rather than scrabbling with a shrimping net, which can damage weed and sea creatures, and replacing stones in position after lifting them. Other events and talks are listed on the website. The Marine Awareness Officer told me that shells found on the beach include cowries, blue rayed limpets and slipper limpets. Wembury Beach and its surrounding coast and sea are designated a Special Area of Conservation and a Voluntary Marine Conservation Area.

The **Old Mill Café**, in an old mill house and with grindstones as outdoor table-tops, is open March to October and some winter weekends. I succumbed happily to a flapjack. There are more substantial snacks too and the usual range of hot and cold drinks.

The Pilgrim Fathers

'Now Johnny, what was the name of the Pilgrim Fathers' ship?'
'Mayflower, Miss.'
'And where did most of the Pilgrims come from, Johnny?'
'They were from the West Country, Miss.'
'And where did they start their voyage?'
'In Plymouth, Miss.'
'Not good enough Johnny – stay in after school.'

The Pilgrims' ship was indeed the *Mayflower*, but they had boarded her in Southampton and didn't originate from the West Country. Of the 102 passengers who then pitched their way across a wintry Atlantic in the 180-ton vessel, 35 were members of the English Separatist Church (a radical faction of the Puritans) who had initially fled to the Netherlands from their homes in and around Lincolnshire to escape religious persecution. Their new life proved less than ideal, however, so they made arrangements to lease two ships: the *Speedwell* to take a group from Holland to Southampton and the *Mayflower* to join her there for the voyage to America. The non-Separatists among the passengers were mainly off to seek their fortune in the New World.

The ships set off together from Southampton on 5 August 1620, but the *Speedwell* began to leak and they had to put in to Dartmouth. Repairs completed, they set off again – but a storm blew up and, *Speedwell* again leaking, they sought shelter in Plymouth Sound. Eventually it was decided to abandon the *Speedwell*; on 6 September the *Mayflower* finally set sail for America. Her first landfall (on 9 November) was Cape Cod, in Massachusetts, but she sailed on and – it is said – eventually put ashore on what later became known as Plymouth Rock. Here her passengers settled, founding the colony of New Plymouth.

Look at a world atlas today and you'll see around twenty towns, mostly in the US, with Plymouth in their names. Just think – if the *Speedwell* hadn't sprung a leak they might, except for ours in Devon, have been called Southampton!
JB

St Werburgh's Church has stood on the cliffside for many centuries, looking across the bay towards the Eddystone lighthouse. It's believed there was a Saxon church on the site in the 9th century, but the present one is described as 14th century on a Norman foundation. The oldest item is the Norman stoup (12th century) inside the north door; there is also a great deal of beautifully carved oak, probably from the 16th century. Among interesting memorials, one chattily commemorates 'a most vertuous Pious Charitable Religious Sweet & lovings Lady Mightily afflicted with a cough & Bigge with child'.

Old Mill Café ☎ 01752 862314.

Lemon Tree Café & Bistro 2 Haye Road South, Elburton, Plymouth PL9 8HJ ☎ 01752 481117 www.lemontreecafe.co.uk. On your return to Plymouth, whether by bus or by car, you could stop off at this friendly little place. It's open Tue–Sat 11.00–14.00 for lunches and snacks, Thu–Sat 19.00–23.00 for dinner (booking essential). Cooking is Mediterranean-style, using fresh local produce; there's a blackboard listing daily 'specials'.

The Tamar Valley

For the fruit markets, cherries, pears, and walnuts are raised in great abundance; especially in the township of Beer Ferrers; which is said to send out of it a thousand pounds worth of fruit (including strawberries) annually.
The Rural Economy of the West of England by William Marshall, 1796.

Bere means spit of land, and this peninsula, locked between the Tamar and the Tavy, is less accessible today than it was two hundred or so years ago when ships regularly carried cargoes of soft fruit down the river to Plymouth. The railway provides the only direct connection between Bere Ferrers, the village near the apex of the triangle, and Plymouth; for car drivers it's a cul-de-sac and they must make a wide detour to Denham Bridge, near Buckland Monachorum, to reach the city, a journey of about twenty miles. This enforced peacefulness means that the walker or cyclist can stroll or pedal the lanes with little danger from cars. It's deservedly one of Devon's Areas of Outstanding Natural Beauty (www.tamarvalley.org.uk).

The Bere peninsula is still a major fruit producer, and walkers will see apple orchards galore, as well as the ever-present river views with clusters of sailing boats. A few centuries back this land between the rivers became valuable for its silver mines; when the silver ran out, lead was discovered. Then, in 1890, the railway arrived and visitors poured in. It is probably quieter now than at any time in its history.

Bere Ferrers has an exceptionally interesting church, a 'Heritage' railway station with displays of memorabilia, and a friendly pub with a beer garden overlooking the Tavy. **Bere Alston** is larger and less picturesque, but has shops where you can buy provisions, and a good pub.

Continuing north, the Tamar remains unbridged, save for the railway, until Gunnislake in Cornwall. The Tavy's first bridge, Denham, opens up the western fringe of Dartmoor and the picturesque village with the grand name, **Buckland Monachorum**. To its south is **Buckland Abbey**.

The Tamar Valley Line

This delightful railway, from Plymouth to Gunnislake, is a commuter service with its roots firmly in yesteryear. On its flower-bedecked and old-fashioned stations you must hail the oncoming train by raising your hand; yet it rescues the residents of Bere Ferrers and its surroundings from a long detour by road to reach workplaces in the city.

The Tamar Valley Line is only 15 miles long, but the changing scenery from viaduct to fruit orchards to rivers is always diverting. The summer service is two-hourly, and the Dartmoor Sunday Rover (see page 79) is valid here.

⑤ Bere Ferrers

The Ferrers were a leading family at the time of the Norman Conquest and Henry de Ferrers was chairman of the Domesday Commission. When he received the Bere estate from Henry II it will have been prime land, situated so close to the river and Plymouth harbour.

The **church of St Andrew** was built – or rather rebuilt since the tower is earlier – by Sir William de Ferrers, who died in 1280. His monument is one of its treasures. He lies, with his wife Isolda de Cardinham, next to the altar, dressed in chainmail, his bare legs crossed and a shield at his side. Both hands are on his sword, ready to draw. His wife wears a simple robe and on one shoulder is a small, disembodied hand, said to be that of a child although it's hard to see where the arm or body could have been. And the fingers are too long for a child; a mystery.

The memorial to his father, Sir Reginald, who died in 1194, seems to have been carved by the same sculptor. This gentleman lies with his body half-turned, his shield over his hands which are also poised to draw his sword. His knee raised, he seems ready to leap from his tomb and defend his honour. Sadly both lower legs are missing, as is the lion on which his feet rested, although the paws and curly tail remain.

Another notable feature of the church is the stained glass in the east window, claimed – rightly or wrongly – to be the oldest in the county apart from some in Exeter Cathedral. The window was a gift of William de Ferrers, and one of the lights shows him – or one of his family – holding a model of the church.

Elsewhere St Andrew's has Tudor carved bench ends, the design echoing the shape of the windows, and lots of granite reflecting its proximity to Dartmoor. The screen has gone, as have the saints in the panels, scraped off at the time of the Reformation.

In the graveyard is a sad little tombstone with no name, just 'Cholera 1849'.

$\bowtie\!\!\!\bowtie\!\!\!\bowtie$

Olde Plough Inn ℡ 01822 840358 🖰 www.oldeploughinn.co.uk. A nicely sited pub next to the church, with a pleasant beer garden. They served us treacle tart at 11.00 in the morning, out of season. Log fires in winter and local guest ales.

Walking the Tamar Valley Discovery Trail from Bere Ferrers

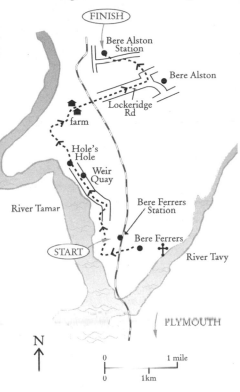

Taking the train to Bere Ferrers and walking to Bere Alston gives you a good overview of the region, with the bonus of a pub at each end. A section of this long-distance trail runs west of Bere Ferrers, across some meadows, and skirts the Tamar (the view of which is often obscured by hedges). You have a choice of path at Liphill Quay; if it has been raining the lower one to the left is very muddy: take the higher. Along a quiet lane you'll pass the intriguingly named Hole's Hole, from where minerals from the Dartmoor mines were shipped, then it's back to the path past orchards and farms to Bere Alston. The walk takes two to three hours, depending how often you stop.

The station is about half a mile north of the town. If you want to continue on the Discovery Trail to Calstock in Cornwall, there's a summer-only pedestrian **ferry** (01822 833331) across the Tamar at Ferry Farm a further mile away. You can follow the route on the OS Explorer map 108; also, according to a notice near Bere Ferrers station, details of the area's walks are available from 'outlets in the village'.

Edgcumbe Hotel Bere Alston ☎ 01822 840252. A handy pub on Cornwall St with a beer garden. Lunches served.

The Bere Ferrers Rail Accident

In 1917 ten servicemen from New Zealand were mown down by an express train at Bere Ferrers. The boys – mostly teenagers – had disembarked from their troopship in Plymouth and were en route to Salisbury Plain for training. They had been told that when the train made its first stop, at Exeter, two men from each carriage should alight and go to the back of the train to distribute rations. When the train made an unscheduled stop at Bere Ferrers they jumped onto the line and were struck by the Waterloo–Plymouth express. They are commemorated in a little rose garden by the station.

197

East of the Tavy

Here we are back on the western edge of Dartmoor, with heather and spacious views only a mile or so away. However, it's still an area of woodland and deep valleys, impregnated with the name of Drake.

⑥ Buckland Monachorum and area

The village street is so narrow that you proceed at your peril, but broadens out at the church and the grand Lady Modyford's School, which she endowed in 1702 with an annual allowance for the schoolmaster of £7.10s.

The church of St Andrew is, at first glance, plain inside with a simple barrel roof, but then you notice the angels. They hang on the horizontal beams, wings half open, merrily playing a range of musical instruments. There's a Saxon font, looking like a cottage loaf, and the rather alarming Drake Chapel (not Sir Francis, but descendants of his brother Thomas) to the south of the nave. The huge Gibraltar Memorial to General Elliot, who successfully defended The Rock against Spain in 1779–83, is thickly planted with dead bodies and heroic words. There's no question which side God was on. The general married into the Drake family.

Close to Buckland Monachorum is **The Garden House** (01822 854769; www.thegardenhouse.org.uk), a gorgeous mixture of formal and informal gardens. It has a wildflower meadow, an area of South African plants, a glade of acers which blaze red in the autumn, and much more.

Before visiting Buckland Abbey, follow the lane south to the almost inaccessible little village of **Milton Combe**, about two miles from Buckland Monachorum, folded into a ravine like a pressed flower. The white cottages find a footing where they can, a stream runs through it, and the pub stands in the square ready to reward your efforts to get here. It's called the Who'd Have Thought It.

⑦ Buckland Abbey

This is a beautiful, peaceful place, with friendly staff. If you don't want to visit the house itself, for a reduced entrance fee you can just park and stroll around the grounds: meadows, orchards, and four woodland walks along the River Tavy. From Plymouth there's a **bus**, the 48, on Sunday only; on weekdays you'll need the 55 from Yelverton. Either the train or buses 83, 84 and 86 will take you to Yelverton from Plymouth. For drivers there's ample parking.

'The outside looks like a church but the inside feels like a home' says one of the introductory displays, and a home is indeed what it became in the hands of

Sir Richard Grenville of *Revenge* fame (see box on page 200). His grandfather (also Richard) had bought the 270-year-old abbey, together with 570 acres of land, from Henry VIII in 1541, but did little to it. It's said that the King had offered it at a good price as a reward for Grenville's services as Marshal of Calais. Eventually the estate passed to the young Richard, when his father drowned in the sinking of the *Mary Rose*. In the 1570s, needing a base near Plymouth, he began developing it, and decided to make his home in the church itself. Throwing himself wholeheartedly into the transformation, he demolished cloisters and monastic buildings on its north side, inserted fireplaces, and added a new

kitchen wing, as well as dividing the interior into three floors and creating the well-proportioned rooms. The great hall, with its fine plasterwork ceiling and decoration, is thought to have been completed in 1576. Then in 1581, the expense of the work having drained his finances, Grenville sold the whole property – reluctantly, by all accounts – to Sir Francis Drake, who paid for it with some of the spoils from his capture of the Spanish galleon *Nuestra Senora de la Concepcion*. He also owned around 40 other properties and, although he did live there on and off for some 14 years, he made no particular mark on it; however it remained in the Drake family (although with periods of disuse) until 1940 when it was presented to the National Trust. Some additional changes were made by subsequent owners over the centuries, particularly in the 1770s, although none so dramatic as Grenville's.

As we arrived at the complex of imposing buildings and stepped down into the courtyard we were clucked at by a cluster of decorative miniature chickens, whose names, we were told, included Petunia, Treacle, Fluff, Cornflake and Lavender. I immediately loved the place.

On the way to the house you pass the Great Barn, a relic of the original Cistercian monastery that was founded here in 1278. 'Great' is inadequate: it's truly massive, with an amazing beamed roof and a huge cider press at one end. Put Petunia & Co inside and they'd seem even smaller. The spirit of the old monastery is evoked more strongly in this building than elsewhere; cowled monks could well be padding on soft sandalled feet through the shadows, their robes swishing in the dust.

Inside the house, memorabilia and objets d'art are attractively displayed. There are paintings, documents, fine furniture, maps, weapons, ornaments – and of course Drake's drum, which, according to legend, will summon the old swashbuckler back to fight for England if his country ever needs his help. It all gives plenty of scope for browsing. The rooms themselves are attractive too, some with beautiful views over the gardens and original Tudor panelling.

One of the paintings shows the surrender of the *Nuestra Señora del Rosario*, captured by Drake off Torbay (see page 118). The cavernous old kitchen gives some idea of the scale of the feasting, with space enough for cooks to handle whole carcases of meat. (The Refectory Restaurant/Tearoom in the grounds uses somewhat more modern equipment!) Outside there are also craft workshops, and even a Letterboxing Trail.

There's a full, year-round programme of events, from bluebell and woodland walks to charcoal making, weaving, storytelling, concerts and historical

Sir Richard Grenville (1542–91) and the *Revenge*

Historian A L Rowse, in his authoritative biography *Sir Richard Grenville of the 'Revenge'* (Jonathan Cape, 1937), lamented the lack of personal records relating to his subject. The Grenvilles seem to have been careless about such things. Over the years family documents were burned, lost, discarded or destroyed, so that Rowse had to ferret out second- or third-hand sources.

When Grenville was three years old, his father Roger, captain of the *Mary Rose*, was drowned when she sank dramatically in 1545, leaving the toddler as sole heir to his estate. As a young man Richard studied at London's Inner Temple, then (aged 24) joined some Devon friends and relatives on a brief 'crusade' against the Turks who had invaded Hungary. Home again, he bought land in Ireland and became involved in organising settlements there. He comes across as a stern, even severe character, proud, obstinate and domineering; but a loyal, courageous and conscientious leader, respected by his peers, although he lacked Drake's charm and easy popularity.

Unlike his cousins Humphrey Gilbert and Walter Raleigh, he was not (apart from his father) from a particularly seafaring family, but he hankered after adventure, and in 1574 requested the Queen's permission to seek new lands and treasure south of the equator. For various military and political reasons, it was not granted. Although he owned ships and financed voyages, until his 40s he spent little time at sea; but then in 1585 he was offered command of a voyage carrying 100 settlers to today's North Carolina, newly acquired for the crown by Raleigh, to establish settlements there. He readily embarked on this new maritime career, for 'the pleasure of God on the seas', but it was short-lived. After he'd organised the settlements, other commitments (he still had responsibilities in Ireland, and was a commissioner for the coastal defences of Devon and Cornwall) kept him at home.

Then, in 1591, came his finest hour. Captaining the *Revenge*, he was appointed second in command (under Lord Thomas Howard) of a small squadron sent to re-enactments – and of course presentations of Sir Francis Drake in all his aspects. Poor old Grenville is much less remembered.

With its variety of attractions, Buckland Abbey is a place for all seasons – and for all weathers too, since you'll be well sheltered inside the house on a rainy day.

Buckland Abbey Yelverton PL20 6EY ☏ 01822 853607 ⌂ www.nationaltrust.co.uk.

tackle Spanish treasure ships off the Azores. The superior Spanish fleet approached them unexpectedly when they were at anchor by Flores; Howard ordered his ships to flee to safety but Grenville lagged behind to pick up crew who were ashore ('waiting to recover the men that were upon the Island that had otherwise bene lost', wrote Raleigh later in his *Report of the Trueth of the fight about the Isles of the Açores*). He then tried to run the *Revenge* forward through the 15 advancing Spaniards but the great ships blocked his way and his wind. Still he could have escaped by turning tail but 'Sir Richard utterly refused to turne from the enemie, alleaging that hee would rather choose to die, than to dishonour himselfe, his countrey, and her Majesties shippe'. An astonishing 15-hour battle then raged, the little *Revenge* firing fiercely into the Spanish galleons and fighting their men hand-to-hand when they swarmed aboard. By dawn next day she had no resources left: her masts and rigging had been shot away and she was badly holed. Sir Richard, grievously wounded, called on his gunner to sink her rather than let her fall into Spanish hands; but his seamen struck a bargain with the Spaniards, deserted their captain and surrendered. Sir Richard was taken to the Spanish flagship *San Pablo*, where he later died.

Many lines in Tennyson's poem *The Revenge* are based closely on Raleigh's report of the battle, but it's another contemporary chronicler, a Dutch merchant named van Linschoten, who provided the dramatic death speech: Linschoten's 'Here die I Richard Greenvil with a joyful and quiet mind, for that I have ended my life as a true soldier ought to do, that hath fought for his countrey, Queene, religion and honor, whereby my soule most joyful departeth out of this body & shal always leave behind it an everlasting fame of a valiant & true soldier that hath done his dutie as he was bound to doe' becomes, under Tennyson, 'I have fought for Queen and Faith like a valiant man and true/I have only done my duty as a man is bound to do/With a joyful spirit I, Sir Richard Grenville, die'.

As the *Revenge* – a considerable prize – was being towed back to Spain, 'the water began to heave and the weather to moan' and a fearful storm arose. The *Revenge* was smashed on to rocks and broke apart, and many Spanish ships and men were also lost. Confrontation had turned to tragedy: there was no prize for the King of Spain, painful loss for the Spaniards, and Sir Richard Grenville passed into heroic history.

JB

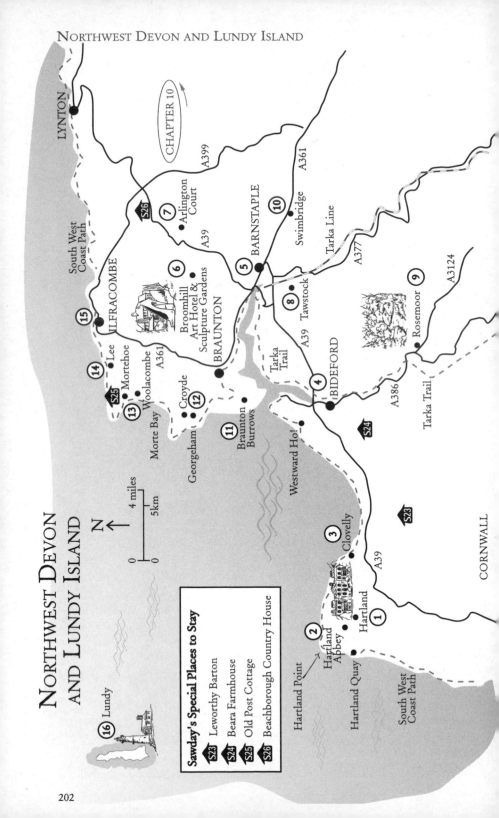

CHAPTER 10

LYNTON

A399

A361

A399

Arlington Court

7

S26

BARNSTAPLE

Swimbridge

10

Tarka Line

A377

A3124

South West Coast Path

ILFRACOMBE

6

5

A39

Broomhill Art Hotel & Sculpture Gardens

BRAUNTON

8 Tawstock

9

Rosemoor

15

Lee

Mortehoe

A361

A39

BIDEFORD

14

S25

13

Woolacombe

Croyde

12

4

A386

Tarka Trail

Morte Bay

Georgeham

11

Braunton Burrows

Tarka Trail

Westward Ho!

S24

N

4 miles

5km

0

0

3

Clovelly

S23

CORNWALL

NORTHWEST DEVON AND LUNDY ISLAND

A39

Sawday's Special Places to Stay

S23 Leworthy Barton
S24 Beara Farmhouse
S25 Old Post Cottage
S26 Beachborough Country House

2

Hartland Abbey

1

Hartland

Hartland Point

Hartland Quay

South West Coast Path

16 Lundy

9. NORTHWEST DEVON AND LUNDY ISLAND

North Devon is holiday Devon. This is where the sandy beaches are, where the best surf is, and the big campsites. But it also provides some dramatic cliff-top walking above the layered and crumpled rocks of **Hartland Quay** and **Hartland Point**, heaved up by geological forces millions of years ago and cut by streams and waterfalls. You need a strong pair of legs to walk here, whereas cyclists have it easy, with the enticingly level **Tarka Trail** and **Braunton Burrows** to pedal along. For those who want to escape the modern world altogether, **Lundy Island** is serenely unchangeable.

This region has, perhaps, fewer traditionally picturesque villages than other parts of Devon, but makes up for it with the one that vies with Cockington (near Torquay) as Devon's most visited: **Clovelly**. This tiny fishing village has no cars, two hotels, and 2,000 visitors a day in summer. While Clovelly is quaint, some of the **great houses** and gardens in the area are splendidly grand. Hartland Abbey is my favourite in all of Devon, but Arlington Court is also impressive, and **Broomhill Sculpture Garden** is thrilling in its combination of art and nature.

The area has strong **literary associations**. Charles Kingsley's name is everywhere, though few 21st-century readers appreciate his flowery, moralistic prose (he wrote *The Water Babies* and *Westward Ho!*). Henry Williamson, on the other hand, was one of the finest nature writers ever. His love for north Devon stemmed from a childhood holiday, and shines through his subsequent writing. Utterly out of his environment as a soldier in World War I he wrote vividly of life in the trenches (*A Chronicle of Ancient Sunlight*, considered, by some, to be one of the greatest series of novels of its time). In the latter part of his life he became embittered and succumbed to extreme right-wing views, but that doesn't diminish the importance of his most famous work, the 1927 *Tarka the Otter*, written in Georgeham where he lived for eight years and is buried. His otter ranged widely over the rivers of north Devon, hence the Tarka label attached to the oblong of countryside stretching from the north coast's sandy shores to the edge of Dartmoor.

The north is the **surfing** capital of Devon, particularly Croyde Beach and Saunton Sands. **South South West** offers lessons to both beginners and improvers: 01271 890400; www.southsouthwest.com.

A meeting with Henry Williamson

Bob Dawe

In a way it feels as though Henry Williamson and I shared a childhood. We both flew kites and tobogganed on Hilly Fields in southeast London even though there was nearly half a lifetime's difference in our ages.

I was keen to meet him and so wrote to him in 1973, shortly afterwards finding myself driving down to visit the lonely hut in which he wrote, high above Georgeham. He lived not far away in a terraced house in Ilfracombe. His mop of white hair and droopy World War I moustache were unmistakable, but I was taken aback by the enormous weariness in his rheumy old eyes, caused by the days and nights he spent writing, writing, often by no more than the light of a candle.

His small basement room was swimming in manuscripts which were piled up everywhere, on tables, the carpet, the floor. *Tarka the Otter* was currently being filmed and, much to his annoyance and confusion, Williamson had been repeatedly badgered to shorten the filmscript, hence the sea of paper as he struggled to complete the work.

Throughout his long life, Williamson had enjoyed the company of women. When I found him fretting in this nest of paper, he was bemoaning the fact that his latest young lady acolyte, who had been doing her best to help him sort it all out, had just left him in the lurch. We retreated to his 'local' where he was not too weary to do his best to impress my girlfriend by squeezing a bread-crust into the shape of an aeroplane and zooming it around her head. Later, we parted company on the sunny edge of Exmoor. As we left the pub, Williamson extravagantly and unnecessarily draped his greatcoat in an overtly protective gesture around my girlfriend's shoulders.

As we drove away, I could see him in my rear view mirror staring after us, a sagging, lonely, world- and work-weary figure. I felt a strange mixture of pity and respect. Not long after this the film of *Tarka the Otter* was completed and not long after that, Henry Williamson died.

Getting there and around

Northwest Devon has excellent **road** links with Tiverton, Exeter and Plymouth, as well as Cornwall. However the **rail** link between Exeter and Barnstaple, the Tarka Line, is so scenic, and the bicycle hire shop in the station so conveniently placed, that a combination of train and bike is an obvious alternative. The local **bus** service isn't bad either.

Barnstaple is the region's public-transport hub. The **Tarka Line** (see page 217) makes frequent stops on its journey, half of which follows the River Taw, so a variety of walks can be made along the way. **Bus routes** fan out from Barnstaple, covering almost all the areas described here. The *North Devon* timetable (www.devon.gov.uk/buses) covers this region. For current bus times (or help) phone Traveline (0871 200 2233). If you get stuck, taxi companies in Barnstaple include A1 Taxi Service (01271 322922), Barnstaple Taxi Service (01271 379455) and Starline Taxis (01271 376070).

Cycling and walking

Mike Harrison, compiler of CroydeCycle maps (www.croydecycle.co.uk), writes: 'Cycling in north Devon is a pleasure, being far from cities so most of the rural lanes are quiet. The Tarka Trail (NCN 3 and 27) is ideal for families and there are other quiet and level lanes around Braunton. Coastal roads can be busy at peak times and often a bike is the quickest way round the narrow lanes but be wary of cars.'

Supplementing the Tarka Trail is the Ilfracombe–Woolacombe cycle circuit. Although part of NCN27, it offers a 15-mile circular route, largely along roads but with a traffic-free section from outside Ilfracombe to Willingcott Cross, along a disused railway, and the coast at Woolacombe Sands. It's very scenic but hilly. The road section takes you to Georgeham, Woolacombe and Mortehoe (the worst hill!) and back via the old railway line to Ilfracombe. This route is described in detail in the free booklet *Cycling Trails in Devon* available from www.visitdevon.co.uk (click on 'brochure request').

The South West Coast Path joins the Tarka Trail to the west of Braunton, but for truly spectacular walking head for Hartland Point. The remote, hilly, and astoundingly beautiful section from Hartland Point to the Cornish border is reckoned, by some, to be the finest in Devon, There are also numerous inland footpaths where you won't meet a soul.

If you prefer a choice of more sociable walks with experienced guides, the **North Devon and Exmoor Walking Festival**, held each year in May and September, is recommended; www.walkingnorthdevon.co.uk or www.west countrywalks.co.uk.

The Tarka Trail

This 180-mile, traffic-free recreational route for cyclists and walkers has some stretches for walkers only; others are so popular with cyclists that walkers may feel crowded out.

The cycle path, shared by walkers, along a disused railway line, goes from Braunton to Meeth. From Braunton, Ilfracombe and Combe Martin the trail is for walkers only, linking up with the South West Coast Path, before joining the Two Moors Way and Macmillan Way from Lynton to Barnstaple. From Meeth the Tarka Trail is again for walkers only, running through the northern edge of Dartmoor to link up with the Tarka Line (see page 217) at Eggesford.

The different sections are described under the relevant towns.

Walking maps and guides

Walkers and cyclists have a bonus in this region – Mike Harrison's marvellous pocket-sized CroydeCycle maps (cost £2). Walkers' maps are Coastal Path map

3, *Westward Ho! to Bude* (scale 1:15,000), and the 1:12,500-scale Walking Maps of *Hartland & Clovelly, Braunton, Croyde, Mortehoe & Woolacombe, Ilfracombe & Berrynarbor*, and *Combe Martin & Hunter's Inn* (Exmoor). There's also a *Braunton & Ilfracombe Cycle Map*, scale 1:30,000. They're widely available but you can also order them direct (01271 891160; www.croydecycle.co.uk).

Ordnance Survey's 1:25,000 Explorer series covers the region in two single-sided maps, 126 and 139. The Landranger 1: 50:000 map 180 doesn't extend to Hartland Point but supplemented by the CroydeCycle map gives you sufficient coverage.

For those who prefer to follow written instructions, there's the 'no map reading' series of walking and cycling leaflets put out by Bryan Cath, Devon's walking expert, who runs West Country Walks (01271 883131; www.westcountrywalks.co.uk).

A number of **guidebooks** detail walks in the area. *Shortish walks in North Devon* (Bossiney Books; www.bosinneybooks.com) is easy to follow with clear maps; *Classic Walks: Devon* (Norton Publishing) has nine walks in this region. The official guidebook for the *South West Coast Path* is published annually by the South West Coast Path Association (01752 896237; www.swcp.org.uk) and includes convenient accommodation.

North Devon Area of Outstanding Natural Beauty ✆ www.northdevon-aonb.org.uk.
North Devon Biosphere ✆ www.northdevonbiosphere.org.uk.
North Devon Marketing Bureau ✆ www.northdevon.com.

Hartland and Clovelly

Hartland Point – or rather its geology – is the focus here. There's no better place in Devon to see the effects of a mighty collision of tectonic plates, around 300 million years ago, which folded the rock like an accordion or pushed it up on its side. Different types of rock erode at varying rates so they tip and slide forming cliffs and sea-stacks.

To experience these remarkable formations fully you need to walk a stretch of the coastal path, but there are two car access points at Hartland Quay and Hartland Point where the less mobile can admire the seascape.

The bus service here is not ideal for coast path walkers since the 319 runs along the A39, necessitating a two-mile hike to reach the coast. However, there are some good walks to/from Clovelly.

① Hartland

The main settlement in the area has a long history. Hartland was a gift from King Alfred to his son Edward, and passed down a line of kings until Canute and eventually William the Conqueror. Seven hundred years later, however, it was described by W G Maton as having 'an air of poverty that depresses it to a level with a Cornish borough'. These days it has regained its confidence and enjoys a nice community feel, an innovative bespoke furniture shop, a village store that stays open late and has a microwave oven for heating your pastics, and a free car park. There are also pubs and teashops.

The principal sights are some distance from Hartland, but both conveniently in the direction of Hartland Quay. The glorious Hartland Abbey is about a mile away and the church, whose tower – at 128 feet the highest in Devon – provides a landmark for walkers, is a mile further on at Stoke. You enter **St Nectan's Church** via an unusual swivel lychgate with a counter-balance weight to keep it closed. Inside are numbered pews from the days when parishioners had to pay 'pew rent' for their seat in church, a huge, intricately carved screen with typical Devon fan vaulting, and carved bench ends. There are memorials, inside and out, to the Lane family who founded Penguin Books.

② Hartland Abbey

W G Maton may have had a poor view of Hartland, but he loved the house, now known as Hartland Abbey:

> *Every advantage has been taken of the spot to create a picturesque and agreeable scene, the slopes on each side being planted very judiciously, and the intermediate lawn opened to a little bridge that crosses a swift, bubbling brook... Though built in a monastic fashion, with Gothic windows, the Priory [sic] is wholly modern, no remains of the old structure being left. It is at present the residence of Colonel Orchard.*

The house was indeed wholly modern when Maton saw it in the 1790s; Paul Orchard had completely rebuilt it only 20 years earlier. Nothing remains of the original abbey, which survived longer than any other monastery in England. When Henry VIII finally dissolved it in 1539 he gave it to the appropriately named William Abbott, who was Sergeant of his Wine Cellar at Hampton Court (nice job; nice perks!). The Orchards held it for a hundred years before it passed to the Stucleys in the mid 1800s; it has been with their family ever since. The Orchards and the Stucleys demolished, rebuilt and altered parts of the house over the centuries, so the current building is a hodgepodge of different designs – but it works, perhaps thanks to architects like Sir George Gilbert Scott who was commissioned by Sir George Stucley to design the entrance and front hall which give the arriving visitor such a positive impression.

Hartland Abbey is gorgeous: far superior to most other great Devon houses, which sometimes struggle to justify their entrance fee. This is indisputedly grand, with magnificent fireplaces, splendid furniture and paintings, many of them from Poltimore House near Exeter (the heiress of Poltimore married a Stucley), and stunning views from the huge windows. The quality of the contents is one of the advantages of a house that has never been sold, but passed down through the centuries by inheritance.

A peep into the guest rooms makes one envious of the wartime evacuees from London's Highgate Junior School, who hit the jackpot when they were sent here. They come back each year to relive those extraordinary days when they acquired a lifelong appreciation of the countryside. Scattered around the house are laminated newspaper cuttings which add snippets of intrigue: Princess Margaret in a bath wearing a tiara, for instance.

The library was built within the walls of the original abbey, and is hung with portraits including one by Sir Joshua Reynolds and two by Gainsborough. And there are quite a few books. Before the war it used to have a lot more – 8,000 more, in fact. In 1939 these books were found to be surplus to requirements and taken to the local tip. A canny farmer intercepted the cart and decided they would be just the thing for building a boundary wall: cheaper than bricks. This literary wall contained such rarities as a copy of a Hebrew grammar from 1597. There will have been some erudite cows in north Devon.

The gardens are as rewarding as the house, and the lived-in, or rather worked-in, feeling is even stronger since almost all of the work has been done by the Stucley family themselves. They only employ 1½ gardeners, so to have achieved this amount of order in such a vast garden is an inspiration to us inept amateurs. The information leaflet describes this challenge in detail; it is clearly written by gardeners for gardeners. Make sure you pick up a copy before setting out to explore. I recommend a visit to the Bog Garden where narrow paths wind around huge stands of giant rhubarb, *Gunnera manicata*, and more delicate ferns and other water-loving plants. Some way from the house is the walled kitchen garden, where runner beans dangled temptingly and a gardener or a Stucley was tying up the raspberry vines. This garden helps to feed the present-day family.

Beyond the car park is a path 'to the beach'. It joins the South West Coast Path at Blackpool Mill, and, since it misses out the first up and down of the Hartland Point walk, makes a sensible alternative to starting the walk at Hartland Quay. On a high point, just before meeting the coast path, is the newly restored gazebo with a super view over the sea to Lundy Island.

Hartland Abbey EX39 6DT ☏ 01237 441264/441234 🖰 www.hartlandabbey.com. Open Apr–Oct; closed Sat. Other opening days/times for the house and gardens vary considerably according to the season, so check the website or phone before visiting.

Walks in the Hartland area

The convoluted slabs of rock washed by the sea, contrasting with the gentle green hills inland, make this one of the most dramatically beautiful walking areas in north Devon. Below is just a sample; you can easily devise your own itineraries using the CroydeCycle *Hartland & Clovelly* map.

Elmscott to Hartland Quay *(3 miles each way)*

There's accommodation at the privately owned **Youth Hostel** (01237 441276) and parking nearby. A clearly signed path runs through a field to join the coast path, where you turn right and keep going. Ahead is the high tower of St Nectan's Church just inland in Stoke, and the dome of the radar station marking Hartland Point. It's a gentle, easy walk, mainly on the level, with a series of inaccessible beaches and jagged rocks below you. I walked it in sunshine after days of rain which had encouraged giant parasol mushrooms to appear among the gorse and heather. Talking of gorse, this was the first time I'd noticed the parasitic common dodder, draped over the gorse like a fragrant mauve bedspread. It kills the gorse, but in this case I prefer the parasite to the host.

After about half a mile you'll come to a seat made from the wreckage of the tanker *Green Ranger* which broke up on the

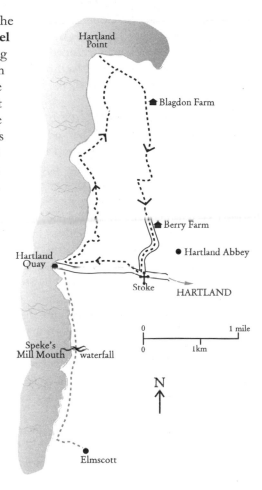

rocks during a gale in November 1962. Heroic Appledore lifeboatmen rescued the crew. Part of the wreck is still visible. The unfolding panorama of rocks at the sea's edge is extraordinary: jagged, furrowed or tilted. At **Speke's Mill Mouth** a spectacular waterfall pours, unhindered, over a vertical rock face, popular with climbers. **Hartland Quay** is only 20 minutes away. The rocks now look like purple ploughed fields, broken by high, smooth chunks topped with green. The closer you get to the quay, the more dramatic the seascape, until you reach Hartland Quay Hotel with a view to die for, and snacks or full meals available from the bar. If you want to linger, there's a small shipwreck museum, a good reminder of the days when this was a busy port. In the late 18th century W G Maton commented that 'Hartland-quay consists of about a dozen decent cottages, and has a commodious little pier, at which commodities of various kinds, for the supply of this part of the country, are landed from Bideford and Barnstaple; and here the fishermen and coasters find good shelter against the south-westerly winds, by mooring under the eminences.' This quay was still in use 50 years later when Hartland Abbey's Sir George Stucley landed a load of Maltese stone from his yacht, destined for the fireplace in the billiard room.

Head inland to look at **St Nectan's Church** in Stoke and/or **Hartland Abbey**, then return to your car via the narrow lanes.

Around Hartland Point (five miles, circular route)

Local walks expert Bryan Cath warned me: 'It may look short but there are five up and downs and no escape route; it's more than some people can cope with.' Indeed, it looks easy to follow the coastal path round Hartland Point to the lighthouse and beyond, but it is certainly strenuous. However, I've known worse elsewhere on the South West Coast Path and the scenery is superlative, so the above is a warning not a deterrent. And it's easy to make it a circular walk, with a chance to see St Nectan's Church and Hartland Abbey too. If you plan to visit Hartland Abbey (do double-check the opening times), you can park there and take the private path to Blackpool Mill, thus cutting out one of the hills. Or achieve the same objective by parking at **Stoke** and taking the path that follows the south bank of Abbey River.

If you park at **Hartland Quay**, take the path round **Warren Beach**. After meeting and leaving the road, start your first climb, admiring the pleated and puckered cliff rocks as you go, to Dyer's Lookout. Dropping down to Abbey River and its bridge, you'll see **Blackpool Mill Cottage** ahead. You may recognise it from the 2007 television film of *Sense and Sensibility* – it played the part of the Dashwoods' Barton Cottage and, as self-catering accommodation, has hardly been empty since.

Another up, another down – and again, and again, and again – and you'll be at **Hartland Point** with its lighthouse sitting coyly at the base of the cliff (closed to visitors) and the big radar 'football' on the hill. This was an important place during World War II (see box opposite). The hills are hard work but from every summit there's a splendid view; remember to stop and look back as well as forward. The steeply sloping rock faces here are used for **climbing and abseiling** run by Skern Lodge (01237 475992; www.skernlodge.co.uk).

At the end of the track to the lighthouse there's a small car park and very welcome refreshment kiosk selling truly wonderful cream teas. This exceptional place, which closes at 17.00, has a range of special teas, and bird and flower guides for visitors to look at.

To return to your car, turn your sights to the church tower and follow it along often muddy tracks to **Stoke**.

Wartime radar at Hartland Point
Patricia Thomas

Well before World War II began, Britain's leaders anticipated invasion and attacks on shipping so radar bases were set up all around the coast to track vessels and aircraft. I served in the WAAF (Women's Auxiliary Air Force) as a radar operator from 1942 to 1946 and spent several months at different stations. In the summer of 1942 I was transferred to Hartland Point where a radar station operated under the control of 78 Wing.

Several of us worked there and we lived in Nissen huts on a sheltered site. We worked four-hour shifts but such absolute concentration was necessary to follow the sweep of the radar beam across the tube that operators were changed hourly to rest their eyes. We were allowed to read, write letters (which were subject to censorship) or play cards. I remember on one occasion a farmer gave us a rabbit, which we cooked with some vegetables on a primus stove, and one of the RAF men produced a bottle of brandy from his first-aid kit to go with it.

The lavatory was outside and we were not allowed to venture to it alone, particularly in bad weather when the wind could be very strong. On a sunny summer's day in peacetime Hartland Point may look an idyllic place to work but in those days Britain's coastline was swathed in entangling rolls of barbed wire with gun sites set at different levels, camouflaged until the brambles, gorse, sea thistles and other natural cover had grown up. We tried to make the best of it: I used to work with a friend called Rosamund and sometimes at the end of our shift if it was a warm day we'd wriggle round the wire to get down to the rocks so we could sunbathe and swim if the tide was up.

③ Clovelly

At Clovelly is a little pier for vessels, and the harbour is noted for the herring-fishery. The land, as it juts out into the promontory of Hartland, is by no means remarkable for fertility, nor is it either novel, or varied enough to be pleasing to the eye.
W G Maton, travelling during 1794–96.

Clovelly has certainly changed, but it took another century for its charms to become widely known. The man credited with this is the Victorian writer Charles Kingsley who, in 1885, described the village in typically overblown fashion in his novel *Westward Ho!* (Yes, the town to the east of Clovelly is named after the book and keeps the same exclamation mark.) Visitors began arriving by boat and as the herrings, which had provided the village with income for centuries, declined in number, so the tourists increased. After Kingsley came

Christine Hamlyn, who ensured that the village remained in a time-warp.

Clovelly has been owned by one family since Zachary Hamlyn, a wealthy lawyer, bought the estate from the last of seven generations of the Cary family in 1738. Christine married Frederick Gosling in 1889, persuading him first to change his name, and secondly to earmark a portion of his large fortune for improving the estate. Many of the cottages were run down, so they and the entire village were restored and prettified according to Christine's taste. Her initials and the date of restoration can sometimes be spotted above a doorway. It was she who ensured that the village remained car-free, the only transport up and down its stepped, cobbled main street being donkeys and sleds. Tourist sentiment has put paid to the pannier-laden donkeys that used to carry supplies and mail; we love seeing working horses, but apparently not working donkeys. The animals now live in a sanctuary and pose for photos or give rides to children. But the sleds are still used, and you'll see them tied up outside the cottages. Souvenir shops are restricted, and all cottages must be leased as the primary home of their owner. Thus, although Clovelly is extraordinarily picturesque, it is a lived-in, working village, but with about 70% of its inhabitants commuting to the real world.

Be warned: in peak season it receives up to 2,000 visitors a day. If you arrive the conventional way, by car, you will be processed through the visitor centre, paying an entrance fee before watching a film about the village's history. Then you're funnelled down the narrow cobbled street to peer into the windows of private houses, choose a few souvenirs, and buy a beer and Devon pasty from the Red Lion pub. If the steep climb up is too daunting a Land Rover service will help you out. And if you resent paying the entrance fee bear in mind that it is this income that keeps the village as it is, free from fast-food outlets and amusement arcades. Or you could come in the evening when the visitor centre is closed and the crowds have gone.

Clovelly Charters ☎ 01237 431405 or 07774 190359 🖥 www.clovelly-charters.ukf.net. Diving or fishing trips, swimming with seals, and visits to Lundy on the *Jessica Hettie*.

Walks to or from Clovelly

If you contrive to arrive in Clovelly on foot you will avoid the feeling of entering a theme park and see it for what it is: an extraordinarily picturesque working village. There's a short circular walk from the car park at Brownsham or two possibilities for bus walks.

Circular walk to Clovelly from Brownsham (5½ miles)

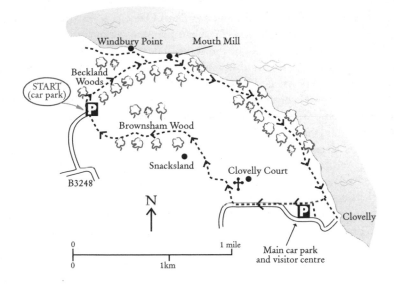

This is mostly straightforward and easy to follow, taking you through woods and along some splendid stretches of the coastal path. There are no particularly strenuous hills.

From the National Trust car park at **Brownsham**, take the path through **Beckland Woods** and follow the signs to **Mouth Mill**; it has some ruined buildings from the old lime kiln in which you can shelter if it's raining, and a pebble beach. The rock formations are splendid, like multi-tiered sandwiches laid on their sides. You are now only about 45 minutes from Clovelly, through Brownsham Wood, owned by the National Trust, and knee-deep in imbecile young pheasants in the late summer. About a third of the way there you'll pass the beautifully carved 'Angel Wings' seat, put there by Sir James Hamlyn Williams in 1826. Soon you'll get glimpses of Clovelly tucked into the cliffs and have a choice of routes into the village: either the road, and a steep walk downhill to emerge near the Red Lion pub by the quay, or the footpath that leads you to the centre of the village.

Returning takes about an hour, and is straightforward except for one confusing bit. Walk out along the road to the main gate of the estate, and pass through the side gate, past the church, then follow the bridleway. Once you see the cottage marked Snacksland on the CroydeCycle map (or Snaxland on the OS map), leave the track and bear right across the field. The bridleway is signposted where it enters Brownsham Wood; after that simply follow it to the car park.

Bus walks to Clovelly from Hartland Quay or Bucks Mills

The 319 bus running along the A39 makes two sorties inland, to Clovelly Visitor Centre and to Hartland, enabling you to do a linear walk between these two points; or you can join it at Bucks Mills or further east, depending on your level of energy.

If you park in Hartland and walk to Hartland Quay to access the coast path the hike is nearly 12 miles. However, you can join it at various places east – the distance along small lanes is about the same. The six-mile walk from the bus stop above Bucks Mills is very different, being mainly inland through woods, including the track known as 'The Hobby Drive': a carriage way constructed, as a hobby, by James Hamlyn, during the Napoleonic Wars, perhaps using the labour of French prisoners-of-war. During those times of high unemployment land-owners thought up schemes to provide work for their labourers, and carriage ways were popular projects. The 1939 Ward Lock guide to the area states that: 'At one time all the inhabitants of Bucks were "Braunds" and many of that name live there still. They seem to be a distinct race, swarthy to a degree, and are held to be descended from a party of Spaniards who some say were wrecked near, and others contend were taken prisoners, at the time of the Armada.' I have no idea whether any Braunds are left in the area. I didn't notice any particularly swarthy individuals.

Bideford, Barnstaple and area

Linked by the Tarka Trail, these two towns are the business focus of the North West and, after the tranquillity of the villages nearby, can feel oppressive with their traffic and multiple roundabouts. They are hard to avoid, however, particularly if you are hiring a bike to cycle part of the Tarka Trail.

④ Bideford

The Bridge at Bedeforde is a very notable Worke... A poore Preste began thys Bridge; and, as it is saide, he was animated so to do by a Vision. Then al the Cuntery about sette their Handes onto the performing of it, and sins Landes hath bene gyven to the maintenaunce of it. Ther standith a fair Chapelle of our Lady at the very ende of it, and there is a Fraternite in the Town for perservation of this Bridge; and one waitith continually to kepe the Bridge clene from al Ordure.
John Leland, travelling during 1534–43.

Bideford's **Long Bridge** is still its most notable feature. It has linked the town with its neighbour across the Torridge, East-the-Water, since about 1280. Two hundred years later the wooden bridge was reinforced with stone; the original wooden arches varied in width, and this irregularity has been preserved with each rebuilding. Leland's 'Fraternite in the Town', the Bideford Bridge Trust, continued to maintain the bridge until 1968 when the western arch collapsed; the Department of Transport decided that enough was enough and took over responsibility.

The Grenville family owned Bideford from Norman times until 1744, but until the late 16th century it was mainly a centre for shipbuilding, and largely overshadowed by Barnstaple. After Sir Richard Grenville's 1585 voyage to establish colonies in Virginia and Carolina, trans-Atlantic trade took off, along with Bideford's fortunes. The Quay was built in 1663 and quantities of tobacco and Newfoundland cod were landed there. The town's surge of prosperity began towards the end of the 17th century when it was the main port for the transport of goods to and from the American colonies. Tobacco was the main import. The attractive houses on Bridgeland Street, climbing up from the broad, tree-lined Quay, date from that era. In the mid 19th century it was exporting emigrants to the USA. The very good **Burton Art Gallery and Museum** is beyond the statue of Charles Kingsley at the north end of the Quay. The town's **Tourist Information Centre** is also here (01237 477676). And there's a Pannier Market on Tuesdays and Saturdays. In East-the-Water **The Royal Hotel** was formerly a rich merchant's house, and still has a fine plaster ceiling on the first floor; Charles Kingsley wrote part of *Westward Ho!* here.

The folks of Bideford become very jolly on **New Year's Eve**, gathering on the Long Bridge in a variety of outlandish fancy-dress costumes to welcome in the New Year.

The Big Sheep Abbotsham ☎ 01237 472366 🖰 www.thebigsheep.co.uk. An imaginatively run family entertainment centred around sheep, including sheep racing.
Burton Art Gallery and Museum Kingsley Rd ☎ 01237 471455
🖰 www.burtonartgallery.co.uk. Combines a tourist information centre, a gallery for changing exhibitions and some permanent displays, and a café. Open Mon–Sat.

⑤ Barnstaple

Historically, Barnstaple has always been compared with Bideford, the fortunes of one rising as the other waned. It, too, has a bridge over the Taw which has an even more exciting history than its rival since it was begun, so they say, by two spinster sisters who spun the first two piers with the assistance of local children. John Leland called it a 'right great and sumptuous Bridge of Stone having 16 high Arches'.

The river silted up in the 19th century and maritime trade switched to Bideford. However, Barnstaple prospered as a market town; it's now the largest town in North Devon and the only one to have a railway connection with the rest of the county. And it is that railway that brings visitors to Barnstaple, and the railway that allows them to escape, for there is little of obvious interest in the town itself, although the **Pannier Market**, held on every day except Sundays, is enjoyable. However, there is a Heritage Trail and a **Museum** (8 Taw Vale; 01271 346747), which has good and varied exhibits on local natural history and archaeology, and a display of boldly decorated Barum Ware from the

Brannam pottery. The town also stages a one-day **North Devon FoodFest** (www.northdevonfoodfest.com) in October.

The Tourist Information Centre is near the railway station (01271 375000; www.staynorthdevon.co.uk).

⑥ Broomhill Art Hotel and Sculpture Gardens

I found myself walking around this magical place with a smile on my face. The early morning sun spot-lit sculptures that would be impressive in a gallery setting, but here, chancing upon them as you wander down meandering paths in the woods, past stands of bamboo and giant rhubarb, or alongside the tree-shaded river, you feel that such a garden is the only setting in which to exhibit large sculptures. Not that they are all large. Sometimes you are alerted to their presence by the sign before you see the piece almost hidden in the shrubbery, such as *Body Stretch*, which is tucked into a bank. Other favourites were the *Three Graces*, a circle of generously proportioned but perfectly formed cavorting ladies, and the menacing graffiti artist caught in the act of embellishing a wall.

Broomhill happened because Rinus and Aniet van de Sande, from the Netherlands, started a gallery to encourage young artists in their home country, but wanted an outdoor venue. Holland was not an option 'because so many galleries and sculpture gardens already existed' so when they found a run-down hotel with a large, overgrown garden on the outskirts of Barnstaple, they knew it was the right place. Broomhill's ten acres are now a mixture of formal garden and natural woodland, and even without the sculptures the steeply terraced and wooded grounds would be a pleasure to stroll in. The combination of the two is stunning, and a must-see for anyone with an interest in art. Or in Slow Food, for its **Terra Madre restaurant**, too, is exceptional, focusing mainly on Mediterranean cooking. An awful lot of restaurants claim 'locally sourced food' nowadays, but here the farms supplying the organic/free-range ingredients are listed, and the philosophy of the Slow Food Movement, of which Rinus is a member, is explained. What could be better for this book: nourishment for the body and soul in one place. Well done Rinus!

Broomhill Hotel and Sculpture Gardens Barnstaple, EX31 4EX ✆ 01271 850262 ⌨ www.broomhillart.co.uk. The hotel is off the B3230 near Muddiford, between Ilfracombe and Barnstaple. Open Wed–Sun, 11.00–16.00. Short closure in Dec/Jan.

⑦ Arlington Court

The Chichester family owned the estate from 1384 until 1949 when Miss Rosalie Chichester bequeathed it to the National Trust. She was the only child of Sir Bruce Chichester, who used to take her on long voyages around the Mediterranean on his schooner, *Erminia*. And, yes, Sir Francis Chichester, the round-the-world yachtsman, was a relative: Rosalie's nephew. Her interest in ships is evident throughout the house in the many exquisite models made from bone and spun glass. Her enthusiasm for animals also appears in the several models and sculptures of questionable beauty, including a truly hideous crystal cat/leopard. The only valuable work of art was found on top of a cupboard in a disused wing of the house: a watercolour by William Blake, painted in 1821. No doubt the mistress of the house didn't like it.

Completed in 1822, the house is described as Neo Greek, and was added to, clumsily, in 1865. More rewarding is the collection of carriages in the old stables. It's one of the best in the country with clear labelling and enough variety to retain interest, from the governess cart which can be compared, in its utility design, to the Morris Minor of later years to the state coaches and even more glamorous state chariots. There are some nice human stories in the inscriptions, such as the footmen who stood at the back of the state coach, bolt upright and immobile, even though they only had two straps to hold on to, and the stable boy who lived in a loft above the stables and had to be available at all times.

Behind the house in a dripping cellar you'll find a batcam. Devon's largest population of lesser horseshoe bats spends its summers here in the roof space, and they hibernate in the cellar. The house and carriage collection is open from March to November; in winter, grounds only, dawn to dusk (01271 850296).

The Tarka Line

This branch railway from Exeter to Barnstaple is one of the most scenic in the county. It runs for 39 miles from the River Exe to the Taw estuary, following much of the river and countryside that featured in *Tarka the Otter*. The leisurely journey takes an hour. Bicycles are carried free, but are normally limited to two.

The Tarka Rail Association (www.tarkarail.org) is a group of enthusiasts who are working with First Great Western and other bodies to improve the service. One of their initiatives is ***Tarka Line Walks***, a guide to 22 linear and circular walks from the railway using the 11 stations along the line as start/finish points. This excellent scheme opens up an area of Devon which is walked much less than the South West Coast Path or the Two Moors Way. As any walker knows, a strategically placed pub can put a spring in the step, and there's a similar booklet describing the **Rail Ale Trail** which recommends the best pubs along the Tarka Line. Go into www.railaletrail.com for details, and make a point of noting the time that the pub's kitchen closes. We've all had the experience of arriving tired and hungry at five past two and finding no food is available. See page 54 for a description of Colebrooke, a very special place near the railway.

Cycling the Tarka Trail

Never has a disused railway line been put to better use! Families who pedal happily in the sunshine have reason to bless Dr Beeching who closed this unprofitable branch line in 1965. Freight trains continued to use it until 1982 and the line was purchased in 1985 by Devon County Council. It must carry far more cycles on its level and scenic route than ever it did rail passengers, and deserves its popularity. From the ease of hiring cycles in Braunton (see page 222), Bideford and Barnstaple, to the informative signs and lovely waterside scenery, this is a great way of spending a summer day.

The stretch of the Tarka Trail between Barnstaple and Bideford is nine miles. I opted for the six miles to Instow, with lunch at The Bar, then back the way I came. The whole trip couldn't have been easier. I found Tarka Trail Cycle Hire right *in* the station – actually occupying the former gents' toilet. John and Margaret Kempson spent 18 months negotiating with Railtrack for some space, but their persistence has paid off. Being able to step off a train and on to a bike with the minimum of fuss has ensured their success. They were pioneers when they started, however. John reckons they were only the fourth business in the country to hire out bicycles, and that 100,000 people have pedalled out of their yard in the 20 years they've been operating.

I asked for 'an old lady's bike' since I didn't want to fuss with lots of gears when the track is level. Maps are provided, but the Tarka Trail is so well waymarked that you mostly don't need them. On a sunny day in May the track was lined with cow parsley and other late spring flowers and fluttering with painted-lady butterflies. Songbirds trilled to our left and water birds lurked in the RSPB Isley Marsh Nature Reserve on our right. There are some hides for proper birdwatching if you want to take a break.

Instow station comes as a surprise. The platform is still there, as is the signal box. There are even some milk churns waiting to be loaded on the absent train. Instow lies at the junction of the Taw and Torridge, and is an agreeable village with a broad sandy beach; **Appledore** across the water is accessible by ferry in the summer. Between them, Instow and Appledore have a large selection of pubs (Appledore has six).

Food and drink on the Tarka Trail

The Bar Marine Parade, Instow ℓ 01271 860624. Boasts a 'quayside location' but the seats are next to a busy road. Good food, Real ales.

The Rolle Quay Inn Rolle St, Barnstaple ℓ 01271 345182. Near the Tarka Trail and serving a range of St Austell's ales and guest ale. Food served 12.00–14.30.

Cycle Hire (Barnstaple and Bideford)

Bideford Bicycle & Kayak Hire Torrington St, East-the-Water, EX39 4DR
ℓ 01237 424123 ✇ www.bidefordbicyclehire.co.uk. Open all year. May offer a pick up/drop off service so you can do a linear route.

Biketrail The Stone Barn, Fremington Quay, nr Barnstaple, EX31 2NH ☎ 01271 372586 ⁿℬ www.biketrail.co.uk. Open daily during school holidays. Will pick up bikes if you want to do a linear route (email mail@biketrail.co.uk beforehand). Fremington Quay is a pleasant two-mile walk along the Tarka Trail from Barnstaple.

Tarka Trail Cycle Hire The Railway Station, Barnstaple, EX34 8DL ☎ 01271 324202 ⁿℬ www.tarkabikes.co.uk. Open daily Mar–Nov.

South of Barnstaple

Driving south from Barnstaple and the coastal resorts, the RHS garden of Rosemoor deserves inclusion, and if you own a Jack Russell terrier you may want to make a pilgrimage to Swimbridge.

⑧ Tawstock

The Erle of Bathe hath a right goodly Maner and Place at Tawstoke on the West side of the Haven.
John Leland, travelling during 1534–43.

This extraordinary place illustrates the historical position of the local aristocracy in its community better than anywhere I know. The entrance is intimidating enough for a modern visitor, so must have been awe-inspiring for a 17th-century labourer. As you drive or cycle down a narrow lane, you pass between stone pillars topped by faithful hounds. To the left are the huge remains of the manor gatehouse with its vast oak door that would admit a carriage and team of horses. Above it is a coat of arms and the date, 1574. A catastrophic fire in 1787 destroyed the rest of the manor, which was rebuilt in 'Gothick' style by Sir Bourchier Wrey. The original lords of the manor were the Bourchiers, created Earls of Bath in 1536; it passed, through marriage, to the Wreys in the 17th century.

Through the centuries the earls could look down on their little **church**, St Peter's, in its lowly position with a sweep of green hills behind it, and feel they had God just where they wanted Him. The inside of the church is so crammed with Wrey memorials that they compete for holy space; uplifting inscriptions, monuments and memorial stones take over the chancel and much of the side aisle. Nor is it just the memorials that make the church so impressive – and different. Its organ is massive, with pipes almost framing a modern stained-glass window. The additional south aisle was formed by knocking holes into the existing side of the church, and creating arches. The pillars that support them are topped with rather smug carved faces and wreaths of foliage. The eagle lectern is ornithologically worrying: this bird would have been unable to close its splendid beak. The chancel is completely paved with inscribed stones commemorating people who died in the 17th and 18th centuries. You can spend a happy half hour reading these, before moving on to the memorials. The most impressive is to the Earl of Bath who died in 1654. His giant sarcophagus is guarded by 'dogs' that spring from the pages of Harry Potter, with curly manes, menacing claws, and oversized canines – another animal that could not have closed its mouth. Only the cropped ears suggest domesticity. Then there are the painted memorials to the third Earl of Bath, William Bourchier, and his wife Elizabeth. Her feet are resting on a goat. At least I think it's a goat. A panel of photos shows how these tombs were restored when the iron holding sections of the stone together started to rust and cause cracking.

Moving on from the Wreys, there are panels listing the charitable actions of the wealthy towards the poor – and the church. In 1677 the Dowager Countess of Bath 'laid out in Land to the benefit of the Poor of this parish for ever' and 'Shee hath also gave the parish a rich embroidered crimson velvet pulpit cloath and cushion and yearly bound out several poor children apprenticed and done many other excellent acts of charity.' Such was the path to the Kingdom of Heaven. Others were less generous – but also certainly less rich; there are several donations of ten shillings. In the side aisle they've also found room for two secular items of rural history: a coffin cart and a plough. Note, too, above the side aisles, the more recent but beautiful plaster ceiling decoration of delicate flowers and tendrils.

If you only see one church in rural Devon make it this one. No other is as rich in visual history inside and rural beauty in its setting. It's as English as you can get, and is only about two miles from Barnstaple station down a quiet lane so you can walk or cycle here with relative ease.

⑨ Rosemoor

The Royal Horticultural Society's showpiece garden, Rosemoor has 65 acres with 200 varieties of rose, decorative vegetable planting, and woodland walks. Come here on a sunny day, any time of the year, and take your time to breathe in the scents and sights. The knowledge of your fellow visitors can be intimidating. On my last visit a voice boomed out 'Did you tell Daddy about the pelargonium?' The child looked about five.

RHS Garden Rosemoor Great Torrington EX38 8PH ✆ 01805 624067
🖰 www.rhs.org.uk/rosemoor. Open year round, but tea room closed Oct–Apr.

⑩ Swimbridge

'No dogs' says a sign on the gate. Unremarkable except that this church is famous because its long-term vicar was the Reverend John Russell, who bred the first Jack Russell terrier (see box opposite). His plain but conspicuous grave is round the corner in the graveyard – follow the arrows – and the original Jack Russell terrier, Trump, has her portrait on the inn sign for the **Jack Russell pub** opposite the church. The pub is full of Jack Russell memorabilia and less strict than the church about canine visitors.

The **church of St James** is unusual in several ways. It has a lead-coated spire rather than the more familiar tower, and an extraordinary font cover, enclosing the font in sort of cupboard, with a canopy above, all beautifully carved. The stone pulpit is very fine, as is the intricately carved wooden screen, and don't forget to look up at the impressive roof. All in all, a church worth visiting, even if you don't give a toss for Jack Russell terriers.

The village itself is most attractive, with a skein of white and cream houses climbing up a lane, and some well-tended allotments. It even has a working post office. 'Yes, they had quite a fight to keep it open.'

The Reverend John (Jack) Russell

By all accounts the Reverend John Russell most perfectly combined his hobby with making a living. He was a popular minister at St James's Church for 46 years, having arrived, with his pack of hounds, in 1833, and indulged his passion for hunting until two years before his death at the age of 87. An estimated 1,000 people attended his funeral. Despite hunting almost daily, he managed to increase the services at Swimbridge from one each Sunday to four, restored the dilapidated church and its school, and was conscientious in visiting his most needy parishioners. He was also remembered for his charity towards gypsies, who were much persecuted in those days. In return they protected the Rectory from thieves.

Not everyone was happy about his obsession with hunting, however, and eventually he yielded to the pressure to give up his pack of hounds, partly instigated by that scourge of licentious clergymen, Bishop Philpotts of Exeter. For two years Russell was without his own pack, which cast him into such depths of depression that when he was offered the gift of 13 foxhounds his resolve faltered. 'There they stood', he said, 'the greatest beauties my eye had ever rested on, looking up in my face so winningly, that I mentally determined to keep the lot and go to work again'. His wife told him that he had as much right to enjoy life as other men, and so he kept them.

These days Jack Russell is famous for the terriers which bear his name. The story goes that while he was at Oxford – doing precious little work but a lot of hunting – he was strolling in Magdalen Meadow trying to memorise some Latin, when he met a milkman with a little terrier bitch and bought it on the spot. The terrier's name was Trump, and she became the first of a distinct breed of dog now called the Jack Russell terrier. Russell was a founder member of the Kennel Club and a respected judge of fox terriers so he knew a thing or two about dog breeding.

In his lifetime this larger-than-life character was better known for his hunting than for his sermons, although he managed to combine both in a visit to Sandringham. At the invitation of the Prince of Wales who asked him to 'put a sermon in his pocket' he danced in the new year with the Princess of Wales and preached his sermon in Sandringham's church the following Sunday.

North Devon's seaside

North of the River Taw's broad estuary are Devon's most popular seaside resorts: the huge expanses of sand at Saunton and Woolacombe, and the more intimate bays of Croyde and Barricane among others. The unique UNESCO Biosphere of Braunton Burrows lures serious naturalists, and there's good birdwatching around Baggy Point, too, together with small coves that are accessible only on foot so are blessedly crowd-free, even in summer. The 308 bus runs frequently from Barnstaple to Braunton, Saunton, Croyde and Georgeham.

⑪ Braunton Burrows

To a nature lover, the very word Biosphere is alluring, conjuring up the image of rare species you wouldn't find elsewhere. And it's true of this UNESCO Worldwide Biosphere Reserve (www.northdevonbiosphere.org.uk) which recognises the uniqueness of this sand-dune ecosystem. 'Sand' is misleading, since the dunes are clothed in vegetation, giving them a pleasing, green, blobby appearance. If you know your stuff, you could happily spend a few hours here. The casual visitor, however, will be hard put to recognise the rare plants or to spot a lizard or unusual insect. Enjoyment is further complicated by the confusing network of paths that crisscross the dunes; you need a good sense of direction and perhaps a compass if you're to avoid getting lost.

Perhaps the most rewarding way to see the reserve is by bike. The flat lanes are a godsend after the hills of Exmoor, and cycling along the canal you'll see a good range of waterfowl. **Braunton** is also the beginning of the cycling section of the **Tarka Trail**. Cycles can be hired in Braunton (Otter Cycle Hire, Station Rd; 01271 813339).

⑫ Croyde and Georgeham

Croyde has 26 listed buildings, mostly old farmhouses and associated barns, and some good pubs, but most visitors only pass through it *en route* to the **beach**, which is renowned for surfing.

Georgeham was just Ham in the Domesday Book, and gained its longer name through the church of St George. So the correct pronunciation is George-ham. It's worth stopping at the church, if only to potter round the graveyard which is as enjoyable to browse in as a second-hand bookshop. Henry Williamson, author of *Tarka the Otter*, is buried here (near the church tower) but it is the graves of ordinary people which are the most interesting. Almost every stone from the 1840s to the 1890s has a four-line (or longer) commemorative poem, usually assuring the reader that the deceased is better off under God's care. It seems no one dared to die in Georgeham at that time without commissioning the local poet to write a verse.

⑬ Morte Bay, Woolacombe and Mortehoe

To see the best of the coast here park near the Heritage Centre (closed

Saturdays) at **Mortehoe**, where a choice of footpaths connects the village with the coastal path: from here **Barricane** and **Grunta Beaches** are accessible (a steepish climb down rough steps and grass to Grunta, a shorter flight of steps to Barricane) with their rippled sand and satiny grey rocks. At low tide you can paddle barefoot along the waterline the whole way from Grunta to Morte Bay (Woolacombe Sands). **Morte Bay** is huge and spacious, but the smaller Grunta is my favourite; it has rocky alleys for children to explore, rock pools, plenty of sand at low tide, and good pickings for painstaking shell hunters. Since all three have road access, if the tide reaches the rocky strips between them you won't be cut off – or at mid tide you can scramble over and around the rocks.

To reach **Woolacombe Sands** by a more inland route, take the footpath that leads from the far end of the Heritage Centre car park. It climbs and then descends steeply through gorse and rocks, dumping you at the edge of the bay. There's a motorable coast road too.

An alternative from Mortehoe is to follow the coast path north and then east around Morte Point, where many careless ships met their ends, and where you might spot seals or even dolphins. On the north side is **Rockham Bay**, perhaps the most rewarding of all the hidden coves in this area, with coarse sand rather than shingle. As you continue to **Bull Point**, you will come upon more hidden coves and secret swimming places. Perhaps the best of these is **Sandy Cove** (shingle and some sand) from where, at low tide, you can walk to Lee.

⑭ Lee

'Go to Lee', said Mike Harrison, and as compiler of the best maps of the region, he should know. 'It's Devon as it used to be.' He's right, Lee is an absolute gem. It was low tide when I arrived, and the sand, seaweed and rock pools stretched invitingly back to the surf, guarded by giant slices of rock. The remains of a concrete slipway provide access over the seaweedy rocks to the sand. You could spend hours here investigating the pools, collecting pink quartz, or walking up the fuchsia-lined footpath to the village and its delightful pub, the **Grampus Inn**. 'Bill was a fiddle player', Mike told me. 'He wanted to play in a pub so he bought one.' So the Grampus has live music from time to time. It also has real ales and cream teas. And owns the village shop.

Driving out of the village I passed a sign for 'Happy eggs'. I thought it summed up Lee rather nicely. It's only three miles via the coastal path to Ilfracombe, and the 35 bus connects the two places.

The Grampus Inn ☎ 01271 862906 🖥 www.grampus-inn.co.uk. Open daily from 11.00 to midnight, lunch served 12.00–15.00. A classic village pub, the centre of the community, serving a wide range of local ale and cider as well as good food.

⑮ Ilfracombe

The situation of Ilfracombe is truly romantic. The port is a beautiful natural basin, sheltered by craggy heights that are overspread with foliage… The town consists chiefly of one street, full a mile long. It has a neat, healthy appearance, and is said to contain about two thousand inhabitants. The church stands on the upper part of the town and there is a chapel on a sort of knoll which may be called St Michael's Mount in miniature, being joined to the main land only by a narrow neck.
W G Maton, travelling during 1794–96.

'Faded Victorian glory' is how people describe this seaside resort these days. As Dr Maton noted, its position is superb. The town fits where it can between giant crags and grassy mounds, with some imposing houses set high on the surrounding hillsides. The arrival of the railway in Victorian times brought up to 10,000 visitors a day, and encouraged the building of some grand hotels. When the railway closed in 1970 the visitors trickled away and the first impression these days can be discouraging, with the pervading smell of fast food, the jangle of amusement arcades and the blast of live music venues.

Escape to **Tunnels Beach**, which is more of a museum than a beach. You pay a small fee to pass through a tunnel built by miners, to emerge, magically, on a beach surrounded by an amphitheatre of vertical black rocks topped with green. There are tide pools galore, and an artificial 'safe' bathing pool fed by the tides. Along the tunnels are some delightful cuttings from the local newspaper of the time, *The North Devon Journal*, reporting various outrages. One (1859) described the intrusion of two gentlemen on the ladies' bathing area. They swam round the point and 'not only mounted the rocks but plunged into the basin while the female bathers were engaged in their ablutions.' (Remember the female bathers would have been covered from neck to knees in their swimwear.) There are also stern rules governing the use of boats by gentlemen: 'Gentlemen unaccustomed to the management of a boat should never venture out with ladies. To do so is foolhardy, if not criminal… Great care must be taken not to splash the ladies… neither should anything be done to cause them fright.' Inevitably this lovely beach gets crowded in the holiday season.

Ilfracombe celebrates **Victorian Week** in June with much dressing up and festivities, and in early August the **Birdman Festival** sees the spectacle of young men (mostly) attempting to take to the air by throwing themselves off the Pier.

Basics

Tourist Information Centre The Landmark, Seafront ☎ 01271 863001
🖰 www.visitilfracombe.co.uk.
Wildlife cruises Pier kiosk, Ilfracombe Harbour ☎ 01271 879727
🖰 ilfracombeprincess.co.uk. Wildlife and coastal cruises. Seals, porpoises and dolphins may be sighted.

Food and drink

The Quay 11 The Quay, EX34 9EQ ☎ 01271 868090 🖰 www.11thequay.co.uk.
Owned by Damien Hirst, this is the smartest restaurant in Ilfracombe. Herbs and
salads come from their own nearby farm.
Seventy One 71 Fore St ☎ 01271 863632 🖰 www.seventyone.biz.
An unpretentious place with terrific food and a loyal clientele.

⑯ Lundy

*I saw the Isle of Lundy
which formerly belonged to
my grandfather, William,
Lord Viscount Say and Seale, which does abound
with fish and rabbits and all sorts of fowls – one bird
that lives partly in the water and partly out, and so may be called an
amphibious creature; it is true that one foot is like a turkey, and the
other a goose's foot; it lays its eggs in a place the sun shines on and
sets it so exactly upright on the small end that there it remains until taken
up, and all the art and skill of persons cannot set it up so again to abide.*
Through England on a Side Saddle by Celia Fiennes, 1695.

One real semi-amphibious bird associated with Lundy is the puffin, which still
appears on Lundy Island brochures even though you would be extremely
fortunate to see one. They were once so plentiful that the island was called after
them: Lunde øy is Norse for Puffin Island. However, there is hope. Puffins and
Manx shearwaters both nest in burrows, and their numbers have been gradually
increasing since rats (which took their eggs) were eradicated a few years ago. So
you just might see puffins in Jenny's Cove during the nesting season.

With or without puffins this island in the Bristol Channel is unique. Those
who know it well are passionate about it. Diana Keast, whose family sold the
island to the National Trust some forty years ago, told me 'I still prefer Lundy
to the mainland. It had been in my family since 1925. My father visited as a
young man in 1903 with two friends – I have a photo of them looking very
formal in their Edwardian collars. He told me he'd said "One day I'm going to
buy this island". And he did.'

The Kingdom of Heaven

Victoria Eveleigh

When the Heaven family owned Lundy, from 1834 until 1918, it was nicknamed
The Kingdom of Heaven. Although the owners have changed, the name is still
appropriate.

A huge amount has been written about Lundy, but it's difficult to find words
to describe why this place, which is only about three miles long and half a mile

wide, is so special. Its credentials are impressive. It is the only island off the North Devon coast, and lies north–south just where the Bristol Channel meets the Atlantic Ocean, creating some unique conditions for wildlife. The waters around Lundy are England's first Marine Nature Reserve and No Take Zone; it is the only place in the UK where you can find all five British species of shallow-water cup coral. Most of the island has been designated a Site of Special Scientific Interest, and also a Special Area of Conservation. It lies within the North Devon UNESCO Biosphere Reserve. About 140 different species of bird are recorded on Lundy every year, and it is the only nesting site in Britain for Manx shearwaters. For some reason there are no reptiles or moles on Lundy, but there are lots of rabbits, with a disproportionate number of black ones.

The Lundy cabbage (which looks remarkably like oilseed rape) is unique to the island. There's a small amount of a particular type of rock called Lundyite, and some of the granite which makes up the bulk of the island is magnetic. Over two-and-a-half miles of granite dry-stone walls have been built on Lundy. Since 1929 it has its own stamps ('puffinage') introduced by the owner at that time, Martin Coles Harman, and for a while it also had its own coinage. Since 2006 Lundy has been the largest rat-free island in Europe... The list of Lundy specials is endless but, like all CVs, reveals little of its true character.

Lundy is so special to me that I get butterflies when I see it from the mainland, and I'm excited for days before a visit. I first went there on my honeymoon, which was a good start, but my feelings for Lundy have grown stronger with each subsequent visit. It's not just that the island is small enough to be personal but large enough to be interesting, or that it provides a tranquillity which is impossible on the mainland; it's everything about this extraordinary place – especially the friendships which have formed with people who also love it. All sorts of people: birdwatchers, divers, climbers, archaeologists, artists, stamp collectors, pony enthusiasts, residents past and present, and people who enthuse about Lundy are joined by this sense of belonging. Lundy is a bit like having your very own *Famous Five* island to explore

Several groups of like-minded enthusiasts have formed over the years, the oldest of which is the Lundy Field Society, co-founded in 1946 by Martin Coles Harman to encourage scientific research into the island's natural history. There is also a Lundy Collector's Club – devoted to the collection of anything to do with Lundy, particularly its stamps – and less formal groups of climbers, divers and birdwatchers.

Visiting Lundy

When Chris and I were on honeymoon in 1986 we seemed to be the only tourists on the island and had the whole of Millcombe House (which was then a hotel) to ourselves. Nowadays there is no hotel, and most of the 23 self-catering buildings are booked all year round; some are reserved more than a year in advance, such is Lundy's growing popularity. The management of Lundy and its buildings (apart from St Helena's Church) is undertaken by the Landmark

Trust, which leases the island from the National Trust. The Harman family sold it to the National Trust in 1969, for £150,000. Diana Keast (née Harman) says, 'The Landmark Trust are doing what we all wanted to do: they're making the island pay for itself without ruining it. We used to have about 18,000 day-trippers to Lundy each year, and that hasn't changed much, but it's the accommodation which makes the difference.

As a visitor, you certainly get a different feeling for the place if you stay for a few nights. An affectionate nickname for day-trippers on Lundy is bluebottles, because they swarm in, buzz around for a while and then buzz off! I'd still rather go on a day trip to Lundy than not go at all, and there are several things you can do to make the most of your day, like trying to book a trip when the weather is good, wearing stout shoes or boots with non-slip soles, carrying waterproofs in a rucksack, taking binoculars, taking a picnic or buying food on the MS *Oldenburg* and planning beforehand what you want to see.

Making the most of a day trip: a guide for bluebottles

The first thing to mention is that there's only one **public loo** on the island, and it's just outside the **Tavern**, so that makes a good starting point. Then it's a question of which way now? That depends on how long you've got (usually about four hours), the weather and what you want to do. For instance, there's no shame in spending the whole time in the Tavern if it's foggy or pouring with rain; it's only a small part of Lundy, but arguably the most important!

But if the weather's fine, there's lots to see. One of the great things about the island is there are no formal waymarked **walks** and no signposts to significant places. You just have to read a map, peer gingerly over the cliffs every now and then and follow the paths trodden by others, hoping they knew where they were going. (Free maps are provided in information leaflets on the MS *Oldenburg*, or more comprehensive guides can be bought in the shop.) A word of warning: the cliffs have taken several lives over the years, so always beware if you are near a cliff, and only look at the view, or the wildlife, when you are stationary.

On a clear day, a place impossible to miss is the **Old Light**. This disused lighthouse near the village is a good starting point, as you can climb to the top of the tower and get a good view of most of Lundy. The house part the lighthouse is a self-catering property.

From the Old Light it's a walk of about one-and-a-half miles round the south end of the island, to look at the **Montagu Steps**, the **Devil's Limekiln** (don't get too close to the edge), the **Rocket Pole** and the deep pond nearby, **Benjamin's Chair** (a sheltered, grassy platform which is a great place for a picnic), the **Castle** and (if you're feeling brave) **Benson's Cave** below it, and then back to the village via **St Helena's Church**.

A more energetic route from the Old Light heads northwards to the **Battery**, over the **Quarter Wall** and along the **West Sideland** to the **Earthquakes** and **Jenny's Cove**, then (if there's plenty of time) carry on northwards and over **Halfway Wall** before cutting across, or (if it's already half-time) head eastwards between Halfway Wall and **Pondsbury**, picking the highest ground with heather and bracken on it, until you reach the main track which runs the length of the island. Once on the track, go north to Halfway Wall, and then east to the slate stile and a chimney-like structure of rocks with one perched on top, known as the **Logan Stone**. From there, pick up the coastal path which runs along the **East Sideland**. This will take you to the **quarries**, which are a fascinating relic of Lundy's recent history. The middle quarry is known as **VC Quarry** because it holds a memorial stone to Lance-Corporal John Pennington Harman (Diana Keast's brother) who was posthumously awarded a VC for his actions during the Siege of Kohima in 1944.

The path then leads upwards, past the **Timekeeper's Hut**, with its circular memorial plaque to Felix Gade (another legendary former Lundy resident), past the **Quarry Pond** to the ruins of the **Quarry Cottages**. From here you have a choice: you can walk inland to the main track and head back to the village, or you can drop down to the small gate south of the Quarry Cottages and carry on along the East Sideland. This route is particularly worthwhile on a fine day, as there are lovely views to the **Landing Bay** and the **South Light**. In May the area is carpeted with bluebells, which makes the view even more stunning. On reaching the steps above **Millcombe**, you can go right-handed to the village if there's time, or left-handed to the waiting ship (if there are a few minutes spare, take a detour to see **The Ugly** – a small shelter built into the hill between Millcombe and the sea, from which there are great views).

One more idea for anyone who hates heights, wants a more or less **level walk** or is afraid of getting lost: take the main track from the village and keep walking northwards. The track is broad enough to take vehicles and is marked by large stones from the Quarter Wall to a spot just above the entrance to the **North Light**. Lundy is divided by three main walls: **Quarter Wall**, **Halfway Wall** and **Threequarter Wall**. The land in between these walls looks very different, from the farmed fields round the village at the south end to rough grazing in the middle and then bare granite encrusted with heather and lichens at the north end. On the way plenty of landmarks will be visible on a clear day: the **Old Light**, the **Quarry Cottages**, the **Old Hospital**, **Pondsbury** and **Tibbett's** (the old Admiralty lookout, now the most remote self-catering property on the island). It's easy to keep on walking without looking at the time, so make sure you turn back in plenty of time for the ship!

Other considerations

There are only a few vehicles on the island, which contributes significantly to a peaceful, stress-free holiday on Lundy. However, if you have mobility problems, you can book a **Land Rover ride** in advance from the jetty to the village 360 feet above. Once there, a happy day can be spent sitting outside or in the Tavern and visiting the shop, St Helena's Church and a small museum in the old Rocket Life-Saving House.

Be warned that it's sometimes impossible to get on or off the island. If the wind is too strong, and especially if it is easterly, the MS *Oldenburg* won't sail. Usually visitors will be flown to and from the mainland for an extra charge. However, if it's foggy, too, the helicopter can't fly, so there's always the possibility of getting stuck. Diana Keast told me that you should never strip a bed on Lundy until the boat or helicopter has left!

The most important building on the island is the **Tavern**. It's the central meeting point for food, drink and conversation. Hot meals can be bought for breakfast, lunch and supper. The roasts on Sunday nights are particularly popular and are usually sold out by eight o'clock. Meals are on a first come, first served basis and you can't book in advance. The Tavern is a focal point in bad weather, with plenty of books and games on offer. Sometimes a terrible day weather-wise can be even more fun than a nice one.

Hints for visiting Lundy

- Take seasick pills and a basic first aid kit, including painkillers. They used to sell seasick pills in the Tavern, but they're no longer allowed to.
- Don't go to Lundy if you feel ill. You could get stranded out there, and you don't want to give your illness to everyone else.
- Earplugs are useful if you're a light sleeper. The foghorn from the lighthouse can be intrusive.
- Take enough warm, waterproof clothes.
- If staying, take a torch. Electrical things like laptops and hairdryers are discouraged because they use too much electricity.
- There is no public phone so bring a mobile.
- If travelling on the MS *Oldenburg*, double-check which harbour you are leaving from and arriving back at: Ilfracombe or Bideford. (There is a bus provided if your car is parked at the other harbour.)
- The long-stay car parks at the harbours require a lot of change, especially if you're staying for a week.
- Make sure your luggage is within the required weight. There is a good shop on the island, so there's no need to pack food.
- Good-quality binoculars can be hired from the office next to the Tavern.

The practical bit

Getting there

The **MS *Oldenburg***, which carries up to 267 passengers, sails from Bideford or, more often, Ilfracombe, depending on the tides, from late March to late

October. Departures are between 08.00 and 10.00 and the journey takes less than two hours. On a fine, calm day it's a beautiful trip, especially from Bideford when you sail up the River Torridge and past Braunton Burrows. On rough days most people are seasick. The *Oldenburg* returns from Lundy between 18.00 and 20.30. To book contact the Lundy Shore Office, The Quay, Bideford EX39 2LY; 01271 863636; www.lundyisland.co.uk.

An alternative is a **wildlife-focused trip** from Clovelly on the *Jessica Hettie*; 01237 431405 or 07774 190359; www.clovelly-charters.ukf.net. Additionally, a **helicopter** departs from Hartland Point on Mondays and Fridays, all year, at 11.00; 01271 863836. During the winter months (November to March) helicopter transport is the main way of getting to and from the island.

Accommodation

The Landmark Trust (01628 825925; www.landmarktrust.org.uk) owns 23 self-catering places, ranging from a 13th-century castle to a lighthouse and fisherman's cottage. All are fairly expensive compared with mainland prices, but for those on a limited budget there is a barn with two dormitories sleeping 14 in all, and also a camping field (these need booking in advance, too). Some of the properties have open fires, but many rely on rather temperamental electric storage heaters, so take as much warm clothing as your luggage allowance will permit. The island has its own electricity supply which is turned off between about midnight and 06.00. Only essential electrical equipment is provided; this doesn't include radios, TVs, washing machines or dishwashers.

John Pennington Harman VC

At the site called VC Quarry on Lundy is a memorial to John Pennington Harman, who was posthumously awarded the Victoria Cross for outstanding bravery in Burma in 1944. During the Siege of Kohima, about 500 men stopped the advance of 15,000 Japanese into India for 15 days until the British 2nd Division could fight their way through to relieve them.

There have been fewer than 1,400 recipients of the Victoria Cross since its inception in 1856, so John Harman has a very special place in history. It is remarkable that an island as small as Lundy produced such an extraordinary man. The quarry was chosen for the memorial as it was John's favourite place to play as a boy.

Diana Keast, John's sister, recalls that he was a keen beekeeper, and kept bees on Lundy. There is a rural superstition that if the owner of a hive of bees dies and the bees are not told they will pine away or desert the hive. The news of John's death was delayed by two weeks, but his father immediately sent word to the resident agent, and asked him to tell John's bees. Felix Gade went to the hives and found that all the bees had vanished.

On the right track

In Devon, and particularly on Dartmoor and Exmoor, several of the smaller roads are single-track with passing places. The hedges or banks edging them may be high, restricting visibility. Driving on them can seem a bit challenging at first, and the important thing to remember – as you should anyway, if you're reading this guide! – is to 'go slow'. Allow yourself plenty of time to brake for bends or oncoming traffic. The other drivers aren't your enemies, no matter how threatening their vehicles may look when you're suddenly nose to nose; you're all involved together in an exercise of skill and co-operation.

The Highway Code instructions for single-track driving are: always keep to the left (if the passing place is on the right, leave it for the oncoming driver); on hills, the descending vehicle should, if possible, give way to the climbing vehicle; if necessary reverse to a passing place behind you so that the oncoming vehicle can get by; slow down when passing pedestrians, cyclists and horse riders; and don't block passing places by parking in them. Also, if there's a vehicle following behind you and you're driving slowly, pull into a passing place so that it can overtake.

In addition, there are some informal points that can be helpful. First, if you're going to pull into a passing place to let either an oncoming or a following driver pass you, do put your left-hand indicator on as soon as possible so that they're aware of your intention. The generally accepted rule is that whoever's closest to the passing place (or gets there first) pulls in, or waits opposite if it's on the right-hand side. Secondly, try to memorise each passing place as you go by, so that you'll know where it is and what it's like if you need to reverse. If it's positioned awkwardly or visibility is poor, you may find it easier to reverse beyond it and then pull forward into it; in this case try to find a spare hand to make a 'stop' sign to the oncoming driver so that he/she doesn't come too close and block you.

There's only one situation when you would pull over to the right instead of the left, and that's if the passing place is on the right but the oncoming vehicle (perhaps a lorry or articulated truck) is clearly too long to fit into it. Then you'll need to go into it yourself so that the on-comer can stay in the centre of the road; but it's important to get your indicator on well in advance, and not to move right until you're absolutely sure the on-comer (and any traffic behind you) knows what you're doing and has slowed sufficiently. Speaking of large vehicles, do be aware that some stone bridges on B roads in central Dartmoor are extremely narrow; don't get your caravan or camper-van jammed!

If visibility is bad (high hedges, blind corners...) use your horn gently on bends to warn oncoming traffic of your presence. Finally, when someone has stopped for you, pulled to one side or performed some other helpful manoeuvre, please don't forget to give them a little wave (or nod, if your hands are full with gears and steering) of acknowledgement. Courtesy and consideration on both sides are what make single-track driving enjoyable rather than tiresome.

JB

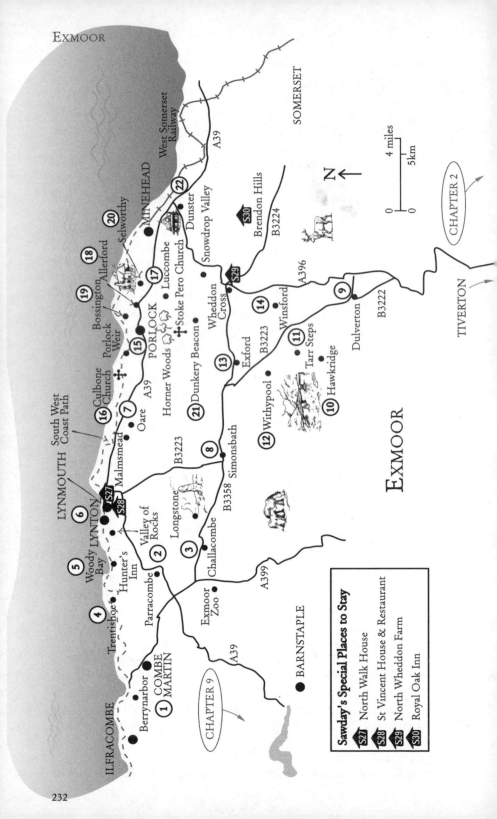

SOMERSET

SOMERSET

West Somerset Railway

A39

4 miles
5km
0   0

N

CHAPTER 2

MINEHEAD

㉒

S27

Selworthy

⑳

Dunster

Allerford

⑱

S30

Snowdrop Valley

Brendon Hills

B3224

⑲ Bossington

⑰

Luccombe

Stoke Pero Church

Wheddon
Cross

S29

A396

Winsford

⑭

⑨

PORLOCK

Porlock
Weir

⑮

Horner Woods

Dunkery Beacon

⑬

Exford

B3223

⑪ Tarr Steps

Dulverton

B3222

South West
Coast Path

Culbone
Church

⑯   ⑦

Oare

A39

㉑

Hawkridge

⑩

TIVERTON

LYNMOUTH

Malmsmead

B3223

⑧

Simonsbath

⑫ Withypool

EXMOOR

S27
S28

LYNTON

⑥

Woody
Bay

Hunter's
Inn

Valley of
Rocks

Longstone

B3358

⑤

②

③

Challacombe

A399

④

Trentishoe

Parracombe

Exmoor
Zoo

A39

Berrynarbor

ILFRACOMBE

① COMBE
MARTIN

CHAPTER 9

BARNSTAPLE

A39

10. EXMOOR

Exmoor is quite different from Dartmoor. Dartmoor is granite; the horizon is pimpled with tors and sometimes it feels as though grey stones grow as crops on every empty space. You can die on Dartmoor, miles and miles from any road or shelter. It would take a certain commitment to die on Exmoor, although you could manage it on the coast where the sea can rise 35 feet during a spring tide and the cliffs are the highest in England. This is a soft landscape of rounded hills, splashed yellow in the spring from gorse and purple in the late summer when the heather blooms, and of deep, wooded valleys. There are red deer here – absent on Dartmoor – and the native ponies are far more distinctive than the more varied Dartmoor breed. Exmoor also has the coast, and the many rivers that race to the sea from the high ground, slicing into the soft sandstone. No sooner are you on moorland than you drop down to a combe. Then up again, so walking can be surprisingly challenging since these sudden clefts may not be visible as you approach.

This is England's smallest national park; you are never far from a village with a shop or pub, or at least a friendly church where you can shelter from the rain. The National Park includes a good network of clearly marked trails, which make walking or cycling a real pleasure, so it's surprising that it's one of England's least visited national parks.

The publication of *Lorna Doone* in 1869 gave Exmoor tourism a marketing high from which it's never recovered. I have a theory that not that many people have read *Lorna Doone,* but perhaps I'm making an excuse for my own ignorance. Certainly Blackmore's novel is more identifiably set in a genuine English landscape than most other literary classics, and the number of visitors to Oare Church testifies that fiction is as powerful as fact.

Early travellers were not impressed by Exmoor, indeed in 1695 Camden, in his *Britannia,* described it as 'a dreary barren tract'. More lyrical in their descriptions were the poets who descended on Exmoor in the age of Romanticism. Samuel Taylor Coleridge and his pal Wordsworth tirelessly roamed the hills above Dunster. In the autumn of 1797 they walked the coastal path to Lynton, and are said to have planned Coleridge's most famous poem, *The Rime of the Ancient Mariner,* during that walk. Coleridge was staying near Culbone when an opium-induced flow of poetry was interrupted by 'a person from Porlock'. He never finished *Kubla Khan.* In 1799 Robert Southey, the Poet Laureate, penned a sonnet in Porlock, and nine years later the 20-year-old Percy Bysshe Shelley burst in on the tranquillity of Lynmouth, scattering pamphlets and scandal. All in all, anyone who had anything to do with poetry at the turn of the 18th century seems to have ended up on the Exmoor coast.

The red deer of Exmoor

The red deer, *Cervus elaphus,* is the largest native British mammal and Exmoor is its last English stronghold. Only in the summer do they have the sleek red coats that give them their name. Hinds and stags live most of the year in separate 'bachelor' groups, splitting up in the autumn when the stags seek mates. Only the stag has antlers or horns as they are (inaccurately) called on Exmoor (see page 253), which it sheds every year. As the animal matures so its annual growth of antlers increases, adding new points each year. All the energy put into growing these antlers each year is important to achieve supremacy over rival stags during the annual rut. In October and November the stags roar out their challenge., and fights ensue. The young are born in June, often remaining hidden in the heather or bracken while the hind goes off to graze, returning from time to time to suckle.

You may come upon deer at any time, particularly in woodlands or at dusk, but an organised safari (see page 243) will increase your chances as will a guided visit during the rutting season. See *Exmoor Visitor* for dates.

Exmoor and the hand of man

Exmoor is not a wilderness; from earliest times humans have changed the landscape through their activities. There are a few remnants of **Bronze Age**

Exmoor Ponies

Victoria Eveleigh

The most obvious thing about Exmoor ponies is that they all look remarkably similar – short and hairy, with brown bodies that are dark on top and lighter underneath, dark legs and hooves and a characteristic 'mealy muzzle' (an oatmeal colour over their muzzles and round their eyes).

Nature tends to select similarities (think of foxes, badgers and other wild animals) whereas Man tends to select novelty, and Exmoor ponies are exceptional amongst the British pony breeds in that they are still as nature intended. In fact, they have the same characteristics as the original British Hill Pony that came to Britain about 130,000 years ago.

Why Exmoor ponies have survived here as an isolated, pure breed is a bit of a mystery, but it may be because, historically, Exmoor has been a sparsely populated area with no significant trade routes and no important towns nearby. Another reason could be that Exmoor people tend to ignore interference from outside. For instance, Henry VIII created 'The Horse Laws', which made it an offence to use stallions under 15 hands high for breeding and ordered that mares not able to bear foals 'of a reasonable stature' should be killed. The Exmoor farmers of the time appear to have had their own definition of what was reasonable!

During the early 20th century it became fashionable to 'improve' native ponies with Arab and Thoroughbred bloodlines, so in 1921 several local breeders got together and formed the Exmoor Pony Society with the purpose of keeping the breed true to type.

barrows, as well as stone circles and standing stones, but nothing like those on Dartmoor where indestructible granite was used.

The climate was warmer and drier in the Bronze Age (2000–650BC), and the area which is now Exmoor was covered with broad-leaved woodland, dominated by alder on damp ground and oak with hazel on better drained ground. Now, only about 25% of Exmoor's original woodland remains, concentrated in the steep valleys. They give us an idea of what Exmoor was like before it was altered by man.

Early man settled on the high ground where the forest was thinner. He managed the woods for grazing, leaf fodder and timber and cleared areas for agriculture. This, together with a progressively wetter climate, led to the decline of woodland on the hilltops and the spread of open moorland vegetation. So the most natural-looking landscapes on Exmoor are often those where man has had the most long-standing and drastic influence. It seems that heather was more dominant on the original moors than it is today, mainly because heavy grazing and burning encourages rough grasses, gorse and bracken. Such changes can be seen along the old Royal Forest boundary, for instance at Brendon Two

The ponies nearly died out during World War II; most of them were killed for food, leaving only about forty-six mares and four stallions, but the local farmers soon re-established their herds with the help of a remarkable lady called Mary Etherington.

Today there are about 300 free-living Exmoor ponies on the moor and about 1,300 worldwide, but only a fraction of these are used for breeding. The number of breeding ponies may increase in future due to new grants under the Higher Level Stewardship scheme for grazing endangered native breeds.

All the Exmoor pony herds which graze the different areas of moorland within Exmoor National Park are free-living (not truly wild) because they are owned by farmers with grazing rights on the moorland. For most of the year the ponies fend for themselves, but in the autumn they are rounded up and the foals are weaned and inspected. Until recently all foals which passed inspection had to be branded, but microchipping is now allowed as an alternative to branding.

As you'd expect of a prey animal designed by nature, Exmoors are well-camouflaged in their natural moorland habitat. However, you will have a good chance of seeing them on Haddon Hill (near Wimbleball Lake), Winsford Hill, Withypool Common, Porlock Common, Dunkery Hill and Brendon Common. If you would like to see ponies at close quarters, visit the Exmoor Pony Centre at Ashwick, near Dulverton (TA22 9QE; 01398 323093; www.moorlandmousietrust.org.uk). It was set up to give the surplus foals from moorland-bred herds a future by training them to be useful family ponies. Visitors can learn about Exmoors, see how they are trained, handle them and (if under about 11 stone) ride one. The Exmoor Pony Society website (www.exmoorponysociety.org.uk) has more information on this breed. A trip to Exmoor isn't complete without seeing these unique ponies; they make history come to life.

Gates where heather is much more plentiful on Brendon Common than it is inside the old Royal Forest.

Saxons began to settle in the early 700s. They introduced the manorial system of land tenure, named many places and established the framework of the Exmoor landscape as we know it today. Trees were cleared in the more fertile valleys, and a network of manors and farmhouses surrounded by small fields were built. The fields were worked in a simple rotation of corn and fallow, with livestock kept on the fallow land and moorland. North Devon cattle, known locally as Red Rubies, are thought to be of Anglo-Saxon origin. The Saxons established moorland common rights of usage for summer grazing, peat cutting and wood gathering. Many of these commons still exist today, with various rights held by adjacent inhabitants. Large areas of unclaimed moor and scrub were set aside as royal hunting grounds, which the Normans formalised into a Royal Forest.

By the beginning of the 14th century nearly all the villages, hamlets and farms on Exmoor today were in existence, except those within the Royal Forest. This pattern remained until the 19th century, although a period of agricultural prosperity in the 16th and 17th centuries, principally due to the thriving **wool industry**, led to some moorland enclosure and the rebuilding of many farms in the traditional 'Devon longhouse' style.

The agricultural revolution had little impact on Exmoor until **John Knight** bought the Royal Forest in 1818. John and his son, Frederic, shaped the landscape within Exmoor Forest and evolved a system of husbandry on which present hill farming methods are based. Large areas of moorland were reclaimed by burning, ploughing, liming and sowing successive rape crops on which sheep were kept so their dung would fertilise the soil. The fields were then used for growing grass and root vegetables. Hereford and Shorthorn cattle, and Scotch Blackface and Cheviot ewes, were imported to breed with the local North Devon cattle and Exmoor horn sheep, and large-scale livestock farming was established in the old Forest. The village of Simonsbath was built, together with a network of tenanted farms. Roads were constructed, a wall was built around the estate and beech hedges were planted on traditional stone-faced earth banks.

During World War II food production was crucial, and a lot of moorland was ploughed up. Exmoor is a relatively 'soft' upland area, and it would be possible to cultivate most of it with modern farming techniques. This is one of the reasons why Exmoor was designated a **National Park** in 1954, to conserve its landscape and wildlife. Today there are about 38,000 hectares of farmland and 19,000 hectares of moorland in Exmoor National Park. The landscape is now influenced by legislation, some of which has unexpected consequences. For example, the change in EU subsidies to farmers from production-based to area-based payments has led to a marked decline in the number of livestock available to graze moorland areas, and some moorlands have become overgrown with gorse and scrub as a result – proof, if any were needed, that Exmoor's landscape has been created and maintained by farming.

Hunting on Exmoor

Victoria Eveleigh

Anyone visiting Exmoor is bound to notice that hunting is deeply embedded in its culture. Nearly all the pubs are decorated with hunting memorabilia of one sort or another, and it's likely that the village shop will sell more copies of *Horse and Hound* than of *Hello* magazine. The history of Exmoor revolves around hunting and farming, and together they've shaped its landscape. The Exmoor Forest (the vast tract of land at the heart of what is now Exmoor National Park) was owned by the Crown and reserved as a royal hunting ground until 1820, when John Knight bought it.

Two of the principal hunts on Exmoor today – the Devon and Somerset Staghounds (D&SSH) and the Exmoor Foxhounds (EFH) – started in the 19th century. Other Exmoor hunts are the Dulverton Farmers Hunt, the Dulverton West Foxhounds, the Minehead Harriers and the North Devon Beagles.

When I moved to our farm on Exmoor 26 years ago, hunting was more or less taken for granted; summer meant tourists and winter meant hunting – and farming benefited from both. The foxhounds were particularly useful to us sheep farmers. Regular meets of the EFH in our area ensured a healthy, fit, well-dispersed and controlled fox population, and meant that we didn't have to control fox numbers by shooting or trapping them ourselves (indeed, it was frowned upon if anyone but the hunt killed a fox!).

We tolerated the damage the red deer did to our hedges and crops because we knew the D&SSH would cull a few during the winter, disperse others and maintain a healthy, wild herd. In return for keeping the deer, we were given venison during the hunting season and if we had dead sheep or cattle, a hunt truck would take them away free of charge.

The system worked; it maintained a healthy, controlled population of foxes and deer on Exmoor at a cost to nobody but the hunting people themselves. Farming and hunting worked well together.

Since then several things have changed – including the law. First, new laws about carcase disposal meant an end to the free collection of deadstock, with far-reaching consequences. Then the Hunting Act of 2004 banned traditional hunting. This meant that the hunts had to adapt so that they continued to operate within the law. The D&SSH have maintained their casualty service for sick or injured deer, and they take part in various scientific studies, such as research into bovine TB in red deer.

It's unhelpful to everyone that the law is incredibly complicated, but the hunts still have a vital role to play on Exmoor. Most still meet two or three times a week during the season, and they welcome visitors to their meets (on foot, in a car or on a horse) and at other events – dances, shows, treasure hunts, point-to-points, ferret racing, fun rides and whist drives, to name a few. For further information, see the D&SSH website www.devonandsomersetstaghounds.net, the EFH website www.foxhunters .net/exmoor and the Endangered Exmoor website www.exmoor.org.uk.

Getting there and around

The dual carriageways that sped you to other parts of the county desert you here, forcing you to take the beautiful and slow approach roads, whether in your own car or in an 'express' bus. The main route from the south, the A396 from Tiverton, winds its way up the Exe Valley to Wheddon Cross. Last time I drove it I stopped to view the river in the early morning sun, and caught a flash of blue as a kingfisher zipped over the dark water. Thrilling! The 398 bus follows the same route, going to Bampton, Dulverton, Wheddon Cross and Minehead.

Exmoor really can be enjoyed without a car, at least in the holiday season, thanks to the Moor Rover (see opposite). There's a good(ish) bus service including an open-topped double-decker that runs in the summer, and some steam trains as well as a main-line service into Barnstaple. It's also more cycle-friendly than Dartmoor (if you can call 25% gradient hills friendly) because most of the lanes are wider so there's less danger from traffic.

Public transport

Exmoor is poorly served by **railways**, a fact which has contributed to its fortuitous lack of development. The nearest regular railway is the Tarka Line from Exeter to Barnstaple, where you can pick up the 309 or 310 bus to Lynmouth (both routes are wonderfully scenic so it's an hour well spent). However, the steam trains of the **West Somerset Railway** (01643 704996; www.west-somerset-railway.co.uk) run from Bishops Lydeard, near Taunton, to Minehead, bringing you to Exmoor's doorstep in an admirably Go Slow manner. The service runs year-round at weekends and regularly during the summer months, sometimes using diesel engines rather than steam. From Minehead the 300 Coastlink bus goes to Lynmouth via Porlock (but only four times a day).

If you prefer the ease of a **taxi** to take you from the station to your destination, there's a large choice including A1 Taxis, Barnstaple (01271 322922), or Value Taxis (01271 327777). In Minehead: 1st Call Lynx Taxis (01643 708888) and 1st 4 A Terrys Taxi (01643 705599) among others.

Exmoor's bus routes and timings are designed more for holiday-makers who want to see the scenery than for people who need to go from A to B. Nothing wrong with that! The **Exmoor Coastal** open-top bus (300) runs along the A39, providing convenient links for walkers doing the South West Coast Path, and there's a twice-weekly summer-only service, the **Exmoor Link** (401), running across Exmoor through most of the popular places such as Tarr Steps and Simonsbath.

The open-top 400 **Exmoor Explorer** bus does a circular route from Minehead, taking in Allerford, Porlock, Exford, Wheddon Cross, Timberscombe and Dunster. Between late May and late September it runs at weekends only, with an additional service on Tuesdays and Thursdays during school summer holidays; the complete journey takes an hour and a half (www.somerset.gov.uk/400exmoorexplorer).

Swathes of Exmoor still have no scheduled bus service but the most beautiful walks. The Somerset part is served by the excellent **Moor Rover** which will pick up you, your bike, your dog or your luggage – and even your wheelchair – at a prearranged place and time and, for a flat fee of £5, drop you anywhere on Exmoor. Currently it runs only in July, August and September, but deserves to be extended. It's operated by Atwest (01643 709701; www.atwest.org.uk).

Do check all bus schedules on Traveline (0871 200 22 33; www.traveline.info or www.devon.gov.uk/buses) before you travel.

Active Exmoor

A dedicated website (www.activeexmoor.com) and an A4-sized magazine *Active Exmoor* are aimed specifically at the more energetic activities for which Exmoor is so suited, covering walking, mountain biking, horse riding, canoeing and sea kayaking, as well as skilled stuff like coasteering and climbing. They're packed with good information including walking and mountain-biking routes. The magazine is available free from National Park outlets.

Cycling

The **West Country Way** (NCN3) traverses the southern part of Exmoor, going through high moorland, and the many quiet lanes on the moor are ideal for cyclists who don't mind hills (of which there are many). Perhaps the most challenging ride is the **Exmoor Cycle Route**, a 56-mile Tour of Britain circuit, or the linear **Culbone Way**, Regional Route 51, which runs from Minehead over Exmoor to llfracombe. The **Millennium Cycle Route** being planned by Sustrans (www.sustrans.org.uk) will use Exmoor's quieter lanes from Dulverton across Molland and Anstey to Mole's Chamber. It is said to be particularly lovely.

Exmoor is ideal for **mountain biking**. Bikes are allowed on bridleways and byways but not on public footpaths or open moorland. Adrian Silvester runs *JustRide Exmoor* in Lynmouth (see page 255 and box on page 244). He hires out only mountain bikes and his ideal is to give people a half-day training to teach them how to get the most out of off-road riding before they head off for the moor. 'I love it when they come back caked in mud, grinning from ear to ear, and saying it was just brilliant.' He will also arrange accommodation, from comfortable B&Bs to a miles-from-anywhere bunkhouse. There are also bicycle hire places in Porlock (page 260) and Minehead (269). Exmoor National Park publishes a number of cycling guides, including *Exmoor for Off-road Cyclists* and a series of single-sheet *Bike It* guides. See www.exmoor-nationalpark.gov.uk; click on to 'online shop'.

Mountain biking on Exmoor

Adrian Sylvester

Riding a mountain bike around Exmoor can be a daunting task. Bridleways that appear almost perfect on the 2D map could turn out to be boggy sheep tracks across exposed moorland. However, without this sort of ground-level exploration I would never have come across the hidden gems that always inspire me to head out in search of somewhere new.

There are two spots local to Lynmouth that I love to ride. The paths that contour around the top of Watersmeet from Brendon to Hillsford are stunning at any time of year. May brings a carpet of bluebells to the woods which give it an enchanted feeling, whilst the thunderous Farley Water in full flow after heavy rains and its contrast with the pretty waterfalls of the summer months are equally captivating. A short bimble along the country lanes will lead you to Malmsmead and the Doone Valley. This gently undulating trail follows the slow-moving Badgworthy Water. With its occasional swimming pools and wide grassy banks, it is the perfect picnic paradise and there are plenty of shady spots in which to put your back against a tree and peruse the map a while or catch a few quiet moments of tranquillity.

Further afield, the terrain between Porlock and Dunkery Beacon, (the highest point on Exmoor) is full of hidden trails that seem hardly used. The woods above Horner never fail to deliver, whether it's the marvel of the ancient woodland which sometimes gives the watchful rider views of deer and other wildlife, or the wonderful twisty single-width track which snakes through it all. Climbing up towards Dunkery Beacon itself the terrain changes and lush greens give way to the browns and purples of open moorland. Another of my favourite trails is called 'Dicky's Path' which contours around the northern side of the beacon. It starts with a short descent into a combe with a small stream crossing before a climb up and out on to more open ground again. This is repeated another three times, each single-track descent more exhilarating than the last, each climb more satisfying as you take in the view northwards across Porlock and the Bristol Channel, before a thrilling descent from Webber's Post. If you're lucky you might find the ice-cream van in the car park.

This is a small selection of what Exmoor offers mountain bikers, but for me it is these trails that define what riding on Exmoor is all about. It takes a certain amount of enthusiasm to tackle the steep and rocky terrain that abounds here but lying just off the beaten track there is a wealth of forgotten trails just waiting to be rediscovered.

Walking and backpacking

Despite its small size, Exmoor has hundreds of miles of footpaths, including several long-distance trails. The 102-mile-long Two Moors Way runs from Lynmouth to Ivybridge on the edge of Dartmoor, the Macmillan Way West (102 miles) enters Exmoor at Withycombe and runs to Barnstaple, and finally there's the superlative 35-mile Exmoor section of the South West Coast Path.

Suggested walks are given in each section. If you plan to do some extensive walking, then it's worth choosing the best seasons: spring or autumn for woodland or the coast, when the landscape is at its loveliest and the crowds have thinned out, but August or early September for the heather. The eastern moors around Dunkery Beacon, and on Winsford Hill, Withypool Common and Trentishoe near the coast, are particularly gorgeous, with a mixture of bell heather and ling so that the landscape glows with different shades of purple.

The Exmoor National Park Association (ENPA) has created a series of 'bus walks' linked to the centres of Dunster, Dulverton and Lynmouth, as well as Combe Martin, Exford and Wheddon Cross. Billed as car-free days, each place has a local circular walk, a linear walk outwards and then back using public transport, and an attraction that can be reached by bus. Downloadable leaflets are available from web: www.exploremoor.co.uk. There are additional suggestions for bus walks in each section.

If you prefer to get to know the moor with experienced guides, the **North Devon and Exmoor Walking Festival**, held each year in May and September, will suit you perfectly. See www.walkingnorthdevon.co.uk or www.westcountry walks.co.uk.

You should be aware that no wild camping is allowed anywhere on Exmoor, although there are organised campsites varying from the comfortable to the very rustic.

Walking maps and guides

The incomparable CroydeCycle walking **maps** at a scale of 1:12,500 cover a good proportion of Exmoor: *Porlock, Lynton & Lynmouth* and *Combe Martin* include all of the coastal area, and *Coast Path Map 1*, at a scale of 1:15,000, covers the entire Exmoor stretch from Minehead to Watermouth. These maps are widely available, or buy online at www.croydecycle.co.uk.

The double-sided OS Explorer map OL9 covers all of Exmoor at a scale of 1:25,000. Like all the Explorer maps, its size makes it unwieldy to use in small spaces, especially cars. If you're driving or cycling, the 1:50,000 Landranger maps 180 and 181 give you just the right level of detail.

Exmoor National Parks publishes a number of walking **guides**, including the handy single-sheet *Golden Walks*; www.exmoor-nationalpark.gov.uk: click on to 'online shop'.

Shortish walks on Exmoor and *Shortish walks in North Devon*, both by Robert Hesketh and published by Bossiney Books (www.bosinneybooks.com), are easy to follow with clear maps. A useful series of self-published walking guides centred round different popular locations is *Exmoor Scenic Walks* by Shirley and Mike Hesman (01271 862421). They are cheap, well organised, clearly written, with easy-to-follow maps. So far the series comprises: The Brendon Hills, Challacombe, Combe Martin, Dunster, Exford, Hunter's Inn, Hawkridge, Horner, Lynton, Lynmouth, North Hill, Porlock, Porlock Weir, Winsford, Withypool, Dulverton, Wheddon Cross and Webbers Post. These and other inexpensive guides for Exmoor walks of varying quality are available from local shops and Tourist Information Centres.

The official guidebook for the *South West Coast Path* is published annually by South West Coast Path Association (01752 896237; www.swcp.org.uk) and includes a listing of convenient accommodation.

Riding

One of my fondest teenage memories is of pony trekking for a week in the 'Lorna Doone country' of Exmoor with my younger sister. I can remember so vividly the woodland rides and the huge sweep of purple moor, and the exhilaration of being able to gallop without worrying about roads or traffic. We started off gently with a couple of hours morning and afternoon, and culminated in a full day trek with lunch at a pub (so grown up!). I can even remember the name of my cob: Satan.

Not much has changed. You can still go for short or long treks across the heather, you can still have lunch in a pub on the long days, and no doubt there are still bolshy cobs called Satan. If you can ride, there's no better way of seeing the moor, and no better way of getting up those steep hills and across the streams.

Here are the major riding stables on Exmoor. Most will take complete novices, but do make it clear how much experience you have had, and underestimate, rather than overestimate, your abilities.

Brendon Manor Riding Stables Nr Lynton ☎ 01598 741246.
Burrowhayes Farm Riding Stables West Luccombe, Porlock TA24 BHT
☎ 01643 862463 www.burrowhayes.co.uk.
Dean Riding Stables Trentishoe EX31 4PJ ☎ 01598 763565
www.deanridingstables.co.uk.
Doone Valley Trekking Oare ☎ 01598 741234 www.doonevalleytrekking.co.uk.
Knowle Riding Centre Dunster TA24 6TZ ☎ 01643 841342
www.knowleridingcentre.co.uk.
Outovercott Riding Stables Lynton ☎ 01598 753341 www.outovercott.co.uk.
West Anstey Farm Stables Dulverton, TA22 9RY ☎ 01398 341354.

Inactive Exmoor

Not everyone can jump on a mountain bike and pedal furiously up Porlock Hill, and even reasonably fit walkers can find the hills on Exmoor a challenge. Of course the moor can be enjoyed in your own **car**; there's good parking at all the well-known places and, out of season, driving here is a real pleasure. In the peak months, you'll have to spend a lot of time in reverse on the narrow lanes, which rob you of the view; the alternative is to let someone else take the wheel.

In the summer months the 400 open-top **bus**, which follows a circular route, gives you a lovely overview with the advantage of being high up – if you can get a seat on the top deck. The 401 also runs on a scenic route, but again only in the summer and only on certain days. The 300 Coastlink bus runs year round, however, from Minehead to Combe Martin.

For a focused drive, two companies offer safaris in **4x4** vehicles; these give you not only an overview of Exmoor's scenery but also inside information on its wildlife, traditions and history. Tours last 2½–3 hours, and the route depends on weather and other factors. Because the driver/guides know the moor so well, you have a good chance of seeing red deer on these trips.

Barle Valley Safaris ☎ 01643 851386 🖰 www.exmoorwildlifesafaris.co.uk. Half- or full-day excursions from Dulverton are available, with a minimum of four people for the full-day one.
Exmoor Safari ☎ 01643 831229/831112 🖰 www.exmoorsafari.co.uk. Trips leave from Exford.

Further information

Exmoor National Park 🖰 www.exmoor-nationalpark.gov.uk.
Exmoor Tourist Association ☎ 01984 633782 🖰 www.exmoor.com.
Visit Exmoor 🖰 www.visit-exmoor.co.uk.
Explore Moor 🖰 www.exploremoor.com. Includes suggestions for car-free days on Exmoor
Exmoor Visitor Published by the National Park, this tabloid-sized publication repeats in newspaper form the information found on the website. It's free, widely available in shops and Tourist Information Centres, and particularly useful for its detailed list of events.
Exmoor Food Festival Early October. 🖰 www.visit-exmoor.co.uk.
Bus and train timetables Traveline ☎ 0871 200 2233 🖰 www.traveline.co.uk. The North Devon timetable (🖰 www.devon.gov.uk/buses) covers the Devon section of Exmoor.

Western Exmoor

From the 'gateway' town of Combe Martin into the heaped and furrowed landscape that lies to the east, this is one of the most dramatic parts of Exmoor though there is no moorland to be seen. Inland are ancient meadows and hanging woods of sessile oaks, accessible by lanes so steep and narrow that even devoted drivers will have second thoughts about taking their cars. The coast, tracked by one of the most scenic stretches of the South West Coast Path, is indented with shingle beaches hidden by the highest cliffs in England. For church enthusiasts there are two little gems: Parracombe for its untouched simplicity, and Trentishoe because it's different – as you will see.

① Combe Martin

We found Combe-Martin placed in a dale, along which it extends at least a mile from the sea-shore. The scenery of the latter is really magnificent: its more prominent parts are singularly striking, and have the happiest accompaniments imaginable. The sea enters a little cove at Combe-Martin, commodious for the mooring of small vessels; and here the produce of the mines is shipped for Wales and Bristol.
W G Maton, travelling during 1794–96.

Squeezed into the crease between two hillsides, this straggly town claims to have the longest high street in England. Once over 70 shops lined this road; now there are only a handful and few noteworthy houses, so that a walk from one end to the other is unrewarding. But Combe Martin has plenty to interest the visitor, including its history.

This was one of England's main silver-producing areas; by the 17th century the place was potholed with mine shafts and the high-quality silver brought considerable wealth to the town. The harbour allowed the metal to be easily transported along with agricultural products, most notably strawberries and hemp. One of the village industries was the spinning of this hemp into shoe-makers' thread.

These days there are only two buildings of interest in the town: the **Pack o' Cards** pub and the church. The Pack o' Cards is a piece of 18th-century eccentricity supposedly created by George Ley, a gambler, in homage to his success. All its numbers echo those in a pack of cards, hence its four floors (suits), 13 doors and 13 fireplaces (cards in a suit), and originally 52 windows (cards in a pack); also the whole thing looks like a house of cards. Ley, who died in 1709, has a memorial in the church of St Peter ad Vincula (St Peter in chains). At the opposite end of the long street from the Pack o' Cards is the town's pretty beach, shingle at high tide and sand at low; cliffs climb steeply up from it on each side. Combe Martin lies within the North Devon Area of Outstanding Natural Beauty, and you really need to approach it on foot to appreciate this setting.

The town also has a good **museum**, recently enlarged with a collection of historical memorabilia; here children can bring in their finds from the beach to study under a microscope, or play around with ropes and pulleys. Combe Martin is also known for its lively **carnival**, taking place during the second week of August, when a giant 'grey mare', ridden by Old Uncle Tom Cobley and All, parades around the town on Wednesday evening, presumably looking for Widecombe Fair. There's also a Strawberry Fayre in June, celebrating the town's history as a major fruit-growing region, and the bizarre but hugely enjoyable Hunting of the Earl of Rone (see box opposite), which takes place on the Spring Bank Holiday (www.earl-of-rone.org.uk). 'They like dressing up in Combe Martin' the lady in the tourist office told me. Indeed!

Hunting the Earl of Rone

Benedict Le Vay

One of the most bizarre, colourful, historical and highly charged events to take place in the British calendar is the Hunting the Earl of Rone which takes over Combe Martin each Spring Bank Holiday.

Men dressed as grenadiers, with muskets that they fire from time to time, hunt down a fugitive who may well be based on the Earl of Tyrone, an Irish traitor who was indeed wanted by the government some 400 years ago. The hunt begins on the Friday, and on Monday, after three days of noisy searching, they catch the man at the top of the village and, dressed in sackcloth, he is put backwards on a donkey and marched along with drums and music through this very long village towards the church.

He escapes now and then and is shot and falls to the ground, only to be revived by a fool with a besom, or an Obby Oss – a dancing figure with a great hooped skirt and a horse's head, complete with clacking, snapping teeth. He's then replaced, again backwards, on the donkey, and continues his sad journey. Women and maidens carry beautiful flower garlands. Eventually the procession reaches the church where people are dancing and the bells ringing and the Earl of Rone is shot once more.

Then it is all the way down to the sea, where the dead Rone is thrown into the waves from the quay, and the women throw their garlands after him. It is an utterly amazing spectacle for what is otherwise a civilised West Country village in the 21st century.

Extracted from Eccentric Britain, *by Benedict Le Vay.*

Next to Combe Martin are some of the highest cliffs in southern England: **Hangman Cliffs**. There's Great Hangman and Little Hangman, and climbing them from Combe Martin Bay is undoubtedly strenuous, but the views make it worthwhile. Having done the hard slog to the top of Great Hangman (1,046 feet) you may be tempted to continue east along the **South West Coast Path**. This is, after all, one of the most spectacular and varied stretches of the entire route. However, there is no bus link until you reach Lynmouth, 13 miles away; given the hilly terrain, this is a lot to do in one day. A good solution is to split the walk into two days.

While in the area, take a look at the lofty village of **Berrynarbor**. The church is one of the most beautifully located in Devon, high on a hill with the billowing landscape behind it, and the village of whitewashed houses, tucked into the hillside, is equally attractive. It has a pub and tearoom.

Tourist Information Centre Cross Street EX34 0AR ☎ 01271 883319
🖰 www.visitcombemartin.com.
Combe Martin Museum Eberleigh House, Cross Street (next to the TIC) ☎ 01271 889031 🖰 www.combemartinmuseum.org.

② Parracombe and ③ Challacombe

Cupped within a bulge of the A39, and almost lost in a maze of steep, narrow lanes, is **Parracombe**, a lovely little village with two churches and a pub. The old church, **St Petrock's**, is rightly the one that draws visitors. It was scheduled for demolition in 1878 when a more conveniently located church had been built, but was saved after a protest led by John Ruskin, and is now cared for by the Churches' Conservation Trust. It stands high above the village, overlooking its usurper church and the scatter of white houses, with the fields of north Devon stretching to the horizon. The squat tower is a landmark from the main road, the pinnacles looking as though they were added as an afterthought by a farmer. They're more like slightly wobbly cairns than a stone-mason's art, and all the more charming for it. Inside, all is plain and unadorned. No one has 'improved' it, but it is clearly cared for and cared about. The first thing you notice on entering is the wooden 'tympanum', boldly painted with a royal coat of arms and improving texts: the Ten Commandments and the Creed. The only carving is the screen and even this is less intricate than usually found in Devon churches. Woodworm has roughened the plain box pews, and at the back there's a musicians' area where a hole has been cut in the panel in front to allow free movement for the bow of the double bass. Note, too, the hat pegs by the door.

Apart from the Black Venus Inn, Challacombe is best known for its **Longstone**, the most spectacular prehistoric monument on Exmoor, standing 9 feet high and remarkably slender. It is marked on the OS map, which you'll need if you're to find it. It's a mile or two from the B3358, northeast of Challacombe, near the source of the River Bray. The area around it can be very marshy, so wear suitable footwear.

In the same area, off the A399, is the well-managed **Exmoor Zoo** (www.exmoorzoo.co.uk), where a black leopard, the 'Exmoor Beast', is the main attraction. Among other rare animals in spacious enclosures is the endangered maned wolf from South America.

The Black Venus, Challacombe ☏ 01598 763251 ⊕ www.blackvenusinn.co.uk. This 16th-century pub is the main reason to visit Challacombe. Good food and atmosphere.
⑤ Fox and Goose, Parracombe ☏ 01598 763239
⊕ www.foxandgoose-parracombe.co.uk. Close to the church and recommended for its above-average food and wide range of beers.

④ Trentishoe

Trentishoe is one of the most isolated communities in Exmoor, best approached from the west to avoid ascending a near-vertical hill. Its church is tiny and, at first glance, pretty ordinary. But at first sniff it's not ordinary. It smells. Bats have taken it over (see box opposite). The human congregation of six or so who attend the once-a-month service co-exist with them as best they can, but cleaning up after them is an impossible task. So be kind when you write your comments in the visitors' book, and remember that this tiny village has supported its church since 1260. Bats are expensive guests, so if you can spare a little more than usual for the upkeep box, please do.

Holy bats

St Peter's church in Trentishoe is one of those tiny Exmoor churches which tug at the heartstrings because they look so vulnerable, set alone in the hills, exposed to the wind and rain. And in this case to bats.

There are often piles of droppings on the carpet, especially in the musicians' gallery. Look up and you'll see the culprits: lesser horseshoe bats clinging to the roof, along with, perhaps, a long-eared bat or a pipistrelle. All three species have been identified as roosting here in the summer. In the visitors' book are comments such as 'In Denmark we don't have dirty churches' along with more generous 'Loved the bats! Never seen them in daylight before.'

I spoke to the local church warden about the bats. 'They weren't a problem until we had the roof repaired in 2006-7 and complied with the regulations to make the church bat-friendly. Since then they're everywhere. I do my best to clean up once a week, but they don't like the hoover and I don't like bats!'

All bats are protected species, but lesser horseshoe bats are particularly rare. They survive only in Wales and the west of England, and churches offer ideal conditions for them. Not only is it against the law to disturb them, they must be actively encouraged to stay in their chosen home. If a church is known to have bats, then before any restoration work can be done a bat expert must visit to assess the situation, identify the species, and set out the requirements. In the case of Trentishoe, special small entrances were created in the roof to allow bats in, while the horseshoe bats enter directly through the slatted vents into the tower. The cost of these alterations falls on the church itself. Think about it: Trentishoe has a congregation in single figures, and a few visitors who generously put coins in the donation box. Complying with the regulations which included paying a fee to DEFRA, paying for the services of the bat expert, and carrying out the required modifications to the church roof cost £1,459.

The plight of churches like Trentishoe was brought to the attention of Parliament by the MP for Northeast Bedfordshire Alistair Burt, in 2004:

'We have no desire to reverse the entire law relating to the protection of bats, as they are indeed one of the glories of our countryside, but there is a clear clash of interests in this corner of England's heritage. We ask simply that our historic churches, which are surely as much a part of England's glory as the bats, have a more equal voice than they have had up to now; otherwise, some of the precious heritage of which we have spoken will not only be pitted and stained but lost for ever.'

The debate continues, but a change in the law is unlikely. Meanwhile, enjoy the bats but spare a thought, too, for the people who must maintain this little church.

Apart from the bats the church has one unique feature. In its musicians' gallery is a hole cut in the woodwork to allow for the bow of the cello or double bass. There's a similar one at Parracombe, but I believe this is the only one in a gallery – so many such galleries were removed by Victorian 'restorers'. The little organ came from the ship *Mauretania*, which was scrapped in 1965.

One of the National Park's Golden Walks series covers this area: *Trentishoe Down*. It's a five-mile circular walk, taking in a level woodland stretch as well as moorland and a section of the coast path. The CroydeCycle map *Combe Martin & Hunter's Inn* shows the lanes and footpaths clearly.

⑤ Hunter's Inn and around

This little pocket of Exmoor is extraordinary. Driving anywhere is challenging, as is walking: the hills are very steep. But the scenery is sublime, and that's why visitors come here.

Hunter's Inn always seems to be swarming with people, either at the beginning or end of their walk or bike ride, or just enjoying a drink or browse in the National Trust shop. The mile-long walk to **Heddon's Mouth**, down the gorge-like Heddon's Cleave, is deservedly one of the most popular on Exmoor, being blissfully level and buggy-friendly.

A longer walk takes you towards **Woody Bay** which reportedly is the perfect place for some wild swimming. There's a small car park on the road above it, but the descent (down a lane marked Martinhoe Manor, and then a path) is so steep that I chickened out and drove west to **Lee Abbey Beach**. This private shingle cove is lovely, and there's parking nearby if you don't feel like walking there along the coast path which, on this stretch, follows the lane. A toll road and a high-level footpath beyond the bay take you to the Valley of Rocks.

Lynmouth, Lynton and area

Without doubt this is the most popular part of Exmoor – and deservedly so. It really does have everything, and all within walking distance: a pretty seaside village, a cliff railway, a tumbling river cutting through forested slopes, the heather-clad moor, and a dollop of recent history. Artists and poets have rhapsodised about its beauty: Gainsborough thought it the perfect place to paint, and Shelley lived there for nine weeks with his first wife.

Lynmouth was 'discovered' in the early part of the 19th century when the Napoleonic Wars had closed the continent to English visitors, and the English gentry had to be satisfied with holidaying nearer to home. The Rising Sun Inn was already there to cope with this influx and other inns were hastily built, but it seems that once the war was over, there was fierce competition between the three lodging houses for potential customers. Murray's travel guide of 1856 warns that 'telescopes are employed at the rival houses for the prompt discovery of the approaching traveller. He had better determine beforehand on his inn, or he may become a bone of contention to a triad of postboys, who wait with additional horses at the bottom of the hill to drag the carriage to its destination.'

The publisher Sir George Newnes lived in Lynton, at Hollerday House, and gave the town its cliff railway in 1890, as well as its town hall. Newnes founded the racy magazine *Tit-Bits* and followed it up with the altogether more serious *Strand Magazine* which was the first to publish Sherlock Holmes stories.

⑥ Lynton and Lynmouth

Hoskins, in 1954, wrote that **Lynton** itself has little to commend it. I disagree. Its sturdy Victorian houses and extraordinary town hall are surprising in a place that otherwise feels like a modern holiday centre with souvenir shops and fast food outlets. And it has a cinema. The **cliff railway** is a masterpiece of simple engineering and a model of 'green' energy. The two carriages are counter-balanced by water. Fill the tank at the top, and it's heavy enough to pull the other carriage up as it descends. We watched the 'driver' at the bottom judge the amount of water to let out to counterbalance not only the weight of the carriage but the passengers as well. Really neat, and a great way to get to the top of a 500-foot cliff. Before the road was built in 1828, tourists were transported to Lynton on donkeys or ponies, as were all the goods arriving in the harbour.

Most people walk down to **Lynmouth** and take the railway up. It's a very pleasant, steepish stroll down, the path lit by solar-powered lamps donated by different organisations. The village is clearly very much older than its partner, with at least one thatched cottage that must surely date from the 15th century, and very pretty with its harbour, cliffs and wooded hillsides. The young **Shelley** brought his 17-year-old wife here a year after the marriage undertaken not so much because he loved Harriet but because he knew it would infuriate his father. He succeeded; his father stopped his allowance. Although he explored the area widely, he seems to have written little poetry, being more interested in disseminating information on radical politics. To this end he would row out from Lynmouth with leaflets sealed into bottles and even suspended from fire balloons. After several brushes with the law the couple fled to Wales by boat, leaving a mass of unpaid debts. There is some debate as to where they lived, but most agree that it was at the cottage now named Shelley's Hotel.

An open-sided display commemorates the great Lynmouth flood of 1952 when, after torrential rain on Exmoor, a wall of water carrying broken trees and boulders washed down the East and West Lyn rivers. It happened in the dead of night, with the electricity supply one of the first casualties, so all the terrified villagers could do was listen to the roar of the approaching torrent. Many houses were destroyed and 34 people lost their lives. As with all major disasters, this has its own Conspiracy Theory: at that time the government was experimenting with cloud seeding...

The Rhenish Tower

Philip Knowling

This folly deceives twice over; it is a seemingly frivolous tower built to serve a purpose and – thanks to tragedy – it is not as old as it seems. Strangely, in a place of precipitous hills, rocky cliffs and fast-flowing waters, the folly here doesn't rise out of the cliffs above you, it stands quietly on the harbour wall, looking out to sea. It's squat and square and built of grey stone, except for the off-set balconies of red brick. The folly was built in the 1850s by a man called General Rawdon. It is often referred to as the Rhenish tower, though whether it is truly in the style of the towers of the Rhine is open to debate. It was built to be of use. It stored salt water for Rawdon's house nearby, used for invigorating baths. Later, the water tower took on an even more useful role as a lighthouse. Then the original folly was swept away in the devastating floods of August 1952. This copy was erected in 1954.

Hollerday Hill and the Valley of Rocks

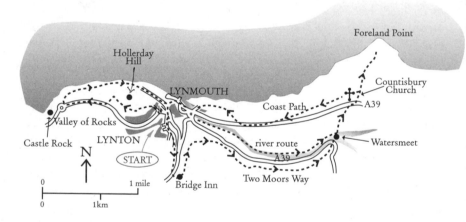

The Valley of Rocks is accessible by car, but it's such a wonderful walk – only about a three-mile round trip – that if you can do it on foot, you should. The valley, which would be unexceptional on Dartmoor, is quite extraordinary on Exmoor where the soft sandstone has left few sharp contours. The most likely explanation for these heaps and castles of rock is that this was once a river valley, the boulders being deposited during the ice age, before the river changed its course. Glaciation and weather erosion did the rest.

The circular walk there starts at Lynton, where a footpath near the town hall leads to Hollerday House. Keep on the lower path, parallel to the sea, and you will see the first sign of the rocks, a monolith aptly known as The Castle. The path drops down to the flat valley bottom, where feral goats and Exmoor ponies graze. Head towards the car park at the end, and then follow the well-maintained path back to North Walk. This is a most beautiful path, cut into the side of the cliff, with benches where you can sit and admire the view. And what a view! Behind you are the rocks, in all shapes and sizes, and ahead is Lynmouth and the Bristol Channel.

Watersmeet and the coast path

This half-day walk takes in the full spectrum of Exmoor: village, river, moor and coast. The path from Lynmouth to Watersmeet is both dramatic, up a deep, wooded gorge, and very easy, following the Lyn gently upstream. If it's hot there are places to paddle. The path is often surfaced, so you can admire the woods and river, and look out for birds, without having to watch where you're going. Start walking on the left side of the river; you'll cross to the right for a stretch, and then back again to the **Watersmeet**, a former fishing lodge and now a National Trust tearoom with excellent snacks. (The Two Moors Way and Tarka Trail follow the wonderfully scenic high-level path along the southern rim of the valley – a highly recommended alternative.)

From the lodge continue upstream, and you'll soon see the sign to Countisbury. Zigzag up the hill through a fairy-tale grove of stunted sessile oaks, all bent and twisted, and emerge on to the moor brightened by clumps of bell heather. Over the hill, and across the A39, is **Countisbury** church, its pinnacled tower peeping above the horizon. The church is unexceptional inside but still worth a peep. A rather sad sign identifies the bell clappers which 'were removed from the bell tower in 1964 when the bells were sold to help pay for repairs to this lovely old church'.

Ahead is Foreland Point. Head up the grassy track toward the radio mast on Butter Hill for the view, then down the other side. A small, rough and exposed path runs round the side of Foreland Point; don't take it. If you want further views, continue straight ahead to Foreland Point itself. The path back to Lynmouth follows the road for the lower part, before zigzagging through woods to make a fine entrance to Lynmouth across Manor Greens.

Cycling

JustRide Exmoor Opposite the car park ☎ 07900 675341 or 01598 752529
🖰 www.justrideexmoor.co.uk. Owned and run by the enthusiastic Adrian Silvester (see page 240), this outfit is a one-stop shop for mountain bikers who want to explore Exmoor. He'll transport baggage if required and also 'Drop at top'. It's a five-mile climb out of Lynmouth, which is, for many people, a bad start to the day.

Eating and drinking

Esplanade Fish Bar 2 The Esplanade, Lynmouth ✆ 01598 753798. A deservedly popular and excellent fish-and-chip shop facing the bay. Huge portions. Beware seagulls if you eat outside!

Le Bistro 7 Watersmeet Rd, Lynmouth ✆ 01598 753302. A small, friendly bistro serving very good food.

On the Steps Church Steps, Lynton. ✆ 01598 753614. Family-run restaurant specialising in locally sourced, top-quality food. Imaginative menu. Highly recommended.

Rising Sun Harbourside, Lynmouth ✆ 01598 753223 ⌨ www.risingsunlynmouth.co.uk. A famous and atmospheric thatched pub with Shelley connections.

Rockford Inn Brendon EX35 6PT ✆ 01598 741214 ⌨ www.therockfordinn.co.uk. A rural pub (east of Lynton and Lynmouth) which is a great favourite with walkers.

Staghunters Inn Brendon. ✆ 01598 741222 ⌨ www.staghunters.com. Very popular with walkers; good atmosphere and food.

Learning and doing near Lynton

Exmoor seems to be a centre for involving visitors in animals and their products. Two places stand out, both near Lynton, where you can learn how to use the inside and outside of an animal.

Alta Lyn Alpacas provide the wool that enables their creative owner, Anne Coombs, to run courses on spinning, felting and weaving with alpaca wool. Anne became interested in alpacas during a sculpture course (she is an accomplished sculptor) when her teacher made one from clay. One thing led to another and she now has 22. Anne says: 'Visitors can learn how we are breeding them for excellence of fleece, which is quite a slow process; they take nearly a year in gestation. New genes can be introduced to aim at improvement with each generation.' I learned that there's still a lot of Peru in British alpacas. For instance they wait for a sunny day to give birth – essential for the survival of the baby in Peru's icy high plain.

I thought that alpacas were just alpacas, but Anne explained: 'We have mainly huacayas, which have soft, fluffy fleeces, but there are also suris where the fleece is more like dreadlocks. The alpacas are shorn once a year, then the fleece needs to be carefully sorted and graded. We teach hand-spinning, felting and weaving so students can appreciate the tactile qualities of the fleece and gain the satisfaction of producing something with their own hands'.

There are three self-catering apartments at the farm, so up to 12 people can stay on the premises for the courses (one apartment is at ground level so suitable for wheelchair users) and there's a campsite next door. The whole set-up is perfect for those of a Slow persuasion: it has solar power, air-source heat pumps, and water comes from their own bore hole. As Anne says 'People can come and stay here on Exmoor and enjoy a wide range of art courses as well as alpaca textiles.'

Whilst Anne's alpacas are not for consumption, the rare-breed Berkshire pigs that rootle so happily in the beech and hazel woods at Barbrook most definitely are. Simon and Debbie Dawson swapped their London lives as estate agent and solicitor for rural Devon and they, and their **Hidden Valley Pigs**, are clearly thriving. Apart from being a self-sufficient smallholding – Simon's book *The Self-Sufficiency Bible* is published in 2010 – the Dawsons offer a variety of courses from a one-day smallholding taster to pig-processing, and butter, cheese and yogurt making. They also offer Rear a Pig. Sadly this doesn't mean you take your piglet home with you, but it remains in the lap of luxury at the farm, growing slowly and naturally, and more or less writing progress reports to its mum (Debbie ensures that you are kept informed on its wellbeing, and you can visit it whenever you want). When the time comes, the slaughterhouse is only a few miles away and the pigs get a special treat the night before. If, like me, you eat meat but want to ensure that the animal has had a good life, this is as humane as you can get.

'I used to be a vegetarian' says Debbie. 'Now my policy is "If we don't rear it we don't eat it." '

><×××<

Alta Lyn Alpacas Anne Coombes, Higher West Lyn, Lynton EX35 6LD
☎ 01598 753654 ⏁ altalynalpacas.co.uk.
Hidden Valley Pigs Simon and Debbie Dawson, East Ilkerton Farm, Barbrook EX35
6PH ☎ 01598 763615 ⏁ www.hiddenvalleypigs.co.uk.

'All his rights'
Victoria Eveleigh

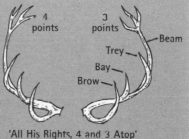

'All His Rights, 4 and 3 Atop'

Although they're technically bones, stags' antlers are called 'horns' on Exmoor. No two sets are the same, but they all follow a basic pattern – adding a new point each year until the animal reaches its prime at about ten years old. Sometimes the horns grow asymmetrically, and sometimes a point never grows. Some stags never grow horns, and they are called 'nott' stags.

On Exmoor, a two year-old male red deer with a pair of uprights is called a 'pricket'. In the third year the 'brow' point usually grows from the beam, with the 'trey' and 'bay' points added in subsequent years until, aged six, he may have the complete six 'rights' and two points atop on each side – or 'all his rights'. He can now properly be called a stag. From then on the number of points on top might increase each year until the stag reaches his prime. A point qualifies as such if a wedding ring can be hung from it.

If you are walking on Exmoor, keep a lookout for horns on the ground. Stags shed them every spring and grow a new 'head' in time for the autumn rut. Collecting horns is a great hobby among Exmoor people, and many local shows have stag's horn competitions.

253

S O S

It was a black January night in 1899 when a message telegraphed from Porlock Weir to Lynmouth Post Office reported 'vessel in distress'. A force-eight gale had raged all day in the Bristol Channel and by Gore point near Porlock, the three-masted barque *Forrest Hall* was tossing helplessly, held only by her sea anchors; she'd been on tow from Bristol to Liverpool when her tug suffered damage and had to abandon her to the storm. The nearest lifeboat, at Watchet, could not launch in the heavy seas, and the telegram requested assistance from the Lynmouth lifeboat, the 3½-ton *Louisa* – but it was clear that she also had no chance of launching. Her crew decided to haul her the 13 miles overland to Porlock Weir, and to attempt a launch from there. Horses were brought – with extra ones for the steep two-mile climb up Countisbury Hill – and ropes were attached to the carriage that bore the lifeboat. Torches and flares were lit. From every home, heedless of weather and darkness, villagers came to help, and within an hour of the telegram's arrival all was set. It seemed barely possible, but everyone agreed: 'We'll try'.

On her carriage, the *Louisa* weighed ten tons. Slowly and laboriously, men and horses together hauled her up the hill. At the summit some men, exhausted, returned home; 20 remained to see her across the moor in the teeth of the storm. Rain and wind extinguished the torches, which had to be continually re-lit. Ropes were slippery and hard to grip. At one point a wheel came off; the load had to be lifted manually so it could be replaced. A small group went ahead with picks and spades to widen the narrow lane at Culbone.

Next came the notorious Porlock Hill, a dizzily steep descent needing all available man- and horse-power to prevent the carriage from hurtling downwards. At the bottom a garden wall had to be demolished – the lady householder enthusiastically joined in the work. Eventually, ten hours after leaving Lynmouth, the *Louisa* was dragged on to the beach at Porlock Weir.

Refusing rest, the 13 lifeboatmen clambered aboard as helpers pushed her into the battering waves. After rowing for an hour they located the *Forrest Hall*, whose anchors had dragged but held firm. To evacuate her 19-man crew in so wild a sea would have risked lives; so the *Louisa* simply stood by. As day broke her tug returned. Some of the lifeboat crew helped to attach her towlines; the *Louisa* then accompanied her – still pounded by the storm – to a place of safety on the Welsh coast. They returned to Lynmouth and a heroes' welcome the following day, after a sound sleep. The cost of the rescue, including repairs to damaged roads and gardens, was £118.17s.6d, of which the owners of the *Forrest Hall* paid £75.

No lives were lost but, sadly, four of the horses that had hauled the boat died from their exertions. Members of the crew each received £5 from local funds and a silver watch donated by a wealthy Lynmouth resident. It was an amazing story of courage and determination. As the old lifeboatmen's saying goes: 'If 'tisn't us, then it's nobody. And it's not never nobody, not in the lifeboat service'.

JB

Central Exmoor

Inland Exmoor is the real thing: high heather- and bracken-clad moorland with lovely glimpses of the sea and the patchwork green fields of the lowlands. On a sunny day it's sublime, in rain it's utterly bleak but at least driving is easier on the high, open-view lanes. The rivers Exe and Barle, and their many tributaries, break up the moorland with deep wooded valleys giving walkers and mountain bikers that perfect combination of high moor and sheltered combes.

⑦ Oare

Even if you've managed to evade Lorna Doone associations until now, if you go to **Oare** you're doomed to get involved. R D Blackmore's grandfather was rector at St Mary's church here from 1809 to 1842 so the author of *Lorna Doone* knew the place well – and used it. See the box below. Setting that aside, the church has lots of interest. Note the box pews: the one for the squire has seats round three sides so he and his family could be fenced off from his labourers, and in a position to ignore the vicar if so inclined.

Note also the Ten Commandments, painted in the 18th century on wooden boards at the entrance to the inner chancel. Shortening of 'the' to 'ye' is common, but here we have 'yt' for 'that'. A head held between two hands forms the unusual piscina. This is thought to be St Decuman, one of those colourful saints who crop up in churches from time to time. St Decuman arrived in Somerset from Wales in the 7th century, sailing across the Bristol Channel on his cloak with a cow for company and sustenance. He and his cow settled in Watchet, to the east of Exmoor. This pastoral life didn't last, however, since he made the wrong sort of enemies and was beheaded. Whereupon the saint picked up his head, washed it, and put it back where it came from. The local people, much impressed, helped him build the church in Watchet, which is dedicated to him. What he is doing in Oare is unclear.

A modern feature of the church is the beautiful carved buzzard lectern by the sculptor Mike Leach (see page 267) replacing the traditional eagle lectern which was stolen.

The lane running east from Oare is particularly scenic, passing over Robbers Bridge and climbing up to the A39 in a series of hairpin bends.

Lorna Doone: fact and fiction

For a fictional heroine, Lorna Doone has had a disproportionately large effect on Exmoor tourism! Little can her creator R D Blackmore have known, as she flowed from his pen, that 21st-century tourists would seek out her home in such numbers. Her romantic tale is so intertwined with factual places and characters that it's hard to know where truth turns to fiction. Some of the characters certainly did exist at the time of the story; others existed but much earlier, so Blackmore will have heard of them and woven them anachronistically into his plot. What is unquestionable is that he caught just the right mixture of love, heroism, villainy and derring-do for his era and the book has remained popular throughout its lifetime, receiving praise from (among others) Thomas Hardy, Robert Louis Stevenson and Gerard Manley Hopkins. In its preface in 1869, Blackmore wrote:

'This work is called a "romance", because the incidents, characters, time, and scenery are alike romantic. And in shaping this old tale, the Writer neither dares, nor desires, to claim for it the dignity, or cumber it with the difficulty of an historic novel.'

The fictional Lorna was kidnapped from a noble family, as a child, by the dastardly Doone outlaws of Exmoor. The Doones seem to have been based in fact: such a family did live in the area around Badgworthy Water and Hoccombe Combe, and terrorised the inhabitants during the 17th century. It's possible they were Scottish miscreants who had fled south to escape the law. Tales of their exploits existed locally and Blackmore, writing *Lorna Doone* in the late 1860s, will have heard them.

Fair Lorna's lover, honest farmer John Ridd, did exist as a boy and went to school in Tiverton – as did Blackmore. In the novel, the Doones murdered John's father when he was 12. Later, now fictional, as a teenager he strayed into Doone country when following a hidden stream in search of loach, and met the young Lorna. Thus their love story began. Naturally, since the paperback version of the book today runs to 627 pages and 75 chapters, it did not flow smoothly! Lorna doesn't get into her wedding gown until page 613 – and then a shot rings out as the dastardly Carver Doone fires his carbine at her through the window of Oare church, where she and John have just exchanged their marriage vows. And no – I am not going to tell you how the story ends: you can visit Doone country, novel in hand, and find out for yourself...

JB

The Doone Valley walk

Two rivers, Badgworthy Water and Oare Water, meet at Malmsmead to become the East Lyn which makes its way to the sea at Lynmouth. A path runs along Badgworthy Water through the Doone Valley to, if you are a fan of the novel, the Doone hideout, an abandoned medieval village mostly hidden in the bracken. Here the path swings right, taking you back over Brendon Common.

The round trip is approximately six miles, and described in *Active Exmoor* (www.activeexmoor.com), or you can make a pleasant short circuit, described in *Shortish Walks on Exmoor*, of 2½ miles which takes in Oare Church and the Cloud Farm tea rooms.

The Buttery Malmsmead ☎ 01598 741106. A continental-style tearoom cum pub, with a sunny garden, draught beer and a simple, tasty menu.

⑧ Simonsbath and the River Barle

Simonsbath (pronounced Simmonsbath) is a relatively modern village that grew up at the crossroads of two tracks across Exmoor Forest. There's the excellent Exmoor Forest Inn, a shop selling ex-army surplus clothing and a car park for the many walks to be enjoyed in the area. For a sample of these buy a copy of *Exmoor Scenic Walks: Simonsbath*.

Exmoor's most popular inland walk starts from here. It combines a riverside walk in one direction and a high-level return with great views. The river section is particularly lovely, with ever-changing views and bits of history, recent and ancient. The recent history belongs to **Wheal Eliza**, a copper mine which was originally called Wheal Maria (why its name was changed is not clear). Wheal Eliza was one of the projects of the Knight family (see page 236). From 1845 to 1854 it mined copper, and when this ran out it switched to iron for three years before being abandoned. A year later the mine was in the news when little Anna Maria Burgess was killed by her father and her body hidden in the one of the mine shafts. He was brought to justice and hanged.

The next landmark is **Cow Castle**, an iron-age hillfort built around 3,000 years ago; from a high point on the walk you can see the enclosing ramparts.

After skirting some conifers you leave the good bridle path that continues to Withypool and turn back towards Picked Stones Farm (pronounced Pickéd) and Simonsbath. The return, I felt, was less rewarding. There are some good views, but over rather bleak, heather-free moorland and conifer plantations. However, the rain and mud probably had quite a bit to do with my disappointment so don't let it put you off. Most people love it.

Exmoor Forest Inn Simonsbath ☎ 01643 831341. In splendid surroundings, a comfortable dog-friendly inn chock full of hunting pictures, trophies, riding gear and antlers; decent bar food (using some own-grown vegetables) and local real ales.

⑨ Dulverton and ⑩ Hawkridge

Dulverton makes a convenient stopping place and you can pick up picnic supplies at Tantivy (01398 323465; www.tantivyexmoor.so.uk), a super delicatessen and general store that's open every day. Nearby is the headquarters of the Exmoor National Park Authority (01398 323665) who can answer any questions and sell you guidebooks, or you might want to visit the Exmoor Pony Centre (01398 323093). Then there's the 17th-century bridge to admire, but finally you'll head off into the moor.

Hawkridge is one of those tiny, high (nearly 1,000 feet) and isolated communities that still exist in Exmoor. It has a population of around 40, and there are just ten houses in the village. A gymkhana has been run on August Bank Holiday for 65 years – a source of great pride for the organisers.

The squat church seems to be hunkered down against the elements, but overlooks a glorious view of the moors. Inside, the visitors' book is full of thanks from tired walkers for keeping the church open (Hawkridge lies on the Two Moors Way). It has a Norman font, but the most notable feature is the stone coffin lid which was found in the wall behind the pulpit in 1877. It has inscriptions in Norman French and Latin, and was probably for William de Plessy, Lord of the Manor, who died in 1274.

Hawkridge is in the same parish as **Tarr Steps**, and the Devil, who caused so many problems to the early users of his bridge (see below), also wreaked havoc with the masons who built the church of St Giles, cutting their apron strings as they carried the stones for the church across the River Barle.

If you're planning to drive to Tarr Steps from Hawkridge be warned: the river can be too deep for an ordinary saloon car to cross the ford, and there is no parking on the west side of the river

✕✕✕✕

S⃝ The Masons Arms Knowstone EX36 4RY ✆ 01398 341231
⛵ www.masonsarmsdevon.co.uk. Southwest of Hawkridge and signposted off the A361 between Tiverton and Barnstaple this award-winning thatched, 13th-century inn is owned and run by Mark Dodson, who spent 12 years as Michel Roux's Head Chef at the three-Michelin-starred Waterside Inn, Bray-on-Thames. Mark's cooking leans towards the classics, and he creates sophisticated French and British dishes with an understated modern edge. Well worth going out of your way for.
S⃝ Woods Bar and Dining Room 4 Bank Square, Dulverton ✆ 01398 324007.
Former tea shop, now with a cosy bar warmed by wood-burners, plus exposed stone walls and pine decor; very good wines, as well as modern British cuisine and Exmoor and Otter ales.

⑪ Tarr Steps

The focus here is the beautifully preserved clapper bridge over the River Barle. Some say it's over a thousand years old but it's more likely to date from the 13th century. Either way, the feat of building it out of giant slabs of stone, brought in from a considerable distance, is remarkable. Some slabs are over six feet long and weigh more than a ton.

This is a great place for paddling, with several deep pools where you can get fully immersed if you wish. Be cautious about sunbathing on the stones, however – that's the Devil's prerogative. Legend has it that he built the bridge, so was understandably peeved when mere mortals tried to use it. The locals asked the vicar to help; he prudently sent a cat across first to test the waters, so to speak, but it disappeared in a puff of smoke. Nothing daunted, the minister set out himself and after a heated argument the Devil agreed to let people use the bridge. Except when he wants to sunbathe.

This is such a lovely area for walking that it makes sense to spend some time here. A 4½-mile walk is described in *Shortish Walks on Exmoor*.

S⊙ Tarr Farm Inn Tarr Steps ℓ 01643 851507 ◌ www.tarrfarm.co.uk. A posh inn in a lovely location. Ideal for lunch or cream teas after a long walk; quite formal in the evenings.

⑫ Withypool

This village ticks all the boxes. It has a good pub, an excellent post office/village shop that sells everything you might need including maps and walking guides, tea rooms, benches in the sun, and some historic Shell petrol pumps looking like the remnants of our civilisation in a post-apocalypse movie. The shop is open seven days a week. This is also a perfect centre for walking. Buy a copy of *Exmoor Scenic Walks: Withypool* and you're all set.

S⊙ The Royal Oak Withypool ℓ 01643 831506. Beamed bars warmed by a good log fire; decent bar food and Exmoor Ale.
Withypool Tea Rooms ℓ 01643 831178. If you get to Withypool outside pub hours or want a light meal, this is the place. Cream teas (or tea's as they prefer to call them), cakes, savoury pastries, really good coffee and a variety of teas. Recommended.

⑬ Exford and ⑭ Winsford

The Exe, a mere stream at Simonsbath, has gathered strength from two tributaries and is a proper river by the time it reaches Exford and Winsford, giving the villages much of their charm.

Exford is quite a bustling village with a good range of shops, two pubs, tearooms and so on, as well as being very picturesque with its river and large village green.

Winsford is often described as one of Exmoor's prettiest villages. Its location, certainly, is idyllic but it seems to lack cohesion and architecturally it has several rivals although its Royal Oak pub is chocolate-box picturesque. It's worth stopping in the village if you're nearby to see if you can find all eight bridges. Or maybe it's six. Or five – I've read various claims. It needs them because not only the Exe but also the Winn flows through the village. Look out for the delightful set of miniature cricket players in a garden with the church as a backdrop: a charming scene, and very English.

Walkers will find the two *Exmoor Scenic Walks* books covering Exford and Winsford useful.

The Royal Oak Winsford ☎ 01643 851455 ✆ www.royaloakexmoor.co.uk. A pretty thatched inn, idyllically placed, with a cosy bar and panelled restaurant, and serving good food such as Exe Valley smoked salmon.

White Horse Inn Exford ☎ 08721 077077. Exmoor ales and a wide choice of malt whiskies at this village pub; the hunting theme prevails strongly in the decor, and there's plenty of outside seating as well as a children's play area.

Porlock, Dunster and area

Back to the coast, **Porlock** makes an excellent base for exploring eastern Exmoor. **Walkers** are spoiled for choice. East is the lozenge of glorious countryside between Porlock, Minehead, the A39 and the sea. It has the coastal path running over Selworthy Beacon and an infinite choice of woodland trails taking you through arguably the prettiest villages of Exmoor: Selworthy, Bossington and Allerford. Walk west along the South West Coast Path for 12 miles and you reach Lynmouth, enjoying some heavenly scenery on the way, including Culbone church. South lie Horner Woods and Dunkery Beacon, with, in August, the best purple-heather views in Exmoor. The *Exmoor Scenic Walks* series has several booklets covering this area: *Porlock, Porlock Weir, Webbers Post* and *Horner*. The long-distance **Coleridge Way** ends in Porlock, so you can follow in the symbolic footsteps of the poet from Wheddon Cross to Porlock, in just under nine miles, and pick up a certificate at the Visitor Centre. The icing on the cake here is that the A39 runs close enough to all the best walking areas to allow for a variety of **bus walks** using the 300 bus; it runs every two hours between Minehead and Lynmouth.

It's quite mouth-wateringly seductive, not just for walkers but for strong **cyclists** – who have the gentler Toll Road if they can't cope with Porlock Hill – and car drivers who try to avoid choking up the roads in the busiest times of the year.

Medieval **Dunster** is packed with official sights and deserves a day to see the town before even beginning to explore the countryside on the extreme east of Exmoor.

⑮ Porlock and Porlock Weir

Porlock, along with Lynmouth and Lynton, is one of the three most populated parishes on Exmoor, and in 2003 was nominated Somerset's Best Large Village out of more than 300 competitors. It combines its villagey feel with wonderful rural surroundings, yet provides all the amenities that visitors need: some delightful cottages and gardens, interesting shops and good restaurants, pubs and tea shops. It is also reached by one of the steepest hills in England: a one-in-four gradient with some sharp bends. The arrival of the motor car to struggle up it must have come as a great relief to the horses that regularly hauled stage coaches to the top. The first car driver to make it to the top apparently did so in 1900, as a dare, and by 1920 motor coaches were managing the climb. Nowadays a very scenic toll road just to the west of the hill offers a gentler route.

For non-car-drivers Porlock is well served by **buses**: the 300 Exmoor Coastlink service passes through, as do the 285 North Exmoor Circular (May–October) and the 38 regular shuttle to Minehead.

The **church** of St Dubricius, an obscure Welsh saint, lost part of its steeple to Culbone (see page 263). Maybe. Or it could have broken off during a storm in 1700. Inside, the clock at the western end of the nave possibly dates from around 1450, but the oldest object in the church is the fragment of a pre-Norman cross set in the wall of the south aisle.

The oldest secular building in Porlock is the delightful **Dovery Manor**, at the eastern end of the town. This 15th-century manor is home to the little local museum, which reopened in 2009 after refurbishment. Its exhibits relate to Porlock and its literary connections, and paintings include one of the launch of the Lynmouth lifeboat which was hauled overland to Porlock Weir (see box on page 264). It also has a small physic garden. Admission is free, but its trustees rely entirely on donations to keep it open so do be generous.

Porlock's annual **Arts Festival** is held in September with distinguished speakers: its patron is Dame Margaret Drabble. Much earlier literary 'names' to visit Porlock included Robert Southey (who wrote a sonnet starting 'Porlock, thy verdant vale so fair to sight' in the Ship Inn while sheltering from the rain) and Samuel Taylor Coleridge, who took such a fancy to the local Porlock speciality, potted laver (seaweed), that he asked a friend for more supplies of it after he'd left. (Perhaps that friend was the 'person from Porlock' who famously interrupted him in 1797 when he was writing *Kubla Khan*.)

Storms in 1996 stripped back shingle in Porlock Bay and revealed underlying blue-grey silt, in which were found the bones of an auroch bull dating to about 1500BC. Aurochs were ancient cattle, now extinct, from which nearly all species of today's domestic cattle are descended. The same storm breached the bay's shingle ridge and allowed a tidal lagoon to form on part of the salt marsh; a great variety of waders and wildfowl can be seen here in winter. Seaward of the ridge are some interesting rock pools, and growing on the ridge – which seems too bare and windswept to harbour any life at all – are tough coastal plants such as everlasting pea and yellow-horned poppy.

The sea left Porlock's working harbour high and dry back in the middle ages, but at neighbouring **Porlock Weir** the shingle bar protected a tidal inlet and kept the harbour open – as it has been now for at least 1,000 years. In the 18th and 19th centuries Porlock Weir was a busy little port, for coasters carrying timber across to South Wales and returning with coal, and there used to be an oyster fleet. Today yachts come and go from its sheltered marina and fishing boats bring in their catch. In the summer pleasure boats ply their trade. The row of thatched cottages next to the harbour provides a strand of brightness between the grey expanse of shingle and the dark woods above. There's a large car park (with toilets), a thatched 14th-century inn, a restaurant, a hotel, a couple of shops, a little maritime museum with some interesting old photos and relics, and a small aquarium. Glassblowing and blacksmithing are also carried out here.

Basics

Porlock Visitor Centre The Old School, West End, High St, Porlock TA24 8QD
☎ 01643 863150 🖥 www.porlock.co.uk. A not-for-profit visitor centre with a good selection of guidebooks and maps.
Dovery Manor Museum open May to September; contact via the visitor centre.
Exmoor Taxis 26 Bay Rd, Porlock ☎ 01643 863355.
Porlock Arts Festival 🖥 www.porlockfestival.org (or the visitor centre as above).
Porlock Cycle Hire High St, Porlock ☎ 01643 862535
🖥 www.porlockcyclehire.co.uk. Mountain bikes, 'ladies comfort bikes', children's bikes and tandems. Drop-off service so you can have your bike delivered to wherever you're staying.

Food and drink

Andrews on the Weir Porlock Weir ☎ 01643 863300. Porlock Weir's best restaurant, offering contemporary cuisine.
Piggy in the Middle High St ☎ 01643 862647. Rightly the most popular restaurant in Porlock, so reservations are recommended. Despite the name, seafood is the speciality.
The Royal Oak High St ☎ 01643 862798. Good beers and reasonably priced food.
The Ship Inn High St ☎ 01643 862507 🖥 www.shipinnporlock.co.uk. A lovely whitewashed and thatched pub; built in 1290, it's one of the oldest inns in England. Its website upholds Porlock's literary heritage by having not a single misplaced apostrophe or comma.

⑯ Culbone Church

The little church of St Beuno is utterly enchanting; the smallest working parish church in the country and surely one of the most remote. Although the vicar and some parishioners can bounce and slither to it by Land Rover, for visitors the only access is on foot via the coastal path, a 2½-mile walk uphill from Porlock Weir. It's a lovely tramp though oak and beech forests with glimpses of the sea, and welcome benches, 'donated by the guests of Anchor Hotel'. These woods were one of the favourite haunts of Samuel Taylor Coleridge, who revelled in the local wildlife and views of Wales across the water. He stayed in a farmhouse nearby where he had his opium-induced vision of a 'stately pleasure dome' which became the unfinished poem *Kubla Khan*, interrupted by the arrival of a 'person from Porlock'.

Shortly after leaving the hamlet of Worthy and its thatched tollhouse, the path passes through two tunnels – intriguing since they seem to serve no possible purpose. The tunnels originally routed tradesmen to the back entrance of the now ruined Ashley Combe, so the Countess of Lovelace (see box on page 264) could be spared the unpleasantness of meeting any of the lower orders as she made her way to her bathing hut.

After about an hour of walking, quite suddenly the little grey church appears below you, squatting in a clearing with its spire, set slightly askew, reaching hopefully towards the treetops. Legend has it that this is actually the top of the Porlock church spire which blew off in a gale and landed here. Or maybe was snapped off by a giant and placed here. An examination of the graveyard is rewarding, with the local family Red being well represented. Look out for the stone of Ethel Red; presumably always unready. And if you've ever wondered what stone carvers do if they make a mistake, there's an example near the path. He put in an extra 'and', tried to change it to … well, it's hard to know what he tried to do, but he obviously thought 'Oh stuff it!' and left it as it is, with a hybrid d and e. The tall cross near the main path served as a useful hitching post for the vicar's horse during the war. The congregation had either to make a detour round the animal or sweeten its mood with a sugar lump before entering.

The interior seats 33 at a pinch. There's no room for anything except the pews, including a box pew for the squire, a tiny harmonium squeezed into a corner, spattered with candle wax, and the Norman font, so roughly carved that the marks of the stonemason's chisel are still visible. A church has probably stood here since Saxon times, and bits have been added through the centuries. One of the oldest features is the twin window on the north side of the chancel which may be a thousand years old, with a strange face carved above it that looks more like a cat than a man. Beyond it is a window where the decorative tracery that holds the glass is made from wood, not stone. And between the two is a 'leper squint' – a tiny window at eye level that allowed the lepers who had been banished to the surrounding woodland to get a glimpse of a church service.

It would be hard not to be moved by this little church. In the booklet telling its story the author writes: 'Its walls are saturated with centuries of worship and it is tended with a care that reveals the devotion of its congregation.' Indeed.

To return to Porlock Weir you can either retrace your steps or take the path up from the bridge, to meet the track to Silcombe Farm (this is a steep climb), then head east along quiet lanes until you reach the toll road. A footpath runs parallel to this road, alongside Worthy Combe through the lovely twisted oaks of Worthy Wood or, if you have energy to spare, take the bridle path deeper into the woods, to emerge east of Porlock Weir. The CroydeCycle map of *Porlock* shows this area very clearly.

Ada, Countess of Lovelace – and computer buff

Augusta Ada Byron was born in 1815, the only legitimate daughter of Lord Byron. Her mother Annabella's short and stormy marriage to the 'mad, bad' poet lasted only a year; they separated five weeks after Ada's birth and she never saw her father again. Annabella feared that her daughter might inherit his unreliable temperament, so had the little girl educated strictly and intensively in mathematics, believing that immersion in such a subject would discipline her mind. Ada did indeed become a formidable mathematician, but also a talented musician and linguist; she loved the arts, and as a young woman moved easily in the London society of the day. It was at a London dinner party in 1833 that she met Charles Babbage (see page 136); she was fascinated by his mathematical 'engines', while he was impressed by the speed with which this charming, accomplished young socialite grasped complex ideas. She saw at once how the machines could work, and developed her knowledge by studying his progress and asking questions.

Meanwhile she had married William King, in 1835. Three years later he was created an Earl and Ada became Countess of Lovelace. Their home was the beautiful Ashleigh Combe at Porlock Weir, which William developed as a romantic country mansion in Italian style to please his young bride. On Sundays they worshipped at tiny Culbone Church, sitting in the VIPs' box pew, probably having travelled there by coach along a rough track that has since fallen victim to a landslip. If they dawdled a little, never mind: the vicar could not start the service until the Earl and his Lady were present.

In 1840 Babbage spoke about his engines to scientists at Turin University; his talks were written up in Italian and then translated into French, which Ada in turn translated into English. Invited by Babbage to add her own comments, she did so comprehensively, outlining the fundamentals of computer programming and the main elements needed in any computer language. She has been called the world's first female computer programmer; but published her findings only under the initials 'AAL', so remained anonymous outside her own circle. Babbage described her as an 'enchantress of numbers' and his 'fairy lady'

By 1844 Ada, never particularly robust, was experiencing health problems. She also began to bet – and lose – on horses. Then cancer was diagnosed and in 1852 she died, just two weeks before her 37th birthday.

Her work faded largely from public memory – until 1953, when her notes on Babbage's engine were republished. In 1979, the US Defense Department named an early, secret software programme 'ADA' after her, her image appears on Microsoft authenticity stickers and she's the subject of a small number of biographies. Tilda Swinton played her in the 1997 film *Conceiving Ada*. It's not much recognition for a talented young woman who was so amazingly ahead of her time.

JB

⑰ Luccombe, ⑱ Allerford, ⑲ Bossington and ⑳ Selworthy

These four National Trust villages are quintessentially rural England with their thatched cottages strung along narrow lanes. Look out for the lateral chimneys, set in the side of the cottage rather than the end, and often incorporating a bulging bread oven. Footpaths and quiet lanes connect all the villages so it's easy and rewarding to devise a walk that includes them all.

Luccombe is an enchanting small village, the essence of unspoiled Exmoor, just far enough off the beaten path to thin the influx of visitors. 'They all go to Selworthy – thank God' said one resident when we complimented him on his village. The church of St Mary is lovely inside and out. Lift the rug at the altar end of the nave, and admire the 17th-century brass of William Harrison, resplendent in his ruff and gown. Next to the church is a thatched cottage; it surely must once have been a long house, with cattle living at one end.

Allerford is famous for its 17th-century packhorse bridge and has a handy car park for walkers. The same is true of **Bossington**, a picturesque little village with particularly good examples on many of the cottages of the local lateral chimneys with bread ovens.

The Holnicote Estate

The Holnicote Estate, which comprises around 5,000 hectares of eastern Exmoor, was inherited by the Acland family in 1745 and owned by them until donated to the National Trust in 1944 by Sir Richard Dyke Acland, the 15th baronet. It includes four miles of coast, a chunk of the moor including Dunkery and Selworthy Beacons, the great Horner Woods – one of the largest National Nature Reserves in Britain – and the villages of Selworthy, Allerford, Bossington, Horner and Luccombe. There are more than 170 cottages and 144 farms on the estate.

The Acland touch is everywhere, from the charming Lynch Chapel of Ease between Allerford and Bossington, which was used as a barn until restored by Sir Thomas Acland, to the memorial shelter above Selworthy Woods. The family seem to have been benevolent landowners. But you'll find few pubs – they didn't approve of them.

Selworthy is probably the best starting point for a walk around the region, giving you a choice of high moorland walking, or valley and village, or a combination of both. It's another chocolate-box thatched village, reminiscent of

Torbay's Cockington, with a spacious green. The church here is a startling sight after the usual typical grey towers. This is whitewashed – or rather lime-washed – as were once most other churches in the region though few are maintained so conscientiously. The interior is full of interest, with a fine wagon roof and bosses, and an hourglass by the pulpit to ensure the sermons ended on time. And there's an absolutely wonderful chest, all worm-eaten wood and ancient iron, straight out of *Treasure Island*. It's thought to be over 400 years old. Lunches and cream teas are served in the garden of Periwinkle Cottage.

From Selworthy you can walk uphill through the woods to the South West Coast Path and Selworthy Beacon, or west to Allerford, Bossington or Luccombe. The paths are all well signposted, and the woods a rewarding mix of mature oak and birch. Near the road at the top you'll come across a 'wind and weather shelter' dedicated to Sir Thomas Dyke Acland who died in 1871; poems by Heber and Keble are engraved on each end.

Horner Woods, ㉑ Dunkery Beacon and Stoke Pero

Of all the places in this chapter, I think these three – which can be linked in one long walk – epitomise the pleasures of Exmoor most satisfyingly. The National Nature Reserve of **Horner Woods** is a magic forest of gnarled oaks, lichens – 330 species – and mosses, networked with inviting paths. The stream, Horner Water, adds to the attraction. Like all places in the Holnicote Estate, the paths are well signposted. Aim for Webber's Post.

Above Horner Woods the moorland stretches in purple swathes towards the high point of **Dunkery Beacon**. From August to mid-September, when the heather is in bloom, this is the most beautiful heathland. Nowhere else on Exmoor has so much heather, nor such a satisfactory contrast with the green, chequerboard fields in the valleys and the sea beyond. It's exhilaratingly lovely, and makes the climb to the beacon a must-do, or you can cheat and stroll up from the car park a bare ten minutes away. The view here can be astonishingly far-ranging: in very clear weather you can see across the Bristol Channel to the Brecon Beacons, and maybe to the jagged mini-range of the Malverns in the northeast; east-southeast is the prominent Wellington Monument on the Blackdown Hills, and further round are the Brendons, Quantocks and Dartmoor.

Stoke Pero is another superlative: Exmoor's highest church at 1,013 feet, and one of the three that were too remote to attract a parson, according to the local ditty: 'Culbone, Oare and Stoke Pero, Parishes three where no parson'll go.' Stoke Pero made do with a curate for much of its history. Not much remains of the original church; it was completely rebuilt by Sir Thomas Acland in 1897, with the help of Zulu the donkey who made the journey from Porlock twice a day carrying the timbers for the roof. It's a most appealing little place, set cosily next to some farm buildings. Inside there's nothing that's centuries old to admire, just a little harmonium and a set of candlesticks because there's no electricity. And a framed drawing of Zulu the donkey on the wall.

Woodland Sculpture Trail

On the outer edge of Horner Woods, at Webbers Post, a series of wooden sculptures hide in the forest. They are unheralded and unlabelled, making them as much part of the landscape as a twisted oak branch or watchful squirrel.

Most of these sculptures are by sculptors from Eastern Europe and were created at Piles Mill, Allerford in 2004 during a week-long Woodcarving Festival. Photographs of the pieces being created and details of the sculptors are on display at Piles Mill (www.wildlifeinthewood.co.uk); it's open Saturdays from 10.00 to 16.00.

The event was sponsored by local businesses, the National Trust and Exmoor National Park Authority. Overseeing the event was Mike Leach, head national park ranger, who was inspired by his participation in various wood-carving symposiums in Estonia. The logs for all the sculptures came from Exmoor, and have weathered through the years to become at one with their environment. The sculptures are beautiful, humorous and intriguing Do seek them out.

The sculpture trails are accessed from the two car parks at Webbers Post, 2½ miles from Porlock, one mile from Luccombe. Look for the signpost pointing to Cloutsham and Exford, and Dunkery Beacon and Wheddon Cross.

㉒ Dunster and around

Dunster is just within the National Park, and deservedly the most touristy small town (or large village) on Exmoor. The medieval town is utterly charming in a slightly self-conscious way, with its car-harassing narrow streets, foot-harassing cobbles, and backdrop of a splendid castle. The shops are tasteful, selling high-quality goods, the traffic is controlled, and there are lots of teashops and snack bars. Strange to think that in the 12th century Dunster Haven was a busy port. When the shore became land, the town switched its activities to the wool trade, so successfully that the local cloth was known as 'Dunsters'. The octagonal **Yarn Market** was built in 1609 to protect the wool traders from the Exmoor weather; it serves a similar purpose for damp tourists today.

Medieval towns like this often feel claustrophobic, but Dunster revels in open spaces and enclosed public gardens. Across one such space, the Village Garden, is the **dovecot**, which probably dates from the 14th century and still has the nest holes. The exceptionally informative leaflet explains that it originally belonged to the Priory but after the Dissolution of the Monasteries was sold to the Luttrells at Dunster Castle. Young pigeon, squab, was a luxury food, and until the 17th century only lords of the manor and parish priests were allowed to keep pigeons.

Near the dovecot is a lovely little church garden, and the red sandstone **church of St George**. First impressions are of a gloriously intricate wagon roof, some good bosses and a font with a complicated cover. And the famous screen. Now most old churches have screens, and many have screens as beautifully carved as this one, with fan vaulting to support the weight of the rood. But none, anywhere, has a screen this length, stretching across the full 54-foot width of the church. The reason it was made had nothing to do with the worship of God but everything to do with sour relations. The Benedictine monks from the priory had used the church since its founding in about 1090; whilst the townspeople, with their vicar, carried out the usual church duties of services, marriages, baptisms and burials in the same church. The dispute arose about who did what where and when. Nasty tricks were played, such as tying up the bells out of the reach of the monks, and even imprisoning them for a time at the east end of the church.

Things got so heated that the matter went to arbitration at Glastonbury in 1498, and the verdict was that a screen should be built to separate the parishioners and their vicar from the monks. The nave belonged to the town and the chancel to the priory. This seems to have left everyone relatively happy – at least until the Dissolution of the Monasteries some 40 years later.

A rural lane running alongside a stream leads to the **Water Mill**. Dating from the 17th century and grinding wheat daily to produce flour for its shop and local bakeries, it's an interesting place to visit and the tea room serves very tasty light meals. Continue past the mill and you enter the spacious gardens of **Dunster Castle**. This is the perfect approach to the castle: peaceful and uncrowded with, when I was there, only the sound of birdsong and the river. A path winds round to the main, steep entrance to the castle, past a sign near a doorway saying 'Ghosts' (I wasn't sure if this was an instruction or a warning) and into the very grand castle itself. Dunster Castle is mentioned in the Domesday Book and was home to 18 generations of the Luttrell family from 1405. And the house, now in the care of the National Trust, is gorgeous. The ornate plasterwork on the ceilings and fireplaces, and the intricately carved grand-scale wooden staircase, are particularly impressive, but so are the paintings, and the furniture, and even the bath. I would rank it with Hartland Abbey as my favourites among the stately homes I visited for this book.

And don't miss, on leaving it, the Dream Garden at the bottom of the hill, created by or for Alys Luttrell. Even in early October it was a riot of flowers – chrysanthemums – penned in by little box hedges, with paths winding between them and a backdrop of the church tower.

After the glories of Dunster, **Wheddon Cross** comes as a bit of an anticlimax. It gained importance as a major crossroads and now consists almost entirely of inns and B&Bs. However, the place comes into its own each February when a woodland valley is carpeted with snowdrops. **Snowdrop Valley**, in the Avill valley north of the village, is owned by the Badgworthy Land Company and is an ESA (Environmentally Sensitive Area). It's a gentle walk, easily accessed from Wheddon Cross from where a Park and Ride scheme operates if you don't want to make the 20-minute walk from the village.

Minehead lies outside the National Park so beyond the scope of this book. However, it is the main gateway to Exmoor so the listings below may be helpful.

Dunster

Dunster Information Centre Dunster Steep ☎ 01643 821835 ⌂ www.visitdunster.co.uk.
Exmoor National Park Authority Dunster Steep ☎ 01643 821835
⌂ www.exmoornationalpark.gov.uk.
Luttrell Arms Restaurant High St, Dunster ☎ 01643 821555. Pleasant garden and view.
Pompy's Cycles Mart Rd, Minehead ☎ 01643 704077 ⌂ www.pompyscycles.co.uk. Mountain bike sales and hire. Escorted rides or self-guiding.
Reeves Restaurant 20–22 High St, Dunster ☎ 01643 821414
⌂ www.reevesrestaurantdunster.co.uk. Reputed to be the best restaurant in Dunster.

Minehead

Minehead Tourist Information Centre Warren Rd, TA24 5BG ☎ 01643 702624
⌂ www.minehead.co.uk.
Exmoor Cycle Hire 6 Parkhouse Rd, Minehead ☎ 01643 705307
⌂ www.exmoorcyclehire.co.uk. A variety of bikes for on- and off-road riding; maps and routes; drop-off service.
West Somerset Railway ☎ 01643 704996 ⌂ www.west-somerset-railway.co.uk. The steam train runs between Minehead and Dunster and on to Bishops Lydeard near Taunton.

Wheddon Cross

Exmoor House Wheddon Cross ☎ 01643 841432 ⌂ www.exmoorhouse.com. This B&B is open to non-residents for exceptional evening meals. Reservations essential.
The Rest and Be Thankful Wheddon Cross ☎ 01643 841222
⌂ www.restandbethankful.co.uk. A popular pub with a lovely name!
Snowdrop Valley ⌂ www.wheddoncross.org.uk.

Index